What
Matters
in College?

Alexander W. Astin

What Matters in College?

Four Critical Years Revisited

JOSSEY-BASS
A Wiley Company
www.josseybass.com

Published by

JOSSEY-BASS
A Wiley Company
989 Market Street
San Francisco, CA 94103-1741

www.josseybass.com

Jossey-Bass books and products are available through most bookstores. To contact
Jossey-Bass directly, call (888) 378-2537, fax to (800) 605-2665, or visit our website
at www.josseybass.com.

Substantial discounts on bulk quantities of Jossey-Bass books are available to
corporations, professional associations, and other organizations. For details and
discount information, contact the special sales department at Jossey-Bass.

We at Jossey-Bass strive to use the most environmentally sensitive paper stocks
available to us. Our publications are printed on acid-free recycled stock whenever
possible, and our paper always meets or exceeds minimum GPO and EPA
requirements.

Jossey-Bass also publishes its books in a variety of electronic formats. Some content
that appears in print may not be available in electronic books.

Library of Congress Cataloging-in-Publication Data

Astin, Alexander W.
    What matters in college? four critical years revisited /
Alexander W. Astin — 1st ed.
        p.   cm. — (The Jossey-Bass higher and adult education series)
    Includes bibliographical references (p.   ) and index.
    ISBN 1-55542-492-9 (alk. paper)
    ISBN 0-7879-0838-X (paperback)
        1. College students—United States.   2. College students—United
States—Attitudes.   3. Education, Higher—United States—Evaluation.
    4. Education, Higher—Social aspects—United States—Evaluation.
    5. College environment—United States—Evaluation.   6. Academic
achievement—United States.   7. Educational surveys—United States.
    I. Title.   II. Series.
    LA229.A7948   1993
    378.1'98'10973—dc20   92-20581

FIRST EDITION
HB Printing   10 9 8 7 6 5 4 3
PB Printing   10 9 8

The Jossey-Bass
Higher and Adult Education Series

To Lena

Contents

Introduction to the Paperback Edition

When the editors at Jossey-Bass first asked me to write this introduction, my initial thought was simply to rewrite and update the original preface. After rereading that preface several times, however, I decided to let it stand as originally written, since it is still a timely and appropriate introduction to the book. My intent in writing this separate introduction is to reflect on some of the book's major findings in light of the rapidly emerging changes in higher education that we have been experiencing just in the four years since this book was written.

Since the first edition was released we have also gained important insights into the age-old problem of teaching "versus" research. While the original study produced a number of findings showing that there is indeed a competition between these two values in most institutions, in my discussion of this conflict (pp. 410–412) I speculated about the possibility that there may well be some unique institutions that have managed to reconcile these two critical functions; in other words, that are able to emphasize *both* research and teaching. If there are such institutions, and if we can understand how they are able to "have their cake and eat it too," such knowledge might be of considerable value to the many other institutions that continue to struggle with this critical problem.

Since that time my colleague Mitchell Chang and I have completed an in-depth study of this issue[1] and we were indeed able to find a handful of institutions that successfully emphasize both research and teaching. Without exception, these are all highly selective, residential liberal arts colleges—prototypic American institutions modeled after the "colleges" that constituted the great British universities. How is it that such colleges have been able to emphasize research and teaching at the same time? To begin with, Chang and I discovered that most of their faculty have achieved a kind of *balance* between research and teaching: they are neither unidimensional in their focus on research (a quality commonly exhibited by faculty in major research universities) nor so devoted to students that they avoid scholarly or other professional pursuits (as one often finds in faculty who work in small, religiously affiliated colleges). But perhaps the most interesting thing about these faculty is that many of the qualities that distinguish them from faculty at other institutions are associated with positive educational outcomes:

- frequent interaction with students
- strong support for student services
- strong humanities orientation
- strong emphasis on "diversity" issues
- student engagement in independent research
- student involvement in faculty research
- written evaluations
- many interdisciplinary courses
- emphasis on history courses
- emphasis on foreign languages courses
- many courses that emphasize writing
- *in*frequent use of multiple choice exams

In effect, what these findings show is that faculty who have effected a balance between research and teaching are also very likely to exhibit exemplary educational practices, more likely even than faculty who are unidimensionally committed to students. But how do we assess the implications of these findings for other types of institutions? Since these selective colleges also have a very high level of per-student educational expenditures, we must confront

[1]A. W. Astin and M. J. Chang, "Colleges That Emphasize Research and Teaching: Can You Have Your Cake and Eat It Too?" *Change*, Sept.-Oct. 1995, *27*, 5, pp. 44–49.

the very practical issue of feasibility: are faculty practices like freshman seminars, team teaching, essay exams, and narrative evaluations less common in other types of institutions because they are highly labor-intensive? A closer look at the above list, however, suggests that none of these practices is *necessarily* precluded by limited resources. If they choose to, faculty at almost any institution can interact more with undergraduates, involve more undergraduates in their research, teach more interdisciplinary courses, give more emphasis on writing in course assignments and exams, or give more written evaluation of their undergraduates' work. And if it chooses to, almost any institution can allocate a higher proportion of its educational expenditures to student services. Finally, students at almost any institution can be encouraged to do more independent research and to take more history and foreign language courses.

This study has shown that neither the institution's overall level of resources, nor the type of institution per se (for example, liberal arts, university), has much direct effect on any student outcomes, once the effects of the specific educational practices such as those listed above are taken into account. In other words, while certain types of institutions are more likely to exemplify these practices than others, a few public institutions, a few universities, and a number of nonaffluent, nonselective liberal arts colleges also use these same practices. The major limiting factors, it would seem, are institutional will, policy, and tradition.

In the original *Four Critical Years*, which was published in 1977, I tried to point out that the policies that had governed the great expansion of American higher education following the end of the Second World War seemed to run counter to most of the study's empirical findings. Thus, while the research suggested that the most effective undergraduate education is associated with such things as small institutional size, private control, a common curricular experience, living on campus, and full-time attendance, the policies that had guided expansion of the system favored larger and larger institutions, public control, an unstructured curricular experience (the "distributional" system), more commuter education, and more part-time attendance. *Four Critical Years* also provided a theoretical basis for understanding these effects: the phenomenon of student *involvement*. According to the theory of student involvement, learning and development is enhanced by such things as living on campus and full-time attendance because the student tends to invest more time and more physical and psychological energy in the educational experience. *What Matters in College?* has further enhanced our understanding of these processes by showing that one of the most powerful sources of student involvement is the *peer group*.

While some observers claim that these findings concerning the peer group and the residential experience are "irrelevant" to large commuter institutions (see the discussion beginning on page 413), since the book was published a number of such institutions have actually begun to *use* these findings to enhance the educational experience for commuter students. Two particularly noteworthy examples are the University of Houston and Portland State University, both of which are large urban institutions that serve commuter populations. The University of Houston has established its "Scholar's Community," which attempts to enhance the peer group experience through the creation of a center where a selected sample of commuter students can study, socialize, take classes together, have access to computer facilities, and interact with faculty and staff. The program also uses peer tutoring, collaborative learning, and "linked" courses that allow students to connect material across courses and to share academic topics with each other. Portland State has focused on the *curriculum* and the local *community* as means of enhancing the peer group experience for its entire commuter population. The highly structured general education program, which uses collaborative learning, peer mentoring, and team-taught interdisciplinary seminars, culminates in a "senior capstone" experience, which involves small teams of students who use their knowledge and skills to work collaboratively on community service projects.

Increasing institutional involvement in service learning and community service is, in fact, one of the most exciting developments in higher education today. In just the past few years the Campus Compact, a consortium of institutions dedicated to promoting service learning and community service, has grown to over 500 members. That student engagement in community service may have a number of education benefits is clearly suggested by the findings of this study (see pp. 391–92). Further, as I write this the Higher Education Research Institute is just completing a number of additional studies which confirm and extend these positive findings. Indeed, it appears that the positive effects of undergraduate service participation extend well into the post-college adult years. Our hope is that these findings will encourage more institutions to incorporate service learning into the curriculum.

The findings concerning peer group effects have taken on special significance in the four years since this book was first released in hardcover form. As discussed in Chapters Ten and Twelve, the socioeconomic status of the peer group (Peer SES) has more and stronger effects on the student's cognitive and affective development than any other environmental characteristic. Since these effects are uniformly positive, it seems reasonable to conclude that students who manage to gain admission to a college that has a high SES peer group are a privileged lot: in general they can look forward to more favorable outcomes—greater satisfaction with their college experience and greater cognitive and affective growth—than can students attending other institutions. Since colleges and universities with high SES peer groups also tend to be highly selective in their admissions policies (see p. 408), these institutions are relatively inaccessible to poor students, African Americans, and Latinos. Despite the fact that most of these institutions have active outreach and affirmative action programs to enhance access for these underrepresented groups, recent economic and political trends are putting such programs at risk.

Most prominent among these trends is the political assault on affirmative action, which is being attacked by its critics for allegedly promoting "racial preferences," "quotas," and "reverse discrimination." In California this campaign has already succeeded not only in eliminating any racial considerations from admissions practices at the University of California, but also in the passage of a state referendum (Proposition 209) outlawing any consideration of race from public education and employment. Similarly, in the Southwest, the *Hopwood* decision, which initially outlawed racial considerations in admission at the University of Texas Law School, now has the force of law in four states.

A parallel trend that promises to further erode access by underrepresented groups to high SES colleges is the escalating cost of higher education. Since federal and state financial aid has not kept pace with growing student costs, institutions have increasingly had to rely on their own resources to meet the financial needs of poor students. As a result, more and more colleges are being forced to take into account the student's "ability to pay" in making admissions decisions.

That these social and economic trends may already be having a negative impact on access to high SES institutions among underrepresented groups is suggested by two pieces of evidence: (1) a decline in applications to the University of California from members of underrepresented students during the past year (1995–96); and (2) Erin Horvat's[2] recent unpublished analysis of data from UCLA's Cooperative Institutional Research Program, which shows that the proportions of both African-American and low-income students enrolling in high SES colleges and universities have been declining in recent years.

Since the book was first released I have also had two rather sobering experiences concerning the use of these research findings by politicians and by our judicial system. The first of these concerns the current debate over "diversity" and "multiculturalism" on the campus. Within the academy, these attacks have been led by a group that calls itself the National Association of Scholars and, in my own state, by an affiliate called the California Association of Scholars (CAS). While the research findings concerning the effects of multiculturalism are clear—students benefit in a variety of ways when their campus emphasizes multiculturalism in its curriculum and cocurriculum (see pp. 429–431)—the CAS has chosen to ignore (or dismiss) these findings in its public pronouncements and to focus instead on a minor finding concerning racial enrollments (see p. 363). When we originally devised the 135 environmental measures for this study, we included three simple measures of racial enrollments: the percentages of African Americans, Asians, and Latinos in the student body. As it turns out, none of these three measures—considered independently—produced many direct effects on student outcomes. The CAS has seized on these negative findings as a means of refuting the claim—typically advanced by proponents of affirmative action—that having a racially diverse student body "enriches" the student's educational experience. The federal courts in the *Hopwood* case recently reached the same negative conclusion as the one propounded by the CAS in their decision to outlaw racial consideration in admission to the University of Texas Law School.

That these measures do not necessarily reflect "diversity" is easily illustrated by considering the percentage of African-American students in the student body. Using this measure, we would have to conclude that the historically black colleges are the "most diverse" institutions, when in fact their student bodies are among the *least* diverse; that is, more than 90 percent of their students are

---

[2]Personal communication.

from the same racial group! Under these circumstances, it is clearly not reasonable to claim that this study proves that diversity has no consequences for student development.

To explore this issue more directly, Mitchell Chang from our institute recently developed a comprehensive measure of student body diversity as part of his doctoral dissertation.[3] Under Chang's definition, the most diverse student body would be one with *equal* representation of students from different racial groups, while the least diverse student body would comprise mostly students from one group. Chang found that white students who attend institutions with diverse student bodies, compared with those who attend institutions enrolling mostly white students, are more likely to discuss racial issues and to socialize with nonwhite students. Since these latter two student experiences are, in turn, associated with a number of positive educational outcomes (see p. 386), it seems clear that diversity can indeed have beneficial effects on student development. It will be interesting to see how the CAS deals with Chang's findings once they are published.

The second experience with misuse of research concerns the much-publicized U.S. Supreme Court decision in 1996 requiring the Virginia Military Institute (VMI) to admit women. When this suit was initiated four years earlier on behalf of women applicants who had been refused admission to VMI, lawyers for VMI cited findings from *Four Critical Years* in support of their argument that the unique educational benefits associated with attending VMI would be lost if women were to be admitted. While *Four Critical Years* had reported a number of positive educational outcomes associated with attending colleges for men, it has not been possible to replicate these results in *What Matters in College* because all but one or two of the two dozen or so men's colleges studied in *Four Critical Years* have since become coeducational.

When I subsequently became involved as an expert witness for the U.S. Department of Justice, I was interested in determining whether the defense claim was indeed true: are the benefits associated with attending a men's college lost if the college becomes coeducational? Using the data base from *What Matters in College*, I was able to find

[3]Mitchell J. Chang, "Racial Diversity in Higher Education: Does a Racially Mixed Student Population Affect Educational Outcomes?" Unpublished Doctoral Dissertation, University of California, Los Angeles, 1996.

nineteen of the men's colleges from *Four Critical Years* that were now coeducational. Using outcome measures that were common to the two studies, I found that the effects of these nineteen institutions are *virtually identical* to what was reported seventeen years earlier in *Four Critical Years*. In other words, these new analyses show clearly that the educational benefits associated with colleges for men are not lost if these colleges become coeducational.

The U.S. District Court in Richmond, which has consistently ruled in VMI's favor, would not allow me to testify concerning this new research evidence on the grounds that the courts had *already* ruled (a) that there are unique educational benefits associated with colleges for men and (b) that these benefits would be lost if a men's college were to admit women. Ironically, these earlier rulings were based in part on the conclusions reported in *Four Critical Years!* While the U.S. Supreme Court has just recently overturned decision of the lower courts and ordered VMI to admit women, the lone dissent by Judge Scalia is based in part on the argument that no evidence was presented to contradict the rulings made by the lower courts. The evidence clearly exists, but unfortunately it was never allowed to become part of the record.

A final word about the book itself. Many readers have told me that they have found the two summary chapters (Ten and Eleven) to be especially useful, while others tell me that the final chapter (Twelve) makes an excellent introduction to "contemporary policy issues in American higher education." Still others say that Chapters One and Three constitute a good methodological introduction to "studying college impact." Having just reread this entire book once again in preparing to write this introduction, I noticed one other thing that readers might want to keep in mind: each of the detailed results chapters—Four through Nine—includes several fascinating "nuggets" of research findings, not mentioned in the summary chapters, that might well suggest potentially useful and even provocative directions for future research and practice. In focusing only on the "big picture" as painted in the final three chapters, it is easy to overlook these nuggets. However, given the considerable amount of detail contained in each of these chapters, I would recommend consuming them in small bites.

November 1996   Alexander W. Astin

Preface

Of the various books and articles that I have written during the past thirty years, none has generated as much interest and commentary as *Four Critical Years* (Astin, 1977). Whenever I visit campuses or address audiences of educators, people mention the book and remark that it has influenced their thinking about higher education in some way. It was especially gratifying to read in the *Journal of Higher Education* a couple of years ago that *Four Critical Years* was the single most frequently cited work in the higher education literature (Budd, 1990). While I do not pretend to understand all the reasons for the interest shown in the book, its popularity convinces me that many educators are indeed interested in how students change and develop in college and what might be done to enhance that development.

As with *Four Critical Years,* the principal purpose of *What Matters in College?* is to enhance our understanding of how undergraduate students are affected by their college experiences. While its organization bears some resemblance to that of the earlier work, this book is an entirely new study. It looks at many important educational issues that simply could not be addressed in the earlier study because of limitations in the data. Chapter

One includes a good deal of material from the first chapter in
Four Critical Years, simply because that original chapter still seems
to me to be a pretty good statement of the basic conceptual and
methodological issues involved in studying college impact. Otherwise, except for an introductory sentence or two here and there,
this is a completely new study and a new book: many new variables are included, and certainly many of the results are different!

Audience

The book is intended for a wide audience. Faculty and student
affairs professionals should find the results of considerable interest, since the study not only addresses a wide range of cognitive and affective outcomes of college but also attempts to show
how those outcomes are affected by the student's peer group experiences and by the faculty's values, interests, and preferred
styles of teaching. Findings of particular relevance for administrators and policy makers include the effects (on students) of
different kinds of institutions, patterns of resource utilization,
and the campus "climate." Finally, in choosing a college, students and their parents may find many of the results useful, especially those having to do with type of college attended and
patterns of student involvement.

Organization of the Book

The book is organized as follows: Chapter One discusses the
complex question of assessing how students are affected by their
college experiences and outlines the overall design of the study.
Chapter Two describes each of the 135 college environmental
measures and 57 "student involvement" measures used in subsequent chapters. Chapter Three presents a detailed analysis
of how the environmental characteristics and the experiences
of involvement affect a single outcome measure: the student's
political identification. The next six chapters present findings
concerning environmental and involvement effects on eighty-
one other outcomes: personality and self-concept (Chapter Four),
attitudes, values, and beliefs (Chapter Five), behavior (Chapter

Six), academic and cognitive development (Chapter Seven), career development (Chapter Eight), and satisfaction with college (Chapter Nine). Chapter Ten summarizes the results separately for each environmental measure, and Chapter Eleven summarizes results separately for each involvement measure. The final chapter (Chapter Twelve) discusses the implications of the study for educational theory and practice. Additional technical details concerning the analyses reported in Chapters Three through Nine are provided in Resources A and B.

Some parts of the book can be read independently of the others. All readers are advised to look over Chapters Three and Twelve. The main purpose of the two summary chapters (Chapters Ten and Eleven) and the final "policy" chapter (Chapter Twelve) is to bring some overall coherence to the entire array of empirical results. Readers can read specific sections (or even subsections) of the two summary chapters without reading the preceding chapters and still capture some of the critical empirical findings. In a sense, these two summary chapters represent a kind of reference work to which readers can go to learn how particular types of colleges, college environments, or educational practices affect a wide range of student outcomes. Readers can also get some sense of the *dynamics* of these effects by seeing what forms of student involvement are encouraged or discouraged by different environmental variables. Readers who are interested in particular types of *outcomes* should, however, consult Chapters Four through Nine. Finally, the last chapter provides a personal commentary on what I see as the major implications of all this information for the future of our higher education system. My real hope is to furnish students, faculty, administrators, and educational policy makers with some new tools for trying to improve and reform our higher education system.

Interpreting the Results

Several things about the findings stand out in my mind. First, the kinds of colleges and college experiences that favorably affect the student's performance on standardized tests are quite different from those that enhance retention and other cognitive and affective outcomes. Second, being in a particular *type* of institution (for example, a research university) does not necessarily limit the effectiveness of undergraduate education; that is, although different types of institutions tend to have particular types of environments, there are notable exceptions, and it is the environment created by the faculty and the students — rather than the type of institution per se — that really seems to matter. Finally, the single most important environmental influence on student development is the peer group. By judicious and imaginative use of peer groups, any college or university can substantially strengthen its impact on student learning and personal development.

In many ways, this book runs the risk of subjecting the reader to information overload. I certainly had to plow my way through a pretty heavy dose of information myself, just to produce a work that is of reasonable length, and — I hope — reasonably intelligible. I must admit that on many occasions I was tempted to limit the content in certain major respects: to cover just a few student outcomes, or to look at just a few environmental variables. I ultimately decided against such alternatives because my real goal has always been to provide a comprehensive portrait of student development in all its complexity. Like it or not, student development is a highly complex, multivariate process, and universities are highly diverse and complex institutions. There are many, many ways in which students are affected by their educational experiences, and many different kinds of curricula, programs, faculty, peer groups, and college environments that can affect students. For the first time in my thirty years as a higher education researcher, we have the data base to look at college impact in all its richness and complexity.

I made several decisions early on, in an attempt to make the reader's task more manageable. The first was the decision to study only bachelor's degree–granting institutions. *Four Critical Years* included a large sample of community colleges, but I am not sure that the book was strengthened in any particular way as a result. Community colleges have changed dramatically in the past two decades, with transfer (bachelor's) education accounting for a rapidly declining part of what community colleges do. Also, some of the unique faculty and peer group measures included in this study would simply not be suitable for community colleges.

Another simplifying decision was to leave out a great deal of technical detail that is not crucial for an understanding of the basic findings. Methodologically inclined readers may be frustrated by the omission of regression tables and by the very selective reporting of various correlation and regression coefficients. (Those who really want all that can get it by writing directly to me, but I warn them ahead of time that the copying and postage costs will be hefty!) I have minimized the reporting of coefficients and other numbers, not only because a great many numbers can numb the reader but also because such numbers would not really enhance the reader's understanding of what was found and what it might mean. Beta and correlation coefficients are provided only when the actual magnitude of an effect seems to be of central interest. Readers who want more detail about the statistical methodology used in the study are advised to consult the appendix to my recent book *Assessment for Excellence* (Astin, 1991). One reviewer of the manuscript for the current book even suggested that large parts of that appendix be included here as well, but space limitations precluded that option.

The reporting of empirical findings in Chapters Three through Nine and the summaries provided in Chapters Ten and Eleven omit a good deal about the effects of "input" variables (entering freshman characteristics). We included more than 140 input characteristics in analyzing each student outcome measure. This "shotgun" approach was motivated by a recognition that the principal methodological limitation of all college impact research (or, indeed, of any social science research that looks at the "real world") is that people are not distributed randomly among different environments. The best way to deal with this problem, it seems to me, is to control everything about the entering student that might possibly bias your results. This, to me, means controlling everything! Some skeptics might still argue that you cannot make causal inferences from correlational (nonexperimental) data, no matter how many input variables you control. To them, I would simply answer: "Yes, you can; people do it all the time." No professor and no administrator can get through a typical day on campus without making dozens of decisions that rely on such inferences. In the world of research, the point of controlling as much of the input bias as possible is to minimize the chances that your causal inferences will be wrong. Methodologists who continue to insist that the only "true science" is experimental must necessarily abandon any attempt to study the world as it is. They forget, however, that astronomers and biologists have developed perfectly good sciences over the years through observing (rather than manipulating or controlling) natural phenomena.

Eighty-two regressions largely form the basis for the content of the book. Each is a rich source of fascinating data, especially if one is able to follow the step-by-step changes in coefficients that occur as the variables from different blocks enter the regression. Given the very large sample size, I have been able to simplify the presentation of each regression (and minimize "Type I" errors) by using a very stringent confidence level ($p < .0005$) for entry of variables. We have been able to develop a way of using regression that confers most of the benefits of path analysis but that also generates an enormous amount of additional information on the dynamics of the variables in the causal chain (see Astin, 1991, Appendix A, for details). One could easily develop separate journal articles — maybe even several articles — from each of these regressions. In particular, it is enlightening to see how the effects of "environmental variables" such as institutional size may be mediated by "involvement" variables, such as student-faculty interaction. While I have given a few examples of such mediating effects in the main results chapters (Chapters Three through Nine), most detail of this kind is withheld until the summary chapters (Chapters Ten and Eleven). Still, it is frustrating, even in those two chapters, not to go into each regression in greater depth. To do so, I fear, would render the work unacceptably long and complicated.

There are, however, hundreds of fascinating further studies that can and should be done, drawing on this rich data base, among them separate analyses by gender. As pointed out in Chapter Twelve, gender affects most of the outcome measures, even after the other entering characteristics of students, including their pretest scores, are controlled. Some of the graduate students who are now doing dissertations and independent study projects relying on these data have already produced strong evidence that suggests significant *interaction effects* involving gender. In nonstatistical terms, an interaction effect involving gender occurs when a particular environmental experience affects men differently from women. It may well be that further studies will identify many other interaction effects involving other student characteristics, such as race or ethnicity, ability, or socioeconomic status. Improving our knowledge of such interaction effects is of particular importance, since it provides guidelines to both students and institutions concerning what kinds of educational experiences are most and least effective for certain kinds of students. As this study involves more than 140 entering student characteristics and more than 190 environmental characteristics, the possibilities for studying interaction effects are virtually limitless.

Because many students these days take five or six years or even longer to complete their baccalaureate degrees, especially in our public institutions, *Four Critical Years* could be regarded as a misnomer. Still, many do complete their undergraduate work in four years, and most students who drop out or transfer do so within the first four years. At the same time, the lives and decisions of even students who take longer than four years to finish college are heavily influenced by what happens during the first four years.

A related issue is that this book focuses almost exclusively on the traditional-age college undergraduate who enters college soon after completing high school. Furthermore, the study is limited to students who begin their college studies on a full-time basis, although many of those students eventually become part-timers. While some readers may regard these qualities of our sample as limitations, I personally do not see them so, any more than I regard our studying only undergraduates and only students in the United States as limitations. Each year, more than 1.5 million young people enter college directly out of high school as full-time students. This is an important population worthy of study in its own right. Despite (or perhaps *because* of) the fact that American higher education has been enrolling increasingly large numbers of adults and part-time students, I believe that it would be a serious mistake to lump these "nontraditional" students together with traditional-age full-time students in a single study. Anyone who has worked with adults and part-timers (as I have and as I assume many readers have) knows full well that the issues and problems confronting the adult and the part-time student are quite different from those confronting the traditional-age full-time student. It is also reasonable to assume that the environmental variables that affect one group may be quite different from those that are important to the other. By combining the two groups, we run a serious risk of confounding these different effects, thus yielding a clouded picture of the actual environmental effects on student development. In other words, it is far better to obtain clear-cut findings on an important and well-defined population (the full-time undergraduate of traditional college age) than a watered-down set of conclusions based on a much more heterogeneous sample.

This is not to say that studies of part-time and adult undergraduate students are not needed. Indeed, in the Cooperative Institutional Research Program (CIRP), we have been trying for several decades to encourage our participating institutions to include such students in the annual student survey in order that they might be singled out for separate study. Unfortunately, the logistics of assessing part-time and transfer students are much more difficult because those students do not usually pass through the same orientation and registration "screens" as traditional full-time undergraduate students do. As a result, most of what we now know about college impact on student development (Pascarella and Terenzini, 1991) tells us little about these newer and expanding populations. We can only hope that institutions will soon find ways to take such students into account in their assessment programs.

What Matters in College? makes no pretense of being a comprehensive review of the literature on college impact. That review task has been admirably performed by Feldman and Newcomb (1969), Bowen (1977), and—most recently—Pascarella and Terenzini (1991). All of us who work in the field owe a debt of gratitude to the scholars who have periodically synthesized its huge and highly diverse literature.

I have tried to make reference to earlier research when the results either replicate or contradict my results, but such references are restricted for the most part to earlier studies that are national in scope. References to relevant prior research are necessarily sparse, however, when it comes to the many environmental and outcome measures that have never before been used in large-scale studies of college impact.

Acknowledgments

This study was supported primarily by grants from the Exxon Education Foundation and the National Science Foundation. I am especially indebted to Dick Johnson of the Exxon Education Foundation, who originally conceived the idea of a national study on the outcomes of general education programs and who provided advice and encouragement during all phases of the project.

A study of this magnitude and complexity becomes possible only through the coordinated efforts of many people. As with so many earlier studies using CIRP data, we are indebted to the hundreds of CIRP representatives and thousands of students and former students who helped to provide us with the questionnaire and retention data. Data on SAT, GRE, and NTE scores were provided by the Educational Testing Service, with financial assistance from the National Education Association. Scores from the ACT, MCAT, and LSAT were supplied by the American College Testing Program, the Association of American Medical Colleges, and the Law School Admissions Council, respectively.

Many people at the Higher Education Research Institute (HERI) made significant contributions to this book. Linda Sax has been a key player in most phases of the study, from running hundreds of complex regressions to reviewing draft chapters. Linda, with able assistance from Marc Chun, was also responsible for generating the "world map" (showing 82 outcomes by 192 environments) that has adorned our walls for all these many months. Linda's intelligence, patience, good nature, and just plain hard work have made the doing of this project much more enjoyable.

Eric Dey was instrumental in helping to mastermind the entire project and in designing the data bases and the complex analyses that followed. Thanks, Eric, for being such a good colleague and consultant. Eric, along with Sylvia Hurtado, did much of the early work on the general education phase of the project. Sylvia also made some helpful suggestions on an early draft of Chapter Ten. Sylvia and Eric are now preparing a book that uses the same data base to explore issues specifically related to general education.

Special appreciation is also due to Ron Opp, who was able, somewhat miraculously, to bring off the sensitive task of persuading the testing companies and professional associations to share their test scores with us. Ron, with considerable help from Jesús Treviño, Tami Wingard Schiff, Lupe Anaya, Jeff Milem, and others, also managed the complex task of collecting faculty survey data. Jeff has also helped in other key phases of the study, especially in factor analyzing student and faculty survey data.

Bill Korn deserves special thanks for all his help in data base design, management, and analysis, and especially for his long-standing enthusiasm for helping produce *Four Supercritical Years,* as he likes to call this book. I have worked with many computer and data processing pros over the years, and Bill is in a class by himself.

Other HERI staff who have made important contributions to various phases of this project include Ellyne Riggs, David Hsieh, and Debra Gomez.

Last, but by no means least, among the HERI staff who have helped in this study is Robin Bailey. Thanks, Robin, not only for all your good work in manuscript preparation and revision but also for the interest you have shown in the results of the study and for the good vibes that you bring with you to the office each day.

Finally, I would like to thank Gary Hanson and Oscar Lenning for their many helpful suggestions on an earlier draft and for their willingness to review the manuscript on a very tight schedule.

Los Angeles, California   Alexander W. Astin
September 1992

The Author

Alexander W. Astin is Allan M. Cartter professor of education at the University of California, Los Angeles; director of the Higher Education Research Institute at UCLA; and director of the Cooperative Institutional Research Program. Previously he was director of research for the American Council on Education and the National Merit Scholarship Corporation. Astin has received awards for outstanding research from the American Personnel and Guidance Association (1965), the National Association of Student Personnel Administrators (1976), the American College Personnel Association (1978), the American College Testing Program-American Educational Research Association (1983), the National Association of College Admissions Counselors (1985), the Council of Independent Colleges (1986), the Association for the Study of Higher Education (1987 and 1996), the American Assocation for Counseling and Development (1992), and the Association for Institutional Research (1992). He has also been a fellow at the Center for Advanced Study in the Behavioral Sciences and a recipient of ten honorary degrees. Astin's work has appeared in more than one hundred articles and seventeen books, including *Assessment for Excellence* (1991), *Achieving Educational Excellence* (1985), *Minorities in American Higher Education* (1982), and *Maximizing Leadership Effectiveness* (1980, with R. A. Scherrei).

Chapter 1

———•·•·•———

Studying
College Impact

Few people will argue with the premise that attending college can have a profound effect on one's life. With the possible exception of getting married or having children, few choices have more far-reaching implications than the decision about college. For most prospective college students, this decision involves three issues: (1) whether or not to go, (2) where to go, and (3) how to go. The matter of "whether" is particularly critical for that substantial minority of young people whose academic interests and achievements are minimal or whose financial situation is tenuous. Will I be able to succeed? Is it likely to be a worthwhile investment of my time and money? Among those for whom college attendance is a foregone conclusion — the college-bound students — the issues of "where" and "how" are paramount. The "where" of college choice involves which kind of institution to attend: large or small, public or private, religious or nonsectarian, and two-year versus four-year. The "how" of college attendance — a critical set of issues often poorly understood by counselors and parents — concerns matters such as financing (whether to borrow money or get a job), where to live (at home, in a dormitory, or in a private room), what to study (choice

1

of major and electives), whether to attend full- or part-time, and which extracurricular activities to pursue.

But what is the impact of college attendance on students' personal, social, and vocational development? Are some students affected differently from others? Do different types of colleges produce different outcomes? And how important is it to attend college away from home, to attend full-time, to work, or to participate in extracurricular activities? Until recently, few research-based answers could be offered.

At the same time, public policy makers have questions of their own about the value of higher education. During the 1950s and early 1960s a substantial national investment in higher education was regarded as an insurance policy in the Cold War and as a way to enhance our technological and scientific position in world trade. Now, however, many public officials are asking whether the soaring costs of higher education are draining off resources that could be better used for other public purposes. Economic pressures have forced legislators to look for programs in which public spending can be cut, and the high level of federal and state investments in higher education underscores the need for better information on how colleges affect students. How does higher education influence students' career opportunities and aspirations? Does it have significant impact on their values, personality, behavior, and life-styles? Do they become more competent and knowledgeable? Are particular types of colleges or programs more effective than others? How can we improve undergraduate education in different types of institutions?

Why Study College Impact?

The sheer volume of publications on college impact (Feldman and Newcomb, 1969; Pascarella and Terenzini, 1991) might tempt one to conclude that a great deal is already known about the answers to these questions. However, since much research is either limited in scope, inadequate in design, or outdated, there is surprisingly little one can say with confidence about the impact of college on contemporary students. Much early research failed to collect the data that would meet the two minimal requirements for adequately designed studies of college impact: (1) multi-institutional data, that is, information collected simultaneously from students at contrasting types of institutions, and (2) longitudinal data, that is, information on the ways in which students change between admission and some subsequent point in time. Other features missing from that research include large and diverse samples of students and institutions; multiple measures of entering student characteristics; multiple follow-up measures of student development, including both cognitive and affective outcomes; multivariate designs for controlling differences among students entering different types of institutions; and methodological provisions for separating college effects from maturational effects or the simple process of growing up. (For a detailed description of requirements for data and methods of analysis, see Astin, 1991.)

The original *Four Critical Years* (Astin, 1977) attempted to correct for these methodological and data limitations by relying on multi-institutional, longitudinal data collected from undergraduates during the late 1960s and early 1970s. (Many of the newer results summarized in Pascarella and Terenzini's 1991 *How College Affects Students* were based on a nine-year follow-up of the 1971 entering freshmen.) While the findings reported in *Four Critical Years* were of considerable value in helping us to understand how students are affected by various types of institutions and by different kinds of educational experiences, the decision to write an entirely new book on the same subject was prompted by several factors. First, considering the numerous ways in which higher education and its students have changed since the early 1970s, I was concerned that many of the earlier findings might now be outdated. And, second, the Higher Education Research Institute (HERI) at the University of California, Los Angeles (UCLA), was recently able to collect some new types of data that make it possible to explore a number of important educational questions and issues that got very little, if any, attention either in the earlier study or in Pascarella and Terenzini's (1991) more recent review, *How College Affects Students.* These new features, not available in *Four Critical Years* or in any other subsequent studies using data from the Cooperative

Institutional Research Program (CIRP) (for example, Astin, forthcoming; Pascarella, 1985b; Pascarella and Wolfle, 1985; Smart, 1986, 1988), include (1) an assessment of the student's cognitive development as measured both by performance on some of the major national tests used for graduate admissions and professional certification as well as by self-reported improvements in knowledge and competence during the undergraduate years, (2) extensive data on the characteristics of each institution's general education program, (3) measures of the characteristics of the student's *peer group* at each institution, and (4) measures of the characteristics of the *teaching faculty* (values, favored teaching methods, relationship with students, and so on) at each institution. The last two features were considered especially important, given the growing body of evidence suggesting that the undergraduate's development is substantially affected by interactions with both peers and faculty.

The purpose of this book is to answer questions about the effects of college that have been raised by students, parents, public officials, and educators themselves — and to answer them on the basis of data from an ongoing research program that was designed to overcome the limitations of earlier studies and to produce data for definitive studies of college impact: the Cooperative Institutional Research Program. CIRP was initiated at the American Council on Education (ACE) in 1966; since 1973 it has been conducted by the Higher Education Research Institute at the University of California, Los Angeles, with continuing sponsorship by ACE. It is now the largest ongoing study of the American higher education system, with longitudinal data covering some 500,000 students and a national sample of more than 1,300 institutions of all types. These data cover a wide range of cognitive and affective student outcomes, affording the opportunity to examine how the college experience affects more than eighty different measures of attitudes, values, behavior, learning, achievement, career development, and satisfaction. The size and scope of CIRP make it possible to employ highly sophisticated multivariate controls over a large number of potentially biasing variables — in particular, the characteristics of the entering students that might predispose them to pick particular types of colleges or programs.

The task of assessing how students are affected by their colleges is composed of three major undertakings: (1) understanding the meaning of student change, (2) developing a model or conceptual framework for studying student outcomes, and (3) designing the analyses of college impact. As an introduction to the findings discussed in later chapters, the following pages of this chapter describe how CIRP deals with each of these three requirements.

Understanding the Meaning of Student Change

In response to the question, How does college affect students? one can legitimately ask, In relation to what? While this response may seem flippant, it captures a fundamental truth regarding research on college impact: if students are not attending college, they are doing something else. Thus the generic concept of "college impact" has meaning only in relation to what would happen if students either did not attend college or attended a different type of college.

In other words, potential students are in a continuous state of growth and change. These developmental processes go on whether or not students attend college and regardless of where they attend. If researchers could somehow put young people who do not attend college in cold storage or in a state of suspended animation, they might be able to obtain a "pure" measure of the effects of college attendance by comparing them after four years with students who went to college. But such a measure would make little sense. In the real world, those who do not attend may get married, join the armed forces or find other work, go on welfare, join communes, raise families, travel abroad, or stay home with parents while they figure out what to do with their lives—but they continue to develop and learn. The real issue in research on college impact is to determine what *difference* college attendance makes in the development of the individual.

Unfortunately, much of the literature on college impact looks merely at *change* or *growth* in students rather than impact as such. Typically, students complete a personality inventory or attitudinal questionnaire when they first enter college (in the jargon of educational research, a pretest) and again after one year, four years, or—in a few cases—many years following graduation (posttest). Change or growth is assessed by comparing the two measures. Most investigators, by equating measured change with college impact, have assumed that any observed changes result from the students' college experience. The major weakness of this approach is that it fails to consider whether the same changes would have occurred if the students had attended different colleges or had not gone to college at all.

For adequate research on "the impact of college," it is essential that observed changes in students over time be seen as having two major components: the first is change resulting from the impact of the college; the second is change resulting from other influences, such as maturation and the environment outside of college. Note that the first component may (1) bring about changes that would not occur under other conditions, (2) exaggerate or accelerate changes originating in other sources, or (3) impede or counteract changes originating elsewhere. One goal of CIRP and this report is to isolate changes brought about by the college experience from changes attributable to other sources.

Some investigators have concluded that the ideal solution to these inferential problems is a control group of young people who do not attend college. Such a college-noncollege research design may have some advantages over the traditional single-institution designs that are discussed later, in the section of this chapter entitled "Assessing the Impact of College Experiences," but the difficulty with the college-noncollege design is that it grossly oversimplifies the issue of college impact. As the proportion of high school graduates who went to college increased during the 1950s and 1960s and as the number and variety of post-secondary opportunities and institutions proliferated, the distinction between college and noncollege experiences grew increasingly blurred. Indeed, for many thousands of students these days, the college experience consists of little more than driving to campus for a few hours of classes and then driving home again. It is not unreasonable to suppose, for example, that the total environmental experiences and life-styles of those commuter students who work at off-campus jobs are much more similar to those of their nonstudent co-workers than to those of students attending, say, residential liberal arts colleges. Thus the variety of experiences possible within the collegiate sphere is so great that it renders virtually meaningless any simple comparison of college attendance with nonattendance. The real issue is not the impact of college but the impact of college *characteristics* or, more precisely, the comparative impact of different collegiate experiences. More information is needed on the relative impact of various *types* of collegiate experiences. The current study seeks to meet this need by focusing not only on differences among different types of institutions but also on differences in students' experiences (faculty, peer group, curriculum) at these institutions.

A Conceptual Framework
for Studying Student Outcomes: The I-E-O Model

For nearly three decades I have been using what I call the input-environment-outcome (I-E-O) model as a conceptual guide for studying college student development. While this model has undergone a number of refinements over the years (Astin, 1962, 1970a, 1970b, 1977, 1991), the basic elements of the model have remained the same. *Inputs* refer to the characteristics of the student at the time of initial entry to the institution; *environment* refers to the various programs, policies, faculty, peers, and educational experiences to which the student is exposed; and *outcomes* refers to the student's characteristics *after* exposure to the environment. Change or growth in the student during college is determined by comparing outcome characteristics with input characteristics. The basic purpose of the model is to assess the impact of various environmental experiences by determining whether students grow or change differently under varying environmental conditions. Studying student development with the I-E-O model provides educators, students, and policy makers with a better basis for knowing how to achieve desired educational outcomes. A key problem, of course, is to specify the relevant outcomes, inputs, and environmental experiences that are to be assessed. In the next section, we examine the specific outcomes, input, and environmental measures used in this study.

Developing Outcome Measures of the College Experience

Trends in the CIRP surveys during the past two decades show that increasing numbers of students believe that the most important outcome of college attendance is economic (Dey, Astin, and Korn, 1991). This view is reinforced by many educators, who argue that having a college degree is supposed to help students develop cognitive skills that enable them to get better jobs and to make more money. But colleges potentially have a much more pervasive influence than this. An eighteen-year-old who is leaving home for the first time to attend college* is subject to wide-ranging influences from faculty, staff, curriculum, and fellow students. The possible influence of parents is reduced proportionately, simply because they are no longer present. Many freshmen experience their first intensive encounter with peers who have markedly different beliefs, backgrounds, and attitudes. For some students, enrolling in college may also provide their first direct experience with drugs, sex, alcohol, or political activism. For others, college presents the first real challenge to their academic motivation and skills. The fact that many students spend four or more years attending college under these circumstances highlights the great potential of the college experience for producing changes not only in knowledge and vocational skills but also in values, attitudes, aspirations, beliefs, and behavior.

A thorough examination of the impact of college must take into account a wide range of possible outcomes. There is no easy way to capture the impact of college adequately in one or

---

*Like the original *Four Critical Years,* the current study will focus primarily on the experience of recent high school graduates who are attending college on a full-time basis. This is not to say that adult and part-time college students, whose numbers have been growing rapidly in recent years, are not important populations that are worthy of study in their own right. There are, however, good theoretical and practical reasons for focusing on the first-time, full-time student. For example, the sampling of part-time students in CIRP surveys is probably not representative of the entire population of such students. Moreover, since the environmental factors affecting full-time traditional-age students may be very different from those that are important to adults and part-timers, lumping these three populations together in a single study may well confound these different effects.

two simple measures, such as credits and degrees earned or job placement. The need for a variety of outcome measures thus was anticipated in the design of CIRP. But rather than simply generating a list of miscellaneous measures, we developed a conceptual scheme to guide the selection of various measures. This "taxonomy of student outcomes," which was proposed several decades ago (Astin, 1970a), was also utilized by Pascarella and Terenzini (1991) in their recent comprehensive review of the college impact literature. It involves three major dimensions: type of outcome, type of data, and time.

Type of Outcome. Behavioral scientists have traditionally classified human performance into two broad domains: cognitive (sometimes called intellective) and noncognitive (sometimes called affective). Since cognitive outcomes involve the use of higher-order mental processes such as reasoning and logic, they are clearly relevant to the educational objectives of most students, faculty, administrators, trustees, parents, and others concerned with higher education. Noncognitive, or affective, outcomes refer to the student's attitudes, values, self-concept, aspirations, and everyday behavior and are important to students as well as to many educators. Information on affective outcomes is relatively easy to obtain through self-administered questionnaires, whereas measurements of cognitive outcomes often require more controlled conditions of administration and larger amounts of the student's time. But both deserve attention in a study of the impact of college.

Type of Data. The second dimension of the taxonomy, type of data, refers to the types of information gathered to assess the cognitive and affective outcomes. Again, two broad classes can be identified: *psychological* data, relating to the internal states or traits of the individual; and *behavioral* data, relating to directly observable activities. The measurement of psychological phenomena is usually indirect, in the sense that the investigator, from the student's responses to questions, infers some underlying state within that student. Behavioral measures, which might also be called sociological, directly reflect transactions between the student and the environment and are usually of intrinsic interest.

Any student outcome measure can be classified simultaneously by the type of outcome involved and the type of data (see Table 1.1). Each cell provides examples of different types of outcome measures obtained using different types of data. The cell on the upper left, for example, includes psychological measures of noncognitive or affective states: the student's ambition, motivation, and self-concept, as well as subjective feelings of satisfaction and well-being. The cell on the upper right includes cognitive measures such as the student's grade point average or performance on multiple-choice tests of ability and achievement. The lower-left cell includes sociological or behavioral features of the individual's development that reflect primarily affective states. Under personal habits, for example, one might include such behaviors as reading, eating, typical interactions with others, and use of drugs, tobacco, and alcohol. Citizenship would include such outcomes as voting behavior, participating in community activities, and earning special awards for community service or, on the negative side, welfare and arrest records.

Table 1.1. Classification of Student Outcomes by
Type of Outcome and Type of Data.

| | Outcome | |
Data	Affective	Cognitive
Psychological	Self-concept	Knowledge
	Values	Critical thinking ability
	Attitudes	Basic skills
	Beliefs	Special aptitudes
	Drive for achievement	Academic achievement
	Satisfaction with college	
Behavioral	Personal habits	Career development
	Avocations	Level of educational attainment
	Mental health	Vocational achievements:
	Citizenship	Level of responsibility
	Interpersonal relations	Income
		Awards or special recognition

Source: Data abstracted from Astin, Panos, and Creager (1967), p.16.

The lower-right cell gives examples of behavioral or sociological measures of cognitive outcomes. Basically, this category contains outcomes that reflect the behavior of the student (or former student) in society and that usually require cognitive skills. Presumably, real-life achievements represent the behavioral manifestations of the cognitive traits listed in the cell immediately above it.

The two dimensions that make up Table 1.1 are really more continua than true dichotomies. For example, a person's earned income probably depends in part on cognitive abilities, but it almost certainly depends as well on noncognitive or personality traits.

Time Dimension. Since attending college can have both short- and long-term effects, the four cells in Table 1.1 could be extended into a third dimension representing temporal differences in student outcomes. Table 1.2 shows examples of related measures taken at two points in time.

Although timing is seldom considered in discussions of educational outcomes, it is of fundamental importance. Most colleges hope to produce long-term rather than short-term changes. The goals stated in college catalogues, for example, imply that the institution is primarily concerned with making an impact

Table 1.2. Examples of Measures
Representing Different Times, Types of Data, and Outcomes.

Type of Outcome	Type of Data	Time 1 (During College)	Time 2 (After College)
Affective	Psychological	Satisfaction with college	Job satisfaction
Affective	Behavioral	Participation in student government	Participation in local or national politics
Cognitive	Psychological	Law School Aptitude Test (LSAT) score	Score on law boards
Cognitive	Behavioral	Persistence in college (staying in versus dropping out)	Income

that will last throughout a lifetime. The college, it would seem, tries to provide experiences that will help the student make the fullest possible use of his or her talents and become an effective, responsible member of society. Presumably, such effects will in turn result in a more satisfying and rewarding life.

For many prospective college students, however, such long-term effects may be too remote and too difficult to comprehend. These students are primarily interested in more immediate goals — their actual experiences during the undergraduate college years — rather than in how these experiences will affect their later development. Educators frequently do not recognize that the two, four, or eight years of college represent a sizable portion of the student's total life span. For students, then, college experiences are important in themselves, not merely for what they will mean later. We might add here that most professors and staff, if they focus at all on student outcomes, limit their attention to outcomes that can be assessed while the student is still enrolled. For these reasons, the study reported in this book will focus on those outcomes that can be observed during the "four critical years" after the student initially enrolls.

This outcome taxonomy, which has guided the selection of CIRP outcomes for the past twenty-seven years, has also been used to organize the major findings from the current study, as reported in Chapters Three through Nine. Affective-psychological outcomes are reported in Chapters Three ("Assessing Environmental Effects"), Four ("Personality and Self-Concept"), Five ("Attitudes, Values, and Beliefs"), and Nine ("Satisfaction with the College Environment"). Affective-behavioral outcomes are included in Chapter Six ("Patterns of Behavior"). Cognitive-psychological outcomes are reported in Chapter Seven ("Academic and Cognitive Development") and cognitive-behavioral outcomes are covered in Chapter Eight ("Career Development").

Outcome data for the study come from three different sources: the CIRP follow-up questionnaire administered during 1989–90 to samples of students who had originally entered college as freshmen in the fall of 1985; retention information on these same students, provided by the registrars of their institutions; and various national testing organizations that supplied us with results from the Scholastic Aptitude Test (SAT) and American College Test (ACT) taken by students prior to entering college, and from the Graduate Record Examination (GRE), Law School Admission Test (LSAT), Medical College Admission Test (MCAT), and National Teacher Examination (NTE) taken by these same students four years later. A total of eighty-two outcome measures was used, including twelve measures of personality and self-concept (Chapter Four), twelve measures of attitudes, values, and beliefs (Chapters Three and Five), nine measures of behavior patterns (Chapter Six), twenty-six measures of competency and achievement (Chapter Seven), nine measures of career development (Chapter Eight), and fourteen measures of satisfaction with the college environment (Chapter Nine). Details of how each outcome measure has been constructed will be provided in the relevant chapter.

Student Input Characteristics

A student's performance on some outcome measure such as the Graduate Record Examination (GRE) is, by itself, of little value in telling us how that student has been affected by the undergraduate experience. However, a GRE score takes on much greater significance when we can compare it to the student's performance on a similar measure, such as the SAT taken four years earlier, prior to college entry. This relationship holds for almost any other outcome measure: when the student's outcome (posttest) performance can be compared with input performance four years earlier, we can develop a measure of *growth* or *change*.

A long history of research on college impact (Astin, 1977; Bowen, 1977; Feldman and Newcomb, 1969; Pascarella and Terenzini, 1991) shows that the student's outcome performance can be affected by a number of other input characteristics besides the pretest performance. Since many of these input characteristics are also related to the kinds of environments to which students are exposed, the possibility remains that any observed correlation between an environment and an outcome measure may reflect the effect of some input characteristic rather than the effect of the college environment. In other words, our assessments of how outcomes are affected by environments will be biased unless we measure and control for as many student input characteristics as possible. The Cooperative Institutional Research Program (CIRP) was initiated in 1966 specifically to collect input data that would make it possible to apply the I-E-O model to a national study of student outcomes in American higher education.

In the study reported here, we had pretests available from the CIRP freshman questionnaire and from various college admissions test scores for approximately half (44) of the eighty-two student outcome measures. The main reason pretests were not available for all eighty-two outcomes is that some outcome measures do not lend themselves to pretesting. A good example is the outcome of student retention (completing a degree versus dropping out): since anybody who drops out of high school (the pretest) will, by definition, be eliminated from the college sample, it is obviously not feasible to have an adequate pretest for an outcome such as college retention. The best alternative in this situation is to make sure that those input characteristics that are known to predict retention (high school grades and admissions tests scores, for example) are available as input measures.

Another way to deal with outcome measures that have no obvious pretest at the input stage is to obtain students' *predictions* or *expectations* with respect to the outcome measure in question. One class of outcomes for which no appropriate pretests are available is measures of student *satisfaction*. In lieu of pretests, one can ask students whether they *expect* to be satisfied with college. One can also ask students to estimate their chances of completing a degree or dropping out. Since self-predictions of this type have some accuracy (Astin, 1977), our input variables included the forty-four pretest measures plus a list of twenty-six different self-predictions by which the student was asked to indicate whether there was a very good chance, some chance, very little chance, or no chance of a particular outcome event occurring during college. Sixty-one other input characteristics included the number of high school courses taken in eight different subject matter fields (8 measures), preliminary choice of a career

(12 measures), the importance (very important, somewhat important, not important) given to each of eleven reasons for attending college (11 measures), religious preference (6 measures), parental occupation (11 measures), parental income, parental education (2 measures), and a variety of demographic measures, including the student's race or ethnicity (6 measures), age, gender, marital status, and citizenship. Altogether, we used a total of 131 input measures. If we also consider the freshman's preliminary choice of a major field of study as an input rather than an environmental variable (see later in this chapter, and Chapter Two), there is a total of 146 input measures.

Environmental Measures

Earlier in this chapter I indicated that one of the major differences between this sequel to *Four Critical Years* and the original work is the inclusion of a number of environmental measures not available in that or any other previous study. The inclusion of these additional measures was made possible in part because of grants from the Exxon Education Foundation and the National Science Foundation, which provided funding for an expansion of the 1989–90 student follow-up questionnaire as well as for a special survey of all teaching faculty in each of the CIRP institutions selected for this study. (A more complete description of the CIRP sample used in the study is given later in this chapter.)

      The 192 environmental measures used in this study include 16 measures of institutional characteristics (such as type, control, size), 35 measures of the student's peer group characteristics (for example, socioeconomic status, academic preparation, values, attitudes), 34 measures of faculty characteristics (such as favored methods of teaching, morale, values), 15 measures of the curriculum (such as true core, type of requirements), 15 measures of financial aid (such as Pell grants, Stafford loans), 16 measures of freshman major field choice, 4 measures of place of residence (for example, college dormitory, private room), and 57 different measures of student involvement (hours spent studying, number of classes taken in different fields, participation in honors programs, and so on). Because of the number and complexity of the various environmental measures used, a detailed description of the construction of each measure will be provided in the next chapter (Chapter Two). Comprehensive summaries of the outcomes affected by each environmental measure are provided in Chapter Ten ("Summary of Environmental Effects") and Chapter Eleven ("Effects of Involvement"). The last Chapter (Chapter Twelve) summarizes the effects by key input variables and discusses the theoretical and policy implications of the major findings.

Assessing the Impact of College Experiences

Assessing the impact of college experiences on students involves two basic problems. The first, as discussed earlier, is to identify the relevant outcome variables. The second and more complex task is to determine how these outcomes are differentially affected by various college programs or experiences. The widespread confusion about how to handle this second task is reflected in the variety of methods and procedures that has been used in research on college impact. Investigators often forget, however, that each methodology implies a somewhat different conception of the purposes of higher education and the nature of the college experience. For this reason, it is important at the outset to describe the particular conception of higher education that underlies this study and to sketch in some detail the methodology employed to assess the impact of higher education on student development.

Two models from outside education are most commonly used in describing the functioning of colleges and universities: those of industry and medicine.

The Industrial Model of Higher Education

Budgetary constraints in recent years have forced many college administrators to come to grips with such issues as institutional accountability and the efficiency of institutional management. Many administrators have responded to these pressures by experimenting with computerized management information systems, by introducing "outcomes assessments," by hiring management consultants, by embarking on elaborate programs of "enrollment management," and by instituting such procedures as program budgeting, management by objectives, and Total Quality Management (TQM). One consequence of this business orientation is that it portrays students and their degrees as "produced" by the institution, in much the same way an automobile is produced at a factory.

Manufacturing is a physical process in which raw materials are fabricated into parts that are put together on an assembly line. The finished product is a result of the manufacturing process. But graduates of college are clearly not produced by the institution in this way. Their personal characteristics at the time of graduation may, to be sure, have been influenced by their college experience, but their physical and psychological makeup depends heavily on background and environmental factors largely independent of the institution. Students, in other words, are fully functioning organisms before they get to college; the purpose of our higher education system is presumably to enhance the student's functioning, or to "develop the talent of its students" (Astin, 1985, p. 60).

A major assumption of the current study is that industrial analogies of this kind are simply not applicable to higher education institutions. Although it is possible to assess the impact of a plant in terms of the number and quality of its products, the actual impact of college is not necessarily reflected in the number of its graduates or even in the quality of their achievements.

The Medical Model of Higher Education

A better institutional analogy for the college is the hospital, clinic, or doctor's office. The main function of both medicine and education is to improve the condition of their clients. Patients (students) are admitted to treatment facilities (colleges) because they need or want medical assistance (education). Medical facilities administer treatment programs based on a diagnosis of the patient's illness; colleges administer educational programs that presumably are relevant to the student's education needs. Just as some patients do not benefit from medical treatment, so some students do not benefit from college education. At the same time, some patients improve and some students learn, even if their treatment (educational) programs are ineffectual.

Although the medical model is clearly inappropriate in one respect — in that students are not ill — students and patients are both seeking some sort of personal service to improve their circumstances. Most important, both colleges and medical treatment facilities attempt to bring about desirable changes in the condition of their clients. For this reason, a critical ingredient in the assessment of college impact is to measure *change* in the characteristics of students over time.

We have already suggested that student change should not be equated with institutional impact. Does the same hold true for patient change? Can the hospital always take credit when the patient gets better? Should the hospital always take the blame if the patient's condition shows no change or gets worse? Can one assume that the hospital has had no impact? In medicine, there is a convenient means for dealing with such conceptual issues: the *prognosis.* When the newly admitted patient has a poor prognosis (input), the treatment program may be judged highly successful if the condition of the patient simply stabilizes (outcome). By the same token, a treatment program could be judged a failure if a patient with a highly favorable prognosis (input) fails to improve after admission (outcome). Thus, a patient whose condition remains unchanged could be judged either a success or a failure, depending on the initial prognosis. In other words, neither the patient's status at discharge nor changes in the patient's condition between admission and discharge provides an adequate indication of the success or failure of a treatment program. Such information has meaning only in the context of the initial prognosis.

The concept of change from admission to discharge is simpler than the relationship between outcome and prognosis (input). For example, a patient with a high fever caused by a bad cold will generally have a favorable prognosis, regardless of treatment. Fevers caused by bad colds usually disappear without any treatment. Thus, the positive change from high to low fever is not remarkable, given that the prognosis was favorable. Fevers caused by other factors (such as pneumonia) may not present such a favorable prognosis in the absence of treatment.

If we recast this last discussion in terms of the I-E-O model, we could say that our initial focus is on a single input measure — the patient's fever — and that we are interested in whether the fever can be reduced (from input measure to outcome measure) through treatment (environment). But it is not enough simply to have a single input measure (the "pretest" fever) in order to make an accurate diagnosis and to prognosticate about what the outcome ("posttest" fever) will be after a period of time. We also need other input data, such as the patient's history, other symptoms, information from a physical exam, and possibly X-rays and laboratory tests of various kinds. By putting together all of this information we are in a much better position to make a prediction (prognosticate) about the outcome (posttest fever). If this other input information leads us to conclude that the patient has a bad cold (diagnosis), we would predict that the fever will disappear after a few days, regardless of what treatment (environment) the patient receives. If we conclude instead that the patient has pneumonia or some kind of bacteriological infection, then we would make a more pessimistic prognosis, especially if no treatment (environment) is administered.

Clinical medicine thus utilizes two types of prognoses: those that assume no treatment and those that assume particular treatment. Diseases for which no effective treatment exists have the same prognosis, regardless of treatment. The essential aspect of an effective treatment is thus that it *changes the prognosis.*

In many ways, assessing the impact of an educational program is analogous. People will continue to grow and develop (from input to outcome) regardless of whether or where they attend college, and, because human behavior tends to be consistent over time, it is possible to predict (prognosticate) from current information (input) what a person will be like at some later time (outcome). High achievers in secondary school (input), for example, tend to be high achievers in college (outcome).

But we can make a better prediction as to whether this high achiever in high school will also be a high achiever in college if we have more input information on the student's ability, motivation, and family background. The basic issue, then, is whether attending a given college or being exposed to a particular type of environment *changes the prediction* of how the student will develop.

Medical prognosticating relies on collective experience showing that the illness of patients who show particular patterns of entry information (medical history, symptoms, laboratory findings, and so forth) frequently follow predictable courses. This is basically a statistical matter: particular illnesses under specified conditions frequently produce similar outcomes. In many ways, studying the development of college students is analogous: particular outcomes (for example, high grades in college) tend to be associated with particular input characteristics at entry (high grades in high school, high test scores, and so forth). The precise weight assigned to each entering freshman characteristic depends on the outcome predicted.

Modern statistical procedures can be used to combine such input information into a "best prediction" (prognosis) about how the entering student will perform later on the outcome measure. Just as the physician arrives at a prognosis using data from a patient's present symptoms, history, physical examination, and laboratory tests, the educational researcher can combine input information on an entering freshman's past achievements and behavior to predict that student's subsequent performance. Separate predictions can be developed for each student outcome. In predicting whether the student will complete a baccalaureate degree, for example, considerable weight will be given to past academic record, degree aspirations, and social background (Astin, 1975). In predicting such affective outcomes as political beliefs at graduation, considerable weight should be given to the student's initial beliefs at college entry. Put more simply, an entering student who espouses conservative beliefs (input) is much more likely to hold similar beliefs at graduation (outcome) than is an entering student who espouses liberal beliefs (see Chapter Three).

Whether such predictions are changed by particular college experiences is analogous to the medical question of whether particular treatments change the prognosis. A conservative freshman's chances of remaining a conservative during college are reduced if she enrolls at a college where her peers are mostly liberals (see Chapter Three). The environmental "treatment" (liberal peer groups) can thus change the "prognosis" (predicted political affiliation four years after entering). One major difference between medicine and education, however, is that the *causal* connections between certain treatments and certain medical outcomes are much better understood than are the causal connections between educational programs (environments) and student outcomes. This difference underscores the need for better studies in education where many student characteristics, such as input pretests, sex, ability, and socioeconomic status, are measured at entry and then statistically controlled in an effort to identify causal connections between educational experiences and outcomes. The actual statistical procedures used to control for entering student characteristics and to assess the impact of environmental experiences are described in Chapters Two and Three.

Data for Assessing College Impact

The need for multiple indicators of the entering student's propensity for change and also the need for multiple outcome measures were major considerations in designing the Cooperative Institutional Research Program. Each fall, the entering freshmen at institutions participating in the CIRP complete an extensive questionnaire composed of three types of input items: pretests on possible outcome measures, self-predictions about possible future outcomes, and personal characteristics (age, race, educational background, and so forth) that might affect the propensity to change or to attain certain outcomes. The sample of entering freshmen used in the current study was taken from the freshman classes entering higher education institutions in the fall of 1985. In addition to data from the freshman questionnaire, we have also been able to obtain SAT or ACT scores from the Educational Testing Service and the American College Testing Program.

The principal source of outcome data is an extensive follow-up questionnaire administered by mail to the 1985 freshmen in the summer and fall of 1989 and the winter of 1990. Other outcome data for retention studies have been obtained from the registrars of each institution that participated in the 1985 freshman survey. Additional data on cognitive outcomes include the students' scores on the Graduate Record Examination (GRE), the Law School Admission Test (LSAT), the Medical College Admission Test (MCAT), and the National Teacher Examination (NTE). These scores were obtained from the respective testing organizations that develop and administer the tests for admission to graduate and professional school. Details of these test scores are presented in Chapter Seven.

Environmental information has been drawn from several different sources. Information on the administrative characteristics of institutions (enrollments, finances, degrees earned, faculty salaries, type, control, and so forth) comes from the U.S. Department of Education. Data on the faculty environment were obtained from a survey of all teaching faculty at 217 of the 309 four-year institutions that were used to compute normative data in the 1985 freshman survey. Additional information about each individual student's environmental experiences comes from the 1989–90 follow-up questionnaire. Details of all of these environmental measures are contained in Chapter Two.

The procedures for mailing out the follow-up questionnaire were these. Starting in the late summer of 1989, a stratified random sample of 16,658 students at four-year colleges who completed the 1985 freshman survey were mailed the follow-up questionnaire to their home addresses. A second copy of the follow-up questionnaire was sent to nonrespondents approximately six weeks later. (Sampling was done to ensure that questionnaires would be received from approximately equal numbers of men and women in each of the twenty-seven stratification cells used for sampling four-year institutions in the CIRP; see Astin, Green, Korn, and Schalit, 1986.)

In addition to this randomly selected national sample, which covered only small numbers of students at each of 309 four-year institutions, follow-ups of much larger samples from

159 of these institutions were conducted between the late summer and early winter of 1989–90 with grants from the Exxon Education Foundation and the National Science Foundation. The 159 were selected so as to include at least four institutions in each of the twenty-six stratification cells used for four-year colleges and universities in the CIRP (Astin, Dey, Korn, and Riggs, 1991). The purpose of these additional follow-ups was to obtain large enough samples at each institution to permit studies of individual institutions.

The total number of students from the normative sample who returned completed questionnaires was 4,093, representing a 24.6 percent rate of response. Because extensive freshman input information is available on both respondents and nonrespondents, it is possible to develop a sophisticated weighting procedure to adjust for nonrespondent bias. In essence, the procedure gives greatest weight to those respondents who most resemble nonrespondents. (For details, see Astin and Molm, 1972; Cartter and Brown, 1976.) Following these corrections for nonresponse bias, additional corrective weights were applied to adjust for differential sampling of students within institutions and differential sampling of institutions within stratification cells. Unless otherwise stated, all normative tabulations reported in subsequent chapters approximate the results that would have been obtained if all first-time, full-time entering freshmen at four-year colleges and universities had participated in the freshman and follow-up surveys. The weighted results, in other words, are designed to be generalizable to the national population of 1985 entering freshmen.

A total of 27,064 students for whom we had institutional environmental data completed either the normative or expanded survey, yielding an overall response rate of 29.7 percent. In order to minimize the effect of any single institution on the results, respondents were excluded from some of the larger institutions so that no individual institution accounted for more than 1 percent of the total respondents. This adjustment resulted in a final longitudinal sample of 24,847 freshmen with completed follow-up questionnaires. Samples of students for whom we had SAT or ACT data and either retention data provided by the registrar or follow-up test scores from the GRE, LSAT, MCAT, or NTE varied for each test (see Table 1.3). These last samples are described in more detail in Chapter Seven.

Statistical Methodology

The statistical analyses that generated the findings reported in Chapters Three through Nine and summarized in Chapters Ten and Eleven involve two stages. First, input information on each entering freshman is combined statistically through multiple-regression techniques to obtain a predicted or expected score (prognosis) on each outcome measure under investigation. Only those variables that add significantly ($p < .0001$) to the prediction are included in the equation. Freshman pretests, when available, usually receive the largest weight in predicting the corresponding posttest outcome measure.

The second stage of the analysis estimates the effects of college experiences (the environment) by determining whether environmental variables add anything to the prediction of the outcome. In essence, we compare predicted outcomes based on entering freshman characteristics with actual outcome measures, and we do these comparisons separately for students in different

Table 1.3. Student Samples Used for Various Purposes.

Sample Used for	Number of	
	Institutions	Students
Descriptive national norms for 1985 freshmen at four-year colleges followed up in 1989	309	4,093
Longitudinal environmental effects analyses on outcomes from the 1989 follow-up questionnaire	217	24,847
Special college effects analyses on		
Retention	478[a]	38,587
GRE scores	478[a]	8,829
MCAT scores	478[a]	1,854
LSAT scores	478[a]	5,854
NTE scores	309[a]	2,477–2,836

[a]Reduced to 217 for analyses involving measures of the faculty environment.

college environments. If an outcome is positively affected by a particular environmental experience, the actual outcome scores should be consistently higher than the expected scores among students exposed to that environment and consistently lower than expected for students exposed to a different environment. Thus, among students who are exposed to a highly liberal peer group, their actual level of liberalism four years after college is higher than the expected level based on their political identification and other characteristics as entering freshmen (Chapter Three). In other words, an environmental effect is said to occur when an environmental variable (liberalism of the peer group) *adds* something to the prediction of the outcome over and above what we can predict from entering freshman characteristics.

To provide readers with a concrete example of just how each of the eighty-two analyses of outcome measures was conducted, Chapter Three is devoted to a detailed discussion of an analysis for a single outcome measure, the student's political identification.

College Impact

So far we have discussed the problem of how to assess the impact of various *environmental characteristics and experiences* on student outcomes. Here we consider the more general question of how to assess the *overall* impact of college attendance. *College impact* is a generic concept that lumps together all the varieties of college experiences and tries to compare their effects with the effects of *noncollege.*

Some scholars in higher education believe that a definitive study of college impact should include a control group of persons who never attended college. By comparing such a group with college attenders, the investigator would presumably be able to differentiate purely maturational changes caused by noncollege influences from changes specifically attributable to the effects of college.

The current study takes a somewhat different approach to the task of identifying college effects. Rather than comparing college attenders with nonattenders, we look at three possible sources of systematic influence on student development: college, maturation, and social change.

College

To estimate the extent to which "college" may influence a particular outcome, we sorted students into groups according to their *degree of exposure* to the college experience. The underlying rationale for this approach is quite simple: if certain outcomes are facilitated by the experience of attending college, the likelihood of such outcomes should be greatest for those students who have the greatest exposure to the college environment. However, if an outcome is not affected by going to college, its occurrence should not depend on how much exposure to college the student has had.

Because of the great diversity of institutional types and the substantial variations in college attendance patterns, students differ widely in their degree of exposure to the college experience. The current study approaches the issue of exposure from two perspectives: *time* of exposure and *intensity* of exposure.

Time of Exposure. Time or degree of exposure can be handled quite simply: How long does the student stay in college? Some students register for college and never show up for their first class. Others drop out before completing the first term. Still others persist as full-time students for the entire four undergraduate years or longer. In subsequent chapters, the presence of college effects is assessed by determining answers to two questions: (1) Are changes in people who stay in college for a short time comparable to changes in people who stay longer? (2) Are the effects of particular college characteristics stronger for people who stay longer?

The lowest point on the time continuum lacks the extreme case of a group that had *no* exposure to college (the control group of the non–college attendees). Nevertheless, this continuum-of-exposure approach has certain advantages over the college-noncollege design. In laboratory experiments, the control group is supposed to be comparable to the experimental group in all respects except the "treatment" variable—in this case, degree of exposure to the college environment. Clearly, high school graduates who enroll in college are different in many respects from their classmates who do not enroll. It may be that a group of students with little exposure to college (say, those who left during their first term) is a less biased control group than one whose members have never attended college. The latter group would differ from college attenders in certain critical respects: most would not have gone through the process of applying to college, and presumably many were never motivated to attend college in the first place. Although it is true that college dropouts differ from nondropouts in such characteristics as ability and achievement (Astin, 1971a, 1975), similar differences between those who do and do not attend college may be even greater (Sewell and Shah, 1968; Trent and Medsker, 1967; Cooley and Flanagan, 1966). Furthermore, since much is known about factors that predispose students to drop out of college (Astin, 1975), this knowledge can be utilized to control for pre-existing input differences between early dropouts and college completers.

One problem with using time of exposure to the college environment is that student dropout rates differ widely among different types of institutions. Students entering private universities, for example, are much more likely to complete four years of undergraduate work than are students initially entering other types of institutions. Ignoring such institutional differences would confound *time of exposure* with *type of institution attended*. To deal with this problem, analyses of the effect of time of exposure to the college environment are conducted only *after* all institutional and other environmental differences have been controlled (see Chapter Three).

Intensity of Exposure. The quality or *intensity* of the student's exposure to the college experience is assessed using two environmental measures: the frequency of interaction with other students and the frequency of interaction with faculty. The rationale for defining intensity of exposure in such terms is that many of the effects of college are mediated through the student's contact with fellow students and with faculty. For example, if being exposed to a particular peer group of fellow college students has certain effects on student development, we would expect the magnitude of these effects to be proportional to the degree of exposure to that peer group: the more frequently the student interacts with peers, the greater the change will be. In other words, if we find that certain overall changes observed in our sample of college undergraduates are greatest for those who have the most exposure to faculty or students and smallest for those who have the least exposure, then we would have some reason to conclude that the observed change can be attributed to the effect of college attendance.

Maturation

One simple way to estimate the possible presence of maturational effects is by the age of the entering student. If a particular change from input to outcome is in part the result of maturation, the older students should show less change than younger students. That is, if a particular change occurs in most young people during the interval from eighteen to twenty, regardless of whether the person attends college, then it is reasonable to expect that students who are already twenty when they first enter college would be less likely to exhibit these changes than students who are seventeen or eighteen. In short, a negative relationship between any given change and age at college entry would constitute evidence that the change is in part maturational.

Social Change

The problem of assessing "the impact of college" is not complicated just by maturational effects. Students can also show systematic changes over time because of social changes that have little to do with either maturation or college impact (Gurin, 1971). What if we had included a question in the 1985 freshman survey that measured something like "fear of the Soviet Union"? If we were to posttest this measure six years later, in 1991, we probably would see a sharp decline in "fear of the Soviet Union." It would make little sense to attribute such a change to college impact and even less sense to attribute it to maturation. Clearly, the change would be primarily attributable to external social events.

Because CIRP assesses the attitude and behavioral patterns of each new entering freshman class, we can monitor such social trends during the same period of time that the 1985 freshmen were attending college. Thus, in attempting to interpret longitudinal changes in the attitudes and behaviors of the 1985 freshmen that occurred between 1985 and 1989, we will look at responses to the same attitudinal and behavioral questions to see how they may have changed in the five consecutive freshman surveys conducted between 1985 and 1989.

Limitations of the Study

One major limitation of this study is that separate analyses have not been done by gender, race, ability, socioeconomic status, or other key student characteristics. While these characteristics have been included among the input variables and their effects on student outcomes summarized in the final chapter (Chapter Twelve), space limitations have made it impossible to do separate subgroup analyses (for example, for men and for women). HERI staff are currently conducting such analyses to identify possible interaction effects, and the highlights are expected to be published in a forthcoming series of journal articles.

Another limitation is the four-year longitudinal span. While the results reported in subsequent chapters show clearly that the first four years of college are indeed critical in many respects, the four-year limit precludes systematic study of other interesting and important phenomena, such as graduate and professional education and the link between higher education and employment. Given the rich data resources that have already been assembled on each of these students, we hope that further funding can be secured to support longer-term studies.

Summary

This chapter has considered a number of conceptual and methodological problems associated with studying college impact, presenting in some detail the general design of the impact analysis used in Chapters Three through Nine.

First, just the fact that students change in certain demonstrable ways while attending college does not mean that college attendance per se has produced the change. One also needs some basis for judging whether the same change would have occurred if the student had attended a different college or no college at all.

Second, because the college experience has the potential to affect any aspect of the students' lives, the impact of college cannot be adequately assessed from one or two simple outcomes, such as attaining a degree or earning a certain income. An adequate assessment requires a variety of cognitive and affective outcome measures.

Third, the factory or production model of higher education, in which credits, degrees, and graduates are "produced" by the institution, has been rejected as a conceptually inadequate representation of the process of higher education. To assess college impacts, a medical or treatment model is a more appropriate analogy, primarily because both medical and educational institutions provide services designed to enhance the development of the individual. The effectiveness of these services cannot be assessed solely in terms of the status of the individual at some end point; rather, the person's final status must be evaluated in relation to initial status at the point of entry into the institution. Initial status (the person's educational potential) is analogous to a medical prognosis.

Fourth, much of the previous research on college impact has produced inconclusive findings, primarily because of limitations in the data and methods of analysis. The I-E-O model (Astin, 1991), which provides the conceptual framework for this new study of college impact, requires three types of information: *input* data describing the student at the point of entry, *environmental* data assessing the student's educational experiences after entering college, and *outcome* data describing the student after exposure to the college environment. The Cooperative Institutional Research Program (CIRP), which provides the principal basis for the findings reported in Chapters Three through Nine, has a number of advantages in studying college impact. Its input data are collected from students as they enter a wide variety of collegiate institutions representing all major types. Environmental data describing the characteristics of each student's institution and experiences within those institutions, together with a variety of outcome measures covering both cognitive and affective as well as psychological and behavioral outcomes, are collected from institutions, faculty, testing organizations, and students via follow-up questionnaires. And CIRP data are longitudinal, with both freshman input pretests and posttests available for most outcome measures. Freshman input data also cover a wide range of personal and background information, which makes possible control of numerous potentially biasing variables.

Fifth and finally, many investigators have assumed that the "ideal" study of college impact requires comparing college attenders with a control group of nonattenders, but that design oversimplifies the college impact problem. Given the great variety of institutions and programs, it is necessary to assess the impact of college *characteristics* and collegiate *experiences* rather than "college" as such. The development of these environmental characteristics is described in the next chapter (Chapter Two). In addition, the matter of attendance versus nonattendance is more a continuum than a dichotomy. Thus, the current study has been designed so students can be compared in terms of their *length of exposure* (minimal time in attendance versus full-time attendance for four years) and *intensity of exposure* (degree of actual involvement in the collegiate experience). Through such comparisons, the following chapters aim to separate changes that are purely maturational or directly societally induced from those that are attributable to college experiences.

This completely new version of the original *Four Critical Years* (Astin, 1977) not only uses much more recent data but also incorporates a number of new features not present in the earlier book: measures of the student's peer group characteristics; extensive measures of the faculty's values, attitudes, and preferred teaching methods; extensive measures of each institution's curriculum; and student performance on college admissions tests and on various tests used for professional certification and for admission to graduate and professional school.

Chapter 2

———•·•·•———

Environmental
Variables

Consider for a moment all the different aspects of the undergraduate student's college experience that have the potential to influence both cognitive and affective outcomes. First we have the kind of institution in which the student enrolls: large or small, research university or liberal arts college, sectarian, independent, or public, and so on. Then there is the curriculum: the number of required courses (and which courses), the presence or absence of a core curriculum, or the availability of interdisciplinary courses. Then there is the faculty: their preferred methods of teaching and student advising, their attitudes, values, and beliefs, and how they interact with each other and with administrators. Finally, there are the student's peers: their academic abilities and interests, their values, attitudes, and beliefs, and their mode of interacting with one another.

Since any or all of these aspects of the environmental experience can make a difference in how the student develops, the challenge to the college impact researcher is to find ways to document the presence or occurrence of as many of these potentially critical environmental factors as possible so that their impact can be assessed. Environmental assessment is not only the most difficult and complex challenge in the field of higher education research, but it is also the most neglected topic in the assessment literature (Astin, 1991). One of the major strengths of the study reported in this book (as well as the book's principal methodological advance over the original *Four Critical Years*) is that we had available a wide range of complex and sophisticated measures of the student's institution, curriculum, faculty, and peer group. In this chapter we shall present and discuss each of these measures in order to prepare the reader for the outcomes analyses presented in Chapters Three through Nine. In essence, the environmental measures described here constitute the independent variables that were used in the outcomes analyses described in the next seven chapters. These environmental variables will be discussed under six general headings: characteristics of institutions; curriculum; faculty; the peer group; residence, major, and financial aid; and student involvement.

Institutional Characteristics

American higher education institutions have traditionally been classified along two dimensions: type and control. Type ordinarily refers to the level of highest degree offered (four-year college, university), whereas control usually refers to the principal source of governance or control (public, Protestant, Roman Catholic, nonsectarian). By combining these two characteristics, we can form six dichotomous measures: public university, private university, public four-year college, Protestant four-year college, Catholic four-year college, nonsectarian four-year college.

Two other dichotomous measures are used to identify historically black colleges (HBCs) and colleges for women. Since there are very few colleges for men left in the American higher education system, we chose instead to create a dichotomous measure indicating that the student body included more than 80 percent male students.

In addition to these dichotomous measures, we also included several continuous measures to reflect various institutional characteristics that are thought to be of potential importance in student development: the size of the institution (two

measures: the total full-time equivalent undergraduate enrollment and the grand total full-time equivalent enrollment), the
student-faculty ratio, percentage of graduate students in the total
student body, the percentage of total expenditures invested in
student services (a measure of the institutional commitment to
student support services), the percentage of total expenditures
invested in instructionally related activities (a measure of the
institutional commitment to the instructional process), and the
average faculty salary (sometimes used as a measure of institutional quality).

Curricular Measures

Until recently there have been virtually no attempts to develop
a systematic description or taxonomy of curricular programs
that lends itself to quantification. Recently, however, a detailed
analysis of data presented in three hundred college catalogues
resulted in an empirical taxonomy (Hurtado, Astin, and Dey,
1991) which has been incorporated into the present study. This
analysis identified three distinctive approaches to designing a
general education curriculum: (1) a *true core,* in which all students
are required to take exactly the same package of courses in order
to satisfy the general education requirement; a *major-dominated*
approach, in which general education requirements are determined by the student's major or area of specialization; and a *distributional* approach, in which general education requirements are
satisfied by selection from an approved list of courses organized
into broad curricular groupings (social sciences, natural sciences,
and so on). True core and major-dominated approaches accounted for only 2 percent and 4 percent, respectively, of the
institutions. Since the distributional approach was found to be
typical of more than 90 percent of all undergraduate institutions, we subjected institutions with distributional systems to
a factor analysis of all their other general education program
characteristics to determine whether there are distinctive ways
in which distributional programs differ. This analysis identified
four different factors or qualities of a distributional system:
progressive offerings (the extent to which general education offer-

ings include contemporary courses on issues such as ethnic studies or gender studies); a *personalized* or *individualized* approach that incorporates such features as an independent research requirement, senior thesis, and written evaluation; an *integrative* or *interdisciplinary* emphasis that includes interdisciplinary courses, field study, and a senior seminar or capstone course; and the *degree of structure* or the number of options available in the distributional system (more structure means fewer options).

In addition to these six measures (major dominated, true core, plus four characteristics of distributional systems), nine other curricular measures were used: use of written evaluations (versus traditional letter grades), existence of a minority or Third World studies program, existence of a women's or gender studies program, and the presence or absence of six different curricular or program requirements (internship, thesis or senior project, comprehensive exam, independent research, minority or Third World course, women's or gender studies course). All of these last nine measures were dichotomous in form.

The Faculty Environment

One of the unique features of the study presented in this book is the comprehensive survey of all teaching faculty that was conducted in 1989–90, concurrently with the four-year follow-up of the 1985 entering freshmen. Comparison of results with a recent national faculty survey conducted by the National Center for Education Statistics (1990) shows that the HERI sample of respondents is representative of the population with respect to age, race, academic rank, and highest degree held (Astin, Dey, and Korn, 1991). Because of the scope and comprehensiveness of the faculty survey, we decided to tap this rich source of environmental information by conducting a series of preliminary analyses of the nearly three hundred items of information contained in the questionnaire.

The first task was to decide which characteristics of teaching faculty would be most likely to have an impact on the undergraduate student. In reviewing the numerous items in the faculty questionnaire, we identified two conceptually distinct categories: information about faculty *behavior* (teaching and examining techniques, for example), and information about the faculty's *satisfaction* (with the administration, for example), *values,* and *perceptions* of the institutional climate. (The dichotomy between behavior and attitudes closely resembles the "type of data" dichotomy that was used in developing student outcome measures; see Chapter One.) An inspection of the questionnaire identified 78 items pertaining to faculty behaviors and 110 items reflecting their values, satisfaction, sources of stress, and perceptions of the institutional climate. Since these items were far too numerous and probably much too redundant to justify their use as separate environmental measures, we decided instead to conduct a series of factor analyses to reduce the number of items and to generate a less redundant list of more general faculty factors. After some debate and discussion, we decided that there were really two conceptually distinct kinds of information in these data: faculty information provided by faculty about themselves, and perceptions about the institution. Accordingly, two new groups of items were formed: those having to do with perceptions of the institutional climate (61 items), and those having to do with the faculty's own behavior, values, sources of stress, and satisfaction (127 items). Separate factor analyses of the two groups of items yielded twenty-one factors (13 behavioral-value-satisfaction and 8 perceptual). Since these factors have not been reported previously in the literature, each one will be presented and discussed separately. The thirteen behavioral-attitudinal factors will be presented first, followed by the eight perceptual factors. To broaden the context for interpreting each factor, we have also computed the correlations between the factors and other characteristics of the institution. Only the largest correlations will be reported.

Research Orientation

Ten items from the faculty survey questionnaire have substantial loadings on the Research Orientation factor. These items, together with their factor "loadings," are shown below. Readers unfamiliar with factor analysis should keep in mind that a factor loading represents the simple correlation (r) of the item with the hypothetical underlying factor. The meaning of any factor is thus revealed in those items with the highest loadings.

	Factor Loading
How many articles have you published in academic or professional journals?	.72
How many of your professional writings have been published or accepted for publication in the *last two* years?	.72
Do your interests lie primarily in teaching or in research? [scored for research]	.71
How important for you (as a personal or professional goal) is engaging in research?	.68
How many hours per week do you spend on research and scholarly writing?	.66
How many chapters have you had published in edited volumes?	.59
How important to you personally is it to become an authority in your field?	.53
Have you received intra- or extramural funds for research?	.52
How many days during the past academic year were you away from campus for professional activities (such as professional meetings, speeches, or consulting)?	.47
How important to you personally is it to obtain recognition from colleagues for contributions to your special field?	.46

Research Orientation is defined primarily by the faculty's publication rate, time spent conducting research, and personal commitment to research and scholarship.

As might be expected, the Research Orientation of the faculty has substantial correlations with institutional size (.66) and selectivity (.56). What is perhaps most remarkable, however, is the correlation of this factor with the average salaries earned by the faculty at the institution (.86). Such a high correlation clearly reflects one of the dominant values in American higher education: differentials in faculty salaries are heavily related to, if not determined primarily by, the amount of research produced.

Use of Active Learning

Active Learning has been a much-discussed concept among higher education faculty and administrators during recent years (Chickering and Gamson, 1987; Study Group, 1984). Following are the ten highest-loading items on this factor:

	Factor Loading
Instructional technique: Cooperative learning (small groups)	.68
Instructional technique: Student presentations	.64
Instructional technique: Group projects	.63
Instructional technique: Experiential learning or field studies	.59
Evaluation technique: Student evaluations of each other's work	.57
Instructional technique: Independent projects	.50
Instructional technique: Student-selected topics for course content	.44
Instructional technique: Class discussions	.42
Instructional technique: Lecture	$-.39$
Instructional technique: Student-developed activities (assignments, exams, and so on)	.36

The term *active,* which is used to distinguish certain learning strategies from the more traditional and passive forms of learning, such as listening to lectures and reading, is meant to encompass a wide range of activities in which students are either (1) actively involved or engaged or (2) required to take a good deal of initiative in enhancing their own learning. Given that virtually all ten items conform to such a definition, we have chosen to call this factor Active Learning. A large body of research suggests that learning and retention are enhanced when active rather than passive strategies are used (Study Group, 1984). Not surprisingly, the extent to which a faculty member relies on lectures is negatively related to the use of active learning strategies.

Active learning strategies are most frequently used at colleges affiliated with the Roman Catholic church and least frequently used in both public and private universities. Use of active learning has negative correlations with institutional size (−.39), selectivity (−.32), and average faculty salaries (−.50).

Faculty Morale

Following are the fourteen highest-loading items on the Faculty Morale factor:

	Factor Loading
Overall job satisfaction	.79
Satisfaction with: Autonomy and independence	.64
Satisfaction with: Undergraduate course assignments	.63
Satisfaction with: Opportunity for scholarly pursuits	.61
Satisfaction with: Working conditions (hours, location)	.61
Satisfaction with: Teaching load	.61
Satisfaction with: Relationships with administration	.60
Satisfaction with: Relationships with other faculty	.56
Satisfaction with: Job security	.54
Satisfaction with: Competency of colleagues	.52
Satisfaction with: Graduate course assignments	.51
Satisfaction with: Visibility for jobs at other institutions or organizations	.49
Satisfaction with: Salary and fringe benefits	.49
Satisfaction with: Quality of students	.45

All these items come from a list of satisfaction questions included in the faculty survey. That this factor is indeed measuring the faculty member's overall level of satisfaction is indicated by the observation that "overall job satisfaction" has the highest loading of all items.

Faculty morale is highest at public universities, at large institutions (.28), and at institutions with high salary levels (.33).

Faculty Commitment to the Student's Personal Development/Altruism

This factor includes two seemingly different clusters of items: goals for undergraduates and personal goals.

	Factor Loading
Goal for undergraduates: Provide for students' emotional development	.71
Goal for undergraduates: Help students develop personal values	.69
Goal for undergraduates: Develop moral character	.68
Goal for undergraduates: Prepare students for family living	.61
Goal for undergraduates: Enhance students' self-understanding	.59
Personal goal: Help others who are in difficulty	.54
Personal goal: Influence social values	.53
Goal for undergraduates: Enhance out-of-class experience for students	.52
Personal goal: Promote racial understanding	.51
Personal goal: Develop meaningful philosophy of life	.49

The five highest-loading items plus one additional item reflect the faculty member's commitment to and interest in the student's affective and personal development (emotional development, personal values, moral character, preparation for family living, self-understanding). The four other items, on the other hand, reflect the faculty member's altruistic tendencies (helping others, influencing social values, promoting racial understanding).

Religiously affiliated colleges (both Catholic and Protestant) tend to receive very high scores on this factor, as do historically black colleges. Both public and private universities, on the other hand, tend to receive low scores. This factor has substantial negative correlations with average faculty salaries ($-.72$), selectivity ($-.61$), and size ($-.47$).

This factor contains two seemingly distinct clusters of items, prompting a decision to develop two factor scores rather than one: a Commitment to Student Development score and a Faculty Altruism score. Although such a decision may not be psychometrically defensible, we felt it important to separate these two groups of items in order to facilitate interpretation of any results. Not surprisingly, the two scores produced a very high correlation ($r = .79$).

Faculty Diversity Orientation

Following are the four items defining Faculty Diversity Orientation:

	Factor Loading
Instructional technique: Incorporated readings on women and gender issues	.74
Instructional technique: Incorporated readings on racial and ethnic issues	.72
Performed research or writing focused on women or gender	.55
Performed research or writing focused on racial or ethnic minorities	.54

Institutional types whose faculties have the strongest diversity orientations are private, nonsectarian colleges and historically black colleges. Faculty Diversity Orientation is negatively related to institutional size (−.23).

Liberalism

Following are the six items with the highest loadings on faculty Liberalism:

	Factor Loading
Political self-label: liberal or far left (versus conservative or far right)	.73
Belief: A national health care plan is needed to cover everybody's medical costs.	.61
Belief: The death penalty should be abolished.	.56
Belief: Wealthy people should pay a larger share of taxes than they do now.	.54
Belief: Abortion should be legal.	.41
Belief: Colleges should be actively involved in solving social problems.	.40

This factor combines a tendency to label oneself either liberal or far left (contrasted with conservative or far right) with support for traditionally liberal issues: a national health care plan, abolition of the death penalty, greater taxation of the wealthy, and legal abortions. One finds the greatest extremes of faculty liberalism within the four-year college sector: non-sectarian colleges have the highest scores and Protestant colleges the lowest scores. Liberalism has moderate positive correlations with institutional selectivity (.41) and average faculty salaries (.40).

Time Stress

The faculty questionnaire included a list of eighteen items designed to reflect possible sources of stress. Eight of these items produced the largest loadings on the faculty Time Stress factor:

	Factor Loading
Stressor: Time pressures	.63
Stressor: Lack of personal time	.63
Stressor: Household responsibilities	53
Stressor: Committee work	.49
Stressor: Teaching load	.42
Stressor: Faculty meetings	.40
Stressor: Research demands	.39
Stressor: Student demands	.32

Time stress has a modest positive correlation with institutional selectivity (.22), whereas faculty at historically black colleges tend to receive relatively low scores. Otherwise, there are only minor differences in Time Stress across different institutional types.

Age

Age was defined by three items:

	Factor Loading
Year tenure was awarded	.88
Year current appointment was made	.79
Year highest degree was awarded	.74

We have taken some liberties with the use of the word *age.* While this factor no doubt has a high correlation with the faculty's chronological age, we felt that length of time at the institution and years since receiving tenure would provide a more meaningful index of the faculty's "age" than would mere chronological age.

The "oldest" faculty are found at the religiously affiliated colleges (both Protestant and Catholic). Faculty age shows moderate negative correlations with institutional selectivity ($-.36$) and size ($-.24$). But the largest and most interesting correlation reveals a negative relationsihp between faculty age and average faculty salary ($-.39$). Given that religiously affiliated institutions generally pay their faculties less than nonsectarian or public institutions do, a negative correlation with faculty salaries is perhaps to be expected. However, for this to be the largest correlation with any institutional characteristic suggests that factors other than institutional control are involved. One possible explanation is that the highest-paid faculty, regardless of age, tend to move more frequently from one institution to another because of the competition among prestigious institutions for nationally visible scholars and researchers. Such an interpretation is consistent with the negative correlations, reported above, between faculty age and institutional size and selectivity.

Involvement in Administration

Following are the five highest-loading items for administrative involvement:

	Factor Loading
Hours per week: Administrative duties	.56
Goal: Have administrative responsibility for the work of others	.51
Have considered a career in academic administration	.45
Hours per week: Committee work	.40
Was previously an academic administrator	.40

The faculty at historically black colleges show by far the highest degree of involvement in administrative work, whereas faculty in private universities show the lowest level. This factor has modest negative correlations with average faculty salaries ($-.33$) and institutional selectivity (-26).

Family Orientation

Family Orientation has only two high-loading items:

	Factor Loading
Have dependent children	.68
Goal: Raise a family	.66

The only institutional characteristic showing even a moderate correlation with this factor is institutional selectivity (−.27).

Humanities Orientation

This factor, Humanities Orientation, should be interpreted with some caution, given the relatively low loadings:

	Factor Loading
Goal for undergraduates: Prepare for employment	−.39
Goal for undergraduates: Teach classics of Western Civilization	.38
Evaluation technique: Midterm essay exams	.35
Taught general education courses	.33
Evaluation technique: Multiple drafts of written work	.30

The nonsectarian private four-year colleges have by far the strongest Humanities Orientation, whereas public institutions (universities and colleges alike) have the lowest scores on this factor. This is one of the few factors that show correlations of opposite sign with institutional selectivity (.30) and size (−.35). In other words, the small, highly selective colleges exhibit the strongest orientation toward the humanities, whereas the larger, nonselective institutions show the weakest Humanities Orientation.

Use of Multiple-Choice Exams

The "doublet" factor for Multiple-Choice Exams speaks for itself:

Factor Loading

Evaluation technique: Multiple-choice mid-
  terms   .53
Evaluation technique: Multiple-choice quizzes   .43

Some of the most dramatic differences in faculty climate by institutional type are found on this factor. Faculty at historically black colleges showed the greatest reliance on multiple-choice tests. Faculty at Catholic and public four-year colleges are also very frequent users of this exam methodology. Faculty at private nonsectarian four-year colleges, on the other hand, are least favorably disposed to the Use of Multiple-Choice Exams. Faculty reliance on multiple-choice tests shows very strong negative associations with institutional selectivity ($-.75!$) and average faculty salaries ($-.58$).

Collegial Stress

The measure of Collegial Stress is not really a factor in the traditional sense, since it contains only one item with substantial loading: the extent to which colleagues are perceived as a significant source of stress (loading = $-.44$). However, because it seems to reflect something about the faculty culture that might have implications for students, we have decided to retain it in our battery of measures of the faculty environment. Collegial Stress does not show substantial differences by institutional type, although it does have a modest positive correlation with institutional selectivity ($.22$).

Up to this point, we have been looking at factors that emerged from the analysis of items concerning faculty behavior, satisfaction, and values. What follows are descriptions of eight factors that emerged from the analysis of faculty *perceptions* about the institutional climate.

Social Activism and Community Orientation

All of the high-loading items on Social Activism and Community Orientation reflect the faculty's perception of their institutions' goals:

Factor Loading

Institutional goal: Teach students how to
   change society   .73
Institutional goal: Develop leadership ability
   among students   .66
Institutional goal: Help solve major social
   and environmental problems   .65
Institutional goal: Develop a sense of com-
   munity among faculty and students   .62
Institutional goal: Help students understand
   their own values   .62
Institutional goal: Facilitate involvement in
   community service activities   .58

Basically, this factor reflects the extent to which the institution is perceived as concerning itself with producing student leaders who will become social change agents. Different types of institutions show substantial differences on this factor. Faculty at historically black colleges, together with faculty at Catholic and Protestant colleges, are most likely to perceive their institutions as emphasizing Social Activism and Community Orientation. Faculty at private universities, public colleges, and especially public universities, on the other hand, are least likely to perceive such an emphasis in their institutions. This factor has a substantial negative correlation with institutional size ($-.55$) and a modest negative correlation with selectivity ($-.28$).

Student Orientation of the Faculty

Faculty concern for students is defined by seven high-loading items:

Factor Loading

Faculty here are interested in students' aca-
   demic problems.   .65
Faculty here are interested in students' per-
   sonal problems.   .62

Faculty here are committed to the welfare of the institution.	.53
Many faculty are sensitive to the issues of minorities.	.47
Faculty are easy to see outside of office hours.	.46
Students are treated like numbers in a book.	−.44
There are many opportunities for student-faculty interaction.	.40

This factor is clearly concerned with the extent to which faculty believe that their colleagues are interested in and focused on student development. All three types of private four-year colleges, but especially the Protestant colleges, have relatively high scores on Student Orientation. The lowest scores were obtained by the public universities, although public four-year colleges and private universities also have very low scores. Not surprisingly, Student Orientation has a very strong negative correlation (−.72) with institutional size. It also has a strong negative correlation (−.64) with average faculty salaries.

Positive Perception of the Administration

The five highest-loading items on this factor all have to do with the faculty's perceptions of the administration:

	Factor Loading
Administrators consider faculty views when making policy.	.69
The administration is open about its policies.	.64
Faculty are often at odds with the administration.	−.60
Administrators don't care about what happens to students.	−.57
Administrators consider student views when making policy.	.52

Two of these items, including the highest-loading one, have to do directly with faculty-administration relationships. Two other items reflect the faculty's views about administrator-student relationships, while the final item has to do with the perceived openness of the administration. This factor might also be labeled Positive Perception of the Administration.

The highest scores on this factor are obtained by the Protestant colleges, whereas the lowest scores are obtained by public institutions (colleges and universities). Not surprisingly, this factor also shows a moderate negative correlation with institutional size (−.40).

Institutional Diversity Emphasis

The five highest-loading items on this factor all have to do with the faculty's perception of the institution's concern with and commitment to diversity issues:

	Factor Loading
Institutional goal: Increase the number of minority faculty	.75
Institutional goal: Increase the number of minority students	.70
Institutional goal: Create a diverse multi-cultural environment	.63
Institutional goal: Increase the number of women faculty	.62
Institutional goal: Develop an appreciation for multiculturalism	.58

Two types of liberal arts colleges anchor the extremes on this factor: private nonsectarian colleges obtain the highest scores, whereas Protestant colleges obtain the lowest scores. Diversity Emphasis has a modest positive correlation with selectivity (.22) and a substantial correlation with Faculty Diversity Orientation ($r = 55$). However, because this second correlation is far from perfect, these two diversity measures are not completely interchangeable.

Lack of Student Community

Lack of Student Community is defined by three items:

Factor Loading

Students here do not socialize with one another regularly.	.80
There is little contact among students outside of class.	.67
Students here are apathetic.	.50

As would be expected, both types of public institutions (universities and colleges) obtain the highest scores on this factor. Protestant colleges obtain the lowest scores. This factor, like Humanities Orientation, shows opposite-sign correlations with size (.26) and selectivity (−.27).

Institutional Emphasis on Resources and Reputation

The Resources and Reputation factor is defined exclusively in terms of perceived goals of the institution:

Factor Loading

Institutional goal: Enhance the institution's national image	.70
Institutional goal: Increase or maintain institutional prestige	.69
Institutional goal: Raise money for the institution	.59
Institutional goal: Hire faculty "stars"	.50

Clearly, this factor reflects the degree of institutional priority given to the enhancement of reputation and the amassing of resources. To a certain extent, this factor confirms the theory expressed in *Achieving Educational Excellence* (Astin, 1985) that reputation building and resource enhancement tend to go together in American higher education.

As might be expected, universities (both public and private) place the greatest emphasis on resources and reputation; public and Catholic four-year colleges put the least emphasis on these goals. Emphasis on Resources and Reputation has moderate positive correlations with both size (.46) and selectivity (.36).

Racial Conflict

Racial Conflict is defined by three items:

Factor Loading

Students from different ethnic backgrounds get along well.	−.50
There is a lot of racial conflict on this campus.	.47
There is little trust between minorities and campus administrators.	.44

The greatest degree of racial conflict is found at public universities, and the least is reported at historically black colleges, Protestant colleges, and Catholic colleges. Racial conflict has substantial positive correlations with institutional size (.47) and selectivity (.39).

Perceived Academic Competence of Students

This factor, Perceived Academic Competence, reflects the extent to which faculty see their students as academically bright and well prepared:

Factor Loading

Most of the students here are very bright.	.60
Most of the students here are well prepared.	.50
There is keen competition among students for grades.	.47

Faculty in nonsectarian and Protestant four-year colleges are most likely to believe that their students are bright and well prepared academically; faculty at historically black colleges and public institutions (both colleges and universities) are least likely to see their students as academically well prepared. Here is the third factor where opposite-sign correlations occur with selectivity (.38) and size (−.32). Considering that selectivity is a direct measure of the average score on nationally standardized college admission tests, it is somewhat surprising to find such a modest correlation ($r = .38$) between selectivity and perceived academic competence of the students. Apparently, faculty are responding to many factors other than the actual level of academic preparation of their students when they answer these questions.

Correlations Between Perceptual and Behavioral-Attitudinal Factors

Since the behavioral-value-satisfaction factor and the perceptual factors are based on independent analyses of the faculty's responses to selected questionnaire items, one might expect some high correlations across the two sets. And indeed there are. The Research Orientation of the faculty, for example, has a substantial negative correlation (−.69) with the Student Orientation of the faculty. Similarly, the faculty's Commitment to Student Development is highly correlated ($r = .72$) with Social Activism and Community Orientation. Use of Active Learning has a substantial correlation ($r = .61$) with Diversity Emphasis, whereas Diversity Emphasis has moderate positive correlations with faculty Liberalism (.55) and Humanities Orientation (.52). Institutional Emphasis on Resources and Reputation, as expected, has a strong positive correlation (.67) with the Research Orientation of the faculty. The largest correlation of all ($r = .78$) involves the Student Orientation of the faculty (as perceived by faculty) and Social Activism and Community Orientation.

Additional Faculty Measures

Twelve additional measures of each institution's faculty have been included because of their intrinsic interest and potential relevance to policy. Seven of these reflect the percentage of faculty who are women, are in some field of science or engineering, have doctoral degrees, teach interdisciplinary courses, team teach, teach general education courses, or involve undergraduates in their research. The other five measures are hours per week spent in teaching or advising students, mean political orientation (average score on the political identification item: 1 = far right, 5 = far left), use of teaching assistants in courses, the mean score of perceived faculty attitudes toward the general education program, and the mean perceived competition among students.

The Peer Group

The extensive literature on the impact of college on students suggests that one of the principal developmental influences on students is the peer group (Astin, 1977; Feldman and Newcomb, 1969; Pascarella and Terenzini, 1991). That fellow students should constitute a major source of influence should not come as any great surprise. Even on a commonsense level, most of us see our peers as important sources of influence, and anybody who has raised children can testify to the tremendous influence that peers can have, even on very young children.

Despite the widespread agreement among researchers and educators about the importance of peer groups, relatively little is actually known about *how* undergraduates are influenced by their peers: What developmental processes are affected by what kinds of peer group experiences? Perhaps the major impediment to extending our knowledge of peer group effects has been the lack of measures of the *characteristics* of the peer group. Accordingly, the analyses reported here were designed to develop a comprehensive assessment of the characteristics of the undergraduate student peer group.

Selectivity

Some of the earlier research on college impact employed simple measures of peer group characteristics based on academic variables. Perhaps the most commonly used among these is the

selectivity of the institution, which has traditionally been measured in terms of the mean score of the entering students on
one of the major national college admissions tests (SAT or ACT).
While Selectivity has often been employed as a measure of quality, it can also be viewed as a peer group measure: the average
ability or average level of academic preparation of the student's
peers.

Another potentially important peer measure that is closely
related to Selectivity ($r = .73$) is the socioeconomic status (SES)
of the peer group. A measure of Peer SES was thus constructed,
consisting of a composite of three peer group characteristics:
father's educational level, mother's educational level, and parental
income. Measures of parental education were coded on an eight-
point scale (1 = grammar school . . . 8 = graduate degree), while
parental income was coded on a fourteen-point scale (1 = less
than \$6,000 . . . 14 = \$150,000 or more). Peer SES for any institution is defined as the sum of the mean scores of its freshmen on these three items.

While the academic ability and SES of the student's peers
can no doubt influence the individual student in many different ways, our primary aim in developing measures of the student's peer environment is to complement these other measures
by focusing the assessment system on personality characteristics.
Our principal goal, then, is to utilize CIRP data to develop a
comprehensive "personality profile" of the undergraduate peer
environment.

Developing Other Peer Measures

The population used to identify the "personality" of the peer
group consisted of the 358 institutions from the 1983 freshman
survey that were judged to have surveyed a representative sample
of their entering freshmen. A total of 190,368 students comprising the entering freshman classes at each institution supplied the basic data for the analysis. The first task was to select
a group of CIRP questionnaire items that would provide a comprehensive picture of the "personality" of the freshman peer group
at each institution. After considerable discussion among the

HERI staff, it was decided that seven categories of question-naire items would be included: behaviors, self-ratings, attitudes, life goals, reasons for attending college, expectations for college, and career choice.

Students' responses to each of the items were aggregated so that mean scores could be computed for each item for each institution. These institutional means became the basic data for the analysis.

Rather than attempting to describe the peer group simply in terms of mean scores, which would be unwieldy and redundant, we decided instead to perform a series of factor analyses of the institutional means, to identify more general character-istics of the peer group. The analysis revealed eight factors. We shall first present and discuss each of the eight factors separately, and then present some extensive data bearing on their construct validity. Readers will note certain similarities between these fac-tors and some of the student peer group "types" described by Clark and Trow (1966) and others. Discussion of these similar-ities will be deferred until Chapter Four.

Peer Factor I: Intellectual Self-Esteem

This first peer factor, Intellectual Self-Esteem, is defined in terms of eight items with very high loadings:

	Factor Loading
Academic ability [self-rating]	.93
Public speaking ability [self-rating]	.91
Drive to achieve [self-rating]	.91
Leadership ability [self-rating]	.90
Intellectual self-confidence [self-rating]	.90
Writing ability [self-rating]	.87
Election to an academic honor society [expectation]	.87
Mathematical ability [self-rating]	.80

Seven of these items are from the list of self-ratings; the remain-ing item is from the list of expectations for college. Three of

the self-ratings have to do with cognitive abilities (academic, writing, mathematical) and two with interpersonal (public speaking
and leadership). Two others have to do with motivation (drive
to achieve and expectation to be elected to an academic honor
society), while the final item — intellectual self-confidence — seems
to summarize the overall content of the factor quite well. Two
other items — high school grade point average, and an attitudinal
question about minimal competency levels for college graduates —
had loadings above .8 but were not included in the factor score
because we wanted to limit the content of this factor to items
that directly reflected the student's Intellectual Self-Esteem.

Peer Factor II: Permissiveness

Permissiveness is defined by six items:

	Factor Loading
A couple should live together for some time before deciding to get married [attitude].	.94
If two people really like each other, it's all right for them to have sex even if they've known each other for only a very short time [attitude].	.87
Marijuana should be legalized [attitude].	.86
Attended a religious service [behavior].	−.86
Divorce laws should be liberalized [attitude].	.80
Abortion should be legalized [attitude].	.75

This factor presented some challenges for labeling. We considered a number of alternatives, such as hedonism, libertarianism, self-indulgence, personal freedom, and others. We eventually settled on Permissiveness, for several reasons. First, five
of the six items have to do with support for individual freedom
in the arenas of sex, drugs, divorce, and abortion. In addition,
the sixth item, "Attended a religious service," which had a negative loading, was considered to reflect a *lack* of permissiveness
in the sense that many organized religions have strong sanctions

against extramarital sex, drug usage, abortion, and divorce. In other words, a person who *did not* attend religious services would be expected to have a more permissive attitude toward such matters.

Peer Factor III: Altruism and Social Activism

The third peer factor, Altruism and Social Activism, was defined entirely through five life-goal items:

	Factor Loading
Participating in a community action program [life goal]	.87
Promoting racial understanding [life goal]	.85
Influencing social values [life goal]	.75
Helping others who are in difficulty [life goal]	.70
Becoming involved in programs to clean up the environment [life goal]	.65

Each of these items implies some kind of personal commitment on the part of the student to action or involvement directed toward altruistic goals (helping others, promoting racial understanding) or toward social change (community action, influencing social values, cleaning up the environment).

Peer Factor IV: Materialism and Status

Five of the six items defining Materialism and Status come from the list of life goals included in the freshman questionnaire; the sixth item comes from the list of reasons that students give for attending college:

	Factor Loading
Being very well off financially [life goal]	.88
To be able to make more money [reason for college]	.79
Being successful in my own business [life goal]	.74

Becoming an authority in my field [life goal]   .71
Obtaining recognition from my colleagues for
    contributions to my special field [life goal]   .65
Having administrative responsibility for the
    work of others [life goal]   .65

The fact that the two highest-loading items have to do with making money prompted the decision to include the word *materialism* in the title of this factor. Because the other items have to do with becoming an authority, obtaining recognition, and being in charge of other workers, we added the term *status* to the factor label.

Peer Factor V: Feminism

Feminism was defined by only three items:

Factor Loading

Women should receive the same salary and
    opportunities for advancement as men in
    comparable positions [attitude].   .71
The activities of married women are best
    confined to the home and family [attitude].   – .64
To meet new and interesting people [reason
    for college].   .51

Labeling factor V presented few problems, given the content of the first two items. Two hallmarks of contemporary feminist thought are that men and women should be treated equally in the workplace and that married women should be free to pursue work outside the home if they so desire. The third item, while not clearly related to feminism, in all likelihood reflects gender differences in the reasons usually given for attending college. The highest-loading (.81) item, the percentage of women in the entering freshman class, was not included in scoring the factor. This decision was prompted by a desire to define the factor exclusively in terms of feminist *attitudes* and *beliefs*.

Peer Factor VI: Artistic Interests

The content for Artistic Interests speaks for itself:

	Factor Loading
Artist (including performer) [career choice]	.88
Creating artistic work (painting, sculpture, decorating) [life goal]	.81
Artistic ability [self-rating]	.73
Becoming accomplished in one of the performing arts [life goal]	.59

All four items are directly concerned either with artistic interests, artistic ability, or an orientation toward artistic accomplishment.

Peer Factor VII: Outside Work

This particular factor, Outside Work, may be of only marginal interest, especially as only two items are used to form the factor score:

	Factor Loading
Get a job to help pay for college expenses [expectation]	.74
Have to work at an outside job during college [expectation]	.73

We decided to include it in the array of peer group measures, however, as the individual student's peer group experience might be substantially affected by the large numbers of fellow students working at jobs off campus.

Peer Factor VIII: Scientific Orientation

This last factor, Scientific Orientation, is defined by three items:

	Factor Loading
Scientific researcher [career choice]	.59
College teacher [career choice]	.52
Make a theoretical contribution to science [life goal]	.49

While the content of the three items used in scoring this factor is consistent with the label Scientific Orientation, this factor must be viewed with some caution because of the modest loadings. Recall that we are dealing here with institutional *means,* which normally produce high correlations and high factor loadings. These loadings were substantially lower than those found for any of the other eight factors, suggesting that this factor score may involve a relatively low degree of internal consistency and/or a substantial amount of error.

Correlations with Institutional Type

Let us first look at how these peer "personality" measures correlate with institutional size and selectivity. Selectivity produced significant correlations with all eight peer factors, including the two largest correlations of the factors with any type characteristic. Peer environments at selective institutions tend to be very high in Intellectual Self-Esteem. They are also high in Feminism, Permissiveness, Scientific Orientation, and Artistic Interests, and low in Materialism and Status, Outside Work, and Social Activism. As far as size is concerned, large institutions also tend to get high scores in Intellectual Self-Esteem and Scientific Orientation and low scores in Social Activism, but — unlike selective institutions — they tend to be above average in Materialism and Status and average in Permissiveness, Feminism, Outside Work, and Artistic Interests.

The peer environments of universities (both public and private) tend to be high in Scientific Orientation and Intellectual Self-Esteem (especially private universities). Public universities tend to be below average in Social Activism.

The peer environments of public four-year colleges (including most of the so-called state colleges and universities) tend to be above average in Materialism and Status and below average in four qualities: Intellectual Self-Esteem, Social Activism, Feminism, and Artistic Interests.

Some of the most interesting patterns occur with different types of four-year private colleges. Both the Protestant and Roman Catholic colleges have peer environments that are substantially below average in Permissiveness. In other words, these religiously affiliated institutions tend to attract peer groups that do not advocate personal freedom in areas of sexual behavior, drug use, divorce, and abortion rights. The peer environments of Protestant institutions also tend to be below average in four other qualities: Scientific Orientation, Materialism and Status, Feminism, and Artistic Interests. Roman Catholic institutions' peer groups, on the other hand, tend to be above average in Social Activism and below average in Intellectual Self-Esteem and Artistic Interests.

The peer environments of the nonsectarian private colleges show an entirely different pattern: they tend to be considerably above average in Permissiveness, Artistic Interests, and Feminism and slightly above average in Social Activism and Intellectual Self-Esteem.

These results demonstrate that schools known as the private colleges represent an extremely heterogeneous grouping of institutions when viewed through their peer environments. Roman Catholic and Protestant institutions show some similarities in their peer environments, but the peers at the nonsectarian private colleges produce an entirely different pattern. These differences may have something to do with the differential selectivity of the sectarian and nonsectarian colleges, given that the pattern of correlations with Selectivity resembles the pattern found with the nonsectarian institutions. The only exception here is the negative correlation of Selectivity with Social Activism, a finding that may well be caused by the predominantly black colleges. That is, predominantly black colleges tend to have very high scores on Social Activism coupled with very low scores on Selectivity. In all likelihood, the negative correlation of Selectivity and Social Activism would be reduced, if not eliminated, by the removal of the predominantly black colleges from the sample.

It may well be that the pattern of correlations shown for public four-year colleges may also be partially the result of their relatively low Selectivity: note that, with the exception of Social Activism, the signs of all of the correlations are reversed when we compare the results for public colleges with the results for Selectivity.

Additional Peer Group Measures

In addition to Selectivity, SES, and the eight measures of the "personality" of the peer group, twenty-five additional measures of the student's peer group were included, making a total of thirty-five peer group measures. One of these additional measures, Political Orientation (liberalism versus conservatism), consisted of the mean score of the entering freshmen on the political self-label: far right, conservative, middle-of-the-road, liberal, and far left, scored 1–5, respectively. This peer measure was included because many of the outcome measures discussed in subsequent chapters (especially Chapters Three and Five) are heavily political in content.

One of the most interesting aspects of the peer environment is the concentration of students in different fields of study. Since earlier research suggests that the institutional environment can be significantly shaped by predominance of various fields of study (Astin and Holland, 1961), we added fifteen additional peer measures based on the percentage of an institution's bachelor's degrees awarded in each of the following fields: agriculture, biology, science, business, education, engineering, English, health professions, humanities, fine arts, mathematics/statistics, physical science, psychology, and other social science and technical (other than engineering). Another related peer measure called Science Preparation was defined as the average number of high school courses taken by the entering freshman class in biological science, physical science, and mathematics.

Three additional peer group measures were concerned with the racial composition of the student body. Specifically, they included three separate measures of the percentages of African-American, Asian, and Hispanic students.

Three additional measures were used to assess the religious orientation of the freshman class: the percentages of Jewish and Roman Catholic students and the percentage of students who indicated that they were born-again Christians.

Two additional measures were included to assess the extent to which students at the institution relied upon various kinds of financial aid. Specifically, we used the percentage who indicated that they were receiving merit-based financial aid and the percentage who indicated that they were receiving need-based financial aid.

The final peer group measure consisted of the percentage of entering freshmen who were living on campus. This measure was included as an indicator of the extent to which the campus was characterized by a residential climate.

Clusters of Environmental Measures

The large number of environmental measures described up to this point may seem a bit bewildering to the reader who is trying to get the "big picture" of how students are affected by the characteristics of their college. While it is tempting to try to simplify the presentation of results by reducing all these measures to a smaller number by means of an overall factor analysis, the use of such factors would actually complicate and possibly obfuscate the interpretation of findings, simply because the reader (as well as this writer) will be hard put to figure out just which variable has in fact "caused" the particular outcome under study. We know, for example, that variables such as size, percentage of graduate students, and Research Orientation will tend to be highly correlated, simply because large institutions tend to enroll high proportions of graduate students and also to emphasize research. Proponents of the factor approach might argue for using a single factor measure that combines all three into a single variable. The problem with this argument is that these three variables, while highly correlated with each other, are not entirely interchangeable. For example, some very large institutions (certain state colleges, for example) enroll relatively few graduate students and put relatively little emphasis on research.

Some very small institutions, such as the California Institute of Technology, on the other hand, enroll a very high percentage of graduate students and place a great deal of emphasis on research. If we substituted a single factor measure for three variables like these and subsequently found that this variable has a significant "effect" on some important student outcome, how would we interpret the finding? Is one of the component variables—size, for example—responsible for the effect? Or is it two of the variables? And which two? Or is it all three working together? Clearly, it would be difficult to base educational policy on such results, simply because we would not know whether to direct the policy at institutional size, graduate student enrollment, Research Orientation, or some combination of these three variables. (See Chapter Ten for more discussion of this problem.)

As a sort of compromise, we are providing here the rough results of a factor analysis that has been performed with the 135 environmental measures described up to this point. The purpose of this analysis is to help the reader understand which of these various environmental measures tend to cluster together. A knowledge of this clustering can be useful in developing a more coherent overview of the findings. In particular, knowing how the variables cluster together will help the reader avoid assuming that a particular environment measure is not important simply because it does not enter the regression equation. Let us take the aforementioned example of institutional size, percentage of graduate students in the student body, and research emphasis. Sometimes the regression results really do not show us which of several highly correlated variables like these is really more important than the other. For example, if percentage of graduate students and research emphasis have virtually identical partial correlations with the outcome measure under study, the computer regression routine will pick the one that has the larger coefficient, even if it must look to the third or fourth digit in the coefficient to find a difference. Obviously, such minuscule differences are not statistically significant and certainly not of any practical significance. However, once the chosen variable is added to the regression equation, the correlation of the other variables in the cluster with the outcome may well be reduced to nonsignificance. In other words, just because Research Orientation enters the regression equation, and size and percentage of graduate students do not, does not mean that these other two variables are not important or that Research Orientation is more important. Such a conclusion depends on the relative sizes of the three partial correlations prior to the entry of Research Orienation into the equation, as well as on other practical considerations, to be discussed in Chapter Ten.

Several different factor analyses were attempted using these environmental variables, and each of them, with minor exceptions, yielded five identifiable factors or clusters of environmental measures. These clusters are briefly examined next.

Cluster I: Liberalism

The cluster of environmental variables denoting Liberalism included faculty measures, student peer measures, and several curricular measures as high-loading variables. The dozen highest-loading variables (with factor loadings shown in parentheses) are as follows:

> Liberalism (versus conservatism) of the student peer group (.86)
> Faculty Liberalism (.77)
> Artistic Interests of the peer group (.75)
> Permissiveness of the peer group (.75)
> Institutional Emphasis on Diversity (.73)
> Feminism of the peer group (.72)
> Faculty Diversity Orientation (.70)
> Progressive offerings (curriculum) (.66)
> Women's or gender studies course requirement (.62)
> Minority or Third World course requirement (.58)
> Percentage of faculty teaching interdisciplinary courses (.56)
> Social Activism of the peer group (.48)

Each of these variables is positively correlated with the others, and the variables with the highest loadings are generally most highly correlated with each other. In other words, on any given regression analysis, one of these may serve as a proxy for one or more of the others or, indeed, for the set.

Cluster II: Research Versus Student Orientation

The cluster for Research versus Student Orientation turned out to be bipolar, meaning that there were variables with very large positive and very large negative loadings. Those with the largest positive loadings are as follows:

> Use of graduate teaching assistants (.84)
> Research Orientation (.73)
> Percentage of graduate students in the student body (.69)
> Size (total undergraduate enrollment) (.63)
> Average faculty salary (.61)
> Student-faculty ratio (.57)
> Resources and Reputation Emphasis (.57)
> Public university (.53)
> Private university (.50)
> Keen competition among students [faculty perception] (.48)
> Faculty Morale (.48)

Clearly, these variables tend to characterize the typical research university: heavy reliance on teaching assistants, large percentage of graduate students, large size, highly paid faculty, and emphasis on resource acquisition and reputational enhancement. Environmental variables making up the negative pole of this factor are as follows:

> Hours per week spent teaching and advising students (−.81)
> Student Orientation (−.69)
> Percentage of expenditures spent on student services (−.69)
> Percentage of faculty involved in teaching general education courses (−.58)
> Faculty Use of Active Learning (−.48)

Each environmental measure making up the negative end of this factor clearly suggests an emphasis on student development. In certain respects, the two poles of this factor reinforce the commonly held notion that, in American higher education, there is a fundamental conflict between research and teaching. That these loadings are substantially less than 1.0, however, suggests that there are a few institutions that are able to emphasize both research and teaching (and a few that emphasize neither). (See Chapter Twelve for a discussion of the significance of this finding.) Nevertheless, the very large loadings suggest that research and teaching have a difficult time existing on a co-equal basis in many higher education institutions.

It is important to realize that we are looking here at *institutional* characteristics, since research done on individual faculty members at single institutions reveals no relationship (or even a weak positive relationship) between Research Orientation and being an effective teacher (Centra, 1981; Feldman, 1987; Pascarella and Terenzini, 1991). The conflict between research and teaching thus becomes apparent only when we look at institutional differences. (See Chapter Twelve for further discussion of this problem.)

Cluster III: Socioeconomic Status, Social Science, Selectivity

This rather unusual cluster of environmental measures suggests that in American higher education there are certain kinds of institutions that combine the following features: high selectivity, students from high socioeconomic levels, and a strong emphasis on the social sciences. Because of the unusual nature of this cluster, we looked to see whether there are particular types of institutions that tend to have high scores. As it turns out, private institutions (both colleges and universities) that are nonsectarian and residential and that enroll high proportions of pre-law students tend to get much higher scores on this cluster than does any other type of institution. The specific environmental measures with the highest positive loadings on this cluster are as follows:

Percentage of students majoring in history or political
science (.82)
Socioeconomic Status of the peer group (.78)
Percentage of students majoring in other social sciences
(.71)
Selectivity (.63)
Percentage of faculty holding Ph.D.s (.59)
Science Preparation of the entering freshmen (.57)
Intellectual Self-Esteem of the peer group (.56)
Humanities Orientation (.52)

This cluster also has a negative pole, but the loadings were
not as high as the highest positive loadings:

Faculty Use of Multiple-Choice Exams (−.57)
Outside Work (peer measure) (−.55)
Percentage of students majoring in education (−.51)

Most of the institutions that occupy the negative pole of
this factor are the so-called state universities or state colleges,
many of which are former teachers colleges.

Cluster IV: Community

In many ways, the cluster dealing with community is the most
interesting one of all, although the loadings are generally smaller
than the loadings on the first three clusters. Small residential private colleges tend to occupy the positive role of this factor, while
many state colleges occupy the negative pole. Environmental
variables with the highest positive loadings are as follows:

Social Activism and Community Orientation (.62)
Positive Perception of the Administration (.63)
Positive faculty attitudes toward the general education pro-
gram (.62)
Percentage of students with need-based aid (.57)
Perceived Academic Competence of Students (.57)
Percentage of students with merit-based aid (.55)
Percentage of students majoring in the humanities (.47)

The negative pole of this cluster provides an interesting contrast:

Materialism and Status (peer group) (–.60)
Lack of Student Community (–.54)
Racial Conflict (–.47)
Size (undergraduate enrollment) (–.46)
Public four-year college (–.45)

Cluster V: Emphasis on Science

The content of the science cluster speaks for itself:

Percentage of the faculty in science fields (.83)
Scientific Orientation of the peer group (.78)
Percentage of students majoring in physical sciences (.71)
Percentage of students majoring in engineering (.70)
Science Preparation of the peer group (.54)
Intellectual Self-Esteem of the peer group (.52)
Percentage of students majoring in math/statistics (.48)
Selectivity (.45)

The reader should note that two characteristics of institutions — size and selectivity — have substantial loadings on more than one cluster. Size, for example, is positively related to the research and graduate education emphasis and negatively related to community. Selectivity, on the other hand, is positively related to both the Socioeconomic Status–social science cluster and the Scientific Orientation cluster. The complexity of these two measures may help to explain why they enter very few of the regressions reported in the next seven chapters (see also Chapter Ten).

Readers should keep in mind that since the environmental variables that make up any cluster tend to be highly correlated with each other, there is a good deal of redundancy within each set of these variables. This means that any environmental variable that turns out to have a significant effect on a student outcome (see Chapters Three through Nine) may well be serving as a proxy for one or more variables in its set. (See Chapter Ten for a fuller discussion of this issue.)

Residence, Major, and Financial Aid

Many studies have already shown the importance of the undergraduate's place of residence (Astin 1975, 1977; Chickering, 1974; Pascarella and Terenzini, 1991). Accordingly, four measures of freshman residence are used: at home with parents, private room or apartment, college residence hall, and distance from home to college.

Financial aid (as revealed in the 1985 freshman questionnaire) covered fifteen measures, including twelve measures reflecting the amount received from specific sources: parents or family, savings from summer work, other savings, full-time work, college work/study, other part-time work, Pell grants, Supplementary Educational Opportunity Grants (SEOGs), state scholarships, grants from the college, Guaranteed Student Loans, and other loans. Three additional measures were added to reflect the *basis* for the aid: academic merit, other special talent, or financial need.

The student's tentative choice of a major field of study at the time of freshman entry was also included in the form of sixteen dichotomous measures: agriculture, biological science, business, education, engineering, English, health professions, history or political science, humanities (other), fine arts, mathematics or statistics, physical sciences, social sciences, other technical, other nontechnical, and undecided.

Measures of Student Involvement

The environmental measures described thus far — characteristics of institutions, curriculum, faculty, residence and financial aid, and student peer groups — are already established at the time the student first matriculates. In other words, all entering students are "exposed" to these environmental characteristics simply by virtue of their enrolling in a particular institution. In the jargon of higher education research, we might refer to these as *between-institution* measures, in the sense that they try to capture environmental attributes that differ from one institution to another.

Once a group of students enrolls at a given institution, however, individual members of that group may have quite different environmental experiences because of the many curricular and extracurricular choices they make. A considerable body of higher education research indicates that these various forms of involvement can have substantial effects on the student's development (Astin, 1975, 1977; Pascarella and Terenzini, 1991).

Most of the information on student involvement comes from the longitudinal follow-up questionnaire completed by students in 1989–90. A total of fifty-seven different measures of involvement have been identified under five general headings (numbers in parentheses after each type of involvement indicate the number of specific measures in that category): academic involvement (22), involvement with faculty (6), involvement with student peers (14), involvement in work (4), and other forms of involvement (11). These measures are described briefly under each general heading.

Academic Involvement

The first three measures of academic involvement are designed to assess the *quantity* of student involvement in academic work. They have been taken from a follow-up questionnaire item that reads as follows: "During your last year in college, how much time did you spend during a typical week doing the following activities?" In response to each activity, the student can give one of eight alternatives: none, less than one hour, one to two hours, three to five hours, six to ten hours, eleven to fifteen hours, sixteen to twenty hours, and over twenty hours per week. The following three activities are included as quantitative measures of academic involvement:

Attending classes or labs
Studying or doing homework
Using a personal computer

Another set of items in the questionnaire has been designed to assess the quantity of student involvement in various

kinds of undergraduate courses. The item instructs the student
to indicate "how many *undergraduate* courses have you taken that
emphasized"

> Writing skills
> Math or understanding numerical data
> Science or scientific inquiry
> History or historical analysis
> Foreign-language skills

To each of the five types of course work, the student could re-
spond along a five-point scale: none, one to two courses, three
to five courses, six to eight courses, nine or more courses.

Nine additional qualitative measures of academic involvement require a dichotomous (yes or no) response: "Since entering college have you enrolled in . . . ?"

> Ethnic studies courses
> Women's studies courses
> Honors or advanced placement courses
> Interdisciplinary courses
> Study-abroad program
> College internship program
> Reading or study-skills classes
> Remedial or developmental courses
> Racial or cultural awareness workshop

The final five measures of academic involvement are included to assess particular academic experiences that can cut
across specific course content areas. Students were instructed,
"For the activities listed below, please indicate how often —
frequently, occasionally, or not at all — you engaged in each during the past year":

> Worked on an independent research project
> Received tutoring in courses
> Gave a presentation in class
> Took a multiple-choice exam
> Took an essay exam

Involvement with Faculty

The first student involvement measure under this category is taken from the time diary:

> Hours per week spent talking with faculty outside of class

Two faculty involvement items have been taken from the dichotomous (yes versus no) list:

> Assisted faculty in teaching a course
> Worked on a professor's research project

Two additional items have been taken from the frequently–occasionally–not at all list:

> Was a guest in a professor's home
> Had a class paper critiqued by an instructor

The final measure of student involvement with faculty is a composite of several follow-up questionnaire items labeled "Frequency of Student Interaction with Faculty." It consists of the sum total of the student's responses to the following items:

> Been a guest in a professor's home
> Worked on a professor's research project
> Assisted faculty in teaching a class
> Hours per week spent talking with faculty outside of class

Involvement with Student Peers

The first three measures of the individual student's degree of involvement with student peers have been taken from the time diary. Specifically, they include the number of hours per week that the student reports spending in the following activities:

> Socializing with friends
> Partying
> Student clubs or groups

The next five measures of involvement with peers have been taken from the dichotomous (yes versus no) list:

> Joined or been a member of a fraternity or sorority
> Participated in campus protests or demonstrations
> Been elected to a student office
> Participated in intercollegiate athletics
> Played intercollegiate football or basketball

Five additional peer involvement measures have been drawn from the frequently–occasionally–not at all list:

> Worked on group projects for a class
> Tutored another student
> Participated in intramural sports
> Discussed racial or ethnic issues
> Socialized with someone of another racial or ethnic group

The final measure of peer involvement attempts to capture the sheer frequency of interaction with the peer group and is called "Frequency of Interaction with Student Peers." Like the final measure of student involvement with faculty, this measure is a composite consisting of the sum of the student's responses to the following items:

> Discussed course content with students outside of class
> Worked on a group project for a class
> Tutored another student
> Participated in intramural sports
> Was a member of a social fraternity or sorority
> Participated in campus protests or demonstrations
> Was elected to student office
> Hours per week spent in student clubs or groups

Involvement in Work

The first of these four measures, which has been taken from the time diary, attempted to capture the sheer quantity of student involvement in work:

Hours per week spent working for pay

The final three measures of work involvement are dichotomous:

Worked full-time while attending college
Had a part-time job off campus
Had a part-time job on campus

The distinction in these last two items is critical, since previous research indicates that off-campus employment has generally negative effects on student development, while part-time employment on campus has generally positive effects (Astin, 1975, 1977).

Other Forms of Involvement

Seven of these final eleven measures of student involvement have been taken from the time diary. Specifically, they include the hours per week that students report spending in the following activities:

Exercising or playing sports
Reading for pleasure
Volunteer work
Watching television
Commuting to campus
Religious services or meetings
Hobbies

Another measure is taken from the dichotomous list:

Got married

The final three student involvement measures have been taken from the frequently–occasionally–not at all list:

Received vocational or career counseling
Received personal or psychological counseling
Use of alcohol (sum of responses to "drank beer" and
    "drank wine or liquor")

Table 2.1 provides a graphic overview of the entire package of 192 environmental measures. The next section explains how these measures are actually used in analyzing environmental effects on student outcomes.

Table 2.1. Summary List of the 192 Environmental Measures.

Institutional Characteristics
  Type and control (6 measures)
  Gender
  Race
  Size (2 measures)
  Student-faculty ratio
  Percentage who are graduate students
  Expenditures (2 measures)
  Average faculty salary

Curricular Measures
  True core
  Major-dominated
  Type of distributional system(4 measures)
  Written evaluations
  Offers Women's Studies or Ethnic Studies (2 measures)
  Specific requirements (6 measures)

Faculty Environment
  Behavior-value-satisfaction factors (14 measures)
  Perceptual factors (8 measures)
  Percentage of women
  Percentage in science fields
  Percentage with doctorates
  Teaching techniques (4 measures)
  Hours per week spent teaching and advising
  Political orientation
  Use of teaching assistants
  Other (2 measures)

Peer Environment
  Selectivity and academic ability
  Socioeconomic status
  Preference for different majors (14 measures)
  Political orientation
  Science preparation
  Racial composition (3 measures)
  Religious preference (3 measures)
  Reliance on financial aid (2 measures)
  Percentage living on campus
  Peer "personality" factors (8 measures)

Table 2.1. Summary List of the 192 Environmental Measures, cont'd.

Individual Involvement Measures
A. Known at time of entry
   Place of freshman residence (4 measures)
   Type of financial aid (12 measures)
   Basis for financial aid (3 measures)
   Freshman major choice (16 measures)

B. Occurring after entry
   Academic involvement (22 measures)
   Involvement with faculty (9 measures)
   Involvement with student peers (14 measures)
   Involvement in work (4 measures)
   Other (11 measures)

Analyses of Environmental Effects

Assessing the effects of between-institution environmental measures, such as the selectivity of the college or the characteristics of the peer group, is a relatively straightforward matter, since the student's initial exposure to these environmental characteristics coincides closely in time with the assessment of input characteristics. In other words, since most institutions administer the freshman questionnaire during freshman orientation or registration or during the first week of classes, there is little if any time lapse between the assessment of pretests and other input characteristics and the student's initial exposure to these between-institution environmental characteristics. The same is true for the student's freshman choice of a major field of study, place of residence, and financial aid: all of these environmental factors are assessed in the freshman questionnaire.

In assessing the effects of other student involvement measures, however, we encounter a number of potential problems. A major difficulty is that we cannot be sure exactly when the student experienced a particular form of involvement as recorded in the follow-up questionnaire. Consider being a member of a social fraternity or sorority as an example. Most students who join such organizations do so only after they have been enrolled in college for a period of time. The analytical problem here is as follows: since the student's input characteristics are assessed at the point of initial entry to college, some of these characteristics may actually change in the interim between college entry and the occurrence of the particular form of involvement in question. In the case of joining a social fraternity or sorority, the personal characteristics that lead students to choose or reject fraternity or sorority membership might well change after they are assessed at input, and these changes could in turn affect the student's decision to join. Subsequent analyses of the data might lead us to the erroneous conclusion that the changes were *caused* by fraternity and sorority membership.

This problem can be illustrated with a hypothetical example. Suppose we are interested in determining whether fraternity or sorority membership affects students' political beliefs. We might pretest political beliefs at the point of initial entry to college and posttest these same beliefs four years later. At the time of the posttest we would also ascertain whether the students had joined social fraternities or sororities. The objective of the analysis would be to determine whether there is still any correlation between fraternity or sorority membership and posttested political beliefs, *after* controlling for the effects of pretested (freshman) political beliefs. What, then, can we conclude if we do find a residual positive correlation between fraternity or sorority membership and conservative political beliefs, after controlling for the effects of the pretest beliefs and other input measures obtained at college entry? Is it legitimate to conclude that this residual correlation reflects the positive effect of fraternity or sorority membership on conservatism?

Interpretive difficulties begin to arise when we observe that the pretest (input) measure of conservatism is also positively associated with joining a fraternity or sorority—that is, that the more conservative students (as reflected in input measures) are more likely to join fraternities or sororities than their less conservative classmates are. Now, if political beliefs had been pretested at the same time the students actually joined (or decided not to join) fraternities or sororities, the finding would not present a serious interpretive problem, since our statistical analysis would have controlled for these pretest belief measures at the same time the decision was made to join or not to join. However, because our pretests were obtained at the point of initial entry to college — some time before students actually made up their minds about joining fraternities and sororities — our causal conclusions become somewhat suspect.

To illustrate this problem, suppose we have two women students who say they are "middle-of-the-road" at the point of entry to college. During the first term, for reasons unrelated to their college experiences, one student becomes substantially more conservative, while the other becomes substantially more liberal. The greater conservatism of the first student might cause her subsequently to join a social sorority during her second term; the second student's greater liberalism might lead her to decide not to join. To complete our hypothetical example, assume that sorority membership really has no effect one way or the other on the first student's political beliefs, and that the conservatism of the first student and liberalism of the second remain unchanged until they graduate. When we posttest the two students' political beliefs at the time of graduation, the one who joined a sorority will check "conservative" and the one who did not join will check "liberal." If the pattern of change described for these two students is replicated for other students in our sample, our subsequent statistical analysis will lead us to conclude that sorority membership strengthens conservatism, when in fact it has no effect one way or the other. In short, the statistical analysis may not fully control for the bias caused by input characteristics if there is a substantial time lapse between the assessment of input and initial exposure to the environment (sorority membership).

Similar interpretive dilemmas are inherent in studying the effects of almost any form of student involvement that occurs subsequent to college entry. While such ambiguities do not necessarily invalidate every attempt to study the effects of involvement, the reader should keep such causal ambiguities in mind when attempting to interpret the results of "involvement" findings reported in subsequent chapters. Readers should be especially cautious of "effects" that are obtained under conditions where the involvement measure in question has a substantial correlation with the pretest measure. We can have the greatest confidence in the observed effects of involvement variables in those cases where the correlation between pretest and involvement is either near zero or of opposite sign from the correlation of involvement with the posttest (Astin, 1991).

Intermediate Outcomes

The basic I-E-O model makes clear temporal distinctions between input, environmental, and outcome variables. That is, the student's input characteristics are assessed prior to any exposure to the college environment, while the college environment is assumed to intervene between input and outcome. A key assumption here is that the environmental variables occur prior in time to the outcome variables. However, our discussion of student involvement measures so far suggests that the environment "occurs" over a considerable length of time, and that some environmental variables (such as between-institution characteristics) occur prior to other environmental variables (such as student involvement). In fact, the earliest-occurring environmental variables, such as institutional size, can even be considered as possible "causes" of later-occurring environmental variables, such as joining sororities. Viewed from this perspective, involvement measures and other later environmental experiences might also be considered as outcomes. Joining a social sorority, for example, can be considered an outcome measure, depending upon how one defines the analytical problem. However, when sorority membership and other later-occurring involvement measures are considered to be part of the student's environmental experiences (that is, as antecedent to some later outcome measure, such as posttest political beliefs), I prefer to designate them as intermediate outcomes. Under these circumstances, the "E" part of the I-E-O model can be elaborated to include two or more different blocks of environmental variables that are ordered according to their known or assumed sequence of occurrence. Thus, for purposes of analyzing the eighty-two different outcome measures discussed in subsequent chapters, input variables will be controlled first, followed by between-institution and other environmental variables known at the time of entry, followed by measures of student involvement and other intermediate outcomes.

Another way of looking at intermediate outcomes is that they can serve to mediate the effects of between-institution variables. Suppose we find a positive effect of attending a large institution on political conservatism, after controlling for pretest political beliefs and other input variables. As we move next to consider the possible effects of intermediate outcomes, we might also find a significant effect of sorority membership. But what if the effect of institutional size on conservatism disappears when we control for the positive effect of sorority membership? What we might conclude under these circumstances is that the effect of size on conservatism is, in the jargon of path analysis, indirect. The size effect, in other words, is *mediated* by sorority membership. In simpler terms, we could conclude that attending a large institution does indeed tend to make students more conservative, but only because it increases the student's chances of joining a sorority; once the effect of sorority membership is controlled, the effect of size disappears. Involvement measures, in other words, can help us to explain *how* and *why* environmental variables affect student outcomes.

Summary

This chapter has described in some detail the development of 192 measures of the undergraduate student's environmental experiences. In all likelihood, this is the largest and most diverse set of environmental measures ever employed in a higher education research project. More than two-thirds of these variables ($N = 135$) are known at the time of the student's initial entry to the institution. They include 16 measures of the characteristics of the institution attended (size, control, and so on), 15 measures of the curricular requirements, 35 measures of the student's peer environment, 34 measures of the faculty environment, and 35 measures of the freshman's place of residence, financial aid, and choice of major.

An additional 57 "involvement" measures have been included to assess environmental experiences that occur only after the student has been enrolled in college for a period of time. These intermediate outcomes are primarily indicative of the quantity and quality of student involvement with academic work (22 measures), faculty (6 measures), the student peer group (14 measures), work (4 measures), and miscellaneous other nonacademic involvements (11 measures).

In the chapters that follow, we shall seek to determine how these various environmental experiences affect a variety of student outcomes.

Chapter 3

———•◦•———

Assessing Environmental Effects: A Prototypical Example

Considering the large number of variables used in this study, there is simply no way that all the important details of the findings can be presented and interpreted, even in a book several times longer than this one. A thorough study of just the 192 environmental variables briefly described in the preceding chapter would be a formidable task. But consider that we have also employed some 146 input variables, not to mention 82 different student outcome variables! We have attempted to introduce some coherence into the presentation of outcome results by organizing the next six chapters around various subgroupings of the 82 outcome measures. But even these six chapters must necessarily condense the findings substantially.

To give the reader a clear idea as to just what is involved in the analysis of each of these eighty-two outcome measures, we are devoting this chapter to a detailed consideration of just one outcome measure: the student's political identification as revealed in answers to a single item from the follow-up questionnaire: "How would you characterize your political views? (mark *one*)." The alternatives, which were scored 1–5, respectively, were far right (1), conservative (2), middle-of-the-road

(3), liberal (4), and far left (5). We have chosen this outcome measure for a variety of reasons. First, much of the previous college impact research studied how the college experience affects students' political views. Second, we have available in our data base not only freshman pretests of this same item but also environmental measures reflecting the political leanings of both the student peer group and the faculty. Finally, we think that political identification will be of special interest to the reader, since students' preferences for various political labels have been undergoing considerable change in recent years, and political identification and political labels are salient issues in contemporary America.

Design of the Analysis

The analyses of the students' political identification and of the eighty-one other outcome measures are performed with several goals in mind. At the simplest descriptive level, it is useful to know how much change takes place during the four-plus years between 1985 and 1989–90: How liberal or how conservative are the students at the time of the follow-up in comparison to their political identification at the time they first enter college as freshmen? It is also important to determine the extent to which these observed changes can be attributed to the experience of being in college, as opposed to other factors, such as maturation or changes in the external political and social climate in the country. Finally, and most important, is the question of why some students change differently from others during the four years. This question really involves two sets of answers: one for student input characteristics, and one for environmental characteristics. From the perspective of student inputs, we are interested in knowing whether different types of students show differential changes in their political identification over time: Do women and men change their political identifications differently during the college years? Are there differential changes by race, ability, or socioeconomic status?

    The second part of the "differential change" question concerns the ultimate purpose of the study: to identify particular aspects of the student's educational experience that affect the manner in which political identification changes over time. Do students change differently in large versus small institutions? In selective versus nonselective institutions? Is the student's political identification influenced by curriculum, peer group, place of residence, type of financial aid, faculty characteristics, or type of involvement in college?

These are questions that will also be asked of the eighty-one other outcome measures that will be discussed in the next six chapters. By increasing our understanding of how particular student outcomes are affected by particular environmental experiences, we substantially enhance our capacity to create more effective institutions and programs. The following section is a discussion of the way in which we approach these questions using our prototypical outcome measure, the student's political identification at the time of the 1989–90 follow-up. In the simple change tables supporting the discussion we are showing the weighted national percentages, which represent estimates of the results that would be obtained if all freshmen entering U.S. colleges and universities in the fall of 1985 had responded to the 1989–90 follow-up survey. Weights compensate not only for differential sampling of institutions within stratification cells and differential sampling of students within institutions but also for nonrespondent bias to the mailed follow-up (see Dey, Astin, and Korn, 1991, for details). More complex cross-tabulations and multivariate analyses use unweighted percentages in order to capitalize on the much larger sample size ($N = 22,328$ versus 4,093 for the weighted national percentages). With a few exceptions, raw change scores for the unweighted sample proved to be very similar to weighted change scores based on weighted national norms (see Resource B).

Change Over Time

Table 3.1 shows how students' political identifications changed between 1985 and 1989. Almost exactly half the students (50.5 percent) checked their political identification as "middle-of-the-road" when they entered as freshmen in 1985. The other stu-

Table 3.1. Changes in Political Identification for 1985 Freshmen.

| Political Identification | Percent in | | Change, |
	1985	1989	1985–1989
Far left	2.3	2.4	+0.1
Liberal	23.8	27.5	+3.7
Middle-of-the-road	50.5	42.6	−7.9
Conservative	22.4	26.8	+4.4
Far right	1.1	0.8	−0.3

Note: Weighted national percentages (abstracted from Wingard, Treviño, Dey, and Korn, 1991) based on unweighted N of 4,093.

dents showed a slight tilt to the left, with those choosing liberal or far left slightly outnumbering those choosing conservative or far right (26.1 percent versus 23.5 percent). This represents a substantial shift since the early 1970s, when freshmen on the left outnumbered those on the right by better than two-to-one (Dey, Astin, and Korn, 1991). By 1989 the percentage of 1985 freshmen checking middle-of-the-road has declined to 42.6 percent, while the percentages choosing liberal and conservative have *both* increased. The left-right balance, however, remains relatively unchanged. These trends indicate that contemporary college students are becoming more politically polarized during the undergraduate years.

What is especially interesting about these changes is that they do not show the "liberalizing" effects of the undergraduate experience reported in previous research (Astin, 1977; Bowen, 1977; Feldman and Newcomb, 1969; Hyman, Wright, and Reed, 1975). Indeed, the increase in liberal and far-left students is slightly less than the increase in conservative and far-right students (3.8 percent versus 4.1 percent). Students who were undergraduates twenty years earlier, by contrast, show substantial increases in liberalism and decreases in conservatism during the college years (Astin, 1977). Similar changes to the left were reported by Feldman and Newcomb (1969) in earlier decades.

Maturation, Social Change, or "College Effects"?

Before considering the effects of the various environmental measures described in the preceding chapter, let us examine the possible "impact of college" on students' political identification. Given that the net change in the left-right balance during the four years is minor, why does the experience of being a college undergraduate no longer have its usual liberalizing effect, at least on this most recent generation of students? If by some chance such an effect has indeed occurred, then it must have been counterbalanced by some other factors (societal change, maturation), such that the overall net change in students' political identification remains minimal.

As mentioned in Chapter One, several techniques can be used to examine the possible influence of maturation, social change, and college attendance on political identification. The first and simplest test of the effect of maturation is to determine whether the student's age at the time of college entry has any measurable effect. Since age might be partially confounded with other variables, such as the type of college attended, that could in turn affect political orientation, our main interest is in whether age carries any significant weight in the longitudinal regression equation (see section on "Environmental Effects") after all other input and environmental variables are controlled. In the case of this particular outcome measure, age proves not to carry any significant weight. Thus, it would appear that maturation per se does not affect college students' political identification one way or the other, at least in the age range of seventeen to twenty-one.

The possible effects of societal change on political beliefs can be assessed by examining changes in the political orientation of five consecutive classes (1985, 1986, 1987, 1988, 1989) that entered college during the same span of years that the 1985 freshmen were being followed longitudinally. The possibility of an effect attributable to social change would be suggested by any systematic changes in the political identifications of consecutive entering classes between 1985 and 1989. As it turns out, trends in the political identification of entering freshman classes between 1985 and 1989 are minimal (Dey, Astin, and Korn, 1991). Using weighted national normative data, we find that the number checking liberal or far left increases very slightly (+1.2 percent), and that the number checking conservative or far right also increases slightly (+1.9 percent). Those checking middle-of-the-road necessarily show an overall decline (-3.1 percent). Clearly, these findings do not reveal any substantial societal change in a conservative direction that might have counterbalanced a "liberalizing" effect of college attendance. They do suggest, however, that the polarization of political identification observed in the 1985 freshmen during college may be attributable in some small degree to changes in the external society between 1985 and 1989.

So far the evidence suggests that maturation has not substantially affected the political identification of the 1985 freshmen during the years between 1985 and 1989, and that social change may have made small contributions both to the polarization and to the slight shift to the right observed in the 1985 freshmen. What about the impact of college attendance? As pointed out in Chapter One, if college attendance affects a particular outcome such as political identification in some systematic way, we would expect to find the greatest change occurring among students who remain in college for the full four years, with minimal change occurring among those who leave college after attending only a short time. For this particular outcome, there is no such effect of number of years completed.

As far as intensity of exposure to college is concerned, we have available three measures: the student's place of residence (lived at home, in a private room or apartment, or campus housing), the frequency with which the student interacts with other students, and the frequency with which the student interacts with faculty. None of these three measures turns out to be associated with the student's 1989 political orientation, once entering freshman characteristics and other environmental factors are controlled.

In short, these analyses all support the argument that the college experience produces no systematic effect on the student's tendency to affiliate with one or the other side of the political spectrum. Consequently, our analyses fail to support the traditional notion that attending college has a liberalizing effect on students' political identification.

One possible reason for this apparent contradiction of earlier studies is the decline, noted earlier, in entering college students' preference for the liberal side of the political spectrum, observed during the 1970s and early 1980s. If we can assume that liberals substantially outnumbered conservatives among undergraduates in the years preceding the 1970s, then it may well be that earlier research was reflecting a peer group effect: the overall effect of college attendance during those years was to "liberalize" students' political identification simply because liberalism was then the dominant political orientation of most student bodies. This explanation is supported by the regression results described below, which indicate that the individual student's political identification is indeed affected by the dominant political orientation of the student peer group. In other words, the net effect of college attendance on the left-right political balance within the total undergraduate population today may be nil, simply because there are just as many "conservative" student peer groups as there are "liberal" student peer groups.

This same peer group effect may also account for the modest tendency toward greater polarization observed in the 1985 freshmen during their undergraduate years. Since students of different political persuasions are not distributed at random among different colleges — liberals tend to congregate in certain colleges, while conservatives tend to congregate in a different set of colleges — students who begin college as middle-of-the-roaders tend to get pulled toward the extremes by their peers. Moreover, in contrast to earlier decades, when liberal peer groups outnumbered conservative peer groups, today's college students may show no net shift toward the left during their undergraduate years because there are roughly equal numbers of liberal and conservative peer groups pulling them in opposite directions.

To summarize: these analyses indicate that the left-right balance in the political identifications of contemporary college undergraduates is not systematically affected by either maturation, social change, or college attendance (considered generically).

Rather, it appears that the particular peer environment encountered by the student, rather than the generic college experience, is the critical factor.

Environmental Effects: Results
of Multiple Regression Analyses

Our main concern in analyzing the effects of environmental factors on student outcomes is to exert as much control as possible over potentially biasing student input variables before examining the possible effects of environmental variables. The technique chosen for this task is stepwise multiple regression analysis. Nontechnical readers should realize that the following description of this methodology is written with them in mind, so that the general logic behind the analysis should be relatively easy to follow. More technically sophisticated readers who are interested in details about how this particular method of analysis is applied to college effects analyses are advised to consult Astin (1991, especially Appendix A) and Astin and Dey (1992).

The basic idea behind the type of regression analysis employed in this study is to control different blocks of variables according to their known or assumed order of occurrence. Thus, since entering characteristics of the 1985 freshmen are known before these freshmen have any significant exposure to the college environment, these input characteristics are controlled in the first block of variables. The second block consists of what I like to call "bridge" variables, as they can be considered both as characteristics of the entering student (inputs) and as characteristics of the student's educational experience (environments). I refer here especially to the entering freshman's financial aid package, place of residence, and initial choice of a major field of study. These measures can be considered "input" characteristics, in the sense that they reflect the student's personal preferences and financial situation at the point of entry to college, but they can also be considered environmental characteristics, in the sense that the student's subsequent development in college can be affected by both the type and amount of financial aid received, as well as by the student's chosen major. Place of residence (dorm, private room, at home), in particular, has been shown in many studies to affect several aspects of the student's personal and academic development (Pascarella and Terenzini, 1991). The major is also a potentially important environmental influence because it can affect which courses the student takes, which professors the student is exposed to, and which student peers the student associates with. Depending on the college attended, initial choice of a major can sometimes also influence such things as housing or the type and amount of academic advising received.

The next (third) block of variables to be controlled consists of *between-college* characteristics of the student's environment that are established at the point of initial entry to the college. As already described in the preceding chapter, this category includes characteristics of the institution, general education curriculum, faculty, and student peer group — environmental measures that are the same for all students at a particular college, but which can vary among student bodies from one college to another.

The final block of variables to be entered into the regression includes all measures of student involvement, as well as any other "intermediate outcomes." The four blocks of independent variables, listed in order of their entry into the regression, are thus as follows:

> Input (entering freshmen) characteristics
> "Bridge" (input-environment) variables
> Between-college environmental variables
> Involvement and other intermediate outcome variables

The basic logic behind this kind of multivariate analysis was discussed earlier, in Chapters One and Two. Entering the first two blocks of variables controls for the potentially biasing effects of entering student characteristics by calculating an "estimated outcome score" based on a weighted combination of all relevant input characteristics. A given student, for example, might have an array of input characteristics that would lead us to expect her to check "liberal" (score of 4) on the follow-up questionnaire. We then compare that estimated score with her actual score to see if there is any discrepancy. Suppose that the student in question actually checks "far left" (score 5) on the follow-up questionnaire. In other words, she scores one point higher than expected from her input characteristics. Another student who happens to have the same expected score of "liberal" (score 4), on the other hand, might check "middle-of-the-road" (score 3) on the follow-up questionnaire. Subtracting the two students' expected scores of 4.0 from their actual scores, we produce a discrepancy (called a residual) of + 1 for the first student and – 1 for the second student. These residual scores, which are computed for all students, indicate the extent to which each student's 1989 response differs from what we would have expected from her or his input characteristics in 1985. What we want to learn is whether these differing residuals have been caused in part by different environmental experiences.

The next stage in the analysis is to determine whether these residuals actually correlate with any environmental characteristics. The purpose of this stage is to answer the following question: Have students with positive residuals had different environmental experiences from students with negative residuals? We might find, for example, that students with positive residuals (more liberal in 1989 than expected from their 1985 input characteristics) were more likely to have attended colleges with highly liberal faculty, while students with negative residuals (more conservative in 1989 than expected) were more likely to have attended colleges with less liberal faculty. In other words, in the second stage of the analysis we correlate each student's residual scores (after controlling for input characteristics) with various environmental measures to see whether we can find any significant correlations. In regression analysis, this process is carried out by determining whether the environmental characteristics (for example, faculty liberalism) add anything significant to the prediction of the outcome (the student's 1989 political orientation) over and above what can be predicted from input characteristics.

In effect, the first stage of the analysis statistically "matches" the students entering different environments according to their input characteristics. The basic purpose of this first (input) stage of the analysis is thus to eliminate any correlation between input and environmental characteristics. Any residual, it should be emphasized, is uncorrelated ($r = .00$) with the input variables that were used to compute it. As indicated in Chapter One, the problem in "natural experiments" like this one is that input characteristics are correlated with environmental characteristics. In "true" experiments, the random assignment of subjects to environments (treatments) eliminates such correlations. Controlling for input characteristics by statistical means (multiple regression) thus serves to remove any correlation between inputs and environments. Basically, we are attempting to simulate through the use of sophisticated multivariate statistics the results that we would obtain if we were able to assign students at random to their different environments.

Another statistical consideration here is measurement error in the input variables, which results in an "undercorrection" for the influence of input variables. Since adjustments for these errors did not substantially change the conclusions about environmental effects in *Four Critical Years*, no such adjustments were used in the current study. (For more details on this problem, see Astin, 1977, Appendix: "A Note on Measurement Error"; Astin, 1970a.)

The next sections explain the results of these various stages in the regression analysis using the student's political identification in 1989 as the outcome measure.

Effects of Input Characteristics

As might be expected, the single entering freshman (input) characteristic that has the strongest simple correlation (r) with 1989 political identification is the pretest measure obtained in 1985. The simple correlation of pretest and posttest political identifications over the four-year period is .42. Table 3.2 shows the relationship between these two measures. Not surprisingly, those students who are most likely to check "far left" in 1989 are the ones who also check the same alternative four years earlier, in 1985. As a matter of fact, in each case the people most likely

Table 3.2. Political Identification in 1985 and 1989.

1985 (Freshman) Identification	N	Percentage Checking Each Identification in 1989				
		Far Right	Conservative	Middle-of-the-Road	Liberal	Far Left
Far left	226	2	10	14	46	29
Liberal	4,900	0	12	25	57	6
Middle-of-the-road	11,267	0	21	52	25	1
Conservative	5,604	1	55	30	14	1
Far right	331	16	52	19	12	2

Note: $N = 22,328$; $r = .42$.

to pick a given alternative in 1989 are those who pick the same alternative in 1985. This is why we find a significant correlation ($r = .42$) between the pretest and posttest measures. However, many students change their political identifications during the four years, and some change quite dramatically. It is for this reason that the correlation is substantially less than perfect (that is, less than 1.0). Note that those who are most likely to change their political identifications over time are the ones who initially pick one of the extremes (far left or far right). Nevertheless, among those freshmen who initially check "far left" but switch to some other choice by the time of the follow-up, well over half check "liberal" four years later. We find a parallel pattern for those initially picking "far right": more than half those who change their choices during the four years change to "conservative." This shows that, even among those who switch their identifications, there is a tendency to stay on the same side of the political spectrum.

In the terminology that is used to describe these regression results, basically three different types of correlations are mentioned. In addition to simple correlations between two variables (usually denoted by the lower-case r), there are also partial correlations and Betas. Partial correlations and Betas show how the outcome is related to some input or environmental variable, after one or more other variables have been controlled.

The I-E-O model is based on the assumption that we are not in a position to interpret the observed correlation between the outcome and any environmental variable until we have first controlled for the effects of input variables. This controlling process means that the environmental-outcome relationship will be expressed in terms of a partial correlation or Beta coefficient rather than a simple correlation. Similarly, we do not attempt to interpret the correlation between an outcome and any measure of student involvement until we have first controlled for the effects of input and environmental variables on that outcome. Once again, these adjusted correlations between outcome and involvement are expressed as either partial correlations or Betas.

After the pretest enters the regression equation for predicting 1989 political identification, twenty-three additional input characteristics add significantly to the prediction, raising the multiple R from .42 to .53. As might be expected, none of these additional input characteristicss is as powerful a predictor as the pretest. Nevertheless, there are some interesting input predictors that should be mentioned.

Keep in mind that these additional input predictors carry significant weight *after* controlling for the effects of freshman political identification. This means that positive predictors are associated with increases in liberalism and that negative predictors are associated with increases in conservatism (the highest scores on this measure are assigned to the labels of liberal and far left, while the lowest scores are assigned to the labels of conservative and far right; since the direction of scoring a bipolar measure like this one is arbitrary, we could just as well reverse the scoring without changing the substantive findings).

Table 3.3 summarizes the additional input variables that are associated with changes in political identification. The entering characteristics associated with becoming more liberal during the college years are being African-American, female, Jewish, having no religious preference, having a mother who is highly educated, and having a father who is a college teacher. The personal values that are associated with becoming more liberal are feminism, having a strong commitment to promoting racial understanding, aspiring to write original works, and

Table 3.3 Freshman Input Variables Associated
with Changes in Political Identification, 1985–1989.

Factors Associated[a] *with*			
Increased Liberalism		*Increased Conservatism*	
Variable	*Beta at Entry*	*Variable*	*Beta at Entry*
Commitment to promoting racial understanding	.14	Desire to have administrative responsibility for others	−.08
Feminism	.12	Born-again Christian	−.08
SAT-Verbal	.11	Desire to become an expert in finance and commerce	−.06
Religious preference: none	.09	Commitment to raising a family	−.05
Desire to write original works	.07	Reason for college: to be able to make more money	−.04
Race: African-American	.07	Parental income	−.04
Hedonism (personality type)	.06	Desire to make a theoretical contribution to science	−.03
Gender: female	.07		
Religious preference: Jewish	.06		
Uncommitted (personality type)	.05		
Reason for college: to gain a general education and appreciation of ideas	.04		
Father's career: college teacher	.03		
Mother's education level	.03		
Artistic orientation (personality type)	.03		
Highest degree planned	.03		

[a]After controlling for 1985 pretest political identification.

saying that a very important reason for attending college is "to gain a general education and appreciation of ideas." Personality characteristics that are associated with increased liberalism include hedonism, artistic orientation, and lack of commitment (this variable reflects the likelihood that the student will change major or career during college or transfer from one college to another; see Astin, forthcoming). It is important to keep in mind that each of the demographic, value, and personality characteristics contributes *independently* to increased liberalism. Obviously, those students possessing many of these characteristics would be most likely to change in a liberal direction during the undergraduate years.

By contrast, those entering freshman characteristics associated with increased conservatism during the undergraduate years are being a born-again Christian, coming from a relatively affluent family, expressing a strong desire to become an expert in finance and commerce, being committed to raising a family, wanting to make a theoretical contribution to science, and saying "to be able to make more money" is a very important reason for attending college.

What these additional input variables mean is that entering college freshmen have differing propensities to change their political identifications during college. To illustrate in more concrete terms how such additional input variables are associated with changes in political identification, Table 3.4 shows how men and women changed their political identifications differentially between 1985 and 1989. While this table shows that both men and women tend to become more polarized in their views, there is a substantially greater tendency for women to increase their preference for the liberal or far-left labels (6.1 percent increase) than is the case with the men (1.1 percent increase). By contrast, men show a greater tendency to increase their preference for the conservative or far-right labels (5.5 percent) than do women (3.1 percent). Men, in other words, enter college with a propensity to become more conservative, while women enter with a propensity to become more liberal.

Table 3.5 shows a similar contrast between African-American and white students. Here we find an even greater

Table 3.4. Differential Changes in Political Identification
for 1985 Freshmen, by Sex.

Political Identification	Percentage among				Change, 1985–1989	
	Women in		Men in			
	1985	1989	1985	1989	Women	Men
Far left	0.9	1.5	3.9	3.4	+0.6	−0.5
Liberal	25.5	31.0	21.7	23.3	+5.5	+1.6
Middle-of-the-road	55.6	46.4	44.5	38.0	−9.2	−6.5
Conservative	17.1	20.6	28.6	34.2	+3.5	+5.6
Far right	0.9	0.5	1.2	1.1	−0.4	−0.1

Note: Weighted national percentages (abstracted from Wingard, Treviño, Dey, and Korn, 1991) based on unweighted Ns of 2,049 women and 2,044 men.

differential change: African-American students increase their preference for the liberal or far-left labels by a net of 9.5 percent, compared to only 6.5 percent for white students. (These figures may deviate somewhat from the data presented in Table 3.1 because we are dealing here with unweighted data in order to have a much larger sample of African-Americans. Unweighted sample sizes shown in Table 3.2 and subsequent tables are slightly smaller than that shown earlier in Table 3.1 because of missing data.) Conversely, white students show a net increase of 4.9 percent in preference for conservative or far-right labels, compared with a net *decrease* of 3.8 percent for African-Americans. Since African-Americans were already more left-leaning when they entered college as freshmen in 1985, the net effect of the four years is to widen substantially the gap in political identification between white and African-American students. Thus, whereas white students by 1989 are only slightly more inclined toward the liberal or far-left labels (32.5 percent) than the conservative or far-right labels (28.1 percent), African-American students in 1989 are tilted far more in the liberal or far-left direction (47.1 versus 12.4 percent).

(Readers should note that the unweighted data in Table 3.5 suggest a modest net shift to the left between 1985 and 1989, whereas the weighted data shown in Tables 3.1 and 3.4 show a slight net shift to the right. In all likelihood, the discrepancy

Table 3.5. Differential Changes in Political Orientation
for 1985 Freshmen: African-American and White Students.

| Political Identification | Percentage among | | | | Change, 1985–1989 | |
| | African-Americans (N = 877) in | | Whites (N = 19,472) in | | African-Americans | Whites |
	1985	1989	1985	1989		
Far left	1.6	2.7	1.5	2.6	+1.1	+1.0
Liberal	36.0	44.4	24.4	29.9	+8.4	+5.5
Middle-of-the-road	46.2	40.5	50.8	39.5	−5.7	−11.3
Conservative	15.2	11.4	22.2	27.4	−3.8	+5.2
Far right	1.0	1.0	1.0	.7	0.0	−0.3

Note: Unweighted percentages.

is attributable to the fact that students in the larger unweighted sample are disproportionately concentrated in institutions with liberal student peer groups; see the next section.)

Environmental Effects

Does any of the environmental measures have a significant effect on students' political identifications once we control for entering student characteristics? As it turns out, only two between-institution measures from the third block enter the regression equation: the political orientation of the student's peer group (Beta = .13) and the political orientation of the faculty (Beta = .12). The reader should be clear about just what these measures are. For any given student, the political orientation of the peer group would consist of the mean response to the political orientation item of *all* 1985 freshmen at that student's institution, and the political orientation of the faculty would consist of the mean response of the faculty at that institution to the same item. A high mean score would indicate that the student's peers (or faculty) lean in a liberal direction, whereas a low mean score would suggest that they lean in a conservative direction. In other words, the political orientations of the peer group and the faculty both vary, depending on which institution the student attends. These significant effects provide clear-cut evidence that the student's political identification can be influenced not only by peers but also by faculty.

To illustrate the magnitude of the effect of the peer group, we have divided the 22,328 students for whom we have complete data into four groups based on the mean political orientation of each student's peer group. Table 3.6 shows how students in each of these four groupings changed their political views between 1985 and 1989. Each row in the table shows students who have a particular political identification in 1985. The percentages in the row show whether there are any differences in how these students identify themselves politically four years later as a function of the degree of liberalism or conservatism of the peer group at the institution they attended. We have arbitrarily chosen the percentage who checked either "liberal" or "far left" as our measure of environmental effect. (We would obtain very similar results if we were to report instead the percentage identifying themselves as either conservative or far right.) Without exception, the highest percentages in each row are found among students who attend colleges with the most liberal peer groups.

Table 3.6. Effect of Political Orientation of the
Peer Environment on Students' Political Identification.

	Percent Who Were Liberal or Far Left in 1989			
Political Identification in 1985	Most Conservative Peer Group (N = 5,992)	Mildly Conservative Peer Group (N = 6,052)	Mildly Liberal Peer Group (N = 4,879)	Most Liberal Peer Group (N = 5,405)
Far left	66.7 (57)	69.3 (62)	67.7 (62)	84.0 (150)
Liberal	54.2 (1,060)	53.9 (1,266)	59.4 (1,235)	74.8 (2,043)
Middle-of-the-road	20.8 (3,022)	22.9 (3,314)	25.1 (2,587)	39.8 (2,344)
Conservative	10.7 (1,774)	12.3 (1,350)	16.4 (944)	22.9 (832)
Far right	11.4 (79)	15.0 (60)	7.9 (51)	23.2 (36)

Note: The Ns on which each percentage is based are shown in parentheses.

As you read from left to right across each row, the percentage checking themselves as "liberal" or "far left" in 1989 increases with increasing liberalism of the peer group. In all of these comparisons there are only three "reversals," and two of them may well be attributable to random errors resulting from the small samples of students who check either "far left" or "far right." One particularly interesting feature of the data in Table 3.5 is that the most powerful effect occurs with the most liberal peer group. While differences between the mildly conservative and mildly liberal peer groups are quite modest, the differences between mildly liberal and most liberal are substantial. This observation shows clearly that the effect of the peer group's political orientation is nonlinear, with most of the effect confined to the high (liberal) end.

Another interesting feature of the data in Table 3.6 is that the *relative* impact of different peer environments appears to be greatest among those who start out identifying themselves as middle-of-the-road, conservative, or far right. For students in each of these groups, the chance of switching to either liberal or far left during the undergraduate years is *twice* as great if they are exposed to the most liberal peer group rather than the most conservative peer group.

Involvement Effects

Do the various involvement measures or intermediate outcomes add any additional predictive power to the regression equation, once we control for the twenty-four entering student and two environmental characteristics? As it turns out, eleven different involvement measures from the fourth block do add significantly to the regression equation. These variables are listed in Table 3.7. Because of the ambiguities in interpreting such intermediate outcome measures, we have written "effects" with quotation marks to indicate the tentative nature of any causal conclusion involving these variables. Nevertheless, it is interesting to see that a tendency toward greater liberalism is associated with participating in demonstrations, enrolling in women's studies courses, discussing racial or ethnic issues with other students, and attending racial or cultural awareness workshops. These "diversity" ac-

Table 3.7. "Effects" of Various Involvement Variables
on Political Identification of 1985 Freshmen.

Variables with Positive Coefficients (Greater Liberalism)	Beta at Entry	Variables with Negative Coefficients (Greater Conservatism)	Beta at Entry
Participated in campus demonstrations	.17	Hours per week spent attending religious services	−.12
Discussion of racial or ethnic issues with other students	.09	Worked on a group project for a class	−.04
Enrolled in women's studies courses	.05	Was a member of a social fraternity or sorority	−.04
Attended racial or cultural awareness workshop	.04	Number of math and quantitative courses taken	−.03
Hours per week spent working for pay	.03	Got married	−.03

tivities are commonly associated with a liberal political outlook. On the other hand, we find the strongest negative effect associated with attendance at religious services, an activity commonly associated with more conservative beliefs. The use of language here is arbitrary. As we are dealing with a bipolar outcome measure — liberalism versus conservatism — we could just as well say that "attending religious services is positively associated with conservatism." The fact that being a member of a social fraternity or sorority is also negatively associated with liberalism supports the commonly held view that membership in such organizations tends to reinforce conservative political beliefs. It is interesting that getting married during college also tends to reinforce conservatism, a finding that might reflect the greater concern about material issues that confronts people who get married at a young age. The association of mathematical or quantitative courses with conservatism might also be a peer group effect, since students in engineering and the sciences tend to have more conservative political beliefs. The effect of working on a group project for a class is somewhat puzzling, given that this item was included as a measure of cooperative learning. Perhaps this variable is serving as a proxy for some other environmental variable, such as the student's final major field of study. Clearly, this is a finding that calls for further investigation.

Do the involvement variables that enter the regression provide any clues to the mechanism whereby the peer group affects the individual student's political identification? By following the step-by-step changes in the Beta coefficient for the peer group's political orientation, we can determine whether any of the involvement measures that entered subsequently might be mediating these peer group effects. Basically, what we seek to determine is whether the Beta for the peer group measure is diminished when particular involvement measures are added to the regression equation. When the Beta for the peer group's political orientation gets smaller, the entering involvement variable that caused it to shrink can be viewed as a possible mediating variable (in the parlance of path analysis, the extent of shrinkage would amount to an "indirect" effect; see Astin, 1991, for a fuller discussion of this procedure).

As it happens, the Beta for the peer group's political orientation was significantly reduced in size when each of four involvement variables entered the regression: participated in campus demonstrations, discussed racial or ethnic issues, took a women's studies course, and hours per week spent attending religious services (only this last involvement measure had a negative effect). In effect, this means that a liberal student peer group may tend to change students' political identifications in a liberal direction, in part because being exposed to such a peer group increases students' chances of participating in protests, engaging in discussions of racial or ethnic issues, and taking women's studies courses, and decreases the amount of time they spend attending religious services.

Summary

This chapter has provided a detailed look at a prototypical "college effects" analysis using a type of outcome measure that has been utilized in many previous studies: the student's political identification (far left, liberal, middle-of-the-road, conservative, far right). Unlike earlier generations of college students, students today show little evidence of the liberalizing effect of the undergraduate experience, at least as far as political self-labeling is concerned. Thus, the left-right balance shows little change during the four years after initial entry to college. Neither maturation, social change, nor "college effects" appears to play a significant role in shifting the overall left-right political balance among today's college students.

Although freshman (pretest) political identification proves to be the most powerful predictor of political identification four years later (posttest), a number of other entering freshman (input) characteristics affect how students change their political identifications during college.

Once the effects of entering freshman characteristics are taken into account, only two characteristics of the college environment are found to exert a significant influence on students' political identifications during the college years: the political leanings of the peer group, and the political leanings of the faculty. Students basically tend to change their identifications in the direction of their peers and their faculty, such that they tend to become more liberal in "liberal" environments and more conservative in "conservative" environments. The regression analyses also provide some evidence suggesting that attraction to the liberal and far-left labels is strengthened by political activism and by engagement in diversity issues having to do with race and gender, and that attraction to the conservative and far-right labels is strengthened by majoring in engineering, by participating in religious services, and by joining social fraternities or sororities.

Peer group effects may also help to explain two potentially important findings: the polarization of political identification that occurs during the undergraduate years, and the failure to replicate earlier college impact studies suggesting that college attendance has a liberalizing effect on students. Unlike the colleges of earlier eras, when liberal student bodies substantially outnumbered conservative ones, American higher education today comprises about equal numbers of liberal and conservative student bodies.

Analyses of the remaining eighty-one student outcome measures will follow exactly the same procedures reported here for students' political identifications, although the reporting of the results (Chapters Four through Nine) will necessarily be much more condensed.

Chapter 4

———•◆•———

Personality and Self-Concept

Chapters Four and Five focus on outcomes from the "affective-psychological" category of the taxonomy of student outcomes described in Chapter One. Twelve outcome measures will be examined here: six personality characteristics, four self-ratings, and two measures of the student's sense of psychological well-being. All of these outcome measures were pretested when the students entered college in the fall of 1985 and posttested four years later in 1989–90.

Since neither the available space nor the perseverance of the reader would tolerate an analysis of each of these outcomes as detailed as the one reported for political identification in the preceding chapter, we will instead summarize only the highlights of the findings from the regression analyses involving these twelve outcomes.

Personality Characteristics

The six measures of personality characteristics—Scholarship, Social Activism, Hedonism, Status Striving, Artistic Inclination, and Leadership—have been adopted from a recent study of student "types" (Astin, forthcoming). These six measures are based on a factor analysis of sixty items from the questionnaire administered to the 1971 entering freshmen. The items include life goals, self-ratings, attitudes, behaviors, expectations, and a measure of the highest degree planned by the student at the time of college entry. The personality types identified through this initial analysis have subsequently been replicated through factor analyses of similar sets of questions from the 1966 and 1986 freshman surveys. These six measures have substantial construct validity and predictive validity over periods as long as nine years after college entry (Astin, forthcoming). Also, considering that the measures are based on three to six items each, they also show a respectable amount of reliability using internal consistency estimates (median Alpha = .66).

Personality Change During College

Since the raw scores on each personality measure will have no particular meaning to the reader, changes in these scores during the undergraduate years would be difficult to interpret. Accordingly, we are instead studying change simply by determining the percentages of students who qualify as being of each "type" in 1985 and in 1989. In the original study in which these personality measures were developed (Astin, forthcoming), "cutting scores" were determined for each personality measure to identify students whose scores were sufficiently high to qualify them as belonging to the personality type represented by the measure. To qualify as belonging to a particular type, a student has to average the next-to-highest possible score on each of the items making up the type. The Social Activism scale, for example, contains four items, each of which is scored from 1 to 4. Any student who has a total score of 12 (average score of "very important" on the four items) or higher is classified as a Social Activist. (The actual items defining each type are shown below.)

Table 4.1 shows the percentage of students who qualify as belonging to each of the six types in 1985 and again in 1989. The data reveal significant increases in the percentages of students qualifying as Social Activists and Scholars. The percent-

Table 4.1. Changes in Student Personality Types During the Undergraduate Years.

| | Percentage Qualifying as Type[b] in | | Net Overall Change, | Percentage Switching from | |
Type	1985	1989	1985–1989	Not Type to Type	Type to Not Type
Social Activist	14.0	22.1	+8.1	16.3	8.2
Scholar[a]	37.4	39.8	+2.4	13.4	10.9
Artist	6.7	8.3	+1.6	5.1	3.5
Status Striver	33.1	34.4	+1.3	15.9	14.5
Leader[a]	35.3	35.9	+0.6	5.2	4.6
Hedonist[a]	17.8	17.5	−0.3	10.0	10.2

Note: N = 4,093.

[a]These type scores have omitted items from original typology (Astin, forthcoming) that cannot be posttested.

[b]Percentages are based on weighted national data abstracted from Wingard, Treviño, Dey, and Korn (1991).

ages qualifying as either Artists or Status Strivers show smaller increases, while the percentages qualifying as either Leaders or Hedonists show virtually no change.

The last two columns of Table 4.1 suggest that these small net changes conceal a great deal of switching around that takes place during the college years. Thus, while the percentage of Hedonists changes very little, more than half of those who qualify as Hedonists when they are entering freshmen are not Hedonists by 1989. At the same time, they are replaced by an equivalent number of freshmen nonhedonists who become Hedonists during the four years, resulting in little net change. Similarly, even though more than half the students who were Social Activists or Artists as freshmen changed to nonactivists and nonartists by 1989, even larger numbers of students switched from nonactivists to Activists and nonartists to Artists during the same period.

To get a better sense of what is actually involved in these changes in student type during the undergraduate years, consider the changes in the individual items making up each type (Table 4.2). For example, the increase in the percentage qualifying as Scholars is accounted for by increased self-ratings on

Table 4.2. Changes in Items Making Up Each Type, 1985-1989.

(Type) Item	Percentage in 1985	Percentage in 1989	Change, 1985-1989	Percentage[a] Changing from Low to High Scores	Percentage[a] Changing from High to Low Scores
(Scholar)					
Academic ability[b]	66.2	73.6	+7.4	14.5	7.1
Intellectual self-confidence[b]	61.8	66.8	+5.0	17.3	12.3
Mathematical ability[b]	45.4	44.0	-1.4	8.0	9.9
Planning a graduate degree	63.0	67.7	+4.7		
(Social Activist)					
Helping others in difficulty[c]	65.2	71.6	+6.4	20.0	13.3
Influencing social values[c]	35.8	50.4	+14.6	26.2	12.2
Participating in community action programs[c]	27.4	34.9	+7.5	20.8	13.5
Influencing the political structure[c]	18.9	23.7	+4.8	13.3	9.0
(Artist)					
Creating artistic works (painting, etc.)[c]	10.4	13.9	+3.5	8.4	4.7
Becoming accomplished in a performing art[c]	11.9	9.9	-2.0	4.8	6.7
Writing original works[c]	13.4	16.8	+3.4	9.9	6.3
Artistic ability[b]	24.2	29.9	+5.7	12.7	6.7
(Hedonist)					
Marijuana should be legalized[d]	20.5	19.5	-1.0	10.3	11.4
Drank beer	66.0	75.0	+9.0	15.8	6.6
Smoked cigarettes frequently	7.2	8.3	+1.1	4.8	3.7
Stayed up all night	75.4	67.2	-8.2	12.8	21.2
(Leader)					
Leadership ability[b]	57.9	63.3	+5.4	16.8	10.8
Popularity[b]	47.0	49.2	+2.2	15.8	13.8
Social self-confidence[b]	50.0	54.7	+4.7	17.7	13.0
(Status Striver)					
Being very well off financially[c]	69.3	62.2	-7.1	10.3	17.3
Obtaining recognition from colleagues[c]	57.9	56.3	-1.6	18.1	19.6
Becoming an authority in my field[c]	75.1	72.3	-2.8	12.9	15.7

Table 4.2. Changes in Items Making Up Each Type, 1985–1989, cont'd.

(Type) Item	Percentage in 1985	1989	Change, 1985–1989	Percentage[a] Changing from Low to High Scores	High to Low Scores
Being successful in my own business[c]	51.0	43.2	−7.8	14.5	22.3
Having administrative responsibility for the work of others[c]	42.8	50.8	+8.0	21.9	14.6

[a]The sum of these two change measures will sometimes deviate slightly from the "net change" column because the sample varied slightly (students who had missing data on either pretest or posttest were necessarily excluded from these computations).
[b]Self-rating "above average" or "top 10 percent."
[c]Rated "essential" or "very important."
[d]Agree "strongly" or "somewhat."
Source: Data abstracted from Wingard, Treviño, Dey, and Korn (1991).

academic ability, intellectual self-confidence, and degree aspirations. Students' ratings of their mathematical ability, on the other hand, actually show a slight decline during the undergraduate years. This finding is consistent with results involving repeated administration of standardized tests of mathematical skill, which have also shown either little change or even decline during the undergraduate years. While the reasons for this decline are not clear, it may well be that the majority of college students manage to avoid undergraduate courses that would significantly challenge their mathematical skills.

The largest and most consistent increases are associated with the items making up the Social Activism scale, a finding consistent with the large increase in the percentage of students qualifying as Social Activists (Table 4.1). By far the largest increase (14.6 percent) is associated with the item "influencing social values." Leadership is the only other type where all of the items show significant increases.

Four of the five items making up the Status Striver scale show declines, but one shows a substantial increase. The largest decreases are associated with the life goals of being successful in a business and being very well off financially. The fact that "having administrative responsibility for the work of others" actually shows a large increase suggests that college undergraduates, as they near the time they will enter the labor force, may expect to seek entry-level managerial positions. In other words, this particular item may be less reflective of status needs than of expectations about employment.

The patterns of item changes for the Artistic and Hedonist types are decidedly mixed. This is especially true in the case of the Hedonist type, where the increases match the decreases almost exactly. The substantial increase in beer drinking, for example, is largely offset by the substantial decrease in staying up all night. Why fewer students should stay up all night in college than in high school is not clear, especially since many students go away from home to attend college. Perhaps all-night parties have lost their allure once students reach college age, or perhaps the academic demands of college preclude such parties.

The last two columns of Table 4.2 once again emphasize that "net change" obscures much that occurs in individual students. For example, while "helping others in difficulty" shows a net change of only 6.4 percent, fully one-third of the students switched either from being low scorers to high scorers (20.0 percent) or from being high scorers to low scorers (13.3 percent).

How do the patterns of change shown in Tables 4.1 and 4.2 compare with the patterns reported nearly twenty years ago in *Four Critical Years*? While the items and scales used in the two studies are somewhat different, there are enough similarities to make some direct comparisons. The increase in Social Activism and the decreases in certain Status Striving items, for example, are very similar to the increase in altruism and the declines in business interests and status needs reported in *Four Critical Years*. It should be pointed out, however, that the declines in certain items making up the Status Striver scale (being very well off, obtaining recognition, becoming an authority, being successful in business) were all much larger in the late 1960s and early 1970s than in the late 1980s. It is especially interesting that the more recent declines are smaller, since the absolute level of popularity of these goals is much higher now than it was in the earlier study. In other words, there is much more room for these items to decline today than was the case eight years ago. What we may be seeing here is a peer group effect: because the overall level of status needs of the typical student peer group today is much higher than it used to be, the peer pressure may serve as more of a deterrent to declining status needs than was the case in the late 1960s and early 1970s.

While the current study shows a very slight decrease in Hedonism during the undergraduate years, *Four Critical Years* reported substantial *increases.* The earlier study took place during the late 1960s and early 1970s, a time when experimentation with sex and drugs was escalating; thus these external societal events may have exaggerated the increases in Hedonism. This interpretation gains credibility from the consecutive freshman surveys conducted between 1967 and 1972, which showed substantial increases in support for the legalization of marijuana (although nowhere near as great, it should be noted, as was observed longitudinally in the 1967 and 1968 freshmen during their undergraduate years). Why today's college students should show much smaller increases in hedonistic tendencies is not clear, although it may once again be attributable to the changed nature of the peer group that many students encounter today. Students entering college in the late 1980s, for example, drank less alcohol and were much more opposed to the legalization of marijuana than were entering students in the early 1970s (Dey, Astin, and Korn, 1991).

There are two additional parallels between the current findings and *Four Critical Years:* the increases in Scholarship and Leadership observed in the current study are consistent with the increases in intellectual and interpersonal self-esteem reported in the earlier study. These more recent increases, however, are much smaller than the increased leadership and interpersonal self-esteem reported in the earlier study.

Scholarship

Scholarship is defined by three self-ratings — academic ability, intellectual self-confidence, and mathematical ability — combined with the highest degree planned by the student (none = 1 . . .

doctorate or advanced professional degree = 5). Scholarship is very similar to the Intellectual Self-Esteem peer group measure (Chapter Two) and the "intellectual self-esteem" individual measure used in *Four Critical Years*. (Because of these similarities, we will use the labels Scholarship and Intellectual Self-Esteem interchangeably throughout the book.) Scholarship also resembles Clark and Trow's Academic (1966), Schumer and Stanfield's Academic and Scholarly Role Orientation (1966), Holland's Investigative Type (1973), Newcomb and others' Scholar (1967), Warren's Academic and Intellectual Orientations (1966), and Katchadourian and Boli's Intellectual (1985). Students who are classified as Scholars tend to come from well-educated families in which the parents are disproportionately concentrated in occupations such as engineering, college teaching, and scientific research. Scholars are far more likely than the other types to rank in the top quarter of their high school classes (88 percent versus 45 percent) and to have A averages (50 percent versus 20 percent). Scholars are disproportionately concentrated in science and engineering and tend to be overrepresented in the private four-year colleges, public universities, and especially in the private universities.

Consistent with the overall increase in the number of students who qualify as Scholars, most of the tests of college effects using the larger unweighted sample suggest that the college experience does indeed have a positive effect on the student's level of Scholarship. Thus, the degree of student interaction with faculty has a substantial positive effect on scholarship: students who interact most with faculty show a net increase between 1985 and 1989 of 3.2 percent in the number who qualify as Scholars, whereas those who interact least with faculty show a net *decline* of 3.9 percent. Similarly, the degree of interaction with other students and the number of years of college completed also have modest positive effects on Scholarship. The degree of overall increase in the number of Scholars observed in the longitudinal sample may well have been attenuated by an apparently *negative* effect of maturation. It may be that this negative impact of maturation is counterbalanced by the positive effect of college attendance, thereby resulting in less net change between 1985 and 1989.

The simple correlation between pretest (1985) and posttest (1989) Scholarship scores is .63. As a number of other input variables besides the pretest also contribute to the prediction of the posttest (increasing the multiple R to .68), different types of students are not equally likely to raise or lower their scores during the four years. Those freshmen who are most likely to increase their Scholarship scores during college are the ones with the highest grade point averages (GPAs) from high school or the highest SAT or ACT scores (either Verbal or Math). In other words, each of these input variables carries significant predictive weight even after the effects of the pretest Scholarship score are taken into account. Other input characteristics with significant positive weights are the student's socioeconomic status (SES) and being a male. One way of looking at these findings is to conclude that American higher education is better-suited to enhancing the Intellectual Self-Esteem of men than of women, of high-SES than of low-SES students, and of students with high GPAs and high test scores than of those with low GPAs and low test scores.

The other two measures of the student's race — black *and* white — both have significant positive weights in the final equation. While neither of these two race measures has significant simple correlations with Scholarship, they carry significant weight once the other input variables have been controlled. This means that both African-American and white freshmen, compared to freshmen of other races with equivalent GPAs, test scores, socioeconomic status, and gender, show greater increases in Scholarship during the undergraduate years.

Several environmental factors have significant effects on Scholarship after input characteristics are controlled, but the magnitude of these effects is generally small. (Adding these variables raises the multiple R from .68 to only .69.) Attending a public university has a negative effect on Scholarship, whereas attending an institution at which the faculty has a strong Student Orientation is associated with an increase in Scholarship. As Scholarship is defined primarily in terms of the student's self-ratings, these last results suggest that faculty who show a strong interest in students' academic and personal problems and who are available to interact with them can impact positively on students' academic self-concept or Intellectual Self-Esteem.

A fascinating pattern of individual and peer group efforts emerges in connection with financial aid. Whereas having merit-based aid tends to increase Scholarship, the *percentage* of student peers who are supported by merit-based aid tends to *lower* Scholarship. In other words, the positive effects of merit-based aid on the individual student's academic and intellectual self-concept appears to be mitigated when many peers also have such aid. While it is not surprising that having a merit-based award can enhance one's Intellectual Self-Esteem, why should the presence of many peers with such aid have the opposite effect? One possibility is that the positive effect on the individual's self-esteem is diminished when such aid is perceived as commonplace. Another is that the individual tends to feel intimidated in the presence of many peers with academic scholarships.

The percentage of peers who are supported by *need*-based aid, by contrast, appears to have a positive effect on Scholarship. Why this peer group measure should have such an effect is not immediately clear.

Adding involvement variables to the equation raises the R to .80. Many of the student involvement measures showing significant relationships with Scholarship (after input and environmental characteristics are controlled) have to do with student-faculty interaction: hours spent talking to faculty outside of class, being a guest in a faculty member's home, assisting faculty in teaching a course, and working on a professor's research project. Here we have an excellent example of the ambiguities inherent in interpreting the "effects" of involvement measures (see Chapter Three). Rather than being a true effect, this finding may indicate that students whose Scholarship increases *after* entering college are more likely to make personal contacts with faculty than are students whose Scholarship shows no change or declines after they enter college. Despite such ambiguities, these findings raise the interesting possibility that frequent involvement with faculty may serve to enhance the student's intellectual self-confidence.

Other involvement measures having positive effects on Scholarship include taking interdisciplinary, science, or math courses, participating in independent research projects, making class presentations, and tutoring other students.

Social Activism

Social Activism is defined by the importance the student assigns to each of four life-goal items: participating in community action programs, helping others who are in difficulty, influencing social values, and influencing the political structure. Each of these values suggests high activity, assertiveness, and social involvement: "participating," "helping," and "influencing." In certain respects, Social Activism resembles Newcomb and others' Political Activist (1967), Warren's Social Protest Orientation (1966), and Holland's Social Type (1973). Students from underrepresented racial or ethnic groups (African-Americans and Chicanos, in particular) tend to obtain high scores on Social Activism. Students with high scores on this scale also show a strong preference for majors in psychology, social sciences, education, and theology and for careers in law, teaching, social work, foreign service, and the church (Astin, forthcoming).

The substantial increases in Social Activism observed during the college years (Table 4.1) appear to be attributable, at least in part, to the impact of the college experience. Social Activism has strong positive relationships (after input and environmental characteristics are controlled) with student-faculty interaction and especially with student-student interaction: students who interact most frequently with other students show a net increase between 1985 and 1989 of 14.9 percent in the proportion who qualify as Social Activists, whereas those who interact least frequently show a net increase of only 4.5 percent. Social Activism has a weak positive residual relationship with number of years completed. It also has a weak negative relationship (after input characteristics are controlled) with living at home, but the relationship is reduced to nonsignificance when other environmental factors are controlled. Neither maturation nor social change appears to have contributed to the increase in Social Activism shown by the 1985 freshmen during their college years.

The pretest-posttest correlation between 1985 and 1989 Social Activism scores is .43. The addition of other input variables to the prediction raises the multiple R to .50. Both black and Chicano students raise their Social Activism scores during college more than do members of other racial or ethnic groups. Otherwise, demographic and family background characteristics show no particular effects on changes in Social Activism.

One environmental measure from the faculty survey, Social Activism and Community Orientation, has a positive effect on the student's Social Activism score. This environmental factor measures the extent to which the institution is perceived as concerning itself with producing student leaders who will become social change agents (see Chapter Two). Here we have clear-cut evidence that institutional values or priorities can have a direct effect on students' values. One peer environment factor also enters the regression equation with a positive weight: the mean Socioeconomic Status (SES) of the peer group. Another peer factor, Altruism and Social Activism, also has a significant partial correlation after input characteristics are controlled, but the correlation shrinks to nonsignificance after Social Activism and Community Orientation and Peer SES are controlled.

The involvement measures showing the strongest residual relationships with Social Activism (after input and environmental variables are controlled) all have to do with activism or "diversity" issues: discussing racial or ethnic issues with other students, taking ethnic studies courses, socializing with students from different ethnic or racial groups, attending racial or cultural awareness workshops, and participating in campus demonstrations. Social Activism is also related to hours per week spent in volunteer work. While we cannot be sure of the direction of causation in these "intermediate outcome" relationships, it is interesting to consider the possibility that students' commitment to social activism can be reinforced through such activities.

Social Activism, as already indicated, is related to student-student and student-faculty interaction. It also has positive relationships with the number of history or writing-skills courses a student takes, and a negative residual relationship with the number of mathematics or numerical courses taken.

Artistic Inclination

Artistic Inclination is defined by the student's self-rating on artistic ability plus the degree of importance attached to three life goals: creating artistic work (such as painting, sculpture, decorating), becoming accomplished in one of the performing arts (acting, dancing), and writing original works (poems, novels, short stories). Artistic Inclination is very similar to Holland's Artistic type (1973) and also bears some similarity to Newcomb and others' Creative Individualist (1967). Students with high scores on Artistic Inclination tend to come from relatively well-educated families and to include a large proportion of women. High scores are also associated with significant artistic or literary achievement in high school (winning art competitions, editing student publications, and having poems published) as well as with having major parts in plays and playing musical instruments. As would be expected, high scorers tend to major in fine arts, music, speech, theater, journalism, and English and to pursue careers in the arts (music, writing, theater), interior decorating, and architecture. That Artists also show an inclination toward careers in school teaching may reflect the paucity of jobs in the performing arts and the decision of many persons with artistic interests to make a living in teaching. People with high scores on Artistic Inclination tend to be disproportionately concentrated in private four-year colleges and underrepresented in community colleges (Astin, forthcoming).

Artistic Inclination is one of the personality measures that changed in a different direction in the larger unweighted sample (decline) than in the weighted norms (slight increase; see Tables 4.1 and 4.2). There is some evidence suggesting that the decline observed during the college years in the unweighted sample is attributable to a mix of college effects and maturational factors. (Evidence from consecutive freshman surveys suggests that, if anything, the decline would have been even greater if it had not been for social changes, since endorsement of all four items increased slightly between the 1985 and 1989 freshman surveys.) Negative college effects are suggested by the finding that the net decline in the number of Artistic types within the unweighted sample is greatest among those who complete four years of college (−8.4 percent) and least among those who complete one or fewer years of college (−1.4 percent). Maturational effects are suggested by a weak but significant positive association with age at the time of college entry: the largest net

decline in the percentage of Artistic types (− 12.2 percent) occurs among students who are younger than eighteen years old
when they start college, whereas the smallest net declines occur
among those who are nineteen (−6.9 percent) and twenty or
older (−7.2 percent). This apparent maturational effect may well
reflect the reality issues that young people increasingly must face
when they consider the problems of trying to make a living in
the arts in a society that does not provide substantial support
for artists. What seems to be a negative effect of college attendance may reflect the influence of the peer group: given that
students in the arts account for a very small fraction of the student body in most institutions, prolonged association with peers
representing a wide range of other career interests may well
tempt the prospective artist to pursue an "easier" career. It may
also be that the academic demands of a traditional liberal arts
education make it difficult for prospective artists to devote the
large amount of time and energy to their special artistic endeavors
that is often required for a successful career in the arts. Whatever
the explanation, the college experience appears to cause, at best,
only a small increase in the artistic inclinations of young people (weighted data) and, at worst, a decrease (unweighted data).
This is a cause for concern. Such effects are certainly incom-
patible with the traditional view of what a "liberal education"
is supposed to accomplish.

The simple correlation between pretest and posttest scores
on Artistic Inclination is .61. The addition of other input variables to the regression equation raises the multiple R to .66.
The student's high school GPA has a weak but significant *negative* effect on Artistic Inclination. This may explain the net decline
observed in the unweighted sample, since students with high
GPAs are overrepresented in this sample (see Wingard, Treviño,
Dey, and Korn, 1991, Table A4). Religious choice of "none"
has a slight positive effect. Otherwise, demographic and family
background characteristics produce no measurable effects on
changes in Artistic Inclination.

One potentially interesting environmental effect concerns
the basis for the student's financial aid. Having aid based on
"other talent" (besides academic or athletic talent) has a significant positive effect on Artistic Inclination. If it is reasonable

to assume that "other" in this case refers to musical or artistic talent, this finding raises the interesting possibility that more young people might be encouraged to sustain their artistic interests during the college years if more financial aid based on artistic merit were made available.

Virtually no other environmental factors show notable effects on Artistic Inclination, although several student involvement measures do show some residual relationships after input and environmental variables are controlled. Specifically, Artistic Inclination is positively associated with a number of measures of activism in college (demonstration, protests) and concern with diversity issues, a finding that is consistent with the traditional involvement of people in the arts with issues of social equity (Astin, Astin, Bayer, and Bisconti, 1975). Artistic Inclination also has positive residual correlations with several items measuring student-faculty interaction. This finding could reflect a curricular artifact: since students who maintain their artistic inclinations over time would be more likely to stay with a major in the arts, these correlations may well reflect the closer association that one normally finds between students and faculty in artistic or literary fields. A similar interpretation could be made of the finding that Artistic Inclination is negatively associated with the number of math or numerical courses taken and positively associated with the number of courses taken in writing, foreign language, and history.

Perhaps the most interesting finding concerning intermediate outcomes was the *positive* association between Artistic Inclination and the fact that the student left school or transferred to another institution sometime between 1985 and 1989. Possibly the only way that some students can maintain their commitment to artistic endeavors is to leave school or to find an alternative institution that is more supportive of the arts. It may also be that Artistic students have less commitment to the more traditional academic demands of college.

Hedonism

Hedonism is defined in terms of three behavioral measures (drinking beer, smoking cigarettes, staying up all night) and support for the view that marijuana should be legalized. The Hedonism scale has some things in common with Newcomb and others' Wild Ones (1967). Otherwise, there do not seem to be any real counterparts in the typologies developed by other investigators. Hedonists have lower high school grades than any of the other types, report a greater frequency of poor study habits in high school, and are often bored in class. Although people with high scores on the Hedonism scale tend to be about average in socioeconomic status, African-American students tend to be *underrepresented* among high scorers. Hedonists show a predilection for majors and careers in fields that are not generally considered academically demanding and which usually do not require postgraduate training: business, nursing, health technology, and secretarial studies.

Although the weighted data show almost no change in the number of Hedonists (Table 4.1), the larger unweighted sample shows a significant increase. There are several lines of evidence from the unweighted sample suggesting that college attendance seems to increase Hedonism. Thus, Hedonism appears to be enhanced by student-student interaction and living in a private room or dormitory, while living at home while attending college tends to have a *negative* impact on Hedonism. This suggests that the "college effect" on Hedonism is positive and accounted for primarily by the effects of leaving home.

Hedonism presents an interesting pattern of relationships to number of years of college completed. A net gain in the percentage of students who qualify as Hedonists occurs among those who complete three years of college (+5.3 percent); completing four years is associated with less than half as much gain (+2.5 percent). Given the link between Hedonism and poor academic performance, noted above, a possible interpretation of this somewhat anomalous finding might be as follows: students who show the largest increases in Hedonism may actually reach a point where they leave college for academic reasons; thus, those who remain for the full four years may represent a more select group, which no longer includes those whose Hedonism increases have made it impossible for them to continue in college.

The simple pretest-posttest correlation between 1985 and 1989 Hedonism scores is .52. The addition of other input variables to the equation raises the multiple R to .56. Men raise their Hedonism scores slightly, while women lower theirs slightly, and students with low high school GPAs raise their scores more than do students with high GPAs. The SAT Verbal score, however, has a slight positive effect on Hedonism scores, as does the educational level of the student's mother. The only other background or demographic characteristic carrying a significant weight in the regression equation is having a religious choice of "none."

Social change appears to have attenuated most of the changes in Hedonism items shown in Table 4.2. Thus, whereas beer drinking increased by 9.0 percent among the 1985 freshmen, it *declined* by 6.2 percent on consecutive freshman surveys between 1985 and 1989. Similarly, staying up all night, which declined by 8.2 percent among the 1985 freshmen, *increased* by 4.4 percent between the 1985 and 1989 freshman surveys. Support for the legalization of marijuana, which declined by only 1.0 percent among the 1985 freshmen, declined by fully 5.1 percent in the consecutive freshman surveys conducted between 1985 and 1989. Only smoking cigarettes frequently showed similar changes: increases of 1.1 percent by *both* indices of change.

What does all this mean in terms of how social change may have affected the shifts shown in Table 4.2? For one thing, it helps to explain why support for legalizing marijuana failed to show an increase and why beer drinking did not increase more: social changes between 1985 and 1989 were affecting students in ways that counterbalanced the normal "college effects" on these outcomes. As far as "staying up all night" is concerned, social change appears to have retarded the decline observed in the 1985 freshmen during the college years.

Several environmental characteristics have significant effects on Hedonism. Students who leave home to attend college, for example, increase their Hedonism significantly while those who live at home lower theirs slightly. The single strongest environmental effect, however, is from the peer group: students attending colleges with a high percentage of born-again

Christians in the student body show reductions in Hedonism, whereas students show increases when they attend colleges where the peer group's socioeconomic status is high. Attending a college for women, by contrast, is associated with decreases in Hedonism. (Men, it should be noted, tend to be more hedonistic than women.)

Only one faculty environmental characteristic enters the regression equation: the Time Stress experienced by the faculty has a weak positive impact on student Hedonism. The meaning of this particular effect is not clear.

A number of involvement measures produce an interesting pattern of relationships with Hedonism, after student input and environmental variables are controlled. Being a member of a social fraternity or sorority, for example, has a positive association with Hedonism, whereas getting married has a negative association.

By far the strongest residual relationships involving Hedonism are the positive effects of hours per week spent partying and the frequency of socializing with friends. Participation in intramural sports is also associated with increased Hedonism.

The strongest negative effect on Hedonism is associated with hours per week spent participating in religious services or meetings. Hedonism is also negatively associated with hours spent commuting and hours spent studying or doing homework.

While issues of causation are, once again, highly ambiguous when it comes to interpreting these findings with involvement measures, the patterns provide highly suggestive evidence concerning forms of student involvement that may enhance or depress students' tendency toward greater Hedonism during the undergraduate years. In short, Hedonism may be increased by joining social fraternities or sororities, socializing and partying, and being involved in intramural sports. The student's hedonistic tendencies may be weakened, on the other hand, by involvement in religious activities, engagement in academic work, commuting, and getting married.

Leadership

Leadership is defined in terms of three self-ratings — leadership ability, popularity, and social self-confidence — and whether the student had been elected to a student office (in calculating the data shown in Table 4.1, this last item has been omitted in order to make the 1985 and 1989 measures comparable). Leadership is very similar to the "interpersonal self-esteem" measure used in *Four Critical Years.* In certain respects it also corresponds to Holland's Enterprising type (1973). Leaders tend to have relatively affluent and well-educated parents. In high school, students with high scores on Leadership excelled in speech and debate, frequently studied with other students, and were far more likely than other students to win varsity letters in sports or to be elected president of some student organization. In college, Leaders show a predilection for majors in pre-law, military science, and communications and a strong preference for careers in law, the church, or military service. Students with high leadership scores tend to be disproportionately concentrated in private colleges and universities and underrepresented in the community colleges (Astin, forthcoming).

Increases in Leadership are somewhat larger in the unweighted sample than in the weighted norms. By almost every indication, increases in Leadership appear to be associated with the college experience. For example, in looking at the net changes between 1985 and 1989 in the percentage of students who qualify as Leaders, we find larger increases associated with living on campus (+4.4 percent) or in a private room or apartment (+3.3 percent) than with living at home (+1.7 percent). The degree of increase is also positively associated with number of years of college completed and with the degree of student interaction with faculty. But by far the strongest effect is associated with student-student interaction: students who interacted most frequently with peers show a net increase of +13.2 in the percentage qualifying as Leaders, whereas those who have the least degree of interaction with peers show a net decrease of −3.6 percent. The lack of any maturational effect is suggested by the observation that age at the time of college entry is not significantly associated with changes in Leadership scores. Clearly, this pattern constitutes strong evidence in support of the argument that increases in leadership skills during the undergraduate years are associated with the college experience rather than with maturation or other environmental factors.

The simple pretest-posttest correlation between 1985 and 1989 Leadership scores is .53. The addition of other input characteristics to the regression equation raises the multiple R to .56. Men and students from high socioeconomic levels show greater-than-average increases in Leadership during the college years. The SAT-Verbal score, on the other hand, is associated with smaller-than-average increases. The only other background or demographic characteristic adding significantly to the prediction is a religious choice of "none," which has a negative effect on Leadership.

As already indicated, leaving home to attend college tends to result in greater-than-average increases in Leadership during the undergraduate years. One peer group factor — the percentage of students who are engaged in outside work activities — has a significant effect (in this case, negative) on Leadership. In all likelihood, when many members of the peer group are engaged in employment off campus, leadership opportunities may be curtailed, and the incentive to seek leadership positions may be reduced.

But the largest environmental effect on Leadership, in this case a negative effect, is associated with a faculty environmental factor: the Research Orientation of the faculty. Why the development of leadership qualities among undergraduates should be attenuated when the faculty is heavily engaged in research and scholarship is not immediately clear. Since involvement with faculty tends to be closely associated with the development of leadership qualities, it may well be that heavy faculty commitment to research simply reduces the amount of time and energy that faculty members can devote to those student-faculty activities that facilitate Leadership development. Whatever the explanation, this finding clearly merits further research.

As might be expected, changes in Leadership (after student input and environmental effects are controlled) are associated with more involvement measures than any other single student outcome. The strong effects of student-student and student-faculty interaction have already been mentioned. Larger-than-average increases in Leadership scores are also associated with being a member of a social fraternity or sorority, playing intramural sports, spending time in volunteer work, tutoring other students, participating in a group project for class, and making presentations to class. Not surprisingly, substantial negative effects are associated with hours spent watching television and hours spent commuting. Both of these activities would limit student opportunities for participation in leadership activities and the development of leadership skills.

Status Striving

Status striving is defined by the importance students give to each of five life goals: being very well off financially, obtaining recognition from colleagues for contributions to one's special field, becoming an authority in one's field, being successful in one's own business, and having administrative responsibility for the work of others. About the only type identified by other investigators that resembles the Status Striver is Holland's Conventional type (1973). African-American and Chicano students and students from families of low socioeconomic status tend to be overrepresented among students with high scores on Status Striving. The academic performance of Status Strivers in high school is poorer than that of all other types except the Hedonist. The strongly materialistic values of the Status Strivers are reflected in their inclination toward college majors and careers in accounting and business. High scores on Status Striving are also associated with majoring in physical education, architecture, and agriculture.

Status Striving is another personality measure for which the changes were different in the unweighted sample (decline) and weighted sample (virtually no change; see Table 4.1). That Status Striving may be negatively affected by maturation is strongly suggested by the negative effect of age: in the larger unweighted sample, a substantial net decline between 1985 and 1989 in the percentage of students qualifying as Status Strivers occurs among those who were younger than eighteen when they entered college, whereas students in this sample who were twenty or older at the time of college entry showed a slight net increase (+0.5 percent).

Has social change affected the changes in items making up the Status Striver scale (Table 4.2)? While "obtain recognition" and "administrative responsibility" showed little variation between the 1985 and 1989 freshman surveys, the other three items showed substantial shifts. In the case of "being very well off financially," it appears that social change retarded the decline observed in the 1985 freshmen during college (–7.1 percent), since endorsement of this value increased by 4.5 percent between the 1985 and 1989 freshman surveys. The reverse seems to be true for the remaining two Status Striver items. If we compare four-year longitudinal changes in the 1985 freshmen during college with changes in consecutive freshman surveys over the same period, we find similar trends: –7.8 percent versus –6.7 percent for "being successful in my own business," and –2.8 percent vesus –5.4 percent for "becoming an authority in my field."

In short, these findings suggest that in the absence of significant social change, the decline in materialism observed in the 1985 freshmen after they entered college would have been even greater, but that the declines in commitment to becoming an authority and being successful in business would have been much smaller.

The evidence concerning the overall effects of the college experience on Status Striving is not only mixed but contradictory. For example, that the college experience might contribute to a decline in Status Striving is suggested by the finding that students who leave college before starting a second year show a net increase in the percentage of Status Strivers (+3.7 percent), whereas those who complete three or four years show the largest decline (–5.3 and –3.2 percent, respectively). Evidence from student-student and student-faculty interaction, on the other hand, suggests an entirely different scenario. Students who interact least frequently with faculty show the largest net declines (–5.3 percent), while students who interact most frequently with faculty show no net change between 1985 and 1989. Similarly, students who interact least with fellow students show an even larger decline (–7.0 percent), whereas students who interact most frequently with fellow students show a slight net increase in the percentage of Status Strivers (+1.8 percent). It thus appears that the college experience works in two different ways: the mere fact of being a college student seems to contribute to a decline in Status Striving (the longer the student stays, the greater the decline), but this effect is mitigated to some extent when the student interacts frequently with fellow students or with faculty. That exposure to peers might now serve to strengthen Status Striving is not surprising, given that contemporary students enter college with much stronger status needs (especially materialistic needs) than did their counterparts of twenty years ago. Why interacting with faculty should also reinforce students' materialistic and status needs is not as clear, but the evidence reported here and later strongly suggests that such an effect in fact occurs. One possibility is suggested by the items that make up the "status" part of this measure: "obtaining recognition from colleagues for contributions to my field" and "becoming an authority in my field." Such values are commonly embraced by many faculty; perhaps in associating with faculty, the student comes to embrace the same values.

The simple pretest-posttest correlation between 1985 and 1989 Status Striving scores is .48. Addition of other student input characteristics to the prediction equation raises the multiple R to .54. Declining Status Striving is associated with having a high score on the SAT-Verbal test and, to a lesser extent, having a high SAT-Math score and a high GPA from high school. (These findings probably explain the net decline in Status Striving observed in the unweighted sample, which overrepresents high achievers.) Women and white students also showed larger-than-average declines between 1985 and 1989. Smaller-than-average declines are associated with having a high family income or a religious preference of Roman Catholic.

The only environmental factors showing significant effects on Status Striving are measures of the peer environment. As might be expected, students will show smaller-than-average declines if they are exposed to a peer group that places a high value on Materialism and Status. By contrast, declines will be slightly larger-than-average when the student is exposed to a peer group with a strong Scientific Orientation or a high score on Permissiveness.

A number of student involvement measures show significant residual correlations with Status Striving after entering student and environmental factors have been controlled. The positive correlations with student-student and student-faculty interaction have already been mentioned. Other involvement measures showing positive relationships with Status Striving are being a member of a social fraternity or sorority, drinking alcoholic beverages, and working at a full-time job; additional positive relationships were with hours spent partying and the number of math or numerical courses taken.

Some clues as to how Status Striving is influenced by Materialism and Status of the peer group is provided by an inspection of step-by-step changes in the Beta coefficient for this environmental variable. It appears that Status Striving is positively affected by a peer group with high scores on Materialism and Status, in part because being exposed to such a peer group enhances the student's chances of joining a social fraternity or sorority and increases the amount of television watching that the student does. Taking multiple-choice exams also diminishes the effects of Materialism and Status when it enters the regression, but it is not clear just why this particular involvement variable should affect Status Striving. One (perhaps far-fetched) explanation might be that the use of multiple-choice exams (in contrast to, say, essay exams) might serve to heighten competition among students.

Self-Concept

While many self-rating items are included in the personality measures just discussed, there are four other self-ratings from the 1989 follow-up questionnaire that are not included in the scoring of any personality measures but that are of interest: drive to achieve, writing ability, emotional health, and physical health. Each of these self-ratings was also pretested when the students first entered college, in 1985.

Four-year changes in the four self-rating items are shown in Table 4.3. There is a substantial increase (8.9 percent) in the percentage of students rating themselves above average in

Table 4.3. Changes[a] in Self-Ratings, 1985–1989.

| Self-Ratings | Percentage Rating Above Average in | | Change, 1985–1989 | Percentage[b] Changing From | |
	1985	1989		Low to High Scores	High to Low Scores
Writing ability	46.8	55.7	+8.9	18.9	9.8
Drive to achieve	68.0	70.7	+2.7	15.1	12.6
Physical health	63.5	58.5	−5.0	12.8	17.2
Emotional health	63.9	57.8	−6.1	12.6	19.3

[a]Weighted national norms (abstracted from Wingard, Treviño, Dey, and Korn, 1991).

[b]The sum of these two change measures will sometimes deviate slightly from the "net change" column because the sample varied slightly (students who had missing data on either pretest or posttest were necessarily excluded from these computations).

writing ability, and a small increase (2.7 percent) in the percentage rating themselves above average in drive to achieve. Self-ratings on both physical and emotional health, on the other hand, show a modest decline after college entry. Is there any evidence suggesting that these changes are attributable to the college experience, maturation, or social change?

As far as maturation is concerned, only one of these self-ratings shows any consistent relationship to age: decreases in ratings of "physical health" are associated with age, with the largest decline (−7 percent) occurring among the students who were younger than eighteen when they entered college, and the smallest decline (0 percent) occurring among those who were older than nineteen at the time of college entry.

What about the possible effects of social change? As it turns out, changes in consecutive entering freshman classes between 1985 and 1989 exactly parallel the changes observed in the 1985 freshmen during the four years after they entered college. Thus, we find increases in the percentage of students rating themselves above average in writing ability (+2.1 percent) and drive to achieve (+2.6 percent), together with decreases in the percentages rating themselves above average in emotional health (−3.3 percent) and physical health (−2.4 percent). This pattern of findings suggests that the self-rating changes observed in the 1985 freshmen may be in part attributable to changes in the larger society (as reflected in how consecutive entering freshman classes changed between 1985 and 1989).

As far as college effects are concerned, the analyses produce mixed results. While there is a weak tendency for students who live on campus to show greater-than-average declines in self-ratings of both physical and emotional health, students who interact frequently with faculty or with fellow students showed the smallest declines. Results with drive to achieve and writing ability were more consistent: frequent student-faculty and student-student interaction is associated with greater-than-average increases in both self-ratings, while place of residence produces no effect one way or the other. In short, these results suggest that increases in the students' self-ratings on writing ability and drive to achieve are partially attributable to the college experience, whereas the role of the college experience in the declines in physical and emotional health is unclear.

Writing Ability

None of the institutional characteristics carries a significant weight in the regression equation for self-rated writing ability. However, a number of involvement measures prove to have substantial weights in the equation, once input variables are controlled. In particular, substantial positive weights are associated with three: the number of courses taken that emphasize the development of writing skills, the frequency with which students report having their class papers critiqued by instructors, and the frequency with which students take essay exams. Weaker but significant positive weights are also associated with hours spent reading for pleasure, hours spent using a personal computer, discussing racial or ethnic issues, and being a member of a social fraternity or sorority. Self-rated writing skills are negatively associated with number of science courses taken, number of math or numerical courses taken, and majoring in engineering. Among other things, this pattern of results highlights the curricular trade-offs involved in the undergraduate experience: self-rated writing skills are enhanced by taking courses that emphasize writing and are diminished by taking courses in science or math.

Drive to Achieve

Two peer group factors have significant effects on the student's self-rating on drive to achieve: Permissiveness has a modest positive effect, while Outside Work has a modest negative effect. Otherwise, institutional characteristics do not carry any significant weight in the regression equation. As far as involvement variables are concerned, the largest positive correlations (after controlling for input and environmental effects) are with hours per week spent studying or doing homework, enrolling in an honors program, giving class presentations, student-student interaction, and student-faculty interaction. Significant negative weights are associated with hours spent watching television and hours spent reading for pleasure.

Physical Health

Self-ratings on physical health are positively affected by having financial aid based on athletic talent. No doubt such aid has the effect of involving students more heavily in team practice and physical conditioning. The peer measure Outside Work has a small negative weight in the regression equation. Otherwise, institutional characteristics are not related to this outcome measure.

As might be expected, by far the largest positive residual correlation of self-rated physical health with any involvement measure is with hours per week spent in sports or exercise (partial Beta = .25). A positive correlation also occurs with participating in intramural sports. Negative involvement correlations were found with hours spent watching television and receiving personal or psychological counseling.

Emotional Health

The student's self-rating on emotional health is negatively affected by two institutional characteristics: Lack of Student Community and the peer measure Scientific Orientation. That Lack of Student Community is likely to prove stressful to the undergraduate is perhaps not surprising, since such an atmosphere would tend to make students feel alienated. Why Scientific Orientation should have a negative effect is not clear, although it may be that having a peer group strongly oriented toward science might serve as a source of stress for the individual student.

Self-ratings on emotional health are also positively associated with several involvement measures, after entering freshman and environmental effects are controlled: hours spent in sports or exercise, participating in intramural sports, working on a group project for a class, hours spent socializing with friends, and hours spent attending religious services. Negative partial correlations involve hours per week watching television, alcohol consumption, and leaving college. (All three of these measures could be the result of poor emotional health, but they could also be a *cause* of it.) The largest negative correlation, however, is with receiving personal or psychological counseling. We have here an excellent illustration of the chicken-egg ambiguities associated with certain involvement measures. While it could be argued that counseling can serve to increase the degree of stress experienced by the student, equally plausible is the argument that those students who seek psychological counseling do so because their emotional well-being has declined since they first entered college. Without another assessment of emotional health at the time the student actually begins counseling, there is no way to resolve such an ambiguity.

This last discussion leads us naturally to a consideration of this chapter's final two outcome measures, both of which are designed to assess the student's sense of psychological well-being.

Psychological Well-Being

The outcome measures considered in this section consist of two items, "felt depressed" and "felt overwhelmed by all I had to do," which are both scored on a three-point scale: frequently (3), occasionally (2), and not at all (1). Table 4.4 shows how "frequently" responses to these questions change during the undergraduate years. Both items show substantial increases, suggesting that the student's sense of psychological well-being actually declines during

Table 4.4. Changes in Psychological Well-Being, 1985–1989.

| Item | Percentage Responding "Frequently" | | Change, 1985–1989 | Percentage[a] Changing From | |
	1985	1989		Low to High Scores	High to Low Scores
Felt depressed	9.7	16.0	+6.3	10.2	5.5
Felt overwhelmed by all I had to do	21.5	35.0	+13.5	23.1	9.5

[a]The sum of these two change measures will sometimes deviate slightly from the "net change" column because the sample varied slightly (students who had missing data on either pretest or posttest were necessarily excluded from these computations).

the college years. (The decline in emotional health just discussed would suggest a similar conclusion.) Such a decline is perhaps to be expected, given the academic and social stresses of the undergraduate experience and considering that, for many students, this is their first experience in being away from the security of the home for an extended period of time.

Is there any evidence that these changes are maturational? As it turns out, the largest increases in "frequently" or "occasionally" responses to both items occur among the *oldest* students (20+ years at the time of college entry), a finding that is the reverse of what one would expect if the changes shown in Table 4.4 are maturational. It should be emphasized, however, that students in the twenty-plus age group started out far below the three younger age groups in positive responses to these items, so that their much larger increase represents more of a "catching up." Most important from the point of view of a maturational hypothesis, however, is the finding that the three youngest age groups (under 18, 18, and 19) showed almost identical increases during the undergraduate years. In short, there is no evidence that the decreased sense of psychological well-being observed in these students is maturational.

Data from the five consecutive freshman surveys conducted between 1985 and 1989 suggest that societal change plays very little part in the declining sense of psychological well-being observed in the 1985 freshmen: compared to the 1985 freshmen, the 1989 freshmen score only slightly higher in the percentage of "frequently" responses to the "overwhelmed" question (+2.8 percent) and virtually the same in their responses to the "depressed" question (+0.2 percent).

To what extent can these increases in stress be attributed to the college experience? The evidence from number of years of college completed is mixed: completing four years of college is negatively associated with feeling depressed, whereas completing two or more years is positively associated with feeling overwhelmed. Two things may be occurring here. First, if a student is *not* able to complete four years of academic requirements during the four calendar years after matriculation, this situation may contribute to a sense of depression. Second, being able to stay in college beyond the first year may ultimately contribute to a feeling of being overwhelmed because of the many responsibilities associated with being a second-year college student.

Results with student-faculty and student-student interaction also fail to provide unequivocal evidence. Interacting frequently with fellow students and interacting frequently with faculty both have weak negative partial correlations (after control for inputs and environments) with feeling depressed, whereas neither "interaction" variable has any residual correlation with feeling overwhelmed. In short, the evidence concerning the possible contribution of the college experience to what appears to be a decline in students' sense of psychological well-being is unclear: remaining in college after the first year appears to be weakly associated with feeling overwhelmed, whereas *not* completing college appears to be associated with feelings of depression. If the college experience does play a role in the declining sense of psychological well-being observed during the four years after entering college, the effect appears to operate through the dropout process: students who fail to complete college show the largest decline, whereas those who manage to complete their degrees show either smaller declines or no change in the reported rate of depression.

Feeling Depressed

Feeling depressed is associated with only one institutional characteristic—the peer measure Scientific Orientation, which has a weak positive effect. When it comes to involvement measures, depression, like the student's self-rating on emotional health, has its strongest positive association with receiving personal or psychological counseling. Once again, the direction of causation here is unclear. Depression is also positively associated with discussing racial or ethnic issues, consuming alcohol, receiving tutoring in courses, and leaving school or transferring. These last two involvement measures may signify academic difficulties, as the student's undergraduate GPA has a negative partial correlation with depression (high depression, in other words, being associated with low grades). Other negative correlates of depression include attending religious services, getting married, participating in intramural sports, and hours spent in sports or exercise. The latter two correlates raise an interesting chicken-egg question: Are depressed students simply less likely to engage in physical activity, or does physical activity help to reduce depression?

Feeling Overwhelmed

Feeling overwhelmed is positively affected by majoring in engineering and by attending an institution with a heavy concentration of students in engineering majors. These results may well reflect the tremendous demands on students' intellectual skills and energies that many engineering programs make. Feeling overwhelmed is also positively affected by the peer measure Outside Work and negatively affected by the percentage of Catholics in the student body.

As far as involvement variables are concerned, feeling overwhelmed has its strongest positive association with hours spent studying or doing homework. It also has positive associations with receiving personal or psychological counseling, giving presentations in class, and hours spent commuting to campus.

Clearly, this pattern suggests that the sense of feeling over-whelmed is closely associated with time pressures. Feeling over-whelmed is negatively associated with hours spent reading for pleasure, hours spent in sports or exercise, and hours spent so-cializing with friends. Again, the direction of causation may be reversed for some of these items, since it may well be that stu-dents who do not feel overwhelmed may feel freer to read, so-cialize, or engage in athletic activities.

Discussion and Summary

Students show a number of changes in personality and self-concept after entering college. The largest increases are in So-cial Activism, with Scholarship (intellectual self-concept), Ar-tistic Inclination, Status Striving, and Leadership showing small increases. Students also show increases in their self-ratings of writing ability and drive to achieve. Undergraduates show mixed changes in Hedonism, with increases in alcohol consumption and cigarette smoking accompanied by decreases in staying up all night. Changes in specific aspects of Status Striving are also mixed, with increases in the desire to have administrative respon-sibility for others being accompanied by decreases in business interests and materialistic tendencies. Most of these changes ap-pear to be attributable to the effects of college attendance rather than to maturation or social change. Indeed, maturation, if any-thing, appears to have a negative effect on intellectual self-confidence.

The most notable declines observed during the college years are in the student's sense of psychological well-being. The role of the college experience in these declines is unclear. Stu-dents also show a slight decline in self-ratings of physical health after entering college, but this change appears to be primarily maturational.

A number of environmental and involvement factors ap-pear to have significant effects on personality development dur-ing the college years. These are summarized in Table 4.5. Both Social Activism and Status Striving appear to be directly affected by the student peer group. Thus, Social Activism is positively

Table 4.5. Summary of Environmental Effects
on Personality and Self-Concept.

Student Outcome	Positively Affected by	Negatively Affected by
Personality		
Scholarship	Student Orientation of Faculty Merit-based aid Percentage of peers with need-based aid	Public university Percentage of peers with merit-based aid
	(Involvement measures)[a] Student-faculty interaction Interdisciplinary courses Science and math courses Independent research Class presentations Tutoring other students	
Social Activism	Social Activism and Community Orientation Peer SES	
	(Involvement measures)[a] Student-faculty interaction History and writing courses Volunteer work "Diversity" activities[b]	Math courses
Artistic Inclination	Aid based on "other talent"	
	(Involvement measures)[a] "Diversity" activities[b] Student-faculty interaction	Math courses
Hedonism	Living away from home Peer SES Faculty: Time Stress	Peers: percentage who are born-again Christians Women's college
	(Involvement measures)[a] Fraternity or sorority membership Partying, socializing Intramural sports	Getting married Attending religious services Commuting Studying or homework
Leadership	Living away from home	Peers: Outside Work Research Orientation
	(Involvement measures)[a] Student-student interaction Student-faculty interaction	

Table 4.5. Summary of Environmental Effects
on Personality and Self-Concept, cont'd.

Student Outcome	Positively Affected by	Negatively Affected by
	Fraternity/sorority membership	
	Intramural sports	
	Volunteer work	
	Tutoring other students	
	Group class projects	
	Class presentations	
Status Striving	Peers: Materialism and Status	Peers: Scientific Orientation Peers: Permissiveness
	(Involvement measures)[a]	
	Student-faculty interaction	
	Student-student interaction	
	Fraternity/sorority membership	
	Partying, alcohol consumption	
	Working full-time	
	Math courses	
Self-Concept		
Drive to achieve	Peers: Permissiveness	Peers: Outside Work
	(Involvement measures)[a]	
	Student-student interaction	Watching television
	Student-faculty interaction	Reading for pleasure
	Studying/homework	
	Honors programs	
	Class presentations	
Writing ability	(Involvement measures)[a]	
	Writing courses	Major: engineering
	Having class papers critiqued by instructors	Science courses Math courses
	Taking essay exams	
	Reading for pleasure	
	Using a personal computer	
	Discussing racial issues	
	Fraternity/sorority membership	
	Student-faculty interaction	
	Student-student interaction	

Table 4.5. Summary of Environmental Effects
on Personality and Self-Concept, cont'd.

Student Outcome	Positively Affected by	Negatively Affected by
Physical health	Aid for "athletic talent"	Peers: Outside Work
	(Involvement measures)[a]	
	Exercise	Watching television
	Intramural sports	
Emotional health		Lack of Student Community
		Peers: Scientific Orientation
	(Involvement measures)[a]	
	Exercise	Watching television
	Intramural sports	Alcohol consumption
	Group class projects	Leaving college
	Socializing	Receiving personal
	Attending religious	counseling
	services	
Psychological well-being		
Feeling depressed	Peers: Scientific Orientation	
	(Involvement measures)[a]	
	Personal counseling	Intramural sports
		Exercise
		Attending religious services
		Getting married
Feeling overwhelmed	Major: engineering	Peers: percentage who are
	Peers: percentage who are	Catholics
	engineering majors	
	Peers: Outside Work	
	(Involvement measures)[a]	
	Studying or homework	Reading for pleasure
	Personal counseling	Exercise
	Giving class presentations	Socializing
	Commuting	

[a]Since the temporal ordering of outcome and involvement measures cannot be precisely determined, causal interpretations should be made with caution.

[b]Includes activities such as discussing racial or ethnic issues, socializing with students from different racial or ethnic groups, participating in campus demonstrations, attending racial or ethnic workshops, and taking women's studies or ethnic studies courses.

affected by the Altruism and Social Activism of peers, and Status Striving is positively affected by the peer group's emphasis on Materialism and Status. The Socioeconomic Status of the peer group also has direct positive effects on Social Activism and Hedonism, while a strong Scientific Orientation and Lack of Community in the peer group appear to impact negatively on the student's psychological well-being.

Leaving home to attend college appears to increase both Leadership and Hedonism, while joining social fraternities or sororities appears to increase both Status Striving and Hedonism. Hedonism is negatively affected, however, by the percentage of the peer group who identify themselves as born-again Christians.

Student involvement appears to have a number of effects on personality development. Interaction with peers is strongly associated with the development of Leadership qualities. While Social Activism also appears to be facilitated by most forms of student-student interaction, the effects of peer involvement on Hedonism and Status Striving seem to vary with the particular form of involvement.

Measures of self-concept and psychological well-being appear to be especially sensitive to different forms of involvement in college. Positive self-ratings tend to be associated with socializing, exercise, and sports, while negative self-ratings tend to be associated with Outside Work and watching television.

Chapter 5

———•◦•———

Attitudes, Values, and Beliefs

Studies of students' values and attitudes account for much of the voluminous literature on college impact (Feldman and Newcomb, 1969; Pascarella and Terenzini, 1991). In this chapter we examine how various college experiences affect student responses to two sets of questions from the 1989 follow-up questionnaire: attitudes about social issues, and level of commitment to various values or life goals. Although several life-goal items were used in scoring the personality measures discussed in the preceding chapter, in this chapter we will examine six particular life goals that are of special relevance to the undergraduate experience.

Attitudinal and Value Change
During the Undergraduate Years

One practical problem in studying student attitudes toward social issues is that the number of specific issues that could be studied is very large. As a matter of fact, the 1989 follow-up questionnaire contains twenty attitudinal items focusing on social issues, seventeen of which were pretested in the 1985 questionnaire. Rather than performing separate analyses on each item, we conducted a factor analysis of these seventeen pretested items to determine whether it would be possible to combine them into a smaller number of more general factors or scales. This analysis was reasonably successful, yielding three factors representing fourteen of the seventeen items. Students' 1985 and 1989 responses to these fourteen items and two additional items are shown in Table 5.1. The largest factor is labeled Liberalism, since it comprises primarily items describing traditional liberal policies: greater government involvement in promoting disarmament, controlling pollution, taxing the wealthy, raising taxes to reduce the deficit, supporting school busing, espousing abolition of the death penalty, and developing a national health care plan.

The second factor has been labeled Libertarianism, since it rejects government regulation of individual behavior (abortion, marijuana use) as well as institutional intervention in the selection of controversial speakers and the regulation of student conduct.

The third factor is labeled Feminism because it includes support for sex equity in pay, assumes a very strong stance on the issue of "date rape," and rejects the proposition that married women should remain in the home. One of two additional attitudinal items, "The chief benefit of a college education is that it increases one's earning power," does not load on a factor but is included here because of its intrinsic interest for a study of undergraduate education. The final attitudinal item, "Realistically, an individual person can do little to bring about changes in our society," is included as a measure of the student's sense of empowerment and control.

Student responses to the items making up these three factors show highly varying patterns of change during the undergraduate years. While the largest changes on the Liberalism factor are in a liberal direction (support for national health care, control of environmental pollution, raising taxes to reduce the deficit), support for certain liberal positions changes very little (promoting disarmament, taxing the wealthy), and some items actually show a trend toward greater conservatism (support for abolition of the death penalty and school busing).

Consistent with Pascarella and Terenzini's (1991) findings,

longitudinal changes also suggest a trend toward greater Libertarianism during college, especially in the area of abortion rights. Support for the legalization of marijuana shows a very small decline, whereas support for the regulation of off-campus behavior shows virtually no change. It should be noted, however, that nine students in ten reject the proposition that college officials have the right to regulate student behavior off campus. There is thus very little room for decrease in support for this question.

By far the most consistent and strongest increases are in Feminism. This trend is especially remarkable, given that between 80 percent and 92 percent of the students gave "feminist" responses to these three statements as entering freshmen in 1985. Thus, despite the very limited room for increases in Feminism, responses to all three items show significant trends in this direction during the undergraduate years. (Freshman data on the "date rape" question are from the 1988 survey, the first year the question was asked. Trends since then — 1988–1991 — show that student agreement has been steadily increasing each year. If we project such trends backward to 1985, the increase shown in Table 5.1 would be even larger.) These changes are consistent, incidentally, with Pascarella and Terenzini's conclusion (1991, p. 326) that students' "sex role attitudes" become more egalitarian during college (see also Thornton and Freedman, 1979; Thornton, Alwin, and Camburn, 1983).

Endorsement of the next item, which states that increased earning power is the chief benefit of a college education, shows a sharp decline during the undergraduate years. Such a change is certainly consistent with the idea that a good liberal education should encourage students to value learning as an intrinsic good rather than merely as an instrumental means to a materialistic end. The decline is also consistent with the general decline in materialistic and status needs noted in the previous chapter. The final item in Table 5.1, "Realistically, an individual person can do little to bring about changes in our society," shows only a small decline in support during the undergraduate years.

The last two columns of Table 5.1 show once again that the simple net change observed during the undergraduate years masks a good deal of switching around in student attitudes.

Table 5.1. Attitudinal Changes, 1985–1989.

(Factor) Attitudinal Statement Scores	(Factor Loading)	Percentage Agreeing[a] in 1985	Percentage Agreeing[a] in 1989	Net Change, 1985–1989	Percentage[b] Changing from Low to High Scores	Percentage[b] Changing from High to Low Scores
(Liberalism)						
The federal government is not doing enough to promote disarmament.	.64	66.3	64.8	−1.5	15.1	15.8
A national health care plan is needed to cover everybody's medical costs.	.53	56.9	65.7	+8.8	22.5	14.3
The federal government is not doing enough to control environmental pollution.	.47	79.0	87.4	+8.4	16.8	8.0
Wealthy people should pay a larger share of taxes than they do now.	.46	72.2	71.5	−0.7	12.2	13.1
The death penalty should be abolished.	.43	27.9	25.2	−2.7	11.1	13.9
Busing is OK if it helps to achieve racial balance in the schools.	.36	50.7	46.5	−4.2	15.1	19.4
The federal government should raise taxes to reduce the deficit.	.35	24.2	29.3	+5.1	16.4	11.9
(Libertarianism)						
Abortion should be legalized.	.50	55.1	72.7	+17.6	23.0	5.3
College officials have the right to ban persons with extreme views from speaking on campus.	−.49	78.7[c]	82.9[c]	+4.2[c]	11.0	16.1
College officials have the right to regulate student behavior off campus.	−.48	89.9[c]	89.5[c]	−0.4[c]	8.8	8.2
Marijuana should be legalized.	.36	20.5	19.5	−1.0	10.3	11.4

(Feminism)

Women should receive the same salaries and opportunities for advancement as men in comparable positions.	.50	92.2	95.9	+3.7	6.9	2.9
Just because a man feels a woman has "led him on" does not entitle him to have sex with her.	.43	83.8[d]	94.3	+10.5	NA	NA
The activities of married women are best confined to the home and family.	-.39	80.1[c]	88.5[c]	+8.4[c]	5.4	14.9

(Other)

The chief benefit of a college education is that it increases one's earning power.	NA	64.9	47.9	-17.0	11.3	28.3
Realistically, an individual person can do little to bring about changes in our society.	NA	32.8	31.1	-1.7	16.0	18.3

[a]Weighted national norms (abstracted from Wingard, Treviño, Dey, and Korn, 1991).

[b]The sum of these two change measures will sometimes deviate slightly from the "net change" column because the sample varied slightly (students who had missing data on either pretest or posttest were necessarily excluded from these computations).

[c]Percentage *disagreeing*.

[d]Data from 1988 freshmen, the first year question was asked.

    In addition to the five outcome measures shown in Table
5.1 (three factors plus two individual items), we have selected
six value items from the list of life goals that were pretested and
posttested in the freshman and follow-up questionnaires (Table
5.2). The item "becoming involved in programs to clean up the
environment" is included because of the current widespread concern about environmental issues such as pollution, global warm-
ing, acid rain, depletion of the ozone layer, and destruction of
the rain forests. Although the item "being very well off financially" was included in the scoring of the Status Striver scale
(Chapter Four), it has been included here, together with "developing a meaningful philosophy of life," because these two
items have shown dramatic and contrasting trends during the
past two decades. "Developing a meaningful philosophy of life"
was the most popular value during the early 1970s but is now
far down on the list. "Being very well off financially," by contrast, has almost doubled in popularity since the early 1970s.
"Helping to promote racial understanding" is included because
of the current interest in "diversity" and "political correctness,"
while "making a theoretical contribution to science" is included
because of the current concern about lack of interest among
American undergraduates in studying science or in becoming
scientific researchers.
    That students become much more interested in involv-
ing themselves in programs to clean up the environment during the college years is consistent with the increases already noted
in Social Activism (Chapter Four) and Liberalism (Table 5.1).
The students' commitment to developing a meaningful philosophy of life, coupled with their decreased interest in being very
well off financially, could well be viewed as consistent with the
goals of a liberal education. The same might be said of the
modest increases in commitment to promoting racial understanding, given that a frequently stated purpose of liberal education is to promote greater tolerance and open-mindedness
among students.
    To what extent can the attitudinal and value changes
shown in Tables 5.1 and 5.2 be attributed to the impact of college? What is the evidence that these changes have been influenced

Table 5.2. Changes in Selected Values, 1985–1989[a].

Life Goal	Percentage Saying Goal Is Essential or Very Important		Net Change, 1985–1989	Percentage[b] Changing from	
	1985	1989		Low to High Scores	High to Low Scores
Becoming involved in programs to clean up the environment	20.6	34.9	+14.3	23.4	9.8
Developing a meaningful philosophy of life	47.9	55.8	+7.9	22.5	15.0
Helping to promote racial understanding	35.3	39.4	+4.1	17.3	14.0
Raising a family	70.5	72.4	+1.9	14.0	11.4
Making a theoretical contribution to science	15.1	14.9	-0.2	8.6	9.5
Being very well off financially	69.3	62.2	-7.1	10.3	17.3

Note: N = 4,093.
[a]Weighted national percentages (data abstracted from Wingard, Treviño, Dey, and Korn, 1991).
[b]The sum of these two change measures will sometimes deviate slightly from the net change column because the sample varied slightly (students who had missing data on either pretest or posttest were necessarily excluded from these computations).

by maturation and social change? We should first consider the possible influence of social change. Concerning the Liberalism factor, it appears that increased liberalism in the 1985 freshmen may be entirely attributable to social change. When we look at the three items showing substantial increases during the undergraduate years — support for a national health care plan, controlling environmental pollution, and raising taxes to reduce the deficit — changes from the 1985 freshmen to the 1989 freshmen were all larger than the changes that occurred among the 1985 freshmen during college. Next, we look at those liberal items that show no change or slight declines during the undergraduate years. In the case of support for school busing, which shows the largest conservative trend during the undergraduate years (–4.2 percent), consecutive freshman classes actually show a small increase (+2.6 percent) between 1985 and 1989. This suggests that social change, if anything, served to retard the decline in support for busing. Comparative results for abolition of the death penalty show a different pattern: consecutive freshman classes between 1985 and 1989 show a larger decline in support (–5.4 percent) than did the 1985 freshmen during the undergraduate years (–2.7 percent), a result suggesting that this decline is entirely attributable to social change. Indeed, the undergraduate experience, if anything, serves to counteract the effects of declining public opposition to the death penalty. In short, these findings suggest that — with the exception of opposition to capital punishment — any tendencies toward increased liberalism observed in the 1985 freshmen during their undergraduate years are entirely attributable to the effects of social change.

What about changes in Libertarianism? Since the items about college regulation of campus speakers and student conduct were not included in the 1989 freshman survey, our analysis of the possible effects of social change on increased Libertarianism must be confined to the items concerning abortion and marijuana. The large increase in support for legalized abortion (+17.6 percent) appears to be in part attributable to social change, since freshman support increased 9.7 percent between the 1985 and 1989 freshman surveys. The slight decline in support for legalizing marijuana observed in the 1985 freshmen (-1.0 percent) appears to be entirely attributable to social change, since freshman support, as already indicated in Chapter Four, declined by a larger amount (-5.1 percent) from the 1985 to the 1989 freshman surveys. These findings suggest, in short, that increased Libertarianism that occurs during the undergraduate years is attributable in part, but not entirely, to social change.

Only one Feminist item, "The activities of married women are best confined to the home and family," is included in both the 1985 and 1989 surveys, and a comparison of results from these two surveys actually shows a slight increase (+2.8 percent) in support from one freshman class to another (as contrasted with a decline of -8.4 percent for the 1985 freshmen). The "date rape" question was not pretested in 1985 (the first year it was included in the freshman survey was 1988). Freshman trends since then show steadily increasing endorsement (from 83.8 percent in 1988 to 86.9 percent in 1990). However, even if we use the 1989 freshman data as the pretest, the "change" figure in Table 5.1 would still be +7.9 percent. These results, in short, indicate that the increase in Feminism observed during the undergraduate years cannot be attributed to social change.

Student support for the proposition that the chief benefit of a college education is monetary changed very little between the 1985 and 1989 freshman surveys (-1.7 percent). Thus it appears that social change is not a major factor in the substantial decline in support for this question observed during the undergraduate years.

Social change does appear to play some role in the changes in values noted in Table 5.2. For example, between the 1985 and 1989 surveys, student commitment to becoming involved in programs to clean up the environment increases substantially (+7.0 percent), and commitment to help promote racial understanding shows a small increase (+3.2 percent). However, with the "philosophy of life" and "very well off financially" items, social change appears to have played no role in the changes shown in Table 5.2, since the trends between the 1985 and 1989 freshman surveys are the opposite of the changes shown in Table 5.2.

Next we come to the issue of maturation. The student's age at the time of entry to college shows weak negative effects on commitment to "raising a family" and "an individual person can do little to bring about changes in our society." It thus appears that maturation may account for the slight increase in commitment to raising a family (Table 5.2), but that the slight decline in "an individual person can do little" (Table 5.1) is not the result of maturation; if anything, maturation has attenuated this decline. Otherwise, maturation does not appear to have played a significant role in any of the other changes shown in Tables 5.1 and 5.2.

What about the "effects of college"? To what extent can these changes in values and attitudes be attributable to the experience of being a college student? The strongest evidence that a college effect is operating was obtained for the increase in commitment to promoting racial understanding and the decreased endorsement of the propositions that the primary benefit of college is monetary and that the individual can do little to bring about changes in society. Virtually every indicator—the residential experience, years completed, student-student interaction, and student-faculty interaction—suggests that college effects are responsible for each of these three outcomes. That the increases in Feminism may also be attributable to the effects of college is suggested by the positive effects of years completed and student-student interaction. Evidence of college effects is also suggested by the positive effects of both student-student and student-faculty interaction on increased Liberalism, increased commitment to becoming involved in programs to clean up the environment, and greater commitment to developing a meaningful philosophy of life. Student-faculty interaction is positively associated with making a theoretical contribution to science and negatively associated with being very well off financially. Student commitment to raising a family is not associated with any of the indices of college impact.

Environmental Effects

To conserve space, we will not include discussions of "input" effects in this section. (Some of these effects will be summarized, however, in Chapter Twelve). Here we consider how each of these attitudinal and value outcomes is affected by differential environmental experiences.

Liberalism

Liberalism appears to be affected by both the faculty and the student peer group. Students will be most likely to strengthen their Liberalism if they are exposed to a peer group that is itself strongly liberal politically. Liberalism is also positively influenced by the degree of Liberalism of the faculty and by an environment characterized by Racial Conflict and by an emphasis on Social Activism and Community Orientation. Having financial aid based on need and participating in the college work-study program also have positive effects on Liberalism. Environmental factors that seem to have a negative effect on Liberalism are majoring in engineering and being exposed to a peer group that is high in Materialism and Status.

Most of the involvement variables that are associated with Liberalism, after student input and environmental characteristics are controlled, have to do with activism and diversity: participating in campus demonstrations, discussing racial or ethnic issues, attending racial or cultural awareness workshops, enrolling in ethnic studies courses, and enrolling in women's studies courses. Other involvement measures having positive associations with Liberalism are receiving personal or psychological counseling, holding a part-time job on campus, and participating in study-abroad programs. Involvement measures having negative associations with Liberalism include being a member of a social fraternity or sorority, number of math or numerical courses taken, and hours per week spent partying. This pattern of effects closely resembles the pattern observed for political identification (Chapter Three).

Libertarianism

By far the strongest environmental effect on Libertarianism is associated with the Permissiveness of the peer group. This finding is especially interesting, given that a "permissive" peer group is one that advocates a good deal of individual freedom in areas such as sex and substance use (see Chapter Two). In effect, Permissiveness represents a measure of the peer group's "libertarianism." Libertarianism is also positively affected by faculty Liberalism. Majoring in elementary education, however, appears to have a negative effect on Libertarianism.

A substantial number of student involvement variables are associated with changes in Libertarianism. The strongest association is with hours per week spent participating in religious services (the correlation in this case, is, of course, a negative one). Other involvement variables having a negative impact on Libertarianism include participating in intramural sports, receiving vocational or career counseling, and getting married.

Several involvement variables have substantial positive associations with Libertarianism: alcohol consumption, participating in campus demonstrations, discussing racial or ethnic issues, hours per week spent working for pay, having class papers critiqued by instructors, hours per week spent partying, and being a member of a social fraternity or sorority. These last two findings are especially interesting, given that partying and fraternity or sorority membership are *negatively* associated with Liberalism (above). Thus, while partying and fraternity or sorority membership appear to increase support for individual freedom in personal conduct (Libertarianism), they are negatively associated with liberal views on governmental and social policy (Liberalism).

Feminism

Feminism is positively affected by the political Liberalism of the faculty and negatively affected by majoring in engineering. No other environmental variable proves to have a significant impact on Feminism.

Involvement measures that show positive associations with Feminism, after entering student and environmental variables are controlled, include socializing with persons from different racial or ethnic groups, hours per week spent studying or doing homework, discussing racial or ethnic issues, holding a part-time job on campus, taking essay exams, and hours per week spent working for pay. Feminism is negatively associated with hours per week spent attending religious services, receiving tutoring, and playing intercollegiate football or basketball. This last effect is of special interest, considering the many professional athletes who have been accused of sexual assaults on women. Could it be that the unique experience of being an intercollegiate foot-ball or basketball player encourages the development of sexist attitudes? This is clearly an area where further research is needed, especially in light of Pascarella and Terenzini's (1991, p. 316) conclusion that "virtually nothing is known" about the effects of within-college experiences on feminist beliefs. Here we have at least some important clues about such effects that could be explored in greater depth in future studies.

Belief That Primary Value of College Is to Increase Earnings

Student acceptance of the idea that the chief benefit of a college education is to increase one's earning power is positively affected by three environmental variables: living at home, majoring in engineering, and a peer environment characterized by a Lack of Student Community. However, the most potent environmental variable, the Humanities Orientation of the environment, has a negative effect. Such an effect is entirely consistent with the values that underlie the humanities component of a liberal education curriculum. Other environmental factors having a negative impact on this value are participating in a college work-study program and the percentage of faculty who are involved in team teaching.

A number of involvement variables show significant associations with the view that the chief benefit of college is to increase earnings, after the effects of student input and environmental variables have been controlled. The single strongest association is with hours per week spent watching television. This is a particularly interesting effect, given the great emphasis on acquisitiveness and materialism that one finds in most commercial television programming. Other involvement variables showing positive associations include taking multiple-choice exams, working full-time while attending college, and being a member of a social fraternity or sorority. Involvement variables that are negatively associated with this belief are heavily verbal: hours per week talking with faculty outside of class, number of courses taken that emphasize writing, number of foreign-language courses taken, having class papers critiqued by instructors, participating in campus demonstrations, and undergraduate GPA.

Belief That Individuals Cannot Change Society

Only a few environmental variables are found to affect student agreement with the statement "Realistically, an individual person can do little to bring about changes in our society." Agreement with this statement is positively affected by majoring in science or engineering and negatively affected by going away from home to attend college and by an environmental emphasis on Social Activism and Community.

The belief that individuals are helpless in trying to change society is positively associated with only one involvement variable: hours per week spent watching television. (This proves to be the strongest association with any involvement variable.) Involvement variables that are negatively associated with this belief include hours per week spent talking with faculty outside of class, number of writing-skills courses taken, participating in campus demonstrations, socializing with persons from different racial or ethnic groups, hours per week spent participating in religious services, and hours per week spent in volunteer work. This last effect is particularly interesting, since it suggests that actual participation in community service activities can help to disabuse students of the notion that they are helpless to do anything about society's problems.

Commitment to Environmental Involvement

Student commitment to getting involved in programs to clean up the environment is affected by a rather unexpected set of environmental variables. Positive effects are associated with the percentage of faculty involved in team teaching, perceived racial conflict on the campus, and majoring in natural science. Faculty use of graduate teaching assistants and the percentage of students majoring in physical science fields both have negative effects on this value question.

One can only guess at the meaning of these effects, although several explanations are possible. Courses that are team taught, for example, may often focus on issues having to do with ecology or the environment. Ecology may well lend itself to team teaching, since ecological issues cut across several disciplines. At the same time, many courses on ecological issues are taught in natural science departments. These interpretations, if correct, suggest that one way to encourage more student interest and involvement in environmental issues would be to require more team-taught courses on the subject.

A substantial number of involvement variables are associated with commitment to getting involved in environmental programs. Many of the variables having positive associations suggest that environmental and "diversity" concerns are linked: discussing racial or ethnic issues, participating in campus demonstrations, attending racial or cultural awareness workshops, socializing with persons from different racial or ethnic groups. Other positive associations involve hours per week spent in exercise or sports, hours per week spent talking with faculty outside of class, number of science courses taken, number of history courses taken, hours per week spent reading for pleasure, and hours per week spent in volunteer work. Involvement factors showing negative associations include undergraduate GPA and hours per week spent socializing with friends, attending religious services, and watching television.

Developing a Philosophy of Life

Student commitment to developing a meaningful philosophy of life is positively affected by Social Activism and Community Orientation and negatively affected by majoring in engineering.

Involvement variables that are significantly associated with developing a meaningful philosophy of life, after control of input and environmental variables, include discussing racial or ethnic issues, participating in campus demonstrations, attending racial or cultural awareness workshops, number of writing courses taken, receiving personal or psychological counseling, and three "hours per week" variables: religious services, reading for pleasure, and studying or doing homework. Many of these activities involve thinking and reflection, activities that might well be associated with attempts to deal with the existential concern suggested by this value statement. The one involvement variable that is negatively associated with interest in developing a meaningful philosophy of life is hours per week spent watching television.

This pattern of effects also provides some possible clues to why student commitment to this value, which used to be the number one value among entering college freshmen, has declined so much in popularity during the past two decades. Thus, it is probably safe to conclude that young people today, compared to their counterparts of twenty years ago, are less active and involved politically, study less and do less homework, spend less time in religious activities, write and read less, and watch more television.

Promoting Racial Understanding

The student's commitment to promoting racial understanding is positively associated with the following environmental variables: going away from home to attend college, the Humanities Orientation of the college environment, the Socioeconomic Status of the peer group, and the Institutional Diversity Emphasis. Commitment to promoting racial understanding is negatively affected by majoring in any of the following subjects: business, nursing, science, or engineering.

As might be expected, most involvement variables that are still correlated with commitment to promoting racial understanding after entering student and environmental characteristics are controlled relate to "diversity" issues: discussing racial or ethnic issues, attending racial or cultural awareness workshops, socializing with people from different racial or ethnic groups, participating in campus demonstrations, and enrolling in ethnic studies courses. While it is entirely possible that some of these involvement variables are the results of increased interest in promoting racial understanding, rather than the causes of this increased interest, it is important to keep in mind that encouraging such activities on the campus may well enhance students' commitment to promoting racial understanding. Three academic variables also have positive partial correlations with this item: hours per week spent studying or doing homework, number of foreign-language courses taken, and number of history courses taken. Two involvement variables have negative associations with commitment to promoting racial understanding: number of math or numerical courses taken, and alcohol consumption.

Raising a Family

Student commitment to the value of raising a family is positively affected by only one environmental variable: majoring in education. Commitment to raising a family is negatively affected by two peer group factors—Permissiveness and Outside Work; it is also negatively affected by majoring in a field of the arts or humanities and by faculty involvement in team teaching. The negative effect of peer Permissiveness is especially interesting, given that this environmental measure reflects the Libertarianism of the peer group. Perhaps raising a family is viewed by some students as a constraint on their individual freedom of action.

Commitment to raising a family has positive partial correlations with several involvement variables: getting married, attending religious services, hours per week spent socializing with friends, hours per week spent watching television, and participating in intramural sports. Getting married, of course, may well be an effect rather than a cause of increased interest in raising a family. Only one involvement variable is negatively associated with raising a family: participating in campus demonstrations.

Contributing to Scientific Theory

As might be expected, the student's desire to make a theoretical contribution to science is significantly affected by several major field variables. Positive effects are associated with majoring in science, nursing, or the health professions; negative affects are associated with majoring in business, pre-law, or arts and humanities. Commitment to making a theoretical contribution to science is also positively affected by two curricular variables — required internship, and the use of written evaluations in grading — and by the peer factor Materialism and Status. As suggested in Chapter Four, this last effect may be attributable to the "Status" part of this measure, which includes two items commonly endorsed by research scientists: "becoming an authority in my field" and "obtaining recognition from my colleagues for contributions to my special field."

A number of involvement variables are significantly associated with wanting to make a theoretical contribution to science, after control for input and environmental effects. The strongest effect (Beta = .33) is associated with number of science courses taken. Other positive associations include working on a professor's research project, hours per week spent talking with faculty outside of class, enrolling in an honors program, tutoring other students, working on an independent research project, assisting faculty in teaching a course, and — surprisingly — taking remedial or developmental courses. With the exception of this last item, we have here a number of interesting possibilities for how students' science interests might be strengthened.

Several involvement variables also have negative effects on students' interest in making a theoretical contribution to science: number of history courses taken, number of writing-skills courses taken, hours per week spent socializing with friends, and hours per week spent attending religious services.

Being Very Well Off Financially

Only one environmental variable proves to have a significant positive effect on the student's commitment to being very well off financially, but it comes as no surprise: the peer emphasis on Materialism and Status. One other environmental variable has a negative effect: the institutional commitment to Social Activism and Community Orientation (as perceived by faculty). This last effect, together with findings reported later in this and subsequent chapters, suggests that there may be inherent conflict between materialism and social concern.

A large number of involvement variables maintain significant correlations with interest in being very well off financially, after student input and environmental variables have been controlled. Positive effects are associated with three "hours per week" variables: partying, watching television, and using a personal computer. Other positive correlations include working full-time while a student, being a member of a social fraternity or sorority, taking multiple-choice exams, number of math or numerical courses taken, and receiving vocational or career counseling. Involvement variables that show negative partial correlations include discussing racial or ethnic issues, participating in campus demonstrations, being a guest in a professor's home, and four "hours per week" variables: participating in religious services, volunteer work, reading for pleasure, and studying or doing homework. Several of these last measures — especially hours per week spent doing volunteer work — offer still further evidence of the negative relationship between materialism and social responsibility.

Table 5.3 provides an overall summary of the environmental and involvement variables that affect students' values, attitudes, and beliefs. Two things stand out in this table: the consistent effects of television watching on values and beliefs (see Chapter Eleven for a discussion of these findings), and the effects of peer group values on the individual student's values. Liberalism is affected by peer Liberalism, Libertarianism by peer Permissiveness, and interest in making money by peer Materialism and Status.

Summary

Undergraduates demonstrate a number of substantial changes in beliefs and attitudes during the college years. The largest positive changes are in Feminism, commitment to participating in programs to clean up the environment, promoting racial understanding, developing a meaningful philosophy of life, and support for legal abortion. The largest declines are in materialistic

Table 5.3. Summary of Environmental Effects
on Attitudes, Values, and Beliefs.

Student Outcome	Positively Affected by	Negatively Affected by
Attitudes and Values		

Liberalism	Peers: Liberalism
	Faculty: Liberalism
	Racial Conflict
	Social Activism and
	  Community Orienta-
	  tion
	Need-based aid
	Work-study aid
		Peers: Materialism and
		  Status
		Major: Engineering

	(Involvement measures)[a] "Diversity" experiences[b] Personal counseling Part-time campus job Study abroad	Fraternity or sorority membership Partying Math courses
Libertarianism	Peers: Permissiveness Faculty: Liberalism	Major: education

	(Involvement measures)[a]
	Alcohol consumption
	Fraternity or sorority
	  membership
	Partying
	Working for pay
	Campus activism
	Discussing racial issues
	Having papers critiqued
	  by instructor
		Attending religious
		  services
		Intramural sports
		Career counseling
		Getting married

Feminism	Faculty: Liberalism	Major: engineering

	(Involvement measures)[a]
	Socializing with differ-
	  ent racial groups
	Discussing racial issues
	Studying or homework
	Part-time campus job
	Working for pay
	Taking essay exams
		Attending religious
		  services
		Being tutored
		Playing varsity football
		  or basketball

Beliefs		

Chief benefit of college
  is making money
	Living at home
	Major: engineering
	Peers: Lack of
	  Community
		Humanities Orientation
		Work-study
		Faculty: percentage
		  who team teach

Table 5.3. Summary of Environmental Effects
on Attitudes, Values, and Beliefs, cont'd.

Student Outcome	Positively Affected by	Negatively Affected by
	(Involvement measures)[a] Watching television Taking multiple-choice exams Working full-time Fraternity or sorority membership	Talking with faculty Writing courses Foreign-language courses Having papers critiqued by instructor Campus activism
Individuals can't change society	Major: science Major: engineering	Leaving home to attend college Social Activism and Community Orientation
	(Involvement measures)[a] Watching television	Talking with faculty Writing courses "Diversity" activity[b] Attending religious services Volunteer work
Life Goals		
To participate in environmental cleanup	Faculty: percentage who team teach Racial Conflict Major: science	Use of teaching assistants Peers: percentage majoring in physical science
	(Involvement measures)[a] "Diversity" activities[b] Exercise Talking with faculty Science courses History courses Reading for pleasure Volunteer work	Socializing Attending religious services Watching television
Developing a meaningful philosophy of life	Social Activism and Community Orientation	Major: engineering
	(Involvement measures)[a] "Diversity" activities[b] Personal counseling	Watching television

Table 5.3. Summary of Environmental Effects
on Attitudes, Values, and Beliefs, cont'd.

Student Outcome	Positively Affected by	Negatively Affected by
	Attending religious services Reading for pleasure Studying or homework	
Promoting racial understanding	Leaving home to attend college Humanities Orientation Peer SES Institutional Diversity Emphasis	Major: business Major: nursing Major: science Major: engineering
	(Involvement measures)[a] "Diversity" activities[b] Studying or homework Foreign-language courses History courses	Math courses Alcohol consumption
Raising a family	Major: education	Peers: Permissiveness Peers: Outside Work
	(Involvement measures)[a] Getting married Attending religious services Socializing Watching television Intramural sports	Campus activism
Contributing to scientific theory	Major: science Major: nursing Major: health professions Required internship Written evaluations Peers: Materialism and Status	Major: business Major: pre-law Major: arts and humanities
	(Involvement measures)[a] Science courses Working on a professor's research Talking with faculty Honors program Tutoring others Independent research	Writing courses Socializing Attending religious services

Table 5.3. Summary of Environmental Effects
on Attitudes, Values, and Beliefs, cont'd.

Student Outcome	Positively Affected by	Negatively Affected by
	Assisting faculty in teaching	
	Remedial courses	
Being very well off financially	Peers: Materialism and Status	Social Activism and Community Orientation
	(Involvement measures)[a]	
	Partying	"Diversity" activities[b]
	Watching television	Guest in professor's home
	Using a personal computer	Attending religious services
	Working full-time	Volunteer work
	Taking multiple-choice exams	Reading for pleasure
	Math courses	Studying or homework
	Career counseling	

[a]Since the temporal ordering of outcome and involvement measures cannot be precisely determined, causal interpretations should be made with caution.

[b]Includes activities such as discussing racial or ethnic issues, socializing with students from different racial or ethnic groups, participating in campus demonstrations, attending racial or ethnic workshops, and taking women's studies or ethnic studies courses.

values: the notion that the chief benefit of a college education is monetary, and commitment to the goal of being very well off financially. Changes in Feminism and Materialism appear to be primarily attributable to the college experience, but changes in support for abortion rights and commitment to getting involved in environmental cleanup programs represent a mix of college effects and changes in societal values.

Students show a number of smaller changes in attitudes (increasing support for a national health care plan, for greater governmental involvement in environmental protection, and for the death penalty), but all of these appear to be attributable to social change rather than to the effects of the college experience. Indeed, the college experience appears, if anything, to weaken slightly student support for the death penalty.

Environmental effects analyses once again demonstrate

the importance of the peer group experience: students' views on social issues generally tend to change in the direction of the dominant view of the peer group. Also, attraction to the idea that the chief benefit of a college education is monetary is strengthened when students are exposed to peer groups that are lacking in a sense of community. Commitment to developing a meaningful philosophy of life, on the other hand, is strengthened by exposure to a peer group that emphasizes Social Activism and Community.

The effect of faculty values and attitudes is also clear: the Liberalism of the faculty (defined in terms of their attitudes on social issues) has positive effects on three student outcomes: Liberalism, Libertarianism, and Feminism. Both student and faculty values may help to explain the negative effects of majoring in engineering on Liberalism, Feminism, and commitment to developing a meaningful philosophy of life. Peer group effects are also suggested by the association of membership in a social fraternity or sorority with decreased Liberalism and increased Libertarianism and commitment to the idea that the primary benefit of college is monetary.

Engagement by the student in diversity activities (discussions of racial issues, participation in racial or ethnic workshops, participation in demonstrations) is positively associated with Liberalism, Libertarianism, Feminism, commitment to promoting racial understanding, and developing a meaningful philosophy of life. Diversity activities are negatively associated with the idea that the individual can do little to help change society. Hours spent watching television, on the other hand, are positively associated with endorsement of materialistic values and interest in raising a family and negatively associated with commitment to participating in environmental cleanup programs and developing a meaningful philosophy of life.

Chapter 6

———•◆•———

Patterns of
Behavior

Human behavior covers an almost infinite range of phenomena. In this chapter we shall consider the behavioral counterparts of the affective outcomes examined in the preceding three chapters. While much of the previous college impact research on affective outcomes has focused primarily on psychological outcomes, it could be argued that changes in psychological processes have little social consequence unless they are somehow reflected in behavior.

Data on behavioral outcomes were obtained by utilizing the students as observers of their own behavior. From the diverse array of possible behaviors, we have selected nine from the follow-up questionnaire for analyses of environmental impact. These nine behaviors were chosen so as to sample from several different domains: political behavior, altruistic behavior, substance use, cultural participation, and social behavior. Behavioral items are basically of two types: discrete events such as getting married or joining a social fraternity or sorority, and activities about which students report frequency of participation (frequently, occasionally, not at all, scored 3, 2, or 1). The reader should keep in mind that some of these variables are used both as outcomes and as environmental variables (that is, intermediate outcomes).

165

Behavioral Changes During the Undergraduate Years

Four of the behavioral questions were pretested with an identical question in the 1985 entering freshman questionnaire. Changes in these four behaviors during the undergraduate years are shown in Table 6.1. The items are arranged in order of the degree of change shown between 1985 and 1989. A modest increase occurs in the percentage of students who drink beer, while a modest decrease occurs in the percentage who attend recitals or concerts. Small increases are also seen in the percentages who tutor other students and smoke cigarettes. Increases in substance use — alcohol and tobacco — have already been discussed briefly in the analysis of changes in Hedonism reported in Chapter Four.

Four other behavioral items from the 1989 follow-up questionnaire are shown in Table 6.2. Rather than providing pretests of these events in 1985, the students were asked to indicate the likelihood (no chance, very little chance, some chance, very good chance) that these events would occur in college. Note that the percentage of students reporting that an event actually occurred in college in every case exceeds the percentage who indicated when they first entered college as freshmen, in 1985, that there was a very good chance the event would occur. The discrepancies here are especially large (more than 17 percent) in the case of being elected to a student office and participating in campus protests. It would appear that these two events are much more likely to depend on the particular environmental circumstances encountered by the student in college than is the case with either getting married or joining a social fraternity or sorority. In all likelihood, the last event produces a much higher level of agreement between expectation and occurrence simply because many institutions do not have social fraternities or sororities. All students predicting "no chance" in such institutions would be right.

Given the large discrepancies shown in Table 6.2, do the students' expectations have any predictive accuracy at all over the four years? Table 6.3 shows the percentages of students actually reporting each of these four events in 1989, with their predictions in 1985. Clearly, the students' expectations have

Table 6.1. Behavioral Changes, 1985–1989.

| Behavior | Percentage Reporting Behavior in Past Year | | Net Change, 1985–1989 | Percentage[b] Changing from | |
	1985	1989		Low to High Scores	High to Low Scores
Drank beer	66.0	75.0	+9.0	15.8	6.6
Tutored another student	49.6	53.5	+3.9	21.2	16.4
Smoked cigarettes[a]	7.2	8.3	+1.1	4.8	3.7
Attended a recital or concert	81.8	73.5	-8.3	9.7	17.9

Note: N = 16,658.
[a]"Frequently" only.
[b]The sum of these two change measures will sometimes deviate slightly from the net change column because the sample varied slightly (students who had missing data on either pretest or posttest were necessarily excluded from these computations).

Table 6.2. Expectation and Occurrences of Various Events in College.

Event	Percentage Predicting Good Chance of Occurrence (1985)	Percentage Reporting Actual Occurrence (1989)	Difference (Occurrence Minus Expectation)
Be elected to a student office	4.2	21.7	+17.5
Participate in campus protests	7.4	24.8	+17.4
Get married during college	3.2	6.6	+3.4
Join a social fraternity or sorority	24.9	26.5	+1.6

Note: Weighted national percentages (abstracted from Wingard, Treviño, Dey, and Korn, 1991).

considerable predictive validity: for each event, the chance of its actual occurrence increases as the student's estimated probability increases. Indeed, when we compare those who said there was a "very good chance" of the event's occurring with those who said there was "no chance" of its occurrence, the percentages of actual occurrences differ by more than three and one-half to one (be elected to a student office) to more than seven to one (get married). The actual simple correlations between expectation and occurrence range from .17 (getting married) to .32 (participating in campus protests). Despite these correlations, students' expectations can also be erroneous. Among those who said there was "no chance" of an event's occurring in college when they entered, the following percentages actually *did* report the event four years later: being elected to a student office (11.7 percent), participating in protests (9.7 percent), getting married (3.6 percent), and joining a social fraternity or sorority (7.7 percent).

One additional behavioral item from the 1989 questionnaire, "voted in the 1988 presidential election," was also included as an outcome measure, although no "expectation" item was included in the 1985 questionnaire. A little more than two-thirds (69.2 percent) of the 1985 freshmen reported that they voted in the 1988 presidential election (weighted percentage).

Note that Table 6.1, which shows weighted national norms, shows a modest increase between high school (1985) and

Table 6.3. College Activities: 1985 Expectations Versus
Actual Participation as Reported in 1989.

1985 Estimate of Chance of Event Occuring in College	Percentage Reporting That Event Actually Occurred			
	Be Elected to Student Office	Participate in Campus Protests	Join Fraternity or Sorority	Get Married
Very good chance	43.0	63.9	44.4	26.8
Some chance	29.1	36.4	27.5	12.1
Very little chance	16.9	17.1	15.4	5.3
No chance	11.7	9.7	7.7	3.6

Note: Unweighted percentages; $N = 21,648$.

college (1989) in the percentage reporting that they tutored other students. With very few exceptions, the direction of change between 1985 and 1989 (+ or −) was the same for the unweighted and weighted samples, although the actual percentages sometimes showed slight differences because of the effects of the weighting procedure. In the case of tutoring other students, however, the change between 1985 and 1989 was *negative* (−4.7 percent). What could cause such an anomaly? The principal difference between the weighted and unweighted samples is that the latter sample includes an overrepresentation of high-achieving students and of students enrolled in selective colleges. Why should such students engage in tutoring less frequently in college than in high school, while the other students increase their involvement in tutoring? Perhaps the answer lies in the highly stratified nature of American higher education. Students who are most likely to tutor others, of course, are the high achievers. Since most of these students attend high schools where there is a diversity of talent and all levels of achievement, there is both the need and the opportunity for tutoring in such schools. However, if a highly able student happens to enroll in a very selective college, where all or most students are high achievers, the need for tutoring services would presumably be less. By contrast, those high-achieving students who happen to enroll in less selective colleges, where there is a greater diversity of students in ability and level of preparation, would be in greater demand to provide tutoring services. Since disproportionate numbers of high-achieving students in our highly stratified higher education system attend selective colleges, fewer of them tutor other students. If this analysis is correct, it would appear that one of the unforeseen consequences of America's highly stratified system of higher education is that many high-achieving students (that is, those who attend highly selective institutions) are deprived of opportunities to assist lower-achieving students.

College Impact, Maturation, or Social Change?

Not surprisingly, all the college effects indicators produced positive results on the following behaviors: joining social fraternities or sororities, being elected to a student office, tutoring other students, and participating in student protests. That is, the likelihood of each of these behaviors was positively associated with leaving home to attend college, number of years completed, student-student interaction, and student-faculty interaction. That these outcomes should be attributable to the effects of college is certainly no surprise, given that each of them virtually requires that the person be a college student. However, drinking beer, which does not depend on being a college student, was also positively associated with all the college effects indicators (except student-faculty interaction), which strongly suggests that the increase in frequency of beer drinking noted in Table 6.1 is attributable at least in part to the effects of being enrolled in college.

Entirely different patterns of results are associated with the other behaviors. Smoking, for example, does not appear to be associated with attending college; indeed, frequency of smoking turned out to be negatively associated with number of years completed. Similarly, getting married is negatively associated with years completed, although in this case the direction of causation is uncertain: staying in college may well delay or prevent marriage, but getting married may well be a cause of leaving college. Voting in the 1988 presidential election had weak but significant positive associations with student-student interaction and student-faculty interaction, but it was negatively affected by leaving home to attend college. This latter finding no doubt reflects the artifacts of voter registration laws: students who leave home (where they are most likely to register) are probably less likely to vote because of the cumbersome procedures for absentee voting required by most states.

An examination of changes in behavioral patterns in consecutive entering classes between 1985 and 1989 indicates that external social change is not a significant factor in any of the behavioral changes discussed above, with one exception: the frequency of reported beer drinking, as already mentioned in Chapter Four, declined substantially (−8.4 percent) between the 1985 and 1989 freshman surveys. Since the 1985 freshmen actually *increased* their frequency of beer drinking during this same period (see Table 6.1), these findings would suggest that, if anything, social change actually serves to attenuate the increase in drinking that would normally occur during the undergraduate years. Indeed, were it not for the effects of social change, as suggested by the decreases in drinking among successive entering classes, the increases observed in the 1985 freshmen could have been twice as large.

Environmental Effects

The environmental variables entering the regression after input variables are controlled are discussed here, with a separate section for each of the nine behavioral outcomes.

Alcohol Consumption

In addition to the item on frequency of beer drinking, the 1989 follow-up questionnaire included one additional behavioral item reflecting frequency of alcohol consumption: "drank wine or liquor." In order to have an outcome measure that reflected more diverse methods of consuming alcohol, these two items have been combined into a single outcome measure that we have labeled "alcohol consumption." Going away from home to attend college has positive effects on drinking, as do several other environmental factors. The single most powerful environmental variable appears to be the percentage of the peer group who are born-again Christians: in this case, the effect is substantially negative. Drinking is positively affected by the average socioeconomic level of the student's peer group.

A number of involvement or intermediate outcome variables show substantial effects on frequency of drinking. The strongest effect is associated with hours per week spent partying. The magnitude of this effect (Beta = .49) is one of the largest in the entire study. It may well be, of course, that this effect represents an artifact, since the student may be interpreting alcohol consumption itself as the equivalent of "partying." Of possibly greater substantive interest is the positive association of alcohol consumption with membership in a social fraternity or sorority, hours per week spent socializing with friends, hours spent watching television or receiving vocational or career counseling, hours per week spent in exercise or sports, and participation in intramural sports. The association of drinking both with sports participation and with watching television is especially interesting, given the frequent sponsorship of sporting events on television by beer companies. Alcohol consumption is negatively associated with hours per week spent attending religious services.

Tutoring Other Students

In addition to the positive effect on tutoring of leaving home to attend college (noted earlier), the likelihood that the student would engage in tutoring other students is positively affected by having a grant from the college. The frequency of tutoring is negatively affected by the research orientation of the institution and by the percentage of students who are receiving merit-based aid. The last two effects are consistent with the interpretation offered earlier in this chapter for the decline in frequency of tutoring observed among students in the unweighted sample.

Majoring in physical science increases the student's likelihood of tutoring other students, whereas majoring in social science decreases that likelihood. In all probability, the differential effects of majors reflect differential demand for tutoring in various subject matter fields.

Tutoring is positively associated with a substantial number of involvement variables, after the effects of input and environmental variables have been controlled. Notable among these is assisting faculty in teaching a class (Beta = .22), hours per week spent talking with faculty outside of class (Beta = .17), and being a guest in a professor's home (Beta = .13). This pattern suggests strongly that faculty may well serve as "brokers" between their best students and students who are experiencing academic difficulties. Tutoring is also positively associated with enrolling in an honors program, college GPA, hours per week spent in volunteer work, holding a part-time job on campus, working on a group project for a class, taking a multiple-choice exam, number of math or numerical courses taken, and number of foreign-language courses taken. The last two effects may reflect the fields in which students are most likely to be tutored by other students. The only involvement variable entering the regression equation with a significant negative weight is hours per week spent watching television.

Smoking Cigarettes

The peer measure Artistic Inclination has a weak positive effect on smoking cigarettes; otherwise, no environmental variable enters the regression equation once the effects of input variables are controlled.

Among the student involvement variables, hours per week spent partying and alcohol consumption have the strongest positive associations with cigarette smoking. Weaker positive associations are found for hours per week spent reading for pleasure, participating in campus demonstrations, working full-time while enrolled as a student, and receiving personal or psychological counseling. The last two variables confirm the notion that smoking is a stress-related behavior.

Several involvement variables prove to have negative associations with smoking cigarettes: number of math or numerical courses taken, hours per week spent in sports or exercise, and college GPA. The last finding replicates previous research suggesting a negative association between smoking and academic performance (Astin, 1975, 1977).

Attending Recitals or Concerts

Not surprisingly, attending recitals and concerts is positively associated with majoring in the arts or humanities. This behavior is also positively associated with having financial aid based on "other talent," a finding that is consistent with the positive effect of such aid on Artistic Inclination reported earlier (see Chapter Four). Other environmental factors positively associated with attending a recital or concert are faculty Liberalism, the percentage of faculty involved in teaching general education courses, the percentage of peers majoring in the fine arts, and attending a historically black college or university. Environmental factors showing a negative effect on attending recitals or concerts include the degree of faculty reliance on the use of teaching assistants and the peer measure, Materialism and Status. The last effect suggests an interesting possibility: Given that Materialism and Status reflects a peer mentality that views a college education in instrumental terms — as a way to gain money and status — could it be that such an environment leads students to view attendance at cultural events as a waste of time?

Involvement measures showing the strongest positive effects on attending recitals or concerts are being a guest in a professor's home, having class papers critiqued by instructors, hours per week spent socializing with friends, socializing with people from different ethnic or racial groups, participating in campus demonstrations, discussing racial or ethnic issues, tutoring other students, working on independent research projects, and four "hours per week" measures: attending religious services, reading for pleasure, working in student organizations, and working on hobbies. The last two involvement measures may well reflect student involvement in musical and/or artistic activities.

Involvement variables that show negative associations with attending recitals or concerts are getting married while in college, hours per week spent commuting, and hours per week spent watching television.

These patterns suggest, in short, that student involvement in musical and cultural events is reflective of a larger pattern of involvement in general.

Being Elected to a Student Office

We have already noted that being elected to a student office is positively affected by leaving home to attend college. Another environmental variable that increases the student's chances of being elected to a student office is attending a women's college. This finding, which replicates a finding reported nearly twenty years ago in *Four Critical Years,* suggests that women are still less likely to achieve leadership positions if they attend coeducational rather than women's colleges. At least two factors could be at work here: women may be more reluctant to aspire to leadership positions when they must compete with men, and students may be biased toward men when voting for leaders. Clearly, this is an area of gender differences that does not seem to have been affected by the women's movement.

Being elected to a student office is also positively affected by the percentage of women on the faculty and by the percentage of faculty who are involved in administrative work. The last finding suggests that the faculty may be providing "role modeling" for student involvement in campus organizations.

The environmental variable having the strongest negative effect on the student's chances of being elected to a student office is the Intellectual Self-Esteem of the peer group. There are several possible reasons that this peer measure should negatively affect students' chances of being elected to a student office. Could it be that institutions whose student bodies have strong Intellectual Self-Esteem simply have fewer elected offices? Is it possible that being part of such a peer group deters students from seeking office because they fear it will detract from their academic work? This is a finding that requires further investigation. The student's chances of being elected to a student office are also negatively associated with the total enrollment of the institution. This finding, which also confirms results reported in the original *Four Critical Years,* underscores a simple statistical fact about large institutions: there are simply fewer leadership opportunities *per student* at such institutions. Negative effects are also associated with two other environmental variables: the use of graduate teaching assistants, and the inclusion of minority and

Third World courses in the curriculum. The meaning of these results is not entirely clear, although it should be pointed out that the effects of reliance on teaching assistants virtually disappear when size and women's college are controlled.

The involvement variable showing the single strongest relationship to being elected to a student office (Beta = .27) is hours per week spent participating in student clubs or groups. This effect could well be artifactual, given that being an elected officer in a student organization may cause the student to spend more time participating in that organization. Here is a clear instance of the ambiguous nature of certain effects associated with involvement measures.

Other involvement measures showing significant positive relationships to being elected to a student office include GPA, attending racial or cultural workshops, being involved in campus protests, participating in campus demonstrations, tutoring other students, working on a professor's research project, participating in a college internship program, and holding a part-time job on campus. Except for GPA, most of these effects may well be artifacts (results, rather than causes, of being elected to a student office).

Participating in Campus Protests

One peer group measure, Political Orientation (liberalism versus conservatism), has a positive effect on the likelihood that the student will participate in campus demonstrations. Participation is also positively affected by Institutional Diversity Emphasis, Racial Conflict, the percentage of students majoring in the humanities, and attendance at a nonsectarian four-year college. In short, it would appear that a student's chances of participating in demonstrations or protests while in college will be maximized if the student lives away from home and attends a nonsectarian college where the peer group is politically liberal, where the curriculum is strongly oriented toward the humanities, and where there is a strong campus emphasis on diversity issues. Not surprisingly, majoring in engineering reduces the student's chances of participating in campus protests.

A large number of involvement variables are associated with participation in protests, once the effects of student input and environmental variables are taken into account. The strongest positive associations involve discussing racial or ethnic issues, attending racial or cultural awareness workshops, enrolling in women's studies courses, hours per week spent in volunteer work, hours per week spent in student clubs or organizations, receiving personal or psychological counseling, taking multiple-choice exams, and being elected to a student office.

Getting Married

Although the percentage of students who got married between 1985 and 1989 was quite small (6.6 percent), a number of interesting factors prove to be predictive of this behavioral outcome. The input factors most predictive of getting married include planning to get married at the time of college entry, being a born-again Christian, being politically conservative, having a Protestant religious choice, being a woman, having low socio-economic status, and planning a career in elementary school teaching. Asian-American and African-American students are less likely than students from other racial and ethnic groups to get married during college. Environmental factors that prove to enhance the entering student's prospects for marriage include not relying on parental support to finance college and having many peers who are majoring in the field of education. Having a peer group that is well prepared in science tends to diminish the student's chances of getting married in college.

We have already mentioned the substantial negative association between getting married and completing four years of college. Other involvement or intermediate outcomes that are positively associated with getting married include commuting to campus, hours per week spent attending religious services, and working full-time while attending college. Involvement factors that are negatively associated with getting married include number of foreign-language courses taken and four "hours per week" measures: partying, student clubs or organizations, volunteer work, and studying or doing homework.

Again, the direction of causation for many of these involvement variables may be reversed: students who get married may simply have less time or less opportunity to party, perform volunteer work, study, or participate in student organizations.

Joining a Social Fraternity or Sorority

Input variables that are positively associated with joining a social fraternity or sorority (over and above the effects of the expectation to join) in many ways conform to the stereotype of the "Greek": having a Protestant religious affiliation, being white, being politically conservative, coming from an affluent family, and scoring high on Leadership, Status Striving, and Hedonism. Negative predictors of joining a fraternity or sorority include a strong commitment to promoting racial understanding, working at an outside job, commitment to writing original works, and having a Catholic religious affiliation.

In addition to going away from home to attend college, environmental factors that increase the student's chances of joining a social fraternity or sorority include having a peer group that is strongly oriented toward Materialism and Status, having a high percentage of peers who are being supported by merit-based financial aid, attending a private university or a Protestant college, and institutional size. Weak positive effects are associated with having a true core curriculum and a women's or gender studies course requirement. A number of other peer group factors appear to reduce the student's chances of joining a social fraternity or sorority: the percentages of either Jewish or Roman Catholic students in the student body, Artistic Inclination, Outside Work, and Altruism and Social Activism. Other environmental factors that reduce the student's chances of joining a social fraternity or sorority include positive faculty attitudes about the general education program, the percentage of faculty involved in teaching general education, average faculty salary, the percentage of student peers with majors in history or political science, the student-faculty ratio, and attending a women's college. Several curricular variables also have negative associations with joining a social fraternity or sorority:

having a minority or Third World course requirement, the use of written (narrative) evaluations, and the presence of an independent research requirement.

But perhaps the most interesting and unexpected environmental effect concerns the positive influence of Racial Conflict on joining a social fraternity or sorority. One possible interpretation of this effect is that the existence of pervasive racial conflict on the campus tends to balkanize the student body, such that students seek out social organizations whose membership is partly racially based. It would be interesting to follow up on this finding to determine whether campuses with a high level of racial conflict have fraternities or sororities that are primarily or exclusively for white students, African-American students, Asian students, Jewish students, and the like.

A large number of involvement measures are also associated with joining a social fraternity or sorority, after the effects of student input and environmental characteristics are controlled. The strongest coefficient (Beta = .25) is associated with hours per week spent in student clubs or groups. This may be an artifact: students are probably interpreting "clubs" or "groups" as equivalent to sororities or fraternities. Other involvement variables showing positive associations with membership in a sorority or fraternity include hours per week spent partying, alcohol consumption, and hours per week spent participating in intramural sports. Involvement variables that show negative associations with joining a social fraternity or sorority include participating in campus demonstrations, discussing racial or ethnic issues, watching television, hours per week spent reading for pleasure, and undergraduate GPA. The direction of causation for many of these involvement variables could easily go either way.

Voting

Those students who were most likely to vote in the 1988 election showed a number of interesting characteristics at the time they entered college as freshmen in 1985: high socioeconomic status, high Scholarship (that is, Intellectual Self-Esteem), an interest in influencing the political structure, high scores on the

SAT-Verbal, involvement in volunteer work, highly educated parents, having a father who is a college professor, commitment to participating in community action programs, and being either Protestant or Jewish in religious affiliation. Negative input factors included the degree of science preparation in high school, wanting to attend college to get away from home, and interest in obtaining recognition from others.

Beyond living at home, only a limited number of environmental factors are associated with voting, and the coefficients were generally quite small. The strongest environmental effect is associated with the Intellectual Self-Esteem of the peer group. Other positive environmental influences include the Diversity Emphasis of the institution and having a high percentage of men in the student body. The percentage of faculty involved in teaching general education courses has a negative effect on student voting.

Involvement factors that are positively associated with students' voting in the 1988 election included number of history courses taken, hours per week spent attending religious services, taking essay exams, undergraduate GPA, participating in campus demonstrations, and attending racial or cultural awareness workshops. The last two factors, together with the positive effects associated with the Diversity Emphasis of the institution, suggest that the student's level of political involvement can be increased by encouraging students to take an interest in political and racial issues. The only involvement variable showing a negative association with voting in the 1988 election is participation in intercollegiate athletics.

Table 6.4 summarizes the environmental and involvement variables that entered the behavioral outcome regressions. Not surprisingly, behavioral outcomes appear to be more dependent on various forms of "involvement" than do attitudinal and other affective outcomes (Chapters Three to Five).

Summary

This chapter has examined the effects of student input and environmental variables on a variety of student behaviors. Between

Table 6.4. Summary of Environmental
Variables Affecting Student Behavior.

Behavioral Outcome	Positively Affected by	Negatively Affected by
Alcohol consumption	Leaving home to attend college Peers: SES	Peers: percentage who are born-again Christians
	(Involvement measures)[a] Partying Fraternity or sorority membership Socializing Watching television Career counseling Exercise Intramural sports	
Tutoring other students	Leaving home to attend college Grant from the college Major: science	Research Orientation Peers: percentage with merit aid Major: social science
	(Involvement measures)[a] Assisting faculty in teaching Talking with faculty Being guest in professor's home Honors program Volunteer work Campus job Group projects for class Math courses Foreign-language courses	Watching television
Smoking cigarettes	Peers: Artistic Inclination	
	(Involvement measures)[a] Partying Alchohol consumption Reading for pleasure Campus activism Working full-time Personal counseling	Math courses Exercise
Attending recitals or concerts	Major: arts and humanities Aid based on "other talent"	Use of teaching assistants

Table 6.4. Summary of Environmental
Variables Affecting Student Behavior, cont'd.

Behavioral Outcome	Postively Affected by	Negatively Affected by
	Faculty:Liberalism Faculty: percentage teaching general education Peers: percentage who are fine arts majors Black college	
	(Involvement measures)[a] Being guest in professor's home Having papers critiqued by instructors Socializing "Diversity" activities[b] Attending religious services Reading for pleasure Student clubs and organizations Hobbies	Getting married Commuting Watching television
Being elected to a student office	Leaving home to attend college Women's college Faculty: percentage who are women Faculty: percentage in administration	Peers: Intellectual Self-Esteem Institutional size Use of teaching assistants Curriculum offers minority or Third World courses
	(Involvement measures)[a] Student clubs and organizations "Diversity" activities[b] Working on professor's research Internship program Campus job	
Participating in campus protests	Peers: Political Orientation Institutional Diversity Emphasis	Major: engineering

Table 6.4. Summary of Environmental Variables Affecting Student Behavior, cont'd.

Behavioral Outcome	Positively Affected by	Negatively Affected by
	Racial Conflict Peers: percentage in humanities Nonsectarian college	
	(Involvement measures)[a] "Diversity" activities[b] Volunteer work Student clubs and organizations Personal counseling Election to student office	
Getting married	Peers: percentage in education	Financial support from parents
	(Involvement measures)[a] Commuting Attending religious services Full-time work	Foreign-language courses Partying Student clubs and organizations Volunteer work Studying or homework
Joining social fraternity or sorority	Leaving home to attend college Peers: Materialism and Status Peers: precentage with merit-based aid True core curriculum Women's studies requirement Racial Conflict	Peers: percentage who are Catholics Peers: percentage who are Jews Peers: Artistic Inclination Peers: Outside Work Peers: Altruism and Social Activism Faculty: positive toward general education program Faculty: percentage teaching general education courses Faculty: average salaries Peers: percentage in history or political science Student-faculty ratio

Table 6.4. Summary of Environmental
Variables Affecting Student Behavior, cont'd.

Behavioral Outcome	Positively Affected by	Negatively Affected by

		Women's college
		Minority or Third World
		  requirement
		Written evaluations
		Independent research
		  requirement

	(Involvement measures)[a] Student clubs and organizations Partying Alcohol consumption Intramural sports	"Diversity" activities[b] Watching television Reading for pleasure

Voting in presidential
  election
	Peers: Intellectual Self-
	  Esteem
	Institutional Diversity
	  Orientation
	Peers: percentage who
	  are males
		Leaving home to attend
		  college
		Faculty: percentage
		  teaching general
		  education courses

	(Involvement measures)[a] History courses Attending religious services Taking essay exams "Diversity" activities[b]	Intercollegiate athletics

[a]Since the temporal ordering of outcome and involvement measures cannot be precisely determined, causal interpretations should be made with caution.

[b]Includes activities such as discussing racial or ethnic issues, socializing with students from different racial or ethnic groups, participating in campus demonstrations, attending racial or ethnic workshops, and taking women's studies or ethnic studies courses.

high school and college there is a substantial increase in alcohol consumption, a small increase in smoking behavior, and a substantial decline in participation in musical activities (attending recitals and concerts). While the overall number of students who tutor other students increases slightly between high school and college, involvement in tutoring appears to decline among highly able students who attend selective colleges. Compared to their expectations when they first enter college, substantially greater

numbers of students are elected to student offices and participate in campus demonstrations in college. (The last finding is
consistent with the substantial increase in Social Activism reported in Chapter Four.) Differences between freshman expectations and actual college experiences are much smaller in the
case of getting married and joining a social fraternity or sorority.

Increased alcohol consumption appears to be directly
related to the effects of college. Smoking and getting married,
on the other hand, appear to be reduced, if anything, by college attendance. That voting in presidential elections is negatively affected by attending college away from home most likely
reflects the effects of voter registration laws.

Widespread peer influences on student behavior in college are once again confirmed by the longitudinal analyses. Living in a campus residence hall (rather than at home) substantially increases the student's chances of being elected to a student
office, tutoring other students, participating in campus demonstrations, consuming alcohol, and joining a social fraternity or
sorority. The Materialism and Status of the peer group has a
positive effect on joining a social fraternity or sorority and a
negative effect on attending recitals or concerts. The percentage of born-again Christians in the student body has negative
effects on alcohol consumption and being elected to a student
office. Finally, the political Liberalism of the peer group has a
positive effect on participation in campus demonstrations.

Chapter 7

———◆•◆•◆———

Academic
and Cognitive
Development

Many educators and policy makers will argue that the principal purposes of higher education are to develop students' academic and intellectual skills and to prepare them for the world of work. Indeed, of all the possible outcomes of higher education, cognitive development and educational credentialing are probably given the most weight by students, parents, educators, and policy makers alike. This emphasis is reflected in the many studies in which the outcome measures are either student retention or grade point average and in the emphasis on cognitive outcomes that one sees in the current "assessment movement."

This chapter examines the impact of the college experience on three areas of academic and intellectual development: academic achievement (traditional grade point average, graduation with honors), educational attainment (persistence versus dropping out, enrollment in graduate or professional school), and cognitive development (performance on standardized tests, self-reported improvements in knowledge and intellectual skills).

Academic Achievement

Academic achievement is surely the most researched topic in higher education. Hundreds of studies using various measure-

186

ments and methodologies have yielded strikingly similar results: college grade point average (GPA) can be predicted with modest accuracy (multiple correlation around .55) from admissions information. The two most potent predictors are the student's high school GPA and scores on college admissions tests. Grades almost always carry more weight than tests.

Few studies of undergraduate grades have involved more than one institution. Indeed, some researchers and educators might argue that predicting grade point averages across different colleges simultaneously makes little sense, since grading systems and academic standards differ so much. Perhaps the most telling argument against the use of grades is that they are relative indices and therefore suspect as measures of the student's intellectual growth and development. Grades, it could be argued, reflect only how the student is performing relative to other students at a given point in time, not necessarily what has been *learned* (Astin, 1974, 1991). The current assessment movement in higher education has witnessed some pressures from educators and measurement specialists to replace traditional grading systems with performance measures that reflect student growth and development through repeated pretesting and posttesting (Astin, 1991). Such "value-added" studies, it is argued, will tell us much more about the effectiveness of our programs than mere letter grades.

In spite of the advantages of measures that reflect student changes over time, institutions continue to rely heavily on traditional letter grades to assess student achievement, and such grades are still weighted heavily by many graduate and professional schools in their selection procedures, as well as by prospective employers. Even the students seem to have accepted the system, since the proposal to abolish college grades, relatively popular during the late 1960s, has declined rapidly and is now endorsed by only a small minority of students (Dey, Astin, and Korn, 1991). Poor grades are still sufficient grounds for dismissal at most colleges, and high grades are necessary for admission to most graduate and professional schools. For these reasons, college grades continue to represent an important index of student accomplishment in college.

**Table 7.1. Average Grades in High School and College
(1985 Freshman Followed Up in 1989).**

| | Percentage Earning Grade in | | Change, High |
Average Grade	High School	College	School to College
A or A+	14.1	6.3	−7.8
A− or B	35.6	25.4	−10.2
B	22.9	34.5	+11.6
B− or C+	21.4	23.0	+1.6
C or less	5.9	10.8	+4.9

Note: Weighted national norms (abstracted from Wingard, Treviño, Dey, and Korn, 1991).

Grade Point Average

How do students' college grades compare with their grades in high school? Table 7.1 shows the national norms for the 1985 freshmen, comparing high school and college grades. Clearly, students' grades decline between high school and college: fewer than half as many students earn A averages in college than did so in high school, and nearly twice as many receive grades of C or less. When we compare individual students' high school and college grades, we find that about one in three obtains the same grades in college as in high school, only about one in five obtains higher grades, and nearly half obtain lower grades (Astin, 1977).

Consistent with hundreds of earlier studies, the two most important input predictors of the students' college grades in our 1985–1989 sample are the high school GPA and SAT Verbal score. High school grades receive more than twice as much weight as SAT Verbal score, producing a two-variable multiple R of .50. Other positive predictors include the student's gender (being female); race (being white); socioeconomic status; Scholarship; self-ratings of academic ability, writing ability, and drive to achieve; commitment to the goals of influencing social values, achieving in a performing art, and obtaining recognition from colleagues; and academic rank in high school (this variable carries very little weight once the effects of high school grades and SAT scores have been controlled). Negative predictors of undergraduate GPA include being committed to being very well off financially and being successful in one's own business; race (Mexican-American/Chicano); being a noncitizen; and the personality measure Leadership.

The single strongest environmental effect is associated with the peer measure Intellectual Self-Esteem. Since the direction of the effect is negative, this result requires a bit of explanation. The positive simple correlation of .13 between this peer measure and undergraduate GPA means simply that students attending colleges where their peers have high Intellectual Self-Esteem tend to get better grades than do students attending college where the peer group has relatively low Intellectual Self-Esteem. However, when input variables are controlled (especially high school grades and SAT Verbal score), the partial correlation involving college GPA and Intellectual Self-Esteem becomes negative. (Intellectual Self-Esteem and selectivity are substantially correlated — $r = .68$ — but the effects of selectivity disappear when Intellectual Self-Esteem enters the equation.) If all colleges graded on the same absolute standard, variables like selectivity and Intellectual Self-Esteem of the peer group would have no (zero) effect on GPA, once input variables like SAT and high school grades were controlled. However, these findings show that while the selective colleges that recruit students with high Intellectual Self-Esteem award higher grades than do the less selective colleges that admit more students with lower Intellectual Self-Esteem, the grading standards of these more selective colleges, considering the caliber of their students, are actually more stringent than those of the less selective colleges. These more stringent standards thus produce a negative effect of Intellectual Self-Esteem (that is, selectivity) on the student's GPA. Similar results have been reported by Anderson (1988).

Environmental factors showing the strongest positive effects on undergraduate GPA include having merit-based aid, having a grant from the college, majoring either in education or in the arts and humanities, the Faculty Diversity Orientation, the percentage of Roman Catholics in the student body, the percentage of Jewish students in the student body, the percentage of students receiving need-based aid, and the percentage of students majoring in biological science. In addition to Intellectual Self-Esteem of the peer group, other negative effects are associated with having need-based aid, majoring in engineering, and attending a public institution (either university or college). Why both types of public institutions should have a negative effect on the student's GPA is not clear. Does this mean that public institutions have more stringent grading standards than private colleges and universities? Or does it mean that the actual achievement level of students in public colleges and universities is lower than would be expected from their entering characteristics? Perhaps we can shed more light on these questions by examining correlations with other cognitive outcomes.

Involvement variables that are associated with the student's GPA, after the effects of input and environmental characteristics are controlled, include tutoring other students, hours per week spent studying or doing homework, participating in a college internship program or a study-abroad program, hours per week spent talking with faculty outside of class, giving presentations in class, enrolling in interdisciplinary courses, and getting married. Negative associations with college GPA include receiving tutoring in courses, hours per week spent partying, working full-time while enrolled as a student, taking reading- and study-skills classes, hours per week spent reading for pleasure, and being a member of a social fraternity or sorority. Some of these correlations might well be the consequences of high or low GPA, rather than the causes. In other words, students who are high achievers would be more likely to tutor other students, while those who are low achievers would be in greater need of tutoring or of taking reading- and study-skills classes. At the same time, high-achieving students might be more inclined to talk with faculty outside of class or to enroll in interdisciplinary courses. Some of the other involvement variables, on the other hand, provide important clues for how to enhance academic performance in college. The positive correlation of GPA with hours per week spent studying has obvious implications, as do the negative correlations with working full-time and partying. The negative correlation of GPA with hours per week spent reading for pleasure is somewhat unexpected. Perhaps some students shortchange their studying and other academic efforts by spending too much time reading for pleasure.

Graduating with Honors

The input, environmental, and involvement variables that predict graduating with honors are very similar to those that predict undergraduate GPA. Such a result is certainly to be expected, given the substantial correlation ($r = .55$) between graduating with honors and undergraduate GPA. One additional input variable carries a small negative weight: being Asian-American or Oriental. Also, majoring in psychology has a positive effect on graduating with honors, whereas two other environmental variables have small negative effects: percentage of born-again Christians in the student body, and having a general education program that is controlled by the major. With these few exceptions, the major input and environmental variables affecting the student's chances of graduating with honors are very similar to those reported above for undergraduate GPA.

Educational Attainment

This study looks at two closely related measures of educational attainment: completing a bachelor's degree, and enrollment in graduate or professional school. What input, environmental, and involvement variables are associated with these two measures?

Completing the Bachelor's Degree

Since the data on degree completion came from a somewhat different sample of students, some discussion of this sample is in order. The names of each of the 95,406 freshmen to whom follow-up questionnaires were sent were also sent to their freshman institutions, with a request for information on three measures of educational progress: whether the student had completed a bachelor's degree, how many years of undergraduate education the student had completed, and whether the student was still enrolled. About three-fourths of the registrars were willing to provide this information, which yielded retention data on 75,752 students (79.4 percent of the original sample). We could not detect any significant bias, within stratification cells, between registrars who did and did not provide the data.

Researchers at the Higher Education Research Institute have experimented with several different ways of measuring "retention": counting only those who completed the bachelor's degree by 1989 as "retained" and all others as "not retained"; counting those who completed four years but did not yet have the bachelor's degree as also "retained"; and adding those who were still enrolled (even if they had not yet completed four years) as "retained." We have experimented with these three measures in a number of different ways over the years, and the most stringent measure (completing the bachelor's degree in four years) always produces the strongest associations with input and environmental variables. A more detailed examination of these different analyses reveals that the input characteristics of those students who are still enrolled after four years but have not yet obtained a bachelor's degree are more like those of students who have dropped out than like those who have earned their degrees. Accordingly, in order to conserve space we will report here only those findings associated with the most stringent retention measure: completing a bachelor's degree in four years. While this is by no means an ideal retention measure, readers should keep in mind that, given the reality that any dropout can return to college at any time and complete a degree, the only perfect measure of retention is one in which everybody either already has the bachelor's degree or has died. Nevertheless, readers who are interested in results using the two less stringent retention measures can obtain them by writing to the Higher Education Research Institute, Graduate School of Education, University of California, Los Angeles.

Several restrictions had to be put on the final sample to be used in the study of retention: community college data were eliminated, institutions without complete environmental data (faculty survey, curriculum, and so on), were removed, and only students for whom we could retrieve SAT or ACT scores were retained. These restrictions generated a final sample of 38,587 students for whom we had complete retention, environmental, and input data.

A little more than half (54.7 percent) of the students had completed their bachelor's degree by 1989–90. That this is somewhat higher than the national retention rates at four-year colleges (Dey and Astin, 1989) is to be expected, given the inclusion in this unweighted sample of a disproportionate number of highly selective institutions that have high retention rates. That we required each student to have an SAT or ACT score also may have contributed to the higher retention rate.

Input Effects

Input characteristics produced a multiple R of .40, which is comparable to multiple correlations obtained in earlier retention studies (Astin, 1971a, 1975). The complexity of the retention phenomenon is underlined by the observation that thirty-three different student input characteristics carried significant weight in predicting degree completion. The single strongest predictor of degree completion is the student's high school GPA ($r = .29$). SAT Mathematical and Verbal scores were also relatively strong predictors (simple $r = .27$ and .27, respectively), but these two measures did not enter the regression equation until the third and ninth steps, respectively. The other input variables entering the regression between the first and the ninth steps included the student's socioeconomic status, being a Roman Catholic, gender (female), being Jewish, scientific orientation (negative), and Hedonism (negative). In other words, those entering freshmen who are most likely to complete a bachelor's degree within four years have high grades in high school and high scores on college admissions tests, come from high socioeconomic levels, are either Roman Catholic or Jewish in their religious preference, are women, are nonhedonistic, and are disinclined toward science. The negative effects of Scientific Orientation may be a reflection that many science and especially many engineering students may take longer than four years to complete their undergraduate degrees (see below).

Other input variables carrying significant positive weights in the regression equation include "to become more knowledgeable about things that interest me" as an important reason for attending college, expecting to change one's career as well as one's major field choice during college, leadership self-rating, science preparation in high school, self-rating of physical health, academic rank in high school, and the Social Activism personality measure. It was also interesting to find that the three components making up the measure of socioeconomic status — father's and mother's educational levels and parental income — all carry significant weight in the regression equation, over and above the effects of socioeconomic status. Once all three had entered the regression, however, the weight for socioeconomic status became nonsignificant. What this means, in effect, is that the index of socioeconomic status that we developed does not optimally take into account the predictive power of the three variables making up the index; it is thus preferable, for predictive purposes, to give separate weights to each of the individual SES measures. Additional negative input predictors of bachelor's degree completion include being a born-again Christian, having an outside job, political liberalism, race (Mexican American/Chicano), and interest in becoming an authority in one's own field.

Environmental Effects

Retention is positively influenced by majoring in either business, psychology, or other social sciences, and negatively influenced by majoring in engineering. Once the effects of these freshman majors are controlled, the negative effect of Scientific Orientation is diminished. This means that Scientific Orientation has a negative effect on retention primarily because people with high scores tend to major in engineering and those with low scores tend to major in business, psychology, and the social sciences. The negative effect of being an engineering major, of course, is in part an artifact: many engineering programs require more than four years for completion.

Retention is enhanced by living in a campus residence

hall, a finding that has been reported in many earlier studies (Astin, 1975, 1977, 1982). Living in a private room, interestingly enough, has a small but significant negative effect on retention.

Retention is significantly affected by more environmental variables than almost any other outcome measure. The largest effect of any institutional characteristic is associated with size, which reduces the student's chances of completing the degree. This finding replicates several earlier studies of retention (Astin, 1975, 1982). Student Orientation of the faculty, on the other hand, has a positive effect on retention. Other weaker but positive effects are associated with the percentage of resources invested in student services and the percentage of graduate students in the student body. Some of the strongest effects are associated with the student peer group. Peer measures showing positive effects on retention include Science Preparation in high school, Socioeconomic Status, Intellectual Self-Esteem, the percentage of Catholics in the student body, the percentage of students receiving need-based aid, and the percentage of students majoring in physical science fields. Negative peer factors include Scientific Orientation, Lack of Student Community, Materialism and Status, and having more than 80 percent men in the student body. (The effects of Scientific Orientation largely disappear when size and Student Orientation of the faculty are controlled.)

Faculty measures showing positive effects on retention include Humanities Orientation, Faculty Morale, Faculty Liberalism, Faculty Diversity Orientation, the percentage of women among the faculty, the percentage of Ph.D.s on the faculty, and — somewhat surprisingly — the faculty perception of Racial Conflict on the campus. Negative influences are associated with Time Stress and — again somewhat surprisingly — Use of Active Learning strategies in the classroom.

Curricular variables having positive effects on retention include a true core curriculum, a distributional system with progressive offerings, a women's or gender studies course requirement, and a required senior comprehensive examination.

Effects of Involvement

In order to examine the possible effects of involvement variables on retention, it was necessary to eliminate students for whom we had no follow-up questionnaire. This reduced the sample for this portion of the retention analysis to 11,079 students. (Since the follow-up questionnaire includes a self-reported question about degree attainment, we used this as the outcome measure, rather than the registrar's report.) Retention is facilitated by both student-student and student-faculty interaction, hours per week spent socializing with friends, partying, talking with faculty outside of class, and being a guest in a professor's home. The single largest negative effect on retention is associated with working full-time as a student. Other negative relationships involved working off campus at a part-time job. Considering that faculty reliance on Active Learning seems to have a negative effect on retention, it is surprising to find that three individual involvement measures signifying Active Learning have positive effects: giving presentations in class, taking essays exams, and working on an independent research project.

Other involvement variables showing positive associations with retention include receiving vocational or career counseling and enrolling in honors programs. Negative correlates include receiving personal or psychological counseling, number of science courses taken, number of math or numerical courses taken, hours per week spent commuting to campus, and hours per week spent reading for pleasure. Once again, we find reading for pleasure to be negatively associated with an academic outcome. Given that most positive correlates signify high involvement (student-student interaction, student-faculty interaction, giving class presentations) and most negative correlates suggest low involvement (working and commuting), it may well be that students who spend a lot of time reading materials unconnected with their studies are not very involved in their academic work.

The pattern of associations reported here is highly consistent with the involvement theory of student retention (Astin, 1975, 1984). Practically all the involvement variables showing positive associations with retention suggest high involvement with faculty, with fellow students, or with academic work. Most of the involvement measures showing negative effects (working full-time, working off campus, commuting, reading for pleasure) represent involvements that take time and energy away from the academic experience. Perhaps the major exception to this general pattern is the negative effect of faculty Use of Active Learning strategies. This finding is indeed a puzzle, and no obvious interpretations suggest themselves. One possibility is that "group projects for a class" does not necessarily signify appropriately designed cooperative learning experiences. Some cooperative learning experts (Johnson, Johnson, and Smith, 1991) have argued that poorly designed cooperative learning—where individual responsibility within the group is not equally shared, and where students are not held individually accountable—can produce worse results than traditional competitive approaches. With the tremendous emphasis now being given to active learning techniques (for example, Chickering and Gamson, 1987), this is a finding that clearly merits a major research effort.

As would be expected, the student's undergraduate GPA shows stronger correlations with retention (Beta = .12), after control for input and environmental characteristics, than any other intermediate outcome or involvement variable. (The reader should keep in mind that the other involvement correlations reported above were obtained *after* GPA had been controlled.) While it stands to reason that the student's decision to remain in or leave college can be directly affected by academic performance, the direction of causation could also work in reverse: a student who decides, for whatever reason, to leave college may consequently lose interest in studies and thereby get a lower GPA.

Admission to Graduate or Professional School

The 1989 follow-up questionnaire contains an item about the student's educational plans for fall 1989. For this particular outcome measure we compare students who indicated that they were attending graduate or professional school with those who were not. Among students entering college as full-time freshmen in the fall of 1985, it is estimated that about 12.3 percent were attending graduate or professional school by the fall of 1989 (Wingard, Treviño, Dey, and Korn, 1991).

While the student's academic preparation in high school (as reflected in high school GPA and SAT Verbal scores) carries significant weight in predicting enrollment in graduate school, even greater weight is carried by personality and motivational variables: freshman plans for attending graduate school, citing "preparation for graduate school" as an important reason for attending college, highest degree planned, and two personality measures: Scholarship and Scientific Orientation. Other input characteristics carrying significant positive weights include the number of biological science courses taken in high school, father's educational level, being either Jewish or Roman Catholic, tutoring other students in high school, and desiring to influence the political structure. Negative predictors of entry to graduate school include Hedonism and career indecision.

As might be expected, the environmental variables having the strongest effects on enrollment in graduate school are associated with the student's major. Majoring in science, premedicine or pre-law has positive effects, while majoring in engineering, business, or nursing has negative effects. Careers in all fields having positive effects require graduate training, while careers in the fields having negative effects do not. In fact, since engineering often requires more than four years of undergraduate study, one would not expect engineering majors to be enrolling in graduate school in 1989, even if they aspired to higher degrees.

Enrollment in graduate school is positively affected by a faculty that is Student-Oriented, by the percentage of Jews in the student body, and by having financial aid based on academic merit. Enrollment in graduate school is negatively affected by the size of the institution, the percentage of students majoring in engineering, and attendance at a public university. Considering that most of the graduate education in the United States is carried out by our public universities, this last finding is indeed ironic: the very institutions that perform most of the graduate education and professional training seem to discourage undergraduates from pursuing such postgraduate study.

The involvement or intermediate outcome variable showing the strongest correlation with enrollment in graduate or professional school is the student's undergraduate GPA. Other involvement measures showing positive associations with enrollment in graduate school include working on a professor's research project, being a guest in a professor's home, enrolling in honors programs, and number of science courses taken. Negative correlations occur with receiving vocational or career counseling and working on a group project for a class.

Performance on Standardized Tests

Cognitive development was assessed with two different types of data: (1) scores on standardized tests taken for professional certification or for admission to graduate or professional school, and (2) self-reported gains in knowledge and intellectual skills, as revealed in the 1989 follow-up questionnaire.

Some readers may wonder whether student performance on tests such as the GRE, MCAT, or LSAT constitute appropriate measures of the "outcomes" of undergraduate education. This issue can be addressed from two different perspectives: content and function. As far as content is concerned, these tests do measure at least three cognitive skills that undergraduate education is supposed to facilitate: facility with language (GRE Verbal and LSAT), scientific and mathematical skills (GRE Quantitative and MCAT), and analytical and problem-solving skills (all three tests). From the perspective of function, these tests represent important "gates" for entry into graduate and professional programs that lead to high-level positions in science, medicine, the law, public service, and college teaching. As a consequence, developing the undergraduate student's ability to perform well on these tests should be an important goal of any undergraduate program that purports to prepare students for postgraduate study. In short, for reasons of both content and function, it is useful to know what kinds of undergraduate institutions and programs facilitate or inhibit the student's ability to perform well on such tests.

It is well known that students entering different kinds of colleges and programs already differ substantially in their performance on standardized tests; therefore, we thought it necessary to have available scores on standardized college admissions tests as input or control data. For this purpose, we were fortunate in being able to obtain from the College Entrance Examination Board and the American College Testing Program the college admissions test scores of those 1985 entering freshmen who completed the fall survey in the Cooperative Institutional Research Program. To match the student's freshman questionnaire data with test score data, a two-stage process was followed: (1) matching students by their social security numbers, and (2) matching on names and addresses.

After all matching had been completed, we found that the ACT Math score could be converted directly into the equivalent SAT Math score, and that the sum of the other three ACT tests (English, Social Sciences, Natural Sciences) could be converted into the equivalent SAT Verbal score. Conversion of ACT to SAT equivalents, which was done by the equipercentile method, was made possible by the existence of a subsample ($N = 14,865$) for whom scores on both tests were available. The SAT and ACT Math scores correlate .85, and the ACT and SAT verbal equivalents correlate .82. (The ACT English subtest by itself correlates only .69 with the SAT Verbal score.) All 1985 freshmen for whom we had both entering freshman questionnaire data and SAT (or equivalent ACT) scores were then matched against the files of the Educational Testing Service to obtain scores on the Graduate Record Examination (GRE). Using social security number as the primary matching criterion and name and address as the secondary criterion, we were able to find 8,829 matches. The unweighted mean scores of this sample on both the SAT and GRE tests are quite high: mean SAT Verbal and Math of 537 and 573, respectively, and mean GRE Verbal and Quantitative of 533 and 590, respectively. Given that our sampling of institutions overrepresents the more selective institutions and that our sample of students includes "fast trackers" who manage to take their GRE tests within four years after first entering college, we would expect this to be a highly select group of students. Nevertheless, it should be pointed out that the variability in test scores is only slightly less than the variability reported by the Educational Testing Service (ETS) for its standardization population (Educational Testing Service, 1987a, 1987b). Thus, the standard deviations were 103 and 106, respectively, for the SAT Verbal and SAT Math (compared to 104 and 114 for the population), and 108 and 123, respectively, for the GRE Verbal and Quantitative tests (compared to 118 and 132 for the population). The fact that the variability in test score performance within our sample has been only slightly constrained indicates that the correlations of these test scores with other variables will not be substantially attenuated by the somewhat select nature of the sample.

Four regressions were carried out using the GRE scores, one for each of the following outcome measures: GRE Verbal, GRE Quantitative, GRE Composite (Verbal + Quantitative), and GRE Analytical. What is perhaps most remarkable about these regressions is how high the correlation is between freshman test scores and GRE test scores:

$$\text{SAT-V} \times \text{GRE-V} = .85$$
$$\text{SAT-M} \times \text{GRE-Q} = .85$$
$$\text{SAT-V} + \text{M} \times \text{GRE-V} + \text{Q} = .88$$
$$\text{SAT-V} + \text{M} \times \text{GRE Analytical} = .73$$

These results are especially remarkable, given that four years have elapsed between the taking of the two tests. (Angoff and Johnson, 1990, obtained almost identical correlations between 1983–1985 GRE scores and 1978–1981 SAT scores in a sample of 22,923 students.) One could argue that these correlations would be impressive even if the students had taken the *same* test four years apart. In short, it seems safe to draw three conclusions from these high correlations: (1) the GRE and the SAT are alternate forms of the same test; (2) better than two-thirds of the variation in GRE performance can be explained in terms of SAT performance; and (3) the relative standing of students on the GRE corresponds quite closely to their relative standing on the SAT.

With these very high correlations between the SAT and the GRE, is it possible to attribute any of the remaining GRE

variation to other student input and environmental characteristics? Surprisingly, there are a number of input and environmental variables that add to the prediction of GRE performance,
over and above the effects of SAT performance. The following
sections summarize these results.

GRE Verbal

The next most important input predictor of the GRE Verbal
score, after the effect of the SAT Verbal Score is controlled, is
the SAT Math score. The SAT Verbal score, however, carries
more than seven times as much weight as the SAT Math score
in the final regression equation. Other input characteristics that
contribute positively to the prediction of the GRE Verbal score,
after controlling for the two SAT scores, include the student's
self-rating in writing ability, commitment to the goal of writing original works, being undecided about a career, highest
degree planned, high school GPA, intellectual self-confidence,
Feminism, commitment to developing a meaningful philosophy
of life, citing "to learn more about things that interest me" as
a reason for attending college, and having no religious preference. Negative input predictors include age, being a woman,
Status Striving, Leadership, citing "to improve my reading and
study skills" as a reason for attending college, interest in being
successful in a business, and commitment to participating in
community action programs. The negative age effect suggests that
cognitive growth in verbal skills, as measured by standardized
tests, is in part maturational.

GRE Verbal performance is enhanced by majoring in social science. Choosing some field of social science as a freshman adds an average of about 15 points to a person's GRE Verbal score, over and above what would be expected from SAT
scores and other input variables. What is interesting about the
effects of these individual majors is that there are also parallel
peer group effects: GRE Verbal performance is also enhanced
when there are high percentages of peers majoring in either history or political science. In other words, in history and political
science, there are separate positive effects of both the individual's major and the concentration of peers in these majors. In

the case of history and political science, it may be that the intellectual climate of an institution that emphasizes these fields is unique in certain respects. Perhaps discussions and debates about social and political issues, social policy, and related matters are very common at such an institution. Also, the course work may put a strong emphasis on critical thinking and the use of language.

Two other curricular variables have significant effects on GRE Verbal scores. Attending institutions that have a personalized or individualized approach to general education has a positive effect, whereas having a structured curriculum (few choices) produces negative effects.

One peer measure has a significant positive effect on GRE performance: Intellectual Self-Esteem. As already mentioned, this variable is strongly associated with the selectivity of the institution. One possible explanation is that having a peer group with very high self-esteem creates an extremely competitive academic environment in which students put a lot of time and energy into preparing for admission into graduate or professional schools. Such an interpretation is consistent with findings for some of the other test scores discussed later.

To assess the effects of environmental variables derived from the faculty survey, there was a certain loss of cases from the analysis (from 8,819 to 6,359), simply because not all institutions participating in the freshman survey administered the faculty survey in 1989–90. Only one faculty measure, Research Orientation, proved to have a significant positive effect on GRE Verbal performance. The interpretation offered for this finding is similar to the one advanced in the case of the Intellectual Self-Esteem of the peer group: an environment characterized by a very strong emphasis on research and scholarship may well engender a high level of competition among students as they compete for admission to graduate or professional schools. Students attending universities that are heavily research oriented are likely to have some firsthand exposure to the realities of graduate admissions (high standards of faculty, many more applicants than places, heavy competition, and so on), especially if they themselves are intending to pursue postgraduate work. This exposure may serve as a strong motivator for them to prepare well for such exams.

Since analyses of involvement variables require that data from the 1989 follow-up questionnaire be available, a substantial additional reduction in sample size was necessitated to create a subsample of students who had SAT scores, 1985 freshman questionnaire data, faculty environmental data, and 1989 follow-up questionnaire data. All such data are available on a subsample of 2,002 students. College GPA has the strongest residual correlation with GRE Verbal (partial Beta = .09), after control of the effects of entering student and environmental characteristics. As shown in later discussions, college GPA is related to *every* standardized test score (GRE, LSAT, MCAT, NTE) after input and environmental effects are controlled. This raises an interesting question: college grades have often been criticized on the grounds that they do not really measure learning, since they are primarily normative measures that rank students in relation to each other. This is especially true in the case of grading on the curve (Astin, 1991). Here we have evidence, however, that the student's undergraduate GPA may in fact reflect cognitive learning, at least to a minor extent.

Other involvement variables showing positive associations with GRE Verbal scores include hours per week spent reading for pleasure, number of foreign-language courses taken, and number of science courses taken. While it is easy to understand why taking foreign-language courses and extensive reading can enhance a student's verbal skills, it is somewhat surprising to find that taking science courses has a similar effect. (Number of math or numerical courses taken had no such effect.) One possible explanation for this finding is in the content and structure of the GRE Verbal test. A major part of this test involves short prose passages which the student is supposed to read before answering several multiple-choice questions based on the passage. As these passages sometimes include scientific or technical content, students who take many science courses in college may have an advantage in taking the GRE, for at least two reasons: (1) they may be more familiar with scientific terminology and scientific concepts, and (2) they may actually know some of the material contained in the GRE reading passages. If this analysis is accurate, it may also help to explain why the Science subtest of the ACT proved to be useful in converting ACT scores into equivalent SAT Verbal scores.

Involvement measures showing negative associations with GRE Verbal scores include hours per week spent in volunteer work, participating in group projects for a class, participating in intercollegiate athletics, hours per week spent attending classes, and receiving tutoring in courses. This last variable may well be the *result,* rather than the cause, of poor verbal skills. Considering the substantial time demands placed on participants in intercollegiate athletics, the negative effect of this activity is understandable. Why taking a large number of courses and participating in group projects for class should have negative effects on GRE Verbal scores, however, is puzzling. These findings clearly merit much further investigation.

GRE Quantitative

Next to the SAT Math score, the strongest freshman predictor of the GRE Quantitative score four years later is the student's self-rating on mathematical ability. Apparently, this self-rating measure contains information about that student's mathematical skills not contained in the SAT Math scores (partial Beta = .21). Other positive predictors that add significantly to the regression equation include the student's high school grades, SAT Verbal score, interest in making a theoretical contribution to science, father's educational level, having a father who is an engineer, tutoring other students in high school, being undecided about a career choice, using a personal computer, number of physical science courses taken in high school, and having no religious preference. Negative input predictors include age, being a woman, race (black/African-American), giving "to improve my reading and study skills" as a reason for attending college, being a noncitizen, interest in writing original works, asking a high school teacher's advice after class, and three personality measures: Leadership, Artistic Inclination, and Social Activism. That these three personality measures should negatively affect the student's GRE Quantitative scores is somewhat puzzling. (Leadership, incidentally, also has a negative effect on GRE

Verbal score.) One simple possibility is that heavy engagement in these activities — student government, artistic pursuits, and social activism — does little, if anything, to enhance development of quantitative skills.

As would be expected, majoring in science, engineering, or other technical fields facilitates the development of quantitative skills, whereas majoring in the arts or humanities has a negative effect. A science or engineering major adds between 10 and 30 points to the student's GRE Quantitative score, depending on whether one discounts the effect of other involvement variables that might be related to choosing a science and engineering career. Majoring in biological science, somewhat surprisingly, also has a negative effect on GRE Quantitative performance, even though the simple correlation between choosing a biological science major and GRE Quantitative score is positive. Once entering freshman characteristics are controlled (especially SAT Math), the coefficient becomes negative. These findings suggest that many biological science majors may avoid courses that challenge their quantitative skills.

Financing college with personal savings is positively associated with GRE Quantitative performance, whereas having need-based aid appears to have a negative effect.

As was the case with GRE Verbal, GRE Quantitative performance is positively affected by both the Intellectual Self-Esteem of the peer group and the Research Orientation of the faculty. Other variables having positive effects include the size of the student body, the percentage of Asians in the student body, and the use of written evaluations. Faculty variables having positive effects include the percentage of faculty in science fields, the faculty's perception that there is keen academic competition among students, and the Institutional Diversity Emphasis. The percentage of women on the faculty has a negative effect on GRE Quantitative performance.

The strongest correlation between GRE Quantitative scores and involvement measures (after input and environmental characteristics are controlled) involves the number of math/numerical courses taken in college. Here is clear-cut evidence in support of the truism that "students learn what they study." The negative effect of taking writing-skills courses on GRE Quantitative performance is perhaps to be expected, although we do not find a similar pattern with math courses and GRE Verbal performance. In other words, taking math or numerical courses does not appear to impede the development of verbal skills in the same way that taking a lot of courses that emphasize writing seems to impact negatively on quantitative skills. These contrasts may reflect something about the modern college curriculum. Whereas all students are required to take at least some courses in the humanities and some courses that emphasize the development of verbal skills (reading, writing, speaking), it is possible in many institutions for those students whose interests lean heavily toward literature, language, the arts, and the humanities to avoid taking any courses that focus on the development of quantitative skills. Apparently, many students do just this. These findings have significant policy implications for curricular committees concerned about the development of students' skills in quantitative reasoning and analysis.

Two other involvement variables show significant correlations with GRE Quantitative performance: college GPA and tutoring other students. The positive correlation with tutoring raises an interesting ambiguity: Do students engage in tutoring *because* they have well-developed quantitative skills, does the tutoring itself enhance the development of such skills, or both? That the students who have well-developed quantitative skills are more likely to tutor other students in college is suggested by the observation that the simple correlation between tutoring and the GRE Quantitative score diminishes considerably (from .14 to .03) when SAT Math and other input and environmental characteristics are controlled. However, the correlation remains highly significant statistically, even after all the other involvement variables are controlled, suggesting that tutoring may indeed help to enhance quantitative skills. Similar theoretical arguments have recently been advanced to explain why cooperative learning seems to benefit all participants, regardless of their achievement levels (Johnson, Johnson, and Smith, 1991).

GRE Analytical

Although there was no entering freshman pretest score available for the GRE Analytical score, more than half the variance in this score could be predicted from the SAT Verbal and the Mathematical scores ($R = .76$), suggesting that the SAT represents a fairly good pretest for the GRE Analytical. Other input characteristics having positive effects on GRE Analytical performance include being white, self-rated mathematical ability, using a personal computer, high school GPA, and two personality measures: Hedonism and Artistic Inclination. Negative input predictors include self-rated physical health, citing "to improve reading and study skills" as an important reason for attending college, being black/African-American, and commitment to creating artistic works.

Gender produces interesting results in the prediction of the GRE Analytical score. Women get much lower scores on the GRE Analytical than men do, as evidenced by the simple correlation of $-.20$. The entry of SAT Mathematical into the regression, however, changes this simple negative correlation to a significant positive partial correlation. The positive correlation survives through the entire regression, suggesting some kind of direct positive effect of gender on Analytical performance during the undergraduate years. In other words, the reason women get lower Analytical scores is because they enter college with much lower SAT Math scores than the men do. Once this differential in math preparation is controlled, being a woman has a positive effect on GRE Analytical scores. This means that women actually get higher Analytical scores than one would expect from their SAT scores. The reason for this positive effect is not at all clear, but it provides interesting material for further studies on gender differences.

As would be expected, majoring in some field of physical science has a positive effect on GRE Analytical scores. Other positive effects are associated with the use of graduate teaching assistants and the percentage of Hispanic students in the undergraduate student body. Conceivably, associating with teaching assistants, many of whom would have taken the GRE relatively recently, may help undergraduates gain useful tips about preparing for the test. The teaching assistants could also serve to motivate undergraduates by stressing that their chances of being admitted to graduate school will be enhanced by a high test score.

No faculty variables are found to be significantly associated with GRE Analytical performance, once the effects of input variables have been controlled.

Only three involvement variables are associated with the GRE Analytical score (following the control of input and environmental variables): undergraduate GPA, hours per week socializing with friends (positive correlations), and receiving personal or psychological counseling (negative correlation). The positive effect of undergraduate GPA suggests once again that college grades, despite their relativistic nature, many indeed reflect cognitive learning.

GRE Composite

Since the GRE Analytical score is normally not included in the GRE total score, the Composite score for this analysis consisted of the simple sum of the GRE Verbal and Quantitative scores. As would be expected, the input and environmental characteristics predicting this Composite were almost identical to the ones that were found to predict the GRE Verbal and Mathematical scores independently. After the effects of the SAT scores are controlled, self-rated mathematical ability carries the largest positive weight, and being a woman carries the largest negative weight. Other positive predictors include average high school grades, Scientific Orientation, father's educational level, having no religious preference, being undecided about a career, tutoring other students in high school, parental income, and two other self ratings: academic ability and writing ability. Additional negative predictors include giving "to improve reading and study skills" as an important reason for attending college, being black/African-American, wanting to be successful in one's own business, wanting to influence social values, and the Leadership personality score.

GRE Composite performance is positively affected by majoring in science, engineering, or social science. But the strongest effect is associated with the peer measure Intellectual Self-Esteem. Other environmental factors having positive effects on GRE Composite performance include the Research Orientation of the college environment, having a general education curriculum that is personalized or individualized, institutional size, the percentage of Asian students in the undergraduate student body, and being supported by parents. The only negative environmental factor is having a general education curriculum that is highly structured (in effect, this is a distributional system that allows little freedom of choice).

The involvement or intermediate outcome variable having the strongest residual correlation with GRE Composite performance (after control for input and environmental effects) is GPA. Other positive correlations are with number of math or numerical courses taken, number of science courses taken, and hours per week spent reading for pleasure. Negative correlations involve working on a group project for a class, receiving tutoring, and hours per week spent in volunteer work.

Medical College Admission Test

Scores on the Medical College Admission Test (MCAT) were obtained from the Association of American Medical Colleges through a matching procedure very similar to the one used for GRE scores. There was a total of 1,854 students for whom we had 1985 entering freshman survey data, SAT or ACT data, and MCAT data. The SAT Math and Verbal scores produce a multiple correlation of .76 with the MCAT, suggesting that the SAT is a reasonably good pretest for this test. The weights assigned to the SAT Verbal and Math scores are nearly equal in size (the weight for Math is slightly higher), indicating that the MCAT is relatively evenly balanced between quantitative and verbal skills. Other entering freshman characteristics having positive weights in the prediction of MCAT scores include high school GPA, self-rated academic and mathematical abilities, and career indecision. Negative weights are associated with being a woman (the largest individual weight except for SAT scores), being black/African-American, and being a noncitizen.

Entering college with plans to major in an allied health field carries a negative weight in predicting MCAT scores, a finding that is somewhat surprising. This result suggests that students who initially aspire to an allied health career but then switch to a pre-med curriculum during college are at something of a disadvantage in their preparation to take the MCAT. One admittedly speculative interpretation is that the basic science courses taken in connection with the allied health major are not as rigorous as similar courses taken in a traditional liberal arts program.

The environmental variable having the strongest environmental effect on MCAT scores is the peer measure Intellectual Self-Esteem. Once again, attending a college where other students are highly able and have high Intellectual Self-Esteem seems to facilitate the student's test-taking skills.

Why should the Intellectual Self-Esteem of the peer group continue to crop up as a facilitator of performance on standardized tests? There are at least three possible (and not mutually exclusive) interpretations. First, being around other highly able, confident, and motivated students may stir up the individual student's competitive juices. Second, verbal interactions among such students may often involve the exchange of information and ideas that are useful in taking such tests. In other words, such students may represent good "teachers" for one another. Finally, since students with high Intellectual Self-Esteem are likely to take graduate admissions tests, there are more individual students in such an environment from whom to learn "tricks of the trade" in preparing to take such tests.

Other variables having positive effects on MCAT scores include having women's or gender studies course offerings, paying for college expenses with personal savings, and the percentage of Asians in the undergraduate student body. It is interesting to note here that *being* Asian or Asian-American as such does not show any significant effect on either the GRE or the MCAT, even though attending a college with a relatively high *proportion* of Asians in the student body positively affects performance on both tests. Apparently, this peer group measure affects Asians and non-Asians alike. The only negative effects on MCAT scores are from being supported by a college work-study grant and attending a college for women.

Studying the effects of faculty environmental variables necessitates a slight loss of students (from 1,854 to 1,785). The strongest effect is associated with the faculty perception of "keen competition" among undergraduate students for grades. This perceptual variable, incidentally, is strongly associated with the Intellectual Self-Esteem of the peer group ($r = .71$). As a matter of fact, at the step where "keen competition" enters the regression, the partial regression coefficients for the two variables were virtually identical ("Beta in" = .13). But when "keen competition" enters the regression, the coefficient for Intellectual Self-Esteem is diminished considerably. In effect, there is little to choose between these two variables in their effects on MCAT scores, since the difference in their partial Beta at the step where "keen competition" enters is insignificant.

The only faculty environmental variable showing positive effects on MCAT performance is the percentage who teach interdisciplinary courses. Two faculty variables have negative effects on MCAT performance: the average age of the faculty and the perception that faculty colleagues are positive about the institution's general education program. In the faculty analysis, two other institutional characteristics entered the regression equation with negative weights: attending a public university, and the percentage of total expenditures devoted to instruction.

Analyses involving the possible effects of involvement variables on MCAT performance required a much reduced sample size ($n = 502$), since it was necessary to have follow-up questionnaire data as well as all the data required for the faculty analysis. The involvement measure showing the strongest correlation with MCAT performance (after the effects of input and environmental characteristics are controlled) is undergraduate GPA (partial Beta = .22). Three other involvement measures have negative associations with MCAT performance: received personal or psychological counseling, hours per week spent in attending religious services, and hours per week spent with student clubs or organizations.

Law School Admission Test (LSAT)

With the assistance of the Law School Admissions Council in Washington, D.C., we obtained scores for the Law School Admission Test (LSAT). Matching procedures were similar to those followed for the MCAT and GRE. A total of 5,854 students were found for whom we had SAT scores, 1985 questionnaire results, and LSAT scores. The multiple R involving SAT Verbal and Mathematical scores as predictors is .72, once again suggesting that the SAT is a reasonable pretest for the LSAT. The SAT Verbal score receives a slightly greater weight in the regression equation than does the SAT Mathematical score. Other input variables making positive contributions to the prediction of LSAT scores include high school GPA, having no religious preference, self-ratings of both academic and mathematical ability, being Jewish, and the Hedonism personality score. Negative input predictors include interest in being very well off financially, self-rated physical health, participation in science contests in high school, two race variables (black or African-American and Puerto Rican-American), interest in creating artistic works, and asking teachers for advice after class. This last variable might be indicative of academic difficulties.

As is the case with both GRE and LSAT scores, the Intellectual Self-Esteem of the student body has a positive effect on LSAT performance. One other peer measure, Social Activism, has a negative effect. Other positive environmental effects are associated with having progressive course offerings and the percentage of students majoring in social sciences. Both these measures may help prepare students for the LSAT. Progressive course offerings, for example, have to do with either women's issues or racial and ethnic issues, both of which may be covered in the LSAT. Similarly, having many peers who are interested in the social sciences may generate student discussions about political, historical, and related matters that are likely to be covered in the LSAT.

Analyses of the effects of faculty characteristics had to be conducted with a somewhat smaller sample ($n = 4,846$). Once again, the Research Orientation has a positive effect on test performance. Otherwise, no faculty variables show significant effects on LSAT performance. Analyses of the intermediate outcome and involvement variables required a further sample size reduction to 1,226. With this group, undergraduate GPA shows the strongest residual correlation with test performance, after control for the effects of input and environmental characteristics. Other involvement variables having significant positive correlations with LSAT performance include hours per week spent socializing with friends, and enrolling in interdisciplinary courses. Negative involvement variables include receiving tutoring, and taking part in intercollegiate athletics. While tutoring may be the result of academic difficulties, rather than a cause of lower test performance, the negative correlation of participation in intercollegiate athletics may well be causal, given the substantial amount of time and energy that athletes must commit to practice.

National Teacher Examination (NTE)

Scores on the National Teacher Examination (NTE) were obtained from the Educational Testing Service with financial support from the National Education Association. To conserve costs, the matching procedure was limited to CIRP institutions located in states where the NTE is required and to students within those institutions who had completed the CIRP questionnaire, had SAT scores, and indicated as freshmen that they planned a career in elementary or secondary school teaching. NTE scores on three subtests were matched with these students' SAT and questionnaire data as follows: Test of General Knowledge ($N = 2,836$), Test of Communication Skills ($N = 2,654$), and Test of Professional Knowledge ($N = 2,477$). Since the results reported here are obtained from a recently completed UCLA dissertation (Opp, 1991), the environmental variables are somewhat different (Opp did not use faculty environmental variables and omitted certain peer measures).

As with GRE, MCAT, and LSAT scores, the SAT scores

turn out to be fairly good pretests for the NTE. Multiple correlations using SAT Verbal and Mathematical scores are .77
(General Knowledge), .71 (Communication Skills), and .60
(Professional Knowledge). Verbal and Math scores are about
equally weighted for the prediction of General Knowledge, but
the Verbal test gets somewhat more weight in predicting the
Communication Skills test and substantially more weight in
predicting the Professional Knowledge test. The only other entering student characteristics to carry significant positive weights
in the prediction of all three NTE scores are the student's high
school GPA, the importance assigned to "raising a family," and
the expectation to change career choice during college. High
school GPA receives much greater weight than do these other
two variables. The student's self-rating on academic ability adds
significantly to the prediction of General Knowledge and Professional Knowledge scores, while self-rating on writing ability adds
to the prediction of Communication Skills scores. Gender has an
interesting pattern of effects on the test scores. As for most of
the other test scores discussed above, being a woman is negatively
associated with performance on the General Knowledge test, after
other input variables have been controlled. However, being a
woman contributes *positively* to the prediction of performance on
both the Communication Skills and Professional Knowledge tests.
These findings suggest an interesting possibility: Since these two
tests are designed to measure competency in classroom teaching — a field that is heavily populated by women — is it possible
that women give higher priority than do the men to the development of these particular skills during college?

Several other input variables carry negative weights in
the prediction of performance on the NTE tests. Performance
on each of the three tests is negatively affected by three variables: student commitment to "being very well off financially,"
indicating "to improve reading and study skills" as an important reason for attending college, and aspiring to a career as
an engineer at the time of freshman entry into college. This last
variable suggests that dropouts from engineering who go into
teaching do not perform as well on the NTE test as would be
expected from their SAT scores.

Choosing a career in secondary education at the time of college entry has a positive effect on the General Knowledge test, but majoring in education has a small negative effect. Majoring in education has a substantial positive effect, however, on Professional Knowledge test scores. Scores on both the General Knowledge test and the Professional Knowledge test are negatively affected by selecting a freshman major in either math or the humanities, while performance on the Professional Knowledge test is negatively affected by majoring in either biological science or fine arts.

The one institutional characteristic that has significant positive effects on all three NTE test scores is institutional size. The percentage of expenditures invested in student services has weak negative effects on both the General and Professional Knowledge tests, while student-faculty ratio has a weak negative effect on the General Knowledge test. The Communication Skills test produces two weak effects with environmental variables: percentage of graduate students (positive), and percentage of black students in the student body (negative).

Why size should impact positively on NTE scores is not clear. It is true that, in this particular sample, the larger institutions enrolled the better-prepared students: the simple correlations between size and NTE scores of .18 (General Knowledge), .17 (Communication Skills), and .11 (Professional Knowledge) are reduced to .07, .06, and .05, respectively, when SAT scores are controlled. Thus, it may be that size is acting as a kind of proxy for the Intellectual Self-Esteem or SES of the peer group.

All students were sent the 1989 follow-up questionnaire, together with a special questionnaire containing items of interest to teacher educators and the National Education Association. Usable follow-up responses were obtained from the following numbers: 1,099 (General Knowledge test), 1,033 (Communication Skills test), and 980 (Professional Knowledge test). All analyses of the possible effects of involvement and intermediate outcome variables are necessarily limited to these smaller samples.

The strongest association between NTE scores and any involvement or intermediate outcome measure involves undergraduate GPA. Once again, we have evidence that the student's undergraduate GPA is a reflection, at least in part, of what he or she learned in college. The only other involvement variables showing positive associations with all three NTE tests are hours per week spent studying or doing homework, and enrolling in interdisciplinary courses.

Two other involvement variables show negative associations with all three NTE tests, after the effects of entering student and environmental variables are controlled: taking remedial or developmental courses, and receiving tutoring in courses. Both these involvement measures may be the *result* of poor performance, rather than the cause of it.

The NTE General Knowledge test shows positive associations with several additional involvement measures: majoring in history or political science, discussing political or social issues, and getting married while in college. Involvement variables showing negative associations with General Knowledge scores include working on an independent research project, talking with faculty outside of class, and playing intercollegiate football or basketball. Again, we have evidence that participation in intercollegiate sports (in this case, the major sports of football or basketball) may contribute negatively to the development of the student's cognitive skills.

Performance on the Communication Skills test is also positively associated with discussing racial or ethnic issues and negatively associated with giving presentations in class and assisting faculty in teaching a course. Scores on the Professional Knowledge test are also negatively associated with assisting faculty in teaching courses and talking with faculty outside of class.

Summary of Standardized Test Results

Are there any consistent patterns in the environmental variables that affect students' performance on standardized tests? Table 7.2 summarizes the results. At least two patterns stand out. First is the tendency for students to "learn what they study": quantitative and analytical skills are enhanced by majoring in math,

Table 7.2. Summary of Environmental Variables
Affecting Performance on Standardized Tests.

Test Score	Positively Affected by	Negatively Affected by
GRE Verbal	Major: social science Peers: percentage in history or political science Personalized or individualized curriculum Peers: Intellectual Self-Esteem Faculty: Research Orientation	Structured curriculum
	(Involvement measures)[a] Reading for pleasure Foreign-language courses Science courses	Volunteer work Group class projects Intercollegiate athletics Being tutored Major: biological science Faculty: percentage who are women
GRE Quantitative	Major: science Major: engineering Major: technical (other) Use of personal savings Faculty: Research Orientation Peers: Intellectual Self-Esteem Institutional size Peers: percentage who are Asians Written evaluations Faculty: percentage in science Competition among students Institutional Diversity Emphasis	
	(Involvement measures)[a] Math courses Tutoring others	Writing courses

Table 7.2. Summary of Environmental Variables
Affecting Performance on Standardized Tests, cont'd.

Test Score	Positively Affected by	Negatively Affected by
GRE Analytical	Major: physical science Use of teaching assistants (Involvement measures)[a] Socializing	 Personal counseling
MCAT	Peers: Intellectual Self-Esteem Women's or gender studies course Use of personal savings Peers: percentage who are Asians Competition among students Faculty: percentage teaching general education courses (Involvement measures)[a]	Major: allied health Work-study grant Women's college Faculty: age Faculty: positive attitude toward general education Personal counseling Attending religious services Student clubs or organizations
LSAT	Peers: Intellectual Self-Esteem "Progressive" general education curriculum Peers: percentage in social sciences Faculty: Research Orientation (Involvement measures)[a] Socializing Interdisciplinary courses	 Being tutored Intercollegiate athletics
NTE General Knowledge	Career: teacher Institutional size	Major: education Major: math

Table 7.2. Summary of Environmental Variables
Affecting Performance on Standardized Tests, cont'd.

Test Score	Positively Affected by	Negatively Affected by
	Major: history or political science	Major: humanities Percentage of all expenditures on student services Student-faculty ratio
	(Involvement measures)[a] Studying or homework Discussing social issues Getting married Interdisciplinary courses	Independent research Talking with faculty Intercollegiate football or basketball Taking remedial courses Receiving tutoring
NTE Communication Skills	Institutional size Peers: percentage who are graduate students	Peers: percentage who are African Americans
	(Involvement measures)[a] Discussing racial or ethnic issues Interdisciplinary courses	Class presentations Assisting faculty in teaching Taking remedial courses Receiving tutoring
NTE Professional Knowledge	Major: education Institutional size	Major: math Major: humanities Major: biological science Major: fine arts Percentage of all expenditures on student services
	(Involvement measures)[a] Interdisciplinary courses	Taking remedial courses Receiving tutoring Assisting faculty in teaching Talking with faculty

[a]Since the temporal ordering of outcome and involvement measures cannot be precisely determined, causal interpretations should be made with caution.

science, or engineering, verbal skills by majoring in social science, professional knowledge in school teaching by majoring in education, and so forth. Second is the apparent effect of the peer group. Three closely related peer group characteristics are found to affect all test scores except the NTE*: Intellectual Self-Esteem, SES, and competitiveness (this last measure is based on faculty perceptions). Performance on three tests — the GRE Verbal, GRE Quantitative, and LSAT — is also positively affected by a closely related faculty characteristic: Research Orientation. Two of these variables — peer SES and Intellectual Self-Esteem — are from environmental cluster III ("SES, Social Science, and Selectivity") and the other two — Research Orientation and Competitiveness — are from environmental cluster II (Research versus Student Orientation) (see Chapter Two). Taken together, this pattern suggests that performance on standardized tests is enhanced in a highly competitive environment.

Especially interesting about this last conclusion is that, with the exception of peer SES (see Chapters Ten and Twelve), none of these "competitive" variables seems to impact positively on any other student outcome or set of outcomes, including the other cognitive outcomes examined in this chapter. In other words, performance on standardized tests is enhanced by a very different kind of college environment than is the case with other cognitive and affective outcomes.

Growth in Knowledge and Intellectual Skills

While we were fortunate in being able to retrieve data on the SAT and ACT taken before entry to college, as well as on the graduate and professional admissions and competency tests taken four years later, the ideal study of college impact on cognitive development would also include before-and-after assessments of such specific skills as critical thinking, problem-solving ability, and knowledge of a discipline. The extraordinary cost

---

*Because the institutional sample for the NTE was quite different and the methodology used in analyzing NTE scores was slightly different (see Opp, 1991), the results are difficult to compare with GRE, MCAT, and LSAT results.

of administering tests to measure such skills makes the collection of input and outcome data of this type impractical, especially in a national study on the scale of this one. One simple alternative is to ask the students themselves to estimate how much cognitive change has occurred between input and outcome. For a number of years, we have been doing this with our annual follow-up surveys by an item which reads: "Compared with when you entered college as a freshman, how would you now describe your_____?" In the 1989 follow-up questionnaire, this statement is followed by a list of nineteen skills and talents. For each skill or talent, students indicate whether they believe their current (outcome) level, compared to their freshman (input) level, is much stronger (5), stronger (4), no change (3), weaker (2), much weaker (1).

Such "quick-and-dirty" assessments of value-added or talent development (Astin, 1991) are clearly not as valid as actual before-and-after assessments of input and output skill levels. However, recent studies indicate that self-estimates of gain do have some modest validity when compared against actual pretest–posttest changes in performance (Anaya, 1992). To reduce the nineteen items describing different areas of knowledge and skill to a more manageable number, we performed a factor analysis that was only partially successful. Two of the resulting factors, Overall Academic Development and Cultural Awareness, were judged to be useful and were therefore included in several regression analyses (see below). However, because many of the nineteen individual skill items are not well reflected in these two factors but are of particular relevance to the goals of a liberal education, we decided to do separate regression analyses on eleven of these items: general knowledge, knowledge of a particular field or discipline, ability to think critically, analytical and problem-solving skills, writing skills, foreign-language skills, public speaking ability, leadership abilities, interpersonal skills, preparation for graduate or professional school, and job-related skills.

Table 7.3 shows the proportions of students reporting that each specific area of knowledge or skill is "much stronger" in 1989 than when they first entered college in 1985. Much greater

Table 7.3. Self-Reported Growth
in Knowledge and Skills During College.

Knowledge or Skill	Percentage Reporting "Much Stronger" in 1989 Than 1985
Knowledge of a particular field	60.5
General knowledge	49.3
Ability to think critically	38.8
Interpersonal skills	37.1
Analytical and problem-solving skills	32.5
Job-related skills	32.5
Leadership abilities	30.8
Writing skills	27.6
Public speaking ability	24.6
Preparation for graduate or professional school	22.7
Foreign-language skills	8.1

Note: Weighted national norms (abstracted from Wingard, Treviño, Dey, and Korn, 1991).

growth is reported for "knowledge" than for "skill." Given that students generally take more courses in their majors than in any other fields, it is not surprising that "knowledge of a particular field" shows the largest increase. Bringing up the rear in terms of the amount of growth reported are writing skills, public speaking ability, and especially foreign-language skills (fewer than one student in ten reports that foreign-language skills are much stronger in 1989 than in 1985). In the following sections, we will report the major findings from the regression analyses involving each of these items, as well as the regression results for the two factor scores, Overall Academic Development and Cultural Awareness.

Before considering the results of the regression analyses involving self-reported growth measures, a comment about the overall regression results with "involvement" variables is in order. First, every strictly "cognitive" or "academic" outcome except foreign-language ability is significantly associated with hours per week studying or doing homework (after the effects of entering student characteristics, environmental characteristics, and years of college completed are controlled). In other words, the only outcomes not associated with hours spent studying are interpersonal skills, leadership abilities, public speaking ability, foreign-language ability, and Cultural Awareness. Among other things, these results suggest strongly that involvement in academic work pays off in terms of greater growth in all cognitive areas.

A second general trend concerns the partial correlations of self-reported growth with another intermediate outcome, undergraduate GPA. After all input and environmental effects are controlled, the student's GPA is associated with every academic or cognitive outcome (including foreign-language skills), but not with Cultural Awareness, public speaking ability, leadership ability, and interpersonal skills.

Finally, years of college completed has significant positive correlations with *every* area of self-reported growth except foreign language. These findings suggest strongly that the effects of college are cumulative: the more years of college one completes, the greater the growth. (In this connection, the reader should be reminded once again that, in each regression analysis reported in this and other results chapters, the effects of years of college completed are *first* controlled, before the correlations between involvement variables and outcomes are computed.)

These results with involvement measures also suggest that the self-reports have some validity, for the following reasons: (1) research on cognitive learning shows that the amount learned is proportionate to "time on task" (that is, hours spent studying and number of years completed), and (2) results reported earlier in this chapter show that undergraduate GPA is also correlated with *actual* cognitive growth as pretested and posttested with standardized tests.

General Knowledge

After entering freshman characteristics are controlled, only three environmental variables show significant partial correlations with self-reported growth in general knowledge: positive effects are associated with Socioeconomic Status of the student's peer group and with the faculty perceptual variable, Social Activism and Community Orientation, and a negative effect is associated with majoring in education. The last finding, which replicates the effect of majoring in education on *tested* general knowledge (see NTE results, discussed earlier), reinforces the commonly held view that majoring in education shortchanges the student's general educational development.

The positive effect of Peer SES on growth in general knowledge, coupled with its positive effect on MCAT performance (discussed earlier), raises an interesting question. Could it be that students from highly educated and affluent families simply have more general knowledge and information that they pass on to each other during the undergraduate years? (See Chapters Ten and Twelve for a fuller discussion of this possibility.)

A number of involvement variables other than GPA and hours per week spent studying have significant residual correlations with self-rated growth in general knowledge, after the effects of input characteristics, environmental variables, and number of years completed have been controlled. Growth in general knowledge is associated with number of courses taken that emphasize writing skills, science or scientific inquiry, and history or historical analysis. Positive correlations are also found with having class papers critiqued by instructors, discussing racial or ethnic issues, and, somewhat surprisingly, alcohol consumption. General knowledge is the only area of academic development associated with this involvement variable. A somewhat far-fetched interpretation of this finding is that the students might enhance their fund of general knowledge and information by means of the lengthy conversations that frequently accompany social drinking. While the size of the correlation is quite small (partial Beta = .04), it is highly significant statistically ($p < .0005$) and certainly warrants further investigation.

Knowledge of a Particular Field or Discipline

Only three environmental variables show significant effects on self-reported growth in knowledge of a particular field or discipline, and all relationships are weak and positive: majoring in either education or nursing, and the percentage of women on the faculty. It is interesting that education shows a positive effect on knowledge of a field or discipline and a negative effect on general knowledge (above). Are education students speaking here of the "field" of education, or of the subject matter fields in which they plan to teach? These data provide no real basis for answering such a question, but the current controversy over the issue of whether teachers-in-training should major in education or in a subject matter field suggests that this finding merits further investigation. Opp (1991) failed to find any consistent effect of majoring in education on NTE performance.

Self-reported growth in knowledge of a particular field or discipline is positively associated with a number of other involvement variables besides GPA and hours spent studying. The strongest positive correlations are with number of science courses taken, hours per week talking with faculty outside of class, giving presentations in class, and having class papers critiqued by instructors. Weaker positive correlations are with hours per week spent attending classes or labs, working on group projects for a class, enrolling in interdisciplinary courses, participating in a college internship program, and socializing with persons from different racial or ethnic groups. Participating in intramural sports has a weak negative correlation with growth in knowledge of a field or discipline.

Ability to Think Critically

The environmental variable showing the strongest positive effect on self-reported growth in ability to think critically is the Humanities Orientation of the institution. This effect is of particular interest, given the great importance that most liberal arts faculty place on developing students' critical thinking abilities. Recall the variables that make up the Humanities Orientation factor: an emphasis on teaching the classics of Western Civilization, heavy faculty involvement in teaching general education courses, the use of essay exams and multiple drafts of written work as evaluation techniques, and a weak emphasis on preparing undergraduates for employment (see Chapter Two). Other environmental factors showing positive effects on critical thinking include Peer SES and Student Orientation of the faculty.

The suggestion that critical thinking skills are enhanced by an emphasis on writing skills is further reinforced by the other involvement measures (besides GPA and hours spent studying) that show significant residual correlations with self-reported growth in critical thinking ability: the strongest correlation is with the number of courses taken that emphasize the development of writing skills. Other involvement variables showing positive associations with this outcome include having class papers critiqued by instructors, number of science courses taken, number of history courses taken, giving presentations in class, being a guest in a professor's home, hours per week spent discussing racial or ethnic issues, enrolling in interdisciplinary courses, and receiving vocational or career counseling. While we cannot be sure of the direction of causation involved in all of these measures, they provide some provocative clues about possible pedagogical strategies that are likely to enhance critical thinking: a strong emphasis on writing, a content focus on science and history, an interdisciplinary emphasis, and active engagement by the student in discussion, debate, class presentations, and talking over vocational and career plans.

Analytical and Problem-Solving Skills

As might be expected, self-reported growth in analytical and problem-solving skills is positively affected by majoring in either engineering or physical science. Negative effects are associated with majoring in either education or the arts. Other environmental variables showing significant positive effects include Student-Oriented Faculty, a positive faculty attitude toward the general education program, and the Artistic Inclination of the student peer group. Why majoring in the arts should have a negative effect and having an Artistically Inclined peer group should have a positive effect is puzzling. The magnitude of these contrasting effects is quite small, but they are highly significant statistically ($p < .0005$), suggesting that they merit further investigation. As we are dealing here with *self-reported* growth measures, the reader should keep in mind the possibility that people in different fields (for example, the arts versus the sciences) may interpret qualities such as analytical skills differently.

Besides GPA and hours spent studying, the involvement measure having the strongest residual association with self-reported growth in analytical and problem-solving skills is the number of courses taken that emphasize mathematics or numerical analysis. Other substantial positive correlations include having class papers critiqued by instructors, working on a group project for a class, and the number of science courses taken. Small positive correlations involve receiving vocational or career counseling, tutoring other students, enrolling in honors programs, using a personal computer, discussing racial or ethnic issues, and student-faculty interaction.

Writing Skills

Self-reported improvement in writing skills is most strongly affected by the Humanities Orientation of the institution. Positive effects are also associated with majoring in psychology, social sciences, or the arts and humanities, whereas a substantial negative effect is associated with majoring in engineering. Other positive effects on writing skills include a Student-Oriented Faculty, a general education program that includes progressive course offerings, having need-based financial aid, and the percentage of institutional expenditures devoted to student services. As would be expected, the other involvement variables (besides GPA and hours spent studying) showing the strongest partial correlations with self-reported improvements in writing skills are number of writing-skills courses taken (partial Beta = .31) and having class papers critiqued by instructors (partial Beta = .12). Other positive associations include taking essay exams, receiving vocational or career counseling, discussing racial or ethnic issues, and hours per week spent using a personal computer. The last finding suggests that the use of word processors may well enhance a student's writing skills.

Overall Academic Development

The factor analysis of the nineteen items describing different areas of self-reported growth in knowledge and skills yielded a factor that we shall call Overall Academic Development. Its highest-loading items (in parentheses) are from the five specific areas just discussed: ability to think critically (.65), analytical and problem-solving skills (.61), general knowledge (.54), knowledge of a particular field or discipline (.51), and writing skills (.37). The score on Overall Academic Development is obtained simply by summing the student's responses to these five items. Although the findings are to some extent redundant to what has already been reported, it is still useful to see which environmental and involvement variables carry the greatest weight when we look at growth in these five areas simultaneously.

Only two environmental variables show positive effects on Overall Academic Development: Student-Oriented Faculty and Peer SES. A number of involvement variables, however, show significant partial correlations with Overall Academic Development, once the effects of entering student and environmental characteristics and years completed have been controlled. Strongest among these are GPA, hours per week spent studying or doing homework, having class papers critiqued by instructors, number of science courses taken, and number of writing-skills courses taken. Other positive associations involve working on group projects for a class, discussing racial or ethnic issues, number of history courses and of math or numerical courses taken, receiving vocational or career counseling, socializing with persons from different racial or ethnic groups, enrolling in interdisciplinary courses, giving presentations in class, tutoring other students, and alcohol consumption.

Cultural Awareness

The factor analysis also yielded an interesting "doublet" factor involving high loadings from only two variables: "cultural awareness and appreciation" (loading = .83) and "acceptance of persons from different races and cultures" (loading = .59). The student's Cultural Awareness score thus consists of the simple sum of responses to these two questions. That self-reported growth in Cultural Awareness is positively affected by going away from home to attend college reinforces the idea that one of the benefits of the residential experience is allowing the student to become familiar with a greater variety of racial and cultural groups. A similar argument can be made to explain the positive effect on Cultural Awareness of having a college work-study assignment; that is, having an on-campus job would tend to bring the student into contact with a wider variety of fellow students and staff.

The strongest positive effects on Cultural Awareness, however, are associated with two environmental measures from the faculty survey: Faculty Diversity Orientation and Institutional Diversity Emphasis. The Materialism and Status of the peer group, on the other hand, has a negative effect on Cultural Awareness. Also producing negative effects is majoring in any of three fields of study: engineering, physical science, and business. These negative effects reinforce the belief that peers and faculty in the sciences, engineering, and business give low priority to issues of Cultural Awareness and diversity.

The involvement measures having the strongest partial correlations with self-reported increases in Cultural Awareness all have to do with "diversity" issues: discussing racial or ethnic issues, attending racial or cultural awareness workshops, socializing with people from different racial or ethnic groups, and enrolling in ethnic studies courses. Weaker positive effects are associated with participating in a study-abroad program, hours per week spent attending religious services, number of history courses taken, and holding a part-time job on campus (other than work-study). Two involvement measures produce negative partial correlations with Cultural Awareness: hours per week spent watching television, and working full-time while enrolled as a student. Both of these activities may limit students' exposure to persons from other cultures. It is also interesting to consider the possibility that the *content* of television programming might also have something to do with this negative effect (the effects of television will be discussed in much greater detail in Chapter Eleven).

Foreign-Language Skills

Not surprisingly, the student's major field of study shows many significant effects on self-reported growth in foreign-language skills. Positive effects are associated with majoring in either the social sciences or the arts and humanities, whereas negative effects are associated with majoring in engineering, nursing, or the health professions.

The sheer concentration of students in the field of engineering (a peer group measure) also shows significant negative effects on foreign-language skills, over and above the effects of majoring in engineering. These effects, however, are nonlinear: having a very high concentration of students in engineering (over 28 percent) is negatively associated with the development of foreign-language skills, whereas having no students majoring in engineering has a positive effect. Concentrations of students between 1 percent and 28 percent produce inconsistent effects.

The student's perceived growth in foreign-language skills is also positively affected by two faculty measures (Liberalism, and having a positive attitude toward the institution's general educational program) and by two peer group measures (SES, and the percentage of born-again Christians in the student body — one wonders whether this finding might not reflect the tendency of some evangelical colleges to encourage their undergraduates to engage in missionary work in foreign countries). One other peer measure, Permissiveness, has a negative effect on self-reported growth in the foreign-language skills. Could it be that this last effect reflects (inversely) the considerable self-discipline required to master a foreign language?

The involvement variable showing the strongest residual correlation with self-reported growth in foreign-language skills is the number of foreign languages taken. The partial Beta of .65 (after entering student and environmental variables and number of years completed are controlled) is the largest in the entire study. Indeed, the fact that the partial Beta coefficient is almost the same size as the simple correlation ($r = .64$) suggests that this is truly a causal relationship (see Astin, 1991, Appendix A). Again, we find support for the truism "students learn what they study."

Other involvement variables showing significant positive correlations with self-reported growth in foreign-language skill include participation in a study-abroad program, and hours per week spent attending religious services.

Public Speaking Ability

The environmental measure having the strongest effect on self-reported increases in public speaking ability (in this case, a negative effect) is Research Orientation. The positive effect that majoring in education has on self-reported growth in public speaking ability may reflect the effects of practice in teaching. Most of the other environmental effects, however, do not lend themselves readily to interpretation. For example, public speaking ability is negatively affected by majoring in science and by the percentage of students who hold merit-based aid, and positively affected by the use of multiple-choice tests. These particular effects are small in magnitude but highly significant statistically ($p < .0005$).

The involvement measures having significant residual associations with self-reported improvement in public speaking ability make much more sense: giving presentations in class (partial Beta = .24), hours per week spent participating in student clubs and organizations, being elected to a student office, working on a group project for a class, number of writing-skills courses taken, and hours per week spent talking with faculty outside of class. Growth in public speaking ability is negatively associated with participating in a study-abroad program and hours per week spent watching television.

Leadership Abilities

The strongest positive effect on self-reported growth in leadership abilities is associated with going away from home to attend college. This finding is consistent with the results for the Leadership personality measure (Chapter Four) and for being elected to a student office (Chapter Six). Other positive effects include attending a women's college, and the percentage of students majoring in the physical sciences. (The last finding may reflect the effect of attending a service academy, since these institutions have a very high percentage of students majoring in physical sciences.) The effect of women's colleges is also consistent with results on being elected to a student office (see Chapter Six). Variables that impact negatively on self-reported improvements in leadership abilities include the use of graduate teaching assistants, the Humanities Orientation of the institution, the concentration of student majors in English, and the peer measure Outside Work.

The three involvement variables showing the strongest residual correlations with self-reported growth in leadership abilities are hours per week spent in student clubs or organizations, being elected to a student office, and giving presentations in class. Other positive associations involve working on a group project for a class, tutoring other students, hours per week spent in exercise or sports, receiving vocational or career counseling, attending racial or cultural awareness workshops, being a member of a social fraternity or sorority, socializing with students from different racial or ethnic groups, and the number of writing-skills courses taken. Like growth in public speaking ability, growth in leadership abilities is negatively associated with participating in a study-abroad program, and hours per week watching television. Almost all of these findings are, once again, consistent with the results reported earlier for the Leadership personality measure (Chapter Four) and being elected to a student office (Chapter Six).

Interpersonal Skills

Environmental variables associated with self-reported growth in interpersonal skills are similar to those associated with leadership abilities. Self-reported growth in interpersonal skills is positively affected by going away from home to attend college and negatively affected by reliance on graduate teaching assistants. Majoring in business also has a weak positive effect on growth in interpersonal skills.

Nearly all involvement variables showing significant residual associations with self-reported growth in interpersonal skills have to do with student-student interaction: hours per week spent in student clubs or organizations, working on group projects for a class, hours per week spent visiting with friends, giving presentations in class, socializing with students from different racial or ethnic groups, participating in a college internship program, participating in intramural sports, discussing racial or ethnic issues, and hours per week spent partying. Number of writing-skills courses taken also shows a positive residual association with interpersonal skills, whereas hours per week spent watching television and participation in a study-abroad program both show negative correlations.

These results with leadership abilities and public speaking skills suggest a corollary to the "you learn what you study" principle: "you learn what you do." Practically all the environmental variables associated with these two growth measures have to do with interpersonal interaction.

Preparation for Graduate or Professional School

Three environmental variables show weak positive effects on self-reported increases in preparation for graduate or professional school: Student-Oriented Faculty, Peer SES, and going away from home to attend college. A weak negative effect is associated with the percentage of students majoring in agriculture.

Nearly all the involvement measures showing significant partial correlations with this outcome measure are academic in nature: GPA, hours per week spent studying or doing homework, number of science courses taken, number of writing-skills courses taken, having class papers critiqued by instructors, enrolling in honors programs, hours per week spent talking with faculty outside of class, tutoring other students, enrolling in interdisciplinary courses, giving presentations in class, working on an independent research project, and working on a professor's research project. Self-reported increases in preparation for graduate or professional school are also positively associated with receiving vocational/career counseling.

Job-Related Skills

It is perhaps to be expected that self-reported improvements in job-related skills would be affected by the student's major field of study. Positive effects are associated with majoring in the professional fields of nursing, education, and engineering, and negative affects are associated with choosing social science and biological science majors. All the other environmental variables showing significant effects on growth in job-related skills are negative: the percentage of students majoring in either social science or biological science, having a general education curriculum that is either personalized and individualized or highly structured, and the percentage of the faculty holding Ph.D.s (institutional scores on this last variable would tend to be low in colleges or universities that offer many programs in applied fields).

A number of involvement variables show significant positive correlations with self-reported improvements in job-related skills, once the effects of entering student and environmental variables and years of college completed have been controlled. Positive correlations occur with working on group projects for a class, participating in a college internship program, receiving vocational or career counseling, holding a part-time job on campus, hours per week studying or doing homework, giving presentations in class, number of math or numerical courses taken, socializing with persons from different racial or ethnic groups, hours per week spent working for pay, and hours per week spent talking with the faculty outside of class. Job-related skills are negatively associated with three involvement measures: taking essay exams, participating in a study-abroad program, and hours per week spent watching television.

Table 7.4 summarizes the environmental variables affecting reported self-growth. Once again, we find confirmation of the finding that "people learn what they study": general knowledge is enhanced by taking science and history courses, critical thinking is enhanced by taking science and history courses, analytical and problem-solving skills are enhanced by taking math and science courses, foreign-language skills are enhanced by taking foreign-language courses, and so forth. What is also of interest are the widespread positive effects of peer SES, taking courses that emphasize writing skills, and taking interdisciplinary courses. The possible significance of these patterns is discussed at greater length in Chapters Ten, Eleven, and Twelve.

Table 7.4. Summary of Environmental Effects
on Self-Reported Growth.

Growth in	Positively Affected by	Negatively Affected by

General knowledge	Peer SES
	Social Activism and
	  Community
	  Orientation
		Major: education

	(Involvement measures)[a] Studying or homework Writing courses Science courses History courses Having papers critiqued by instructors Alcohol consumption	

Knowledge of field
  or discipline
	Major: education
	Major: nursing
	Faculty: percentage
	  who are women	

	(Involvement measures)[a]
	Studying or homework
	Science courses
	Talking with faculty
	Having papers critiqued
	  by instructors
	Number of classes taken
	Group class projects
	Interdisciplinary courses
	College internship
	Socializing with stu-
	  dents from different
	  racial or ethnic groups
		Intramural sports

Critical thinking ability	Humanities Orientation Peer SES Faculty Student Orientation	
	(Involvement measures)[a] Studying or homework Writing courses Having papers critiqued by instructors Science courses History courses Class presentations	

Table 7.4. Summary of Environmental Effects
on Self-Reported Growth, cont'd.

Growth in	Positively Affected by	Negatively Affected by
	Being guest in professor's home Discussing racial or ethnic issues Interdisiciplinary courses Career counseling	
Analytical and problem-solving skills	Major: science Major: engineering Faculty Student Orientation Faculty: positive attitude toward general education program Peers: Artistic Inclination	Major: education Major: fine arts
	(Involvement measures)[a] Studying or homework Math courses Having papers critiqued by instructors Group class projects Science courses Career counseling Tutoring others Honors program Using a personal computer Discussing racial or ethnic issues Student-faculty interaction	
Writing skills	Humanities Orientation Major: psychology Major: social science Major: arts and humanities Faculty Student Orientation "Progressive" general education curriculum Need-based aid	Major: engineering

Table 7.4. Summary of Environmental Effects
on Self-Reported Growth, cont'd.

Growth in	Positively Affected by	Negatively Affected by
	Percentage of all expenditures on student services	
	(Involvement measures)[a] Studying or homework Writing courses Having papers critiqued by instructors Taking essay exams Career counseling Discussing racial or ethnic issues Using a personal computer	
Cultural Awareness	Faculty Diversity Orientation Institutional Diversity Emphasis Leaving home to attend college Work-study aid	Peers: Materialism and Status Major: engineering Major: business Major: physical science
	(Involvement measures)[a] "Diversity" activities[b] Study abroad Attending religious services History courses Part-time campus job	Watching television Working full-time
Foreign-language skills	Major: social science Major: arts and humanities Faculty Liberalism Faculty: positive attitude toward general education program Peer SES Peers: percentage who are born-again Christians	Major: engineering Major: nursing Major: allied health professions Peers: percentage in engineering Peers: Permissiveness
	(Involvement measures)[a] Foreign-language courses	

Table 7.4. Summary of Environmental Effects on Self-Reported Growth, cont'd.

Growth in	Positively Affected by	Negatively Affected by
	Study abroad Attending religious services	
Public speaking ability	Major: education Taking multiple-choice exams	Faculty Research Orientation Major: science Peers: percentage with merit-based aid
	(Involvement measures)[a] Class presentations Student clubs and organizations Being elected to student office Group class projects Writing courses Talking with faculty	Study abroad Watching television
Leadership abilities	Leaving home to attend college Women's college Peers: percentage in physical science	Use of teaching assistants Humanities Orientation Peers: percentage who are in English Peers: Outside Work
	(Involvement measures)[a] Student clubs and organizations Being elected to student office Class presentations Group class projects Tutoring others Exercise Career counseling Fraternity or sorority membership Writing courses "Diversity" activities[b]	Study abroad Watching television
Interpersonal skills	Leaving home to attend college	Use of teaching assistants Major: business

**Table 7.4. Summary of Environmental Effects
on Self-Reported Growth, cont'd.**

Growth in	Positively Affected by	Negatively Affected by
	(Involvement measures)[a]	
	Student-student interaction	Watching television
	Writing courses	Study abroad
Preparation for graduate or professional school	Faculty Student Orientation	
	Peer SES	
	Leaving home to attend college	
	(Involvement measures)[a]	
	Studying or homework	
	Science courses	
	Writing courses	
	Having papers critiqued by instructors	
	Honors program	
	Tutoring others	
	Interdisicplinary courses	
	Class presentations	
	Student-faculty interaction	
	Career counseling	
Job-related skills	Major: nursing	Major: social science
	Major: education	Major: biological science
	Major: engineering	Peers: percentage in social science
		Peers: percentage in biological science
		Personalized and individualized general education program
		Highly structured general education program
		Faculty: percentage with Ph.D.s
	(Involvement measures)[a]	
	Group class projects	Taking essay exams
	College internship	Study abroad
	Career counseling	Watching television

Table 7.4. Summary of Environmental Effects
on Self-Reported Growth, cont'd.

Growth in	Positively Affected by	Negatively Affected by
	Part-time campus job	
	Studying or homework	
	Class presentations	
	Math courses	
	Socializing with students from different racial or ethnic groups	
	Working for pay	
	Talking with faculty	

[a]Since the temporal ordering of outcome and involvement measures cannot be precisely determined, causal interpretations should be made with caution.
[b]Includes activities such as discussing racial or ethnic issues, socializing with students from different racial or ethnic groups, participating in campus demonstrations, attending racial or ethnic workshops, and taking women's studies or ethnic studies courses.

Summary and Discussion

Not only is cognitive development a multidimensional phenomenon, there are also multiple ways of measuring it: gains in test scores, self-reported gains, and actual achievement. In this chapter, we have looked at several dimensions of cognitive development, using a variety of measurement techniques.

Students get substantially lower grades in college than they do in high school. Factors that contribute to even lower grades include attending a public institution or an institution where the peer group has very high Intellectual Self-Esteem (such institutions also tend to be highly selective). Factors that impact positively on grades include majoring in education, the arts, or the humanities and having merit-based financial aid.

Although the college GPA has been subjected to a great deal of criticism over the years (this writer has been one of those critics; see Astin, 1991), it should be pointed out that undergraduate GPA is positively related to nearly all measures of cognitive and academic growth covered in this chapter, *even after the effects of all other input, environmental, and involvement measures have been controlled.* What this tells us is that the GPA, despite its limitations, appears to reflect the student's actual learning and growth during the undergraduate years.

Retention in college (degree attainment) is enhanced by a number of factors reported in earlier studies: the residential experience, and student involvement with peers and with faculty. A number of environmental variables not available in earlier studies also have positive effects on retention: the Science Preparation and SES of the peer group, and the Student Orientation and Humanities Orientation of the faculty. Retention is negatively affected by institutional size and by working full-time, working part-time off campus, and commuting.

Enrollment in graduate or professional school is also affected positively by having merit-based aid, by attending an institution with a Student-Oriented Faculty, and by frequent student-faculty contact. Like retention, graduate school attendance is negatively affected by institutional size.

Scores on standardized tests used for admission to graduate and professional school (GRE, LSAT, MCAT) and for professional certification (NTE) are predicted with considerable accuracy from college admissions tests taken four years earlier (SAT, ACT). Small but highly significant effects on test performance are associated with a variety of environmental variables, including the peer environment, the major, and the number of courses taken in various fields of study. The two environmental measures that seem to have the most consistent positive effects on standardized test performance are the Intellectual Self-Esteem of the student's peer group and the Research Orientation of the faculty.

Majoring in professional fields such as education, business, and nursing does not have negative effects on GRE, LSAT, or MCAT scores, suggesting that Adelman's finding (1984) that students majoring in these fields get low scores on such tests is attributable to uncontrolled "inputs": we find similar correlations in our own sample, but the correlations disappear when SAT and ACT scores are controlled.

Self-reported gains in most areas of cognitive functioning are positively affected by two environmental measures:

Student-Oriented Faculty, and Peer SES. The Humanities Orientation has positive effects on self-reported gains in critical thinking and writing skills, and a negative effect on growth in leadership abilities. Majoring in engineering has positive effects on self-reported growth in analytical and problem-solving skills and job-related skills, and negative effects on growth in writing skills and Cultural Awareness. Majoring in education, on the other hand, has a positive effect on self-reported growth in knowledge of a field or discipline, and negative effects on growth in general knowledge and analytical and problem-solving skills.

Some of the most fascinating results concern the partial correlations of self-reported growth measures with involvement measures. While causal interpretations of these patterns must be made with some caution, they are highly suggestive. For example, the number of courses taken that emphasize the development of writing skills is positively associated with self-reported growth, not only in most of the academic or cognitive areas (general Overall Academic Development, critical thinking, writing, general knowledge, preparation for graduate school) but also in several affective areas: public speaking, Leadership, and interpersonal skills. This pattern certainly reinforces the idea that the current emphasis on "writing across the curriculum" is a positive force in undergraduate education today.

A closely related involvement measure is "having class papers critiqued by instructors." This measure, which implies not only that students are being given writing assignments but also that they are receiving direct feedback from faculty, has positive partial correlations (beyond the effect of number of writing-skills courses taken) with most academic outcomes: general knowledge, knowledge of a field or discipline, analytical and problem-solving skills, writing skills, preparation for graduate or professional school, and Overall Academic Development. Having class papers critiqued, however, is not associated with affective growth areas, once the effects of the number of writing-skills courses taken are controlled.

Number of science courses taken has an almost identical pattern: positive partial correlations with self-reported growth in general knowledge, knowledge of specific field or discipline, critical thinking ability, analytical and problem-solving skills, Overall Academic Development, and preparation for graduate or professional school. Once again, this involvement measure shows no significant correlations with affective outcomes.

The number of courses taken that emphasize math or numerical analysis is positively associated with growth in analytical and problem-solving skills, job-related skills, and Overall Academic Development, but is negatively associated with the development of writing skills.

Participating in group projects for a class shows a very different pattern of partial correlations with self-reported growth: positive effects on public speaking ability, Leadership, interpersonal skills, knowledge of a particular field or discipline, and Overall Academic Development, but negative effects on SAT Verbal scores and enrollment in graduate school. Number of history courses taken shows a mix of positive partial correlations: general knowledge, critical thinking, Overall Academic Development, and Cultural Awareness.

But certainly the most interesting and potentially most important set of results concerns the involvement measure of hours per week spent watching television. The uniformly negative effects of television watching involve only one cognitive outcome (job-related skills) but include practically all the affective outcomes: Cultural Awareness, public speaking ability, leadership abilities, and interpersonal skills. If these partial correlations are indeed causal, one can only speculate at this point as to what the causal mechanisms might be. On the one hand, watching a great deal of television clearly limits the student's opportunity to interact with others, at least on an active verbal level. At the same time, the content of television programs and commercials may not be conducive to the development of Cultural Awareness and interpersonal skills. Such an interpretation is consistent with the correlation between television watching and the development of materialistic values reported earlier (Chapter Five). Whatever the explanation, these findings suggest that frequent television watching may impede the personal development of the undergraduate student, especially in the areas of Cultural Awareness and interpersonal skills.

Chapter 8

Career Development

Many students attend college primarily to prepare for a career. Entering freshmen have always cited "to get a better job" as an important reason to go to college, and the percentage of students who hold this view of the college experience is on the increase. Of the freshmen entering college in the fall of 1991, for example, 79 percent (compared to 71 percent in 1976) say that getting a better job is a "very important" reason for their decision to go to college. Fully 75 percent (compared to only 54 percent in 1976) also say that "to make more money" is a very important reason for attending college. Institutions attempt to facilitate this career development process in various ways: by developing special skills and competencies needed in various career fields, by certification or the awarding of credits and degrees required to enter particular professions, and through guidance and counseling to help students crystallize career plans.

This chapter focuses on factors influencing students' choices of eight different career fields: business, college teaching, engineering, law, medicine, nursing, school teaching, and scientific research. These fields account for more than half the careers chosen by the students in the 1985 and 1989 surveys; if undecided students are excluded, the named professions account for well over 60 percent of the students' career choices. Analyses reported here examine several related questions. What characteristics of the entering students are associated with changes in career choice between 1985 and 1989? How are students' career choices in 1989 influenced by their curricular, faculty, and peer group experiences during the undergraduate years? Are some types of institutions more successful than others in encouraging students to pursue particular types of careers?

The chapter also examines an additional outcome that is closely related to career development: the student's degree plans. Here we are interested in a similar set of questions. How do different types of entering students change their degree plans during the undergraduate years? What characteristics of the undergraduate institution and its environment raise or lower students' degree aspirations?

Change in Career Choice During the Undergraduate Years

A substantial literature on career development during the undergraduate years indicates that students frequently change their plans after they enter college (Astin, 1977; Astin and Panos, 1969; Davis, 1965; Pascarella and Terenzini, 1991). These changes are more systematic than random: students who change majors or career plans usually change to related fields. Fields differ markedly in their retention and recruitment of students, with business and law generally showing the greatest gains and science and engineering the greatest losses during the undergraduate years.

Changes in students' career choices during college are of particular interest today, as the choices given by contemporary entering freshmen are markedly different from the choices reported by their counterparts two decades ago. When we compare the 1985 freshmen who constitute the focus of this study with their *Four Critical Years* counterparts who entered college in 1968, we find dramatic differences in the distribution of choices. The 1985 freshmen, for example, were much more interested in careers in business (22.0 versus 11.0 percent), law (6.0 versus 3.0 percent), and medicine (7.0 versus 3.0 percent), and much less interested in careers in school teaching (6.0 versus 23.0 percent), college teaching (.3 versus 1.2 percent), and scientific research (1.9 versus 3.1 percent).

With these dramatic differences in freshman career choices, it is of interest to know whether contemporary students' career choices change during college in the same fashion as their predecessors' choices did. Table 8.1 shows the career choices of the 1985 freshmen at the time they entered college and four years

Table 8.1. Changes in Career Aspirations, 1985–1989.

Career	Percent Choosing in		Percent Change, 1985–1989	
	1985	1989	Absolute	Relative
Business	21.5	27.7	+6.2	+ 27.3
School teacher	6.4	8.9	+2.5	+39.1
College teacher	.3	1.9	+1.6	+533.3
Research scientist	1.9	2.1	+.2	+10.5
Nurse	2.4	2.2	−.2	−8.3
Lawyer	5.8	4.6	−1.2	−20.6
Engineer	9.2	6.3	−2.9	−31.5
Physician	7.0	3.5	−3.5	−50.0

Note: N = 16,658.

Source: Weighted national percentages abstracted from Wingard, Treviño, Dey, and Korn (1991).

later, in 1989. The largest relative and absolute increases occur in the fields of business, school teaching, and college teaching; the biggest absolute and relative declines occur in law, engineering, and medicine. These changes are in certain respects similar to those observed in the 1968 freshmen, but there are some dramatic differences. The greatest similarities are the substantial increases in popularity of business and college teaching and the substantial declines in popularity of engineering and medicine. The 1985 freshmen, however, show much larger relative declines in the fields of medicine (−50 percent versus −24 percent for the 1968 freshmen) and much larger relative increases in interest in college teaching (533 versus 200 percent). For these two career fields, it would appear that changes in entering freshman choice patterns between 1968 and 1985 have been compensated for in part by differential changes in the 1985 freshmen during the undergraduate years.

The greatest differences in change can be observed in the careers of lawyer and school teacher. Whereas school teaching declined substantially in popularity during the college years among 1968 freshmen (from 23.0 to 16.0 percent), it actually increased substantially in popularity among the 1985 freshmen (from 6.4 to 8.9 percent). This differential change pattern is reversed for the career of law. The 1968 freshmen showed a slight increase in preference for law during the undergraduate years (from 3.4 to 3.8 percent), while law decreased in popularity (from 5.8 to 4.6 percent) among the 1985 freshmen during the college years.

These findings show that differences between the 1968 and 1985 freshmen in their preferences for careers in medicine, law, school teaching, and college teaching are narrowed somewhat by changes in career shifts that occur during the undergraduate years: four years after entering college, the preferences of the 1968 and 1985 freshmen for those four careers are much more alike than when they first entered college as freshmen.

Factors Influencing Career Choice

Why do we see such dramatic changes in career interest during the undergraduate years? Do different types of students (as reflected in their input characteristics) change differently during the undergraduate years? What environmental factors and involvement factors influence career decision making? We explore these questions below, with a separate discussion for each of the eight career choice categories.

Business

The initial 1985 freshman choice of a career in business has a modest correlation with the 1989 choice four years later ($r = .41$). A number of other entering freshman characteristics add to the prediction of the 1989 choice of a business career, after the freshman choice has been controlled. Students are more likely to choose a business career in 1989 if they come from a high-income family or if their religious preference is Roman Catholic. Several personality and value measures also add positively to the prediction of a business career choice: wanting to be an expert in finance and commerce, wanting to be successful in one's own business, valuing having administrative responsibility for others, giving "to make more money" as an important reason for going to college, and high self-ratings on social self-confidence and mathematical ability. The freshman expectation that there will be a change in career choice during college is also positively related to a 1989 choice of a business career, a finding that helps to explain the substantial increase in business career choices observed during college (Table 8.1). In other words, business appears to be a "receptive field" for dropouts from other career fields during the undergraduate years.

A very interesting pattern of entering freshman characteristics is negatively associated with choosing a business career in 1989. (Readers should keep in mind that the variables mentioned here, as well as those having positive effects reported in the preceding paragraph, contribute significantly to the prediction of the 1989 follow-up career choice, independently of the freshman choice and of each other.) The negative weight of the SAT Verbal score is consistent with the observation that business majors tend to be less well prepared academically than students in other fields (Astin, 1982). Students are also less likely to choose a business career if their fathers are doctors, if they place a high value on promoting racial understanding, if they have high degree aspirations when they enter college, or if they value writing original works or making a theoretical contribution to science. Other negative predictors of choosing a business career include performing volunteer work in high school and the personality measure Artistic Inclination.

Not surprisingly, choosing a freshman major in business enhances the student's prospects of having a business career choice four years later. Choosing a freshman major in education has the opposite effect. The only other environmental variable showing a significant effect on choice of a business career is the percentage of the peer group majoring in engineering, which proves to have a negative effect on choosing a career in business. The meaning of this effect is not entirely clear, since one normally expects a good deal of one-way traffic from careers in engineering to careers in business during the undergraduate years. One possible explanation is that schools with very large engineering schools have more holding power over their engineering students. This could well be a peer group effect, through which an engineering student who is considering a switch to business would be discouraged from doing so if many peers are also engineering students.

A substantial number of involvement variables are significantly associated with a business career choice, after entering freshman and environmental characteristics have been controlled. The strongest partial correlations involve curricular variables: students are more likely to choose a business career if they take a lot of courses emphasizing math or numerical content, but they are less likely to choose a business career if they take many courses in science. This pattern suggests that the typical business curriculum involves a considerable amount of quantitative content but is largely devoid of scientific content. It may also have to do with the aforementioned effect of large engineering departments: those students who remain in engineering will almost certainly take more science courses than those who switch into business. Other involvement variables showing positive correlations with choosing a business career include being a member of a social fraternity or sorority, hours per week spent partying, receiving vocational or career counseling, hours per week spent using a personal computer, working on a group project for a class, and taking multiple-choice exams. The last three variables may well reflect some of the departmental differences between business and other fields: business departments may more frequently require their students to use personal computers, work on group projects, and take multiple-choice exams than do departments in other fields.

Involvement measures showing negative partial correlations with choosing a business career include hours per week spent attending classes, being a guest in a professor's home, talking with faculty outside of class, participating in campus demonstrations, participating in a college internship program, and undergraduate GPA. The last variable raises the possibility that some students may shift out of other fields into business because of poor academic performance. Such an interpretation is consistent with the negative effect, noted above, of the SAT Verbal score on choosing a business career.

College Teaching

Very few freshmen in 1985 aspired to careers as college professors (only .3 percent). The small percentage may help to explain why the pretest-posttest correlation involving this particular career choice is so low ($r = .13$). One other entering freshman characteristic, the student's score on the SAT Verbal test, actually produced a slightly higher correlation ($r = .14$) with the posttest career choice of college teacher than the pretest itself. College teaching proves to be the most difficult 1989 career choice to predict from input and environmental characteristics, as indicated by the final multiple R of only .29.

Other entering freshman characteristics that add to the prediction of a career choice in college teaching include having a father who is also a college teacher, aspiring to a high-level degree, placing a high value on writing original works, Scholarship (Intellectual Self-Esteem), having a liberal political orientation, and placing a high value on influencing the political structure. That expecting to change career choice at the time of college entry also is a positive predictor suggests an interpretation similar to the one offered in the case of a business career: since college teaching is a substantial "net gainer" during the undergraduate years, students initially picking other choices as entering freshmen will be more likely to switch into college teaching than other careers if they are not strongly committed to their initial choices.

Negative predictors of a career choice in college teaching include wanting to be successful in one's own business, citing "to make more money" as an important reason for attending college, taking computer science courses in high school, studying with other students, and having a Jewish religious preference. The last variable is somewhat puzzling, given the very high proportion of Jews among teaching faculty in higher education (Astin, Dey, and Korn, 1991). Actually, the simple correlation between being Jewish and a 1989 career choice of college teacher is not statistically significant. What happens is that, as other entering freshman characteristics are controlled, the correlation becomes significant and negative. This means, in effect, that although Jewish freshmen are no more or less likely to pick college teaching four years after entering college than other freshmen are, they are less likely to pick college teaching than one would expect from their high SAT scores, high degree aspirations, liberal political orientation, and fathers' occupations (a disproportionate number of fathers of Jewish students are college teachers).

Freshmen increase their chances of pursuing a college teaching career four years later if they start out majoring either in the physical sciences or in some field of the arts or humanities. Students initially aspiring to careers in secondary education are also more likely to end up in college teaching, a finding that probably reflects the undergraduate "traffic" between secondary teaching careers and college teaching careers (see Astin, 1977).

Two curricular variables have positive effects on choosing a career in college teaching: having an independent research requirement, and using written (narrative) evaluations of student performance. These two variables suggest interesting possibilities for increasing the supplies of students going into teaching careers at the higher education level. In essence, both of these variables would appear to bring undergraduates and faculty into closer contact with each other. Students who are required to carry out an independent research project, for example, will almost certainly have to consult regularly with faculty on the design and implementation of such projects. Faculty who must provide their undergraduates with written evaluations of their academic performance would most likely have to know their students well in order to write such evaluations.

Only one other environmental variable has a significant effect on choosing a career in college teaching: the size of the institution has a negative effect. This finding is especially ironic, since the vast majority of college professors receive their graduate training in the large universities. Apparently, the professor in the small college provides a more appealing role model for the undergraduate than does the professor in the large university.

The suggestion that personal contact between undergraduates and faculty enhances the student's desire to pursue a college teaching career is strongly reinforced by the involvement measures that are positively associated with choosing a career in college teaching (after controlling for freshman and environmental variables): hours per week spent talking with faculty outside of class, being a guest in a professor's home, and working on an independent research project. The significant correlation of this last individual involvement measure with college teaching, even after the curricular requirement of independent research is controlled (discussed earlier), indicates that independent research projects have positive effects even when they are not part of the formal requirements.

Other involvement variables showing positive correlations with choice of a college teaching career include number of foreign-language courses taken, number of courses taken that emphasize writing skills, and undergraduate GPA. Involvement measures with negative associations include participating in a college internship program, working on group projects for classes, and taking multiple-choice exams.

For choosing a career in college teaching to be positively affected by the student's SAT Verbal score as well as by the undergraduate GPA raises interesting possibilities for speculation. Is high academic achievement simply a requirement for entry into graduate school, or are more subtle motivational processes at work? Does the student's sense of mastery over academic materials stimulate the pursuit of that same subject matter in greater depth? Does succeeding in the academic setting reinforce the student's inclination to remain in that setting? Do professors single out their best students for special attention, and does the student reciprocate by identifying with and wanting to emulate the professor? To what extent do the best students simply feel more comfortable initiating contacts with their professors? We should note, however, that several curricular measures (independent research, written evaluation) and several different measures of student-faculty contact maintain significant relationships with choosing a college teaching career, over and above the effects of SAT scores or GPAs, suggesting that the effects of curriculum and student-faculty contact on this career outcome are not merely matters of student self-selection.

Engineering

The choice of a career in engineering has one of the highest correlations between freshman and follow-up measures ($r = .49$). Other positive predictors include having a father who is also an engineer, a high self-rating on mathematical ability, SAT Mathematics score, high school grades, scientific orientation (a measure of interest in science), and citing "my parents wanted me to go" as an important reason for attending college. Negative entering student predictors include being a woman and citing "to make me a more cultured person" as an important reason for attending college. Clearly, academic prowess (SAT Math, high school GPA, and self-rated math ability) are important determinants of choosing a career in engineering during the undergraduate years.

The most powerful environmental predictor of an engineering career choice in 1989 is *majoring* in engineering at the time of college entry. Majoring in a vocational or technical field is also a positive predictor, but majoring in biological science is a negative predictor.

The next most important environmental factor affecting a final career choice of engineer is the percentage of peers majoring in engineering. This environmental effect appears to be nonlinear, so that the strength of the effect accelerates substantially as the proportion of students majoring in engineering surpasses 25 percent. Thus, freshmen will be most likely to maintain an initial career choice of engineer (or to switch from some other choice into engineering) if they attend an institution where a very high percentage of peers are also engineering majors. This finding, which replicates earlier research on environmental determinants of career choice (Astin, 1977; Astin and Panos, 1969), may reflect a peer group effect. Such an effect can operate in at least two ways: (1) students who are considering switching from engineering to some other career choice may be discouraged from doing so if many of their peers are also pursuing engineering careers, and (2) students who decide to leave other career fields may be attracted into engineering if many of their peers are engineering majors.

Other environmental factors having positive effects on the choice of an engineering career include the Institutional Emphasis on Resources and Reputation and the percentage of peers majoring in mathematics or statistics. A rather unexpected finding arises, however, in the case of the percentage of peers majoring in physical science fields. Although this environmental measure has a small positive simple correlation with a 1989 career choice of engineer, it has a negative effect once other input and institutional characteristics are controlled. A closer look at this phenomenon reveals some remarkable results (Table 8.2). Among the 1,376 students in our sample who started college in 1985 intending to pursue a career in engineering, 36 percent still planned on being engineers four years later. However, among freshman engineering students who enrolled in colleges with a very strong emphasis on the physical sciences (more than 16

Table 8.2. Effect of Peer Interests in Science and Engineering on Choice of an Engineering Career.

Percentage of Peers Majoring in Engineering	N	Percentage Pursuing Engineering Careers in 1989 Among Students Enrolling at Institutions Where the Percentage of Peers Majoring in Physical Science Fields is			
		Less Than 5 Percent	5–16 Percent	Over 16 Percent	Total Sample
More than 28	259	46	53	13	40
17–28	541	42	43	*	42
1–16	391	33	36	*	33
Less than 1	179	17	13	*	15

*Sample size too small to compute reliable percentages.
Note: N = 1,370 freshmen intending to become engineers in 1985.

percent majors), only 13 percent were still pursuing engineering careers in 1989.

Why should students be *less* likely to pursue a career in engineering if they happen to attend a college where many student peers are studying some field of physical science? A possible explanation concerns the status differences that one typically encounters among the different scientific fields. Within the broad field of science and engineering, engineering is often regarded as having lower status because it is an "applied" or "professional" field rather than a "pure" or "academic" discipline. When an institution simultaneously operates an engineering program and a large undergraduate program in the physical sciences, perhaps many students are tempted to leave engineering to enroll in the more prestigious physical science fields.

As might be expected, an engineering career choice is positively associated with the number of science and math or numerical courses taken, and negatively associated with the number of writing-skills and history courses taken. An engineering career choice is also positively correlated with hours per week spent studying and working on a group project for a class, and negatively correlated with taking multiple-choice exams and essay exams. Possibly most, if not all, of these involvement variables are the *results,* rather than the causes, of pursuing a career in engineering. Thus, students who are studying engineering, compared to students taking other fields, may spend more hours studying, take more courses in science and math and fewer courses in writing and history, work more often on group projects, and take fewer essay exams. The negative association with multiple-choice exams is unexpected; perhaps engineering courses, many of which require problem solving, typically ask students to supply the correct answer rather than find it among a set of predetermined answers.

One notable difference between the findings of the current study and those of the original *Four Critical Years* concerns the effect of undergraduate GPA. In the earlier study, the student's undergraduate GPA produced one of the largest correlations with an engineering career choice (with other variables controlled) of all involvement or intermediate outcome measures. In the current study, undergraduate GPA shows no significant relationship to an engineering career choice, once other factors are controlled. Although the simple correlation of GPA with the 1989 engineering choice is significant and positive, this correlation shrinks to nonsignificance when the 1985 choice and self-rated math ability are controlled.

Law

Freshman and follow-up choices of a career in law produce a modest correlation of .35. The next most powerful input predictors are the student's SAT-Verbal score, the importance attached to "influencing the political structure," level of degree aspiration, and being Jewish. Other positive predictors include the student's socioeconomic status, being male, checking "to prepare for graduate or professional school" as an important reason for attending college, and the personality characteristic Leadership. Negative predictors include being white, Liberalism, the student's Scientific Orientation, self-rated artistic ability, and having a father who is a college professor. (The last variable was also a negative predictor in the original *Four Critical Years.*)

Students are more likely to pursue careers as lawyers if they start college with the intention to major in some field of social science. The only other positive environmental factor is the SES of the peer group. Why associating with peers who are from high socioeconomic levels should encourage the student to pursue a career as a lawyer is not entirely clear. Could it be that such peer groups tend to include a large proportion of students pursuing legal careers? As the individual student's SES is also predictive of the choice of a legal career, this may be the case. However, this peer effect may operate in a somewhat more subtle fashion than mere imitation of the career preferences of one's peers. If peers also tend to come from well-to-do families, the peer climate thus created could discourage students from pursuing lower-paying (and lower-status?) professional fields such as college teaching or science.

Several curricular variables are related to choosing a career in law, once the effects of entering student and environmental variables have been controlled. Most of the positive variables would be typical of students undertaking a pre-law curriculum: the number of history courses taken, the number of courses taken that emphasize writing skills, and taking essay exams. Similarly, pre-law students would not ordinarily be characterized by the curricular variables with negative associations: number of science courses taken, and number of math or numerical courses taken. Choosing a career as a lawyer is also positively associated with being elected to a student office, being a member of a social fraternity or sorority, and undergraduate GPA. Negative correlates include working on a group project for a class, assisting faculty in teaching a course, and receiving personal or psychological counseling.

That pursuing a career in law is predicted from the SAT Verbal test, as well as from the student's undergraduate GPA, may reflect the highly competitive nature of law school admissions and the heavy dependence on the Law School Admission Test (LSAT). Because of the crush of applications, many law schools have been forced to rely on the relatively mechanical use of admissions formulas based on college grades and LSAT scores.

Medicine

The 1985 and 1989 choices of a career as a physician produce a moderate correlation of .49. A number of other freshman characteristics add to the prediction of the 1989 choice of this career. Positive predictors include having a father who is also a physician, the Scholarship personality score, SAT Mathematics score, number of biology courses taken in high school, and being either Asian or African-American.

Three environmental variables also have positive effects on choosing a career as a physician: private university, historically black college (HBC), and the percentage of Jews in the student body. A possible explanation for these effects is that (1) the student bodies entering both private universities and private HBCs include higher proportions of students aspiring to medical careers (13.2 and 14.6 percent, respectively, compared to only 4.4 percent for all freshmen) than any other type of institution (Astin, Dey, Korn, and Riggs, 1992), and (2) Jewish students are highly predisposed to pursue careers in medicine (Drew, 1970). Private university, HBC, and the percentage of Jews in the student body, in other words, may all serve as crude proxies for the percentage of students pursuing careers as physicians.

Three of the involvement variables positively associated with choosing a medical career, once entering student and environmental characteristics have been controlled, would be expected of pre-medical students: number of science courses taken, working on a professor's research project, and undergraduate GPA. One other positive correlate, hours per week spent in volunteer work, raises an interesting question: Does participation in volunteer work encourage students to pursue careers as physicians, or is volunteer work simply more likely to be performed by pre-medical students? Since neither Status Striving nor wanting to be very well off financially predicted choosing a medical career, the positive effect of volunteer work reinforces the idea that students are motivated more by altruism than by materialistic motives when they pursue careers in medicine.

Negative involvement correlates of choosing a medical career include number of history courses taken and hours per week spent using a personal computer. The results with one other involvement measure, the number of math or numerical courses taken, are rather unexpected. Although this measure has a significant positive simple correlation with choosing a medical career, the correlation becomes significantly negative after number of science courses taken is controlled. This means, in effect, that pre-med students take fewer math courses than one would expect, given the very large number of science courses they take.

Some of the predictors of choosing a medical career may help to explain why there is a 50 percent loss of students pursuing medical careers between 1985 and 1989 (Table 8.1). Substantial predictors include not only college admissions test scores (SAT Mathematical) but also undergraduate GPA. Possibly many students abandon their plans to pursue a medical career simply because they do not have the college GPA or the scores on the Medical College Admission Test (MCAT) that qualify them for admission to medical school.

Nursing

Nursing produces the highest pretest-posttest correlation between 1985 and 1989 choices ($r = .62$), suggesting that students make a firm decision about nursing careers earlier than they do other careers. However, there are fewer additional predictors of this career choice than for any other. Positive input predictors include being a woman, number of biology courses taken in high school, and choosing a freshman career in one of the health professions other than nursing.

Only one environmental measure has a significant effect on choosing a career in nursing: the peer measure Artistic Inclination, which has a negative effect.

Involvement measures that have positive partial correlations with choosing a career in nursing include number of science courses taken, hours per week spent attending classes or labs, having class papers critiqued by instructors, and taking multiple-choice exams. Negative involvement measures include number of math or numerical courses taken, taking essay exams, participating in a college internship program, and hours spent in student clubs or groups.

Scientific Research

Many of our country's research scientists can be found working as professors in colleges or universities; consequently, limiting this category to those students who indicate "research scientist" as a career choice risks overlooking students headed for higher education careers who will indeed be functioning as research scientists in an academic setting. Accordingly, our definition of the career choice of "research scientist" has been expanded to include all students who indicate "college teacher" as a career choice and who are majoring in some field of science. Even with this broadened definition, the pretest-posttest correlation involving this career choice is quite modest ($r = .28$). Other positive predictors include an interest in "making a theoretical contribution to science," SAT Mathematics score, giving "preparation for graduate or professional school" as a very important reason for attending college, and commitment to "becoming involved in programs to clean up the environment" to "becoming an authority in my field" and to "obtaining recognition from my colleagues for contributions to my special field." Having a mother who is a research scientist and having a father who is a research scientist are both predictive of choosing a career in scientific research. The only negative predictors among entering student characteristics are two personality measures: Status Striving, and Social Activism.

This interesting pattern of predictors suggests that while prospective scientists are not motivated by "status," in the sense of having money and power, they are clearly motivated by the need to be recognized by others for their accomplishments. The "status needs" of people who are motivated to pursue careers in science are thus highly specialized.

The most potent environmental predictor of choosing a research career is having an initial freshman choice of a natural science major. Since being undecided about one's career choice is also a significant predictor, the indecision may involve uncertainty about an academic versus a straight research career. Having a grant from the college is also a positive predictor, suggesting that financial aid may represent one potential tool for increasing the number of undergraduates who pursue careers as research scientists.

One environmental variable that has a small but significant negative effect on choosing a career as a scientific researcher is having a peer group in which many students are engineering majors. Here we have the mirror image of the finding discussed earlier, in our analysis of career choices in engineering: an institution that has a very high concentration of majors in engineering may siphon off some of the student talent that might otherwise be devoted to careers in scientific research.

One final environmental factor having a positive effect on choosing a career as a research scientist is the use of written evaluations in grading. This positive effect on science careers may be similar to the positive effect of the same factor on careers in college teaching: increased student-faculty contact. The interpretation is reinforced by some of the involvement variables that have positive correlations with choosing a career in research (after entering freshman and environmental variables are controlled): working on a professor's research project, assisting faculty in teaching a course, and hours per week spent talking with faculty outside of class. Each of these activities puts students in more of a "colleague" role in their relationships with professors. Choosing a scientific career is also positively associated with number of science courses taken, working on an independent research project, and number of math or numerical courses taken.

Involvement variables showing negative partial correlations with pursuing a career as a research scientist include taking multiple-choice exams, number of history courses taken, working on a group project for a class, number of courses taken that involve writing skills, holding a part-time job off campus, and hours per week spent in volunteer work. Most of these negative correlates may reflect artifacts, in the sense that they are most likely to characterize students who are not studying science.

School Teaching

The 1985 and 1989 choices of a career in school teaching produce a moderate correlation of .45. Among the other significant predictors, gender is by far the strongest: women are much more likely to stay with an initial freshman choice of school teaching (or to switch from some other freshman choice into school teaching) than are men. Among the 898 women and 167 men who started college in 1985 intending to become school teachers, 66.4 percent of the women but only 52.7 of the men retained their intention to become teachers by the 1989 survey. Among those with no intention to pursue teaching careers in 1985 (5,982 men and 9,154 women), 9.7 percent of the women and only 3.6 percent of the men had switched to school teaching by 1989.

Other positive predictors of pursuing a career in school teaching include the student's degree of commitment to raising a family, being a born-again Christian, being white, and being a guest in a teacher's home during high school. The last predictor suggests that close student-teacher contact may foster the development of the high school student's interest in pursuing a career in teaching. Perhaps the process here is similar to that postulated in the case of student-professor interaction and the development of interest in a career in college teaching (see above).

Negative predictors of choosing a career in school teaching include the personality measure Status Striving and the student's score on the SAT Verbal test. Earlier studies (Astin, 1982) have shown that secondary school students who express an interest in teaching careers tend to get relatively low marks in school and low scores on college admissions tests. The current finding concerning SAT scores suggests that the selective process continues during the undergraduate years, with high-scoring students being more likely than low-scoring students to switch from school teaching to other careers during the undergraduate years. With the current concern about the quality of our primary and secondary schools, this finding is troubling.

The strongest environmental predictor of choosing a career in school teaching is majoring in education. Majoring in one of the health professions also carries a small predictive weight.

Attending a public four-year-college has a positive effect on the student's choice of a career in school teaching. This finding, which has been replicated in several earlier studies going all the way back to the early 1960s (Astin, 1977; Astin and Panos, 1969), suggests that institutions that have historically assumed primary responsibility for teacher training — the public colleges — still have significant holding power on prospective teachers, even though they are no longer identified as "teachers colleges." As the career field of school teaching is now a "net gainer" during the undergraduate years, possibly many public four-year colleges, because they still operate substantial teacher-training programs, are able to attract dropouts from other career fields during the undergraduate years. This effect may also reflect the influence of the peer group, as the students enrolling at public colleges include a higher proportion of people planning to become school teachers than any other type of institution (14.1 percent compared to 8.7 percent for students in general; see Astin, Dey, Korn, and Riggs, 1992).

Two other environmental factors show significant effects on the career choice of school teacher: faculty Use of Multiple-Choice Exams shows a positive effect, whereas the peer group measure Scientific Orientation has a negative effect. Students appear to be discouraged from pursuing careers in school teaching when they are exposed to peers who are strongly oriented toward science. The reason for this peer effect is not clear, but it is a cause for concern, particularly given the current shortage of science teachers in our public schools.

Involvement variables showing positive partial correlations with a career choice in school teaching include number of history courses taken, giving presentations in class, and tutoring other students. Negative correlations are found with hours per week spent using a personal computer, hours per week spent partying, and working on a professor's research project. Once again, we find evidence of a negative association between scientific work and choosing a career in school teaching.

Degree Aspirations

An important aspect of career development is the highest degree that the student seeks and is able to attain. The entering freshmen of fall 1985 reported very high degree aspirations: nearly two-thirds (63 percent) aspired to postgraduate degrees, and more than one in four (28.2 percent) aspired to doctoral or advanced professional degrees (Table 8.3). This represents a substantial increase over the freshmen of the 1960s and early 1970s, only about half of whom reported such aspirations (Dey, Astin, and Korn, 1991).

By the time of the 1989 follow-up, more than two-thirds of the 1985 freshmen (67.7 percent) aspire to postgraduate degrees, even though there has been a modest increase in the number who aspire to less than a bachelor's degree. These figures are all the more remarkable when one considers that, by the time of the 1989 follow-up, only about half (51.7 percent) of the 1985 freshmen had actually attained their bachelor's degrees.

The small change in proportion aspiring to doctorates or advanced professional degrees (from 28.2 to 27.5 percent) masks

Table 8.3. Changes in Degree Aspirations
of 1985 Freshmen, 1985–1989.

Highest Degree Aspired to	Percent Choosing in		Change
	1985	1989	
None or less than bachelor's	1.8	4.2	+2.4
Bachelor's[a]	35.0	28.1	−6.9
Master's	34.9	40.2	+5.3
Doctoral or advanced professional[b]	28.2	27.5	−0.7

[a]Includes "other."
[b]Ph.D., Ed.D., M.D., D.O., D.D.S., D.V.M., J.D., B.D., or M.Div.
Source: Weighted national percentages abstracted from Wingard, Treviño,
Dey, and Korn (1991).

substantial differences in specific degrees. While students were
showing increased interest in doctoral degrees (from 13.2 to 15.0
percent) and law degrees (from 5.4 to 7.3 percent), interest in
medical degrees dropped sharply (from 9.1 to 4.9 percent). This
decline is consistent with the comparable decline of student interest in medical careers cited earlier (Table 8.1).

Freshman Predictors

What entering characteristics are predictive of the student's
degree aspirations four years after entering college? As the pretest
measure of degree aspirations in 1985 has only a modest correlation of .35 with 1989 aspirations, it suggests that there is a
great deal of switching among individual students between 1985
and 1989. What other entering characteristics are associated with
these changes in aspirations? The largest weights are associated
with the following three input characteristics: Intellectual Self-
Esteem, SAT Verbal score, and checking "to prepare for graduate or professional school" as an important reason for attending college. Substantial positive weights are also associated with
high school grades, socioeconomic status, being African-American, and the personality measure Social Activism. Other positive but weaker predictors include having a father who is a physician, Feminism, tutoring other students, number of biology

courses taken in high school, number of physical science courses taken in high school, and checking "to make me a more cultured person" as an important reason for attending college.

Environmental Effects

Environmental variables that are associated with increased degree aspirations include majoring in natural science, psychology, social science, arts or humanities, or pre-law. Students are also more likely to increase their degree aspirations if they go away from home to attend college and if they are recipients of state scholarships. Although majoring in education has a simple negative correlation with degree aspirations, the correlation becomes significantly positive when variables such as SAT Verbal, socioeconomic status, and high school grades are controlled.

The most potent environmental variable influencing students' degree aspirations is Humanities Orientation. Other positive environmental factors are the percentage of women in the student body and the peer measure Science Preparation. The only environmental factor having a negative effect on degree aspirations is the percentage of students majoring in agriculture.

The size and consistency of the effect of Humanities Orientation on degree aspirations can be seen in Table 8.4.

Table 8.4. Effect of Humanities Orientation on
Aspiration to Advanced Degrees (Unweighted Data).

1985 Degree Aspiration	N	Percentage Aspiring to Advanced Degrees[a] in 1989 by Level of Institutional Humanities Orientation			
		Very low (N = 4,487)	Low (N = 5,088)	High (N = 4,782)	Very High (N = 4,758)
Doctoral or advanced professional	6,509	46	58	61	66
Master's	7,349	21	23	27	35
Bachelor's	5,041	10	13	15	19
None or less than bachelor's	216	11	16	19	38

[a]Ph.D., Ed.D., M.D., D.O., D.D.S., D.V.M., J.D., B.D., or M.Div.

Regardless of the student's initial level of degree aspirations in 1985, the Humanities Orientation has a consistent positive effect: with each increasing level of Humanities Orientation, higher proportions of students indicate in 1989 that they plan to obtain the doctorate or an advanced professional degree. Without exception, every percentage increases with each increasing level of Humanities Orientation. This may be, at least in part, a peer group effect, since the percentage of freshmen aspiring to the doctorate or an advanced professional degree increases regularly with each increasing level of Humanities Orientation: 25, 29, 35, and 48 percent of freshmen, respectively, entering institutions with very low, low, high, and very high Humanities Orientation.

Effects of Involvement

A number of involvement measures are significantly associated with degree aspirations, after control for the effects of entering student and environmental characteristics. Most potent among these is the student's undergraduate GPA. While we cannot be absolutely certain about the direction of causation involving GPA, it certainly seems likely that students' undergraduate grades can influence their plans for further education (Drew and Astin, 1972). A number of other involvement measures highlight the importance of student-faculty interaction in raising students' degree aspirations: hours per week spent talking with faculty outside of class, working on professors' research projects, and having class papers critiqued by instructors. Other positive correlates of degree aspirations include enrolling in interdisciplinary courses, taking essay exams, tutoring other students, enrolling in honors programs, participating in campus demonstrations, socializing with students from different racial or ethnic groups, number of science courses taken, and number of history courses taken.

The only involvement variables showing negative associations with degree aspirations are working on group projects for a class and hours per week spent working on hobbies.

Summary

Compared to freshmen of twenty years ago, today's college fresh-men express much greater interest in careers in business, law, and medicine and much less interest in school teaching, college teaching, and research careers. College attendance appears to reduce some of these generational differences, however, since today's students switch out of law and medicine and into teach-ing in greater numbers during the college years than did stu-dents of other generations.

The analyses of input effects also produce substantial evidence of "occupational inheritance," particularly in fields that are science-related. Independent of all other variables, having a father who is in the same career field positively af-fects students' choices of careers in medicine, engineering, col-lege teaching, and scientific research. In the case of research careers, both fathers' and mothers' careers are significant pre-dictors.

The environmental and involvement variables that affect career choice and degree aspirations are summarized in Table 8.5. The involvement variables shown in this table should be interpreted with caution, since they may well be the *results* of changed career plans, rather than the causes of these plans. Nevertheless, these results once again highlight the importance of peer group effects. The percentage of students majoring in en-gineering has a positive effect on choice of an engineering career and negative effects on choosing a career in either business or scientific research. Choosing a career in law is positively affected by the Socioeconomic Status of the peer group. Public colleges, which enroll the highest proportion of students planning teach-ing careers, have a positive effect on the student's decision to pursue a career in elementary or secondary school teaching. Finally, private universities and historically black colleges, which enroll the highest proportions of students planning careers in medicine, have positive effects on the student's decision to pur-sue a career as a physician.

Certain career choices also appear to be affected by the faculty and the curriculum. Frequent student-faculty contact,

Table 8.5. Summary of Environmental Effects
on Career Development.

Career Choice	Positively Affected by	Negatively Affected by
Businessperson	Major: business	Major: education Peers: percentage in engineering

	(Involvement measures)[a]
	  Math courses
	  Fraternity or sorority
	    membership
	  Partying
	  Career counseling
	  Using a pesonal com-
	    puter
	  Working on a group
	    project
	  Taking multiple-choice
	    exams
		Science courses
		Hours spent attending
		  classes
		Being a guest in
		  professor's home
		Talking with faculty
		"Diversity" activities[b]
		Required internship

College Teacher	Major: physical science Major: arts or humanities	Institutional size

	(Involvement measures)[a]
	  Independent research
	    requirement
	  Written evaluations
	  Student-faculty
	    interaction
	  Independent research
	  Foreign-language courses
	  Writing courses
		Required internship
		Group class projects
		Taking multiple-choice
		  exams

Engineer	Major: engineering
	Major: vocational or
	  technical
	Peers: percentage in
	  engineering
	Resources and
	  Reputation Emphasis
	Peers: percentage in
	  math or statistics
		Major: biological
		  science
		Peers: percentage in
		  physical science

	(Involvement measures)[a]
	  Math courses
	  Science courses
		Writing courses
		History courses

Table 8.5. Summary of Environmental Effects
on Career Development, cont'd.

Career Choice	Positively Affected by	Negatively Affected by
	Studying or homework Group class projects	Taking multiple-choice exams Taking essay exams
Lawyer	Major: social science Peer SES	
	(Involvement measures)[a] History courses Writing courses Taking essay exams Elected to student office Fraternity or sorority membership	Science courses Math courses Group class projects Assisting faculty in teaching Personal counseling
Physician	Private university Black college Peers: percentage who are Jews	
	(Involvement measures)[a] Science courses Working on professor's research Volunteer work	History courses Using a personal computer Math courses
Nurse	(Involvement measures)[a] Science courses Attending classes or labs Having papers critiqued by instructors Taking multiple-choice exams	Peers: Artistic Inclination Math courses Taking essay exams Required internship Student clubs or organizations
Research Scientist	Major: natural science Major: undecided Grant from the college	Peers: percentage in engineering
	(Involvement measures)[a] Written evaluations Student-faculty interaction Math courses Science courses Independent research	Taking multiple-choice exams History courses Group class projects Part-time job off campus Volunteer work

Table 8.5. Summary of Environmental Effects
on Career Development, cont'd.

Career Choice	Positively Affected by	Negatively Affected by
School Teacher	Major: education Major: health professions Public four-year college	Peers: Scientific Orientation
	(Involvement measures)[a] Taking multiple-choice exams History courses Class presentations Tutoring others	Using a personal computer Partying Working on professor's research
Degree Aspirations	Major: natural science Major: psychology Major: social science Major: arts or humanities Major: education Major: pre-law Distance from home to college State scholarship Humanities Orientation Peers: percentage who are women Peers: Science Preparation	Peers: percentage in agriculture Group class projects Hobbies
	(Involvement measures)[a] Student-faculty interaction Interdisciplinary courses Taking essay exams Tutoring others Honors program "Diversity" activities[b] Science courses History courses	

[a]Since the temporal ordering of outcome and involvement measures cannot be precisely determined, causal interpretations should be made with caution.

[b]Includes activities such as discussing racial or ethnic issues, socializing with students from different racial or ethnic groups, participating in campus demonstrations, attending racial or ethnic workshops, and taking women's studies or ethnic studies courses.

for example, seems to encourage students to pick careers in both college teaching and scientific research. Choosing a career in scientific research also appears to be positively affected by the use of written evaluations in grading. Finally, the student's aspiration to higher degrees is substantially strengthened by the Humanities Orientation of the faculty and by attending college away from home.

Chapter 9

---•·•·•---

Satisfaction with
the College
Environment

Contemporary discussions of the "outcomes" of higher education or of improved "assessment" in higher education frequently
overlook student satisfaction. This area covers the student's subjective experience during the college years and perceptions of
the value of the educational experience. Given the considerable investment of time and energy that most students make in
attending college, their perceptions of the value of that experience should be given substantial weight. Indeed, it is difficult
to argue that student satisfaction can be legitimately subordi-
nated to any other educational outcome.

The student's subjective response to the college environment is assessed in two different ways: satisfaction with the environment, and ratings of the college environment. Satisfaction
measures include the student's level of satisfaction with the total undergraduate experience, as well as with specific aspects of
that experience, such as the quality of instruction, contacts with
faculty and fellow students, curriculum, college administration,
and facilities. Ratings of the college environment cover such
areas as the degree of faculty interest in students, relationships
with the administration, and the degree of institutional priority

given to issues such as diversity, social change, resource acquisition, and enhancement of institutional reputation. The second set of subjective outcomes is similar to "climate" measures
used in previous studies of college environments (Astin, 1968;
Pace and Stern, 1958) in that the object is to obtain the student's perception of the academic and intellectual climate of the
institution.

Student Satisfaction

Since 1967 the Cooperative Institutional Research Program has
regularly conducted longitudinal follow-ups of entering freshman
classes that have focused on student satisfaction. The 1989 follow-
up of the 1985 freshmen includes twenty-seven different areas
of student satisfaction, with the following instruction: "Please
rate your satisfaction with the college you entered as a freshman on each of the aspects of campus life listed below." Students were permitted to offer one of five responses: very satisfied; satisfied; neutral; dissatisfied; can't rate, no experience.
Students responding "can't rate, no experience" are excluded
from the analysis of any given item. The remaining students'
responses are scored from 1 (dissatisfied) to 4 (very satisfied).

Because of the very large number of satisfaction items and
the likelihood of considerable redundancy among them, we
decided to perform a factor analysis of these twenty-seven items
to determine whether it was possible to use a limited number
of general satisfaction measures that would combine related items
from the list. This analysis proved to be successful, as we were
able to identify five general satisfaction factors that accounted
for much of the information contained in the twenty-seven individual items. These factors and their associated items are
shown in Table 9.1. The specific areas generating the highest
levels of student satisfaction (75 percent or higher) include
courses in the major field, opportunities to participate in extracurricular activities, and the overall college experience. The
specific areas producing the lowest levels of satisfaction (less
than 50 percent) include regulations governing campus life and

Table 9.1. Student Satisfaction with Various Aspects
of the Undergraduate Experience.

(Factor) Area of Satisfaction	Factor Loading	Percentage "Satisfied" or "Very Satisfied"
(Relationships with Faculty)		
Amount of contact with faculty and administrators	.82	62.7
Overall relationships with faculty and administrators	.77	66.5
Opportunities to discuss course work and assignments out of class with professors	.64	77.3
(Curriculum and Instruction)		
Humanities courses	.64	74.6
Social science courses	.62	73.0
Overall quality of instruction	.52	74.0
General education requirements	.45	63.3
Relevance of course work to everyday life	.45	52.8
Courses in your major field	.38	83.8
Opportunities to take interdisciplinary courses	.35	55.7
(Student Life)		
Campus social life	.77	64.4
On-campus opportunities to attend films, concerts, and so on	.50	73.4
Opportunities to participate in extracurriculuar activities	.48	80.0
Regulations governing campus life	.44	43.1
(Individual Support Services)		
Career counseling and advising	.82	42.2
Personal counseling	.60	45.8
Academic advising	.58	44.1
Job placement services for students	.50	46.2
Tutoring help or other academic assistance	.41	59.3
(Facilities)		
Library facilities	.62	73.1
Computer facilities	.61	73.1
Laboratory facilities	.59	63.9
Overall college experience	—	78.1

Source: Weighted national norms for four-year colleges abstracted from
Wingard, Treviño, Dey, and Korn (1991).

virtually all the items making up the Individual Support Services factor: career counseling, personal counseling, academic
advising, and job placement services. The four other broad areas
identified in the factor analysis—Relationships with Faculty,
Curriculum and Instruction, Student Life, and Facilities—all
produce moderate levels of satisfaction (average of about 65–70
percent), but there are wide discrepancies within each area in
satisfaction with particular aspects of the undergraduate experience. For example, in the area of Curriculum and Instruction, more than 80 percent of the students are satisfied with
courses in the major, but fewer than 60 percent are satisfied
with the relevance of course work to everyday life and with opportunities to take interdisciplinary courses. Similarly, in the
general area of Relationships with Faculty, more than three-
fourths of the students are satisfied with opportunities to discuss
course work with professors, but fewer than two-thirds are satisfied with the amount of contact with faculty and administrators.

The reader should note that satisfaction with the overall
college experience has a factor loading of .51 on the Student
Life factor, but we excluded it from the scoring of that factor
because it also has significant loadings (up to .34) on the other
four factors. Rather than including it in the scoring of any factor, we shall treat satisfaction with the overall college experience as a separate outcome measure for purposes of analyzing
environmental effects. Other areas of specific satisfaction that
do not produce loadings on any factor sufficiently high to justify
their inclusion in the scoring of any factor include financial aid,
student housing, campus health services, and science and math
courses. These satisfaction items will not be considered further
in this particular chapter.

Scores on each of the five factors were obtained by simply adding together the students' scores on each of the relevant
items shown in Table 9.1. Separate regression analyses were
performed using each of these five factor scores, as well as the
student's score on satisfaction with the overall college experience. Two other individual satisfaction items were used as outcomes in separate regression analyses because they were of special interest to the project staff and to the sponsoring agency

(the Exxon Education Foundation): student satisfaction with general education requirements, and satisfaction with opportunities to take interdisciplinary courses. One final satisfaction measure for which a separate regression analysis was performed was the student's response to the question "If you could make your college choice over again, would you still choose to enroll at the college you entered as a freshman?" Possible answers were scored on a five-point scale: definitely yes (5), probably I would (4), don't know (3), probably not (2), and definitely not (1). The percentages of students selecting each of these alternatives were as follows:

Response	Percent
Definitely yes	36.0
Probably I would	30.7
Don't know	4.6
Probably not	16.4
Definitely not	12.2

These figures suggest a somewhat more negative view than the 78.1 percent satisfaction with the overall college experience shown in Table 9.1. As one possible explanation, even if some students say that they are "satisfied" with their overall college experience, they still might feel that they could benefit more from attending a college different from the one they initially entered in the fall of 1985.

Effects of Entering Characteristics on Satisfaction

Consistent with earlier studies of student satisfaction (Astin, 1977), the student's degree of satisfaction with the college experience proves to be much less dependent on entering characteristics than other outcomes and more susceptible to influence from the college environment (see Resource A). Nevertheless, some entering student characteristics do carry significant weight in predicting student satisfaction. For example, whether the college entered in 1985 was the student's first, second, or third choice is positively related to eight of the nine satisfaction out-

comes. Several variables having to do with academic preparation are also present in many of these regressions: one or
both SAT scores (seven regressions), high school grades (six
regressions), and Intellectual Self-Esteem (three regressions).
At least one of these "ability" variables was present in all nine
regressions.

Another interesting category of predictors that enter many
of the satisfaction regressions is indices of mental health: the
student's self-rating on "emotional health" enters six of the nine
regressions with positive weights, whereas the frequency with
which the student reports being depressed enters four regressions with negative weights. Socioeconomic status carries a positive weight in five regressions, whereas being a woman carries
a positive weight in four regressions. For the most part, however, the effects of these input characteristics are much smaller
than the effects of environmental characteristics.

It is important to note that virtually all measures of satisfaction with the undergraduate experience are significantly
related to number of undergraduate years completed, after the
effects of entering student and environmental characteristics are
controlled. For many of the satisfaction items there is also a significant partial correlation with the involvement item "left school
or transferred." In other words, there appears to be a direct association between student satisfaction and retention in college.
While we cannot be absolutely sure that satisfaction is a direct
causal agent in the student's decision to remain in or leave college (students, for example, might be more inclined to say that
they are dissatisfied if they know that they have already left college), the strength of these associations and their prevalence
across all measures suggest that one promising way to reduce
an institution's dropout rate is to focus more attention on student satisfaction as an "intermediate outcome." The analyses
reported later in this chapter provide a number of potentially
useful clues as to what institutions might actually do to enhance
student satisfaction. In the following sections we consider how
each of these satisfaction outcomes is affected by various environmental experiences.

Overall Satisfaction with College

The environmental variable having the strongest positive effect on overall satisfaction is leaving home to attend college. The distance of the student's college from home is also positively related to overall satisfaction, over and above the effects of living away from home. Thus, it would appear that it is not just living somewhere other than at home that positively affects satisfaction but also the sheer distance of the college from the student's home. Other environmental variables having a positive effect on overall satisfaction include Institutional Diversity Emphasis, having a minority or Third World course requirement, having a positive faculty attitude toward the institution's general education program, and majoring in education.

The environmental variable with the strongest negative effect on overall satisfaction is Lack of Student Community. Satisfaction is also negatively affected by an Institutional Emphasis on Resources and Reputation, majoring in engineering, and the proportion of engineering majors in the student body. The last two findings suggest that the heavy academic demands and curricular requirements that characterize many engineering programs may create an environment in which students tend to be dissatisfied with their overall experience.

Many involvement variables are associated with overall satisfaction, after the effects of input and environmental variables have been controlled. Two of these have to do with student-faculty interaction: hours per week spent talking with faculty outside of class, and being a guest in a professor's home. Several others have to do with student-student interaction: hours per week spent in student clubs or organizations, socializing with friends, hours per week spent partying, socializing with persons from different racial or ethnic groups, attending racial or cultural awareness workshops, participating in intramural sports, and hours per week spent attending religious services. Overall satisfaction is also positively related to college GPA, number of writing-skills courses taken, and receiving vocational or career counseling, but negatively related to receiving personal or psychological counseling (the last finding is consistent with the negative effect, mentioned above, of the student input variable feeling depressed). Other negative involvement factors include hours per week spent watching television, and holding a part-time job off campus.

Willingness to Re-enroll in Same College

Whether the student would choose to enter the same college is related to some of the environmental and involvement measures associated with overall satisfaction, but there are also some notable differences. Students are more likely to be satisfied if they go away from home to attend college and if their college is located some distance from home. Satisfaction is also positively associated with Institutional Diversity Emphasis and having a minority or Third World course requirement. Lack of Student Community on the campus is associated with *not* wanting to re-enroll, as is the percentage of bachelor's degrees awarded in engineering. However, once the effects of Lack of Community and Diversity Orientation are controlled, students are slightly more likely to say that they would be willing to re-enroll if they attend a public university and if they are frequently taught by graduate teaching assistants in their undergraduate courses. Even though these effects are weak, they are nevertheless somewhat puzzling, given the other outcome measures with which these two variables are associated (see Chapter Ten). While public universities are frequently critized for their impersonality, lack of community, and neglect of undergraduate teaching, could it be that exposure to teaching assistants is a positive factor in the undergraduate experience, once the Lack of Community that usually accompanies frequent use of teaching assistants is taken into account? Willingness to re-enroll is negatively affected by the percentage of Jewish students in the student body. Again, the meaning of this finding is not clear.

As was true with overall satisfaction, willingness to re-enroll in the same college is positively associated with student-faculty interaction (being a guest in a professor's home, hours per week spent talking with faculty outside of class) and student-

student interaction (hours per week spent socializing with friends, attending religious services, and participating in student clubs or organizations), and negatively associated with holding a part-time job off campus and hours per week spent watching television. Working full-time while attending college is also negatively associated with willingness to re-enroll in the same college.

Relationships with Faculty

Like the previous two measures, satisfaction with faculty is positively associated with distance from home to college, but the effects of place of residence are more complex: living in a campus residence hall has a positive effect on student satisfaction with faculty, but living off campus in a private room or apartment has a negative effect. In all likelihood, these differential effects have to do with the differential proximity to faculty associated with the two types of living arrangements. Satisfaction with faculty is also significantly associated with several financial aid measures: being supported by a grant from the college or by a state scholarship enhances satisfaction with faculty, but having to rely on one's own savings to attend college reduces satisfaction with faculty.

By far the strongest environmental effect on student satisfaction with faculty involves the environmental measure Student Orientation of the Faculty. This measure produces one of the strongest effects in the entire study (partial Beta = .37). At this point it is worth reviewing the item content that would be associated with a high score on this environmental factor: faculty are interested in students' academic problems, faculty are interested in students' personal problems, faculty are committed to the institution, faculty are sensitive to issues of minorities, faculty are easy to see outside of office hours, and there are frequent opportunities for student-faculty interaction. The fact that Student Orientation of the Faculty is based on information that has been obtained completely independently of the student satisfaction measure (that is, from the faculty questionnaire) makes this finding all the more impressive. Consistent with this result, the strongest negative effect (partial Beta = .13) on satisfaction with faculty is associated with Research Orientation (another measure derived from the faculty questionnaire). It is important to keep in mind that even though these two environmental measures are highly correlated ($r = -.69$), each contributes *independently* to student satisfaction (or dissatisfaction). Other environmental variables having a positive effect on satisfaction with faculty include the percentage of institutional expenditures invested in student services, the percentage of students majoring in business fields, Peer SES, and Social Activism and Community Orientation (another measure derived from faculty responses; see Chapter Two).

Size also has a negative effect (partial Beta = $-.09$) on satisfaction with faculty over and above the effects of Student Orientation of the Faculty and Research Orientation. Also, unlike the results for the student's willingness to re-enroll in the same college, the reliance on graduate teaching assistants has a negative impact (partial Beta = $-.10$) on student satisfaction with faculty. In all likelihood, heavy reliance on teaching assistants serves to separate and alienate students from faculty. Two additional measures have negative impacts on satisfaction with faculty: majoring in engineering, and the peer measure Intellectual Self-Esteem.

As might be expected from the environmental effects just discussed, several measures of faculty-student involvement have positive associations with satisfaction with faculty: hours per week spent talking with faculty outside of class, having a class paper critiqued by an instructor, and being a guest in a professor's home. Undergraduate GPA is also positively associated with satisfaction with faculty, as are several measures of student-student interaction: being elected to a student office, participating in campus demonstrations, socializing with students from different racial or ethnic groups, and tutoring other students. Additional involvement measures having positive correlations with satisfaction with faculty are number of writing-skills courses taken, and receiving vocational or career counseling. No involvement measures show significant negative effects on satisfaction with faculty, once the effects of input and environmental variables are controlled.

Curriculum and Instruction

Satisfaction with curriculum and instruction is positively affected by going away from home to attend college. Three financial aid measures also show positive effects: having a grant from the college, having support from parents or family, and having aid based on financial need.

Like satisfaction with faculty, satisfaction with Curriculum and Instruction has its strongest positive association with the faculty-based measure Student Orientation of the Faculty. Other environmental measures having positive effects include a positive faculty attitude about the general education program, Humanities Orientation of the environment, Social Activism and Community Orientation, the percentage of students majoring in biological science fields, and Peer SES (the last measure has a stronger effect than any other environmental measure except Student Orientation of the Faculty).

The strongest negative factor in satisfaction with Curriculum and Instruction is the size of the student's institution. Other negative environmental factors replicate findings from overall satisfaction: majoring in engineering, and attending a college that awards a high percentage of degrees in engineering fields.

Involvement measures having positive associations with satisfaction with Curriculum and Instruction (after the effects of entering student and environmental characteristics are controlled) are similar to those related to overall satisfaction: hours per week spent talking with faculty outside of class, being a guest in a professor's home, undergraduate GPA, number of writing-skills courses taken, receiving vocational or career counseling, and socializing with persons from different racial or ethnic groups. One additional involvement measure not found in earlier analyses is hours per week spent studying or doing homework. Although the correlation with this variable is positive, the direction of causation is especially unclear, since the amount of time and energy that students devote to studying may also be a result, rather than merely a cause, of their level of satisfaction with Curriculum and Instruction.

Student Life

Satisfaction with Student Life is affected by more environmental variables than any other satisfaction measure. Unlike the last two measures discussed, however, none of these variables stands out by having a very large weight in the regression. Like previous measures, satisfaction with Student Life is positively affected both by leaving home to attend college and by distance from home to college. Other environmental variables showing positive effects on satisfaction with Student Life include the Political Orientation (liberalism versus conservatism) of the student peer group, Institutional Diversity Emphasis, the percentage of undergraduates majoring in English, having a women's or gender studies requirement, the percentage of faculty involved in teaching general education courses, Peer SES, and majoring in education. Negative factors in satisfaction with Student Life include Lack of Student Community, the percentage of faculty in science fields, having a thesis or senior project requirement, the percentage of Catholics in the student body, the percentage of Jewish students in the student body, and majoring in either nursing or engineering.

Unlike satisfaction with faculty, satisfaction with Student Life is *positively* affected by the size of the institution. If one looks at the content of this outcome measure, the reason for this effect becomes clear: Student Life includes social life, opportunities to attend cultural events, opportunities to participate in extracurricular activities, and regulations governing campus life. In all likelihood, large institutions, in comparison to small ones, offer more diverse social opportunities (social organizations, parties, and so on), more frequent cultural events on campus, a greater number of extracurricular activities, and fewer regulations governing campus life.

Involvement variables showing positive associations with satisfaction with campus life lean heavily toward student interaction and social life: hours per week spent in student clubs or organizations, participating in intramural sports, hours per week spent attending religious services, socializing with persons from different racial or ethnic groups, hours per week spent socializing with friends, being elected to a student office, working on group projects for a class, participating in intercollegiate athletics, and attending racial or cultural awareness workshops. Hours per week spent talking with faculty outside of class also shows a small positive association with satisfaction with Student Life. The only involvement measure showing a negative association with satisfaction with Student Life is hours per week spent watching television.

Individual Support Services

By far the strongest environmental effect on student satisfaction with Individual Support Services is associated with the faculty-based measure Student Orientation of the Faculty (Beta = .18). Satisfaction with individual support services is also positively associated with distance from home to college, but not with any of the residential measures (once distance is controlled). Of special interest, however, is the positive effect of the percentage of expenditures devoted to student services. Here is one of those rare instances where we find a direct link between a resource measure and an educational outcome measure: spending generously on student services apparently "pays off."

Environmental factors having negative effects on satisfaction with Individual Support Services include majoring in science or engineering, receiving financial support from parents or family, the percentage of faculty involved in team teaching, and the peer measure Outside Work. The last finding raises an interesting question: Does heavy involvement of students in outside work tend to relieve the institution of the normal student demand to develop effective individual support services, or is it more difficult to deliver such services effectively if students do not spend much time on campus?

One peculiar finding is the negative effect of the percentage of students majoring in social science fields on student satisfaction with Individual Support Services. This effect is especially puzzling, given that many personnel who deliver such services (counselors, psychologists, social workers) come from social science fields. One would expect an institution that emphasizes the social sciences to have a sophisticated and well-supported program of Individual Support Services. Is it possible that a peer group that is heavily involved in the social sciences has very high standards for such services? Clearly, this puzzling finding merits much further investigation.

Involvement variables showing positive associations with satisfaction with Individual Support Services include receiving vocational or career counseling, receiving tutoring in courses, hours per week spent talking with faculty outside of class, hours per week spent attending religious services, and undergraduate GPA. Among other things, these variables suggest that students who avail themselves of individual services are more likely to report being satisfied with such services. The direction of causation could, of course, be reversed: students may not bother to seek out such services if they are perceived as being inadequate. The only involvement measure showing a significant negative association with satisfaction with Individual Support Services is hours per week spent watching television.

Facilities

The pattern of environmental effects on satisfaction with Facilities is very different from the pattern found for other satisfaction measures. The two environmental variables having the strongest positive effect on student satisfaction with this measure are the Research Orientation of the institution and average faculty salaries. When one realizes that "facilities" in this outcome measure are defined as libraries, computers, and laboratories, these effects are easy to understand: institutions that have highly paid faculty and that place a strong emphasis on research are much more likely than other institutions to have first-class research facilities, simply because their faculty will expect and demand them. Under these conditions, it is not surprising that student satisfaction with Facilities is also positively affected by the use of graduate teaching assistants and by the percentages of students majoring in physical science or agriculture. Other positive effects on satisfaction with Facilities are associated with the Intellectual Self-Esteem of the student peer group; the percentages of students majoring in history or political science, in biological science, in social science, or in education; Institutional Diversity Emphasis; majoring in either biological science or education; and a variety of curricular variables: having a minority or Third World requirement, having a general education program that is personalized and individualized, and the use of written evaluations of student performance.

One of the most interesting environmental effects on satisfaction with Facilities is the positive effect associated with having a high proportion of men (more than 80 percent) in the student body. Why this variable should have such an effect is not clear. Why should institutions that primarily or exclusively enroll men tend to have better facilities than other institutions? That this may be a holdover from the days of single-sex colleges is suggested by the pattern of results associated with attending a women's college. While the simple correlation between attending a women's college and student satisfaction with Facilities is negative, attending a women's college tends to have a *positive* effect on this variable once other environmental variables such as Research Orientation and faculty salaries have been controlled. These findings indicate that the physical facilities of single-sex (or formerly single-sex) institutions may, for a variety of historical and geographical reasons, be superior to those of institutions that have always been coeducational.

A number of other environmental variables prove to have negative effects on satisfaction with Facilities. One of the strongest negative effects is associated with the peer measure Materialism and Status. Perhaps a highly materialistic student body sets unrealistically high standards for physical facilities. Other peer measures showing negative effects include Outside Work and Altruism and Social Activism. Several curricular measures also have negative effects: the requirement of a thesis or senior project, having a "major-dominated" general education program, and having a women's or gender studies requirement. Following this atypical pattern, we also find that both the Student Orientation of the Faculty and a Lack of Student Community have negative effects on satisfaction with Facilities.

Only a few involvement variables are significantly associated with satisfaction with Facilities, and the coefficients are quite small. Socializing with students from different racial or ethnic groups is positively associated with satisfaction with Facilities, whereas participation in campus demonstrations is negatively associated. The general lack of involvement variables in this analysis suggests that students are indeed making judgments about the physical facilities, rather than responding indirectly to their experiences with other students and with faculty.

General Education Requirements

Among the environmental variables having the strongest effects on satisfaction with general education requirements are two faculty measures: Student Orientation of the Faculty, and positive faculty attitudes toward the general education program. Here we have clear evidence that the faculty's attitudes regarding the general education program can directly affect students' reactions to that program. Other environmental factors having positive effects on students' satisfaction with the general education program include Peer SES, the Scientific Orientation of the peer group, majoring in science or pre-med, having a grant from the college, going away from home to attend college, and attending a women's college. One type of general education program — the interdisciplinary or true-core curriculum — also has a positive effect on student satisfaction. This is a potentially important finding for curriculum development, considering that the idea of a true core, where students are offered no choice but are all required to take the same assortment of general education courses, is often criticized on the grounds that the students would resent not being allowed to exercise at least some degree of choice. Choice within some form of distributional system is, as already noted, the norm: more than 90 percent of general education programs in the United States are of this type (Hurtado, Astin, and Dey, 1991). Perhaps the lack of student choice is more than compensated for by the care with which most true-core programs are designed and implemented, and by the heavy involvement of key faculty members in teaching such a program.

Environmental variables having negative effects on students' satisfaction with general education requirements include having a women's or gender studies course requirement, the size of the institution, the percentage of faculty who involve students in their personal research, and the percentage of students majoring in technical fields (other than engineering). Each of these variables offers provocative possibilities for interpretation. The negative effects of size may well reflect the cursory treatment that general education is likely to receive in large institutions where large departments emphasize disciplinary specialization. A similar process may be at work in institutions where faculty engage undergraduates in their personal research. Finally, institutions with a strong technical emphasis in the curriculum may well shortchange the general education program, in part because insufficient numbers of faculty and courses are available in nontechnical fields such as the arts and humanities.

Involvement variables showing positive relationships to satisfaction with the general education program include undergraduate GPA, socializing with students from different racial or ethnic groups, receiving vocational and career counseling, number of writing-skills courses taken, hours per week spent partying, and hours per week spent attending religious services. Working full-time while enrolled as a student is negatively associated with satisfaction with general education requirements.

Opportunities to Take Interdisciplinary Courses

The environmental variable showing the strongest effect on student satisfaction with opportunities to take interdisciplinary courses is, not surprisingly, the percentage of faculty reporting that they teach interdisciplinary courses (partial Beta = .15). Other positive environmental factors include Peer SES, Institutional Diversity Emphasis, Social Activism and Community Orientation, and faculty morale. Once again, having an interdisciplinary true-core general education curriculum has a positive effect, although in this instance the "opportunity" for interdisciplinary studies may be a bit of a euphemism, since under a true-core curriculum students really have no choice but to take interdisciplinary courses. Other environmental variables having positive effects on satisfaction with opportunities to take interdisciplinary courses include going away from home to attend college and having need-based financial aid. Negative effects are associated with majoring in either engineering or nursing and with the student-faculty ratio. The latter finding, in effect, means that students tend to be more satisfied with opportunities to take interdisciplinary courses when there are relatively few students per faculty member. Among other things, this finding suggests that it is easier to undertake a program of interdisciplinary courses when there are abundant faculty available to teach them.

The involvement variable showing the strongest partial correlation with satisfaction with opportunities to take interdisciplinary courses is the number of interdisciplinary courses actually taken by the student. Other positive associations involve having a class paper critiqued by an instructor, being a guest in a professor's home, and number of writing-skills courses taken.

Perceptions of the Environment

So far we have been looking at how students are *affected* by their college experience, as revealed in their levels of expressed satisfaction with various aspects of that experience. In this section we examine another aspect of the students' subjective experiences at the institution: how they *perceive* their college environment. To examine this issue in depth, the 1989 follow-up questionnaire was designed to include three lists of perceptual items. The first list contains eighteen items describing various aspects of the student's experience of the environment, such as "It is easy to see faculty outside of office hours" or "Students have little contact with each other outside of class." Students are asked to indicate whether each item is very descriptive (score 3), somewhat descriptive (score 2), or not descriptive (score 1) of the college they entered as freshmen in 1985. The second set of items is somewhat more judgmental. Included here are eighteen different statements, such as the following: "Most faculty here are sensitive to the issues of minorities" or "Campus administrators care little about what happens to students." Students are asked to indicate their extent of agreement with each item along a four-point continuum: agree strongly (4), agree somewhat (3), disagree somewhat (2), and disagree strongly (1). The third set of items includes twenty-one statements reflecting possible priorities of the institution as perceived by the student. These include both general priorities ("to promote the intellectual development of students" or "to maintain a campus climate where differences of opinion can be aired openly") as well as very specific priorities, such as "to raise money for the institution" or "to recruit more minority students." Students are asked to indicate how much priority they feel the institution assigns to each goal along a four-point scale: highest (4), high (3), medium (2), and low (1) priority.

Because of the large number of perceptual items in these three lists, it would be impractical to do a separate analysis of each item. Accordingly, the fifty-seven items were factor analyzed to develop more general measures of students' perceptions of the college environment. These analyses resulted in five clearly distinguishable factors: Student Orientation of the Faculty, Social Change Orientation, Trust in the Administration, Diversity Orientation, and Resources and Reputation Emphasis. That these factors very closely resemble certain factors obtained in the analyses of faculty questionnaire responses (see Chapter Two) is perhaps inevitable, since many of the fifty-seven items used in the factor analysis of student perceptions were also included in the faculty questionnaire. There is an important difference, however, between the student perceptual factors and the faculty environmental measures. Whereas the student perceptual measures consist of the responses of each *individual student* to these items, the faculty measures are institutional *means* based on the responses of the entire faculty. In other words, since the faculty environmental measures are institutional, there is therefore no variation in scores *within* an institution. The student measures, on the other hand, allow for variation in student perception within an institution, since the analyses are based on individual students rather than the entire institution.

Another distinction between the student perceptual measures and the faculty environmental measures is their manner of utilization in the study. The student measures are being used as *outcome* measures that can be affected by entering student and environmental variables. The faculty measures, on the other hand, are being used as *environmental* measures that can potentially influence student outcomes. Because both sets of measures are based on perceptions, however, we are required to make some modifications in the way we analyze the student perceptual measures. Specifically, we are not using any of the faculty perceptual measures as independent (environmental) variables in the analyses of student perceptions; by doing so, we would almost certainly be misled by the results. Since both the students and their faculty are rating the same institution, it stands to reason that there will be a correlation between the faculty means and the individual student responses. But would such a correlation justify a causal inference? For example, if we were to find that the faculty's perception of Diversity Orientation was significantly correlated with the individual student's perception of Diversity Orientation (after controlling for entering student characteristics), would we be justified in concluding that the faculty environmental measure "caused" the student perception? While it is certainly true that faculty perceptions might influence student perceptions, it is also the case that both groups are observing the same phenomena and making similar judgments about them. Just because the results show a high level of agreement cannot be taken as proof that the judgments of one group "affect" the judgments of the other. The inherent ambiguity involved in such correlations thus prompted a decision to omit the faculty perceptual measures from the environmental effects analyses in which the five student perceptual measures are used as outcome variables.

In the following sections we examine the results of these modified regression analyses separately for each of the five student perceptual outcomes.

Student-Oriented Faculty

To learn students' perceptions of how student-oriented the faculty were, six items were used:

Faculty here are interested in students' personal problems.

Faculty here are strongly interested in the academic problems of undergraduates.

There are many opportunities for faculty and students to socialize with one another.

It is easy to see faculty outside of office hours.

[negative] Most students are treated like "numbers in a book."

[negative] There is little or no contact between students and faculty.

This and the other factors are scored simply by summing the student's responses to all the items making up the factor. The direction of scoring for the negative items is reversed. The regression analysis in which entering student characteristics are controlled generates a multiple R of only .25. Adding the environmental characteristics, however, raises the coefficient to .59. If we want to assess the relative importance of input and environmental variables in terms of percentage of variance accounted for, input characteristics account for only 6 percent, while environmental characteristics account for an additional 29 percent. Clearly, the students' perceptions of how Student-Oriented the faculty are depend far more on their actual experiences during college than on any predisposition they might have had to see faculty in a certain light.

These are the most potent environmental factors shaping the students' perceptions of how Student-Oriented the faculty are: institutional size, use of graduate teaching assistants, and Research Orientation. Each of these three variables, of course, carries a negative weight in the regression equation. In effect, these results mean that those faculty who are most likely to be perceived as Student-Oriented work in small institutions that are not strongly oriented toward research and that do not rely on teaching assistants in undergraduate courses.

The simple correlation of the Student-Oriented Faculty outcome with attending a public university ($-.40$) is comparable to the correlations involving size ($-.48$), use of graduate teaching assistants ($-.42$), and Research Orientation ($-.37$), but most of the effect of attending a public university is accounted for when these other three characteristics are controlled. Nevertheless, attending a public university still contributes independently (and negatively) to the prediction of Student-Oriented Faculty, even after these other three characteristics are controlled. By way of comparison, the largest simple correlation involving an input characteristic is $-.11$.

Environmental variables having the strongest positive effects on the perception of a Student-Oriented Faculty include Humanities Orientation, the percentage of faculty involved in teaching interdisciplinary courses, the percentage of women on the faculty, and the percentage of institutional expenditures devoted to student services. Other positive factors include Peer SES and the percentage of students living on campus during the freshman year. Other negative factors include Permissiveness (a peer measure), the degree of science preparation of the peer group, the percentage of faculty in the sciences, the percentage of Asians in the student body, the percentage of African-American students in the student body, and attending a public four-year college.

Many curricular variables affect the student's perception of Student-Oriented Faculty. Positive effects are associated with majoring in either psychology or some other social science, whereas negative effects are associated with majoring in engineering and with the percentages of students majoring in engineering, the health professions, or other technical fields. These patterns may reflect the teaching and mentoring styles of faculty in these particular fields. Positive effects are also associated with having a true interdisciplinary core curriculum, whereas having a minority or Third World course requirement is negatively associated with this outcome.

Living on campus and attending college far away from home both have positive effects on the student's perception of a Student-Oriented Faculty, whereas living at home and living in a private room or apartment both have negative effects.

It is somewhat surprising to find that the student's perception of a Student-Oriented Faculty is significantly affected by a number of financial aid variables, both at the individual and the peer group level. For example, a positive perception is associated with having a grant from the college and having a state scholarship, and with two peer group measures: the percentage having merit-based aid, and the percentage having need-based aid. Negative effects are associated with reliance on savings, although the effect here is much weaker than are the positive effects of the other eight variables.

A number of involvement variables are also positively associated with the student's perception of Student-Oriented Faculty, after the effects of entering student and environmental characteristics are controlled. Not surprisingly, the two strongest partial correlations are with measures of student-faculty interaction: hours per week spent talking with faculty outside of class, and being a guest in a professor's home. Positive effects are also associated with GPA, receiving vocational or career counseling, socializing with students from different racial or ethnic groups, and hours per week spent socializing with friends. Negative correlations include hours per week spent commuting to campus, and — surprisingly — being a member of a social fraternity or sorority (this last effect is quite weak, although statistically significant).

As is the case with most satisfaction measures, the Student Orientation of the Faculty is positively associated with number of years completed and negatively associated with leaving school or transferring. This finding raises the interesting possibility that student retention might well be enhanced if faculty priorities could be shifted more in the direction of a concern with student development.

Social Change Orientation

Orientation to social change is defined by six items from the list of institutional priorities:

> To facilitate student involvement in community service activities
> To help students learn how to bring about changes in American society
> To help solve major social and environmental problems

To help students examine and understand their personal
   values
To develop a sense of community among students and
   faculty
To develop leadership ability among students

Entering student characteristics have somewhat more
predictive power for Social Change Orientation (11 percent of
the variance; $R = .33$) than was the case with Student-Oriented
Faculty, but the environmental characteristics still account for
a larger share of the variance (13 percent; R increased to .49).
As a likely explanation of the greater relative importance of input characteristics, note that the most powerful environmental
factors influencing the student's perception of the institution's
Social Change Orientation are peer group factors: Altruism and
Social Activism (the strongest positive effect of all environmental variables; Beta = .27), Peer SES (positive effect), and the Permissiveness of the peer group (negative effect). Other positive
effects are associated with the percentage of students planning
to live on campus, the percentage of women in the student body,
the percentage of undergraduates majoring in each of the following: humanities, biological science, and—somewhat surprisingly—business.

The faculty variable with the strongest effect (in this case,
a negative one) on the student's perception of the institution's
Social Change Orientation is Research Orientation. The perception of Social Change Orientation is also negatively affected
by majoring in science or engineering.

Social Change Orientation is positively affected by attending either a historically black college or a college for women,
and negatively affected by the size of the institution. Other positive effects are associated with the percentage of faculty who use
active learning techniques, the percentage of institutional expenditures invested in student services, having a grant from the
college, having need-based financial aid, attending a college
away from home, and distance from home to college.

As would be expected, involvement variables having positive partial correlations with the perception of a Social Change

Orientation include items having to do with "diversity" issues: socializing with someone from a different racial or ethnic group, and discussing racial or ethnic issues. The strongest partial correlations, however, are with hours per week spent talking with faculty outside of class, receiving vocational or career counseling, and working on group projects for class. Other positive correlations include number of history courses taken, being a guest in a professor's home, and four "hours per week" measures: sports or exercise, religious services, partying, and hobbies.

As was the case with Student-Oriented Faculty, Social Change Orientation is positively associated with number of years completed and negatively associated with leaving school or transferring, although the partial correlations are much smaller than is the case with Student-Oriented Faculty.

Trust in the Administration

Before presenting results of environmental effects on the student's perception of Trust in the Administration, it is worthwhile to mention a few of the entering student characteristics that affect this outcome. High perceived Trust in the Administration is associated with being a woman, white, and a born-again Christian; with self-rated emotional health; and with enrolling in one's first-choice college. Low Trust in the Administration is associated with SAT Verbal scores, being Jewish, attending college to "get away from home," placing a high value on writing original works, and Hedonism. However, this perceptual factor is one of the hardest to predict: input variables account for only 5.7 percent of the variance ($R = .24$), compared to an additional 7.2 percent ($R = .36$) attributable to the environment.

The environmental variable having the strongest effect (in this case, negative) on perceived Trust in the Administration is use of graduate teaching assistants. But perhaps the most interesting environmental effect concerns the positive effect of the percentage of women on the faculty. Is it possible that having a substantial representation of women on the faculty creates a more trusting environment? Or could it be that having more women on the faculty leads to having more women administrators who, in turn, create a more nurturing and trusting environment? Other positive environmental factors include going away from home to attend college, having a grant from the college, the percentage of faculty involved in teaching interdisciplinary courses, the use of written evaluations in grading, the percentage of freshmen living on campus, the percentage whose financial aid is based on need, having a minority or Third World course requirement, the percentage of bachelor's degrees awarded in fields of business, and the percentage of expenditures devoted to student services. Attending a women's college has a positive impact on Trust in the Administration, but so does attending a college with more than 80 percent men in the student body. Once again, we have what seems to be a curvilinear relationship between the sex ratio of the student body and an outcome measure. In this case, it appears that coeducation tends to be associated with not trusting the administration.

Several peer group measures are negatively associated with Trust in the Administration: Materialism and Status, Permissiveness, the percentages of Roman Catholics and of blacks in the student body, and the student body's Political Orientation (liberalism versus conservatism). Trust in the Administration is also negatively affected by majoring in science or engineering, Research Orientation, and two characteristics of the general education program: having general education requirements under the control of the major, and having "progressive" course offerings.

Several involvement variables have significant partial correlations with student Trust in the Administration, after the effects of input and environmental characteristics are controlled. Positive correlations involve hours per week spent participating in religious services, receiving vocational or career counseling, hours per week spent exercising or in sports, socializing with persons from different racial or ethnic groups, and number of math or numerical courses taken. By far the largest negative correlation is with participating in campus demonstrations. Other negative factors include holding a part-time job off campus and taking a women's or gender studies course.

Diversity Orientation

The student's perception of the Diversity Orientation of the college is defined by seven items. Two of these concern the curriculum:

> Many courses include minority perspectives
> Many courses include feminist perspectives

The other five items measure students' perceptions of institutional priorities:

> To create a diverse multicultural environment
> To increase representation of minorities in the faculty or administration
> To develop among students and faculty an appreciation for a multicultural society
> To recruit more minority students
> To increase representation of women in the faculty or administration

Entering student characteristics account for less than 6 percent of the variance in students' perceptions of Diversity Orientation ($R = .24$), whereas environmental characteristics account for an additional 15 percent of the variance (multiple R raised to .46). Five environmental variables stand out because of their substantial positive effect on Diversity Orientation: the Political Orientation (liberalism versus conservatism) of the student body, the Altruism and Social Activism of the peer group, Liberalism, the percentage of women on the faculty, and attending a women's college. While each of these five environmental variables is positively associated with the others, each one contributes independently to the perception of Diversity Orientation. Other positive factors affecting the perception of a Diversity Orientation include having progressive course offerings (recall that this variable is defined primarily by offerings in the areas of gender or ethnic studies), the percentage of students receiving need-based aid, having a women's or gender studies requirement, the percentage of freshmen living on campus, the percentage of faculty involved in teaching general education, and having a true-core curriculum. Diversity Orientation is also positively affected by going away from home to attend college, and by receiving aid based on financial need.

Environmental factors having negative effects on the student's perception of the college's Diversity Orientation include the Materialism and Status of the peer group, Faculty Morale, the percentage of students majoring in the health professions, receiving merit-based financial aid, having a required internship, and majoring in either business or engineering.

As would be expected, students' perceptions of campus Diversity Orientation are positively associated with socializing with persons from different racial or ethnic groups and discussing racial or ethnic issues. Other positive associations involve hours per week spent in sports or exercise, receiving vocational or career counseling, hours per week spent in religious services, talking with faculty outside of class, number of writing-skills courses taken, and working on a group project for a class.

The fact that the campus Diversity Orientation is negatively associated with leaving school or transferring suggests that enhancing the institutional emphasis on diversity may be one further way of increasing retention rates.

Resources and Reputation Emphasis

The factor measuring the school's Emphasis on Resources and Reputation is defined by five items from the list of institutional priorities:

> To increase or maintain institutional prestige
> To enhance the institution's national image
> To raise money for the institution
> To hire faculty "stars"
> To conduct basic and applied research

This perceptual factor obviously duplicates, almost precisely, the faculty measure Institutional Emphasis on Resources and Reputation. What kinds of students are attracted to institutions with a strong Emphasis on Resources and Reputation? Positive input correlates include SAT Verbal, SAT Mathematical, Status Striving, Intellectual Self-Esteem, parental income, having a Jewish religious preference, and citing "to make more money" as an important reason for attending college. About 8 percent of the variance ($R = .29$) in Resources and Reputation Emphasis is accounted for by these input measures, while the environmental variables account for an additional 14.5 percent ($R = .48$).

The strongest positive environmental effect on the student's perception of Resources and Reputation Emphasis is attributable to the faculty measure Research Orientation (partial Beta = .32). Several peer group measures also contribute to this perception: the percentage receiving merit-based aid, Materialism and Status, SES, Science Preparation in high school, and Intellectual Self-Esteem. Other positive influences include requiring a thesis or senior project, the percentage of faculty who involve students in their research, having progressive course offerings, and degree of reliance on graduate teaching assistants.

Environmental factors having a negative effect on the perception of a Resources and Reputation Emphasis include the percentage of Roman Catholics in the student body, attending a college with over 80 percent male enrollment, faculty Involvement in Administration, Collegial Stress, and the peer measure Outside Work. Having a true-core curriculum also has a negative impact on the perception of a Resources and Reputation Emphasis.

Involvement variables retaining positive associations with Resources and Reputation Emphasis after control of input and environmental characteristics include having class papers critiqued by instructors, discussing racial or ethnic issues, giving presentations in class, and hours per week spent talking with faculty outside of class.

Table 9.2 summarizes the environmental and involvement variables that affect the student's satisfaction with and perceptions

Table 9.2. Summary of Environmental Effects on Satisfaction.

Satisfaction with	Positively Affected by	Negatively Affected by
Overall college experience	Leaving home to attend college	Lack of Student Community
	Distance from home to college	Resources and Reputation Emphasis
	Institutional Diversity Emphasis	Major: engineering
	Minority or Third World course requirement	Peers: percentage in engineering
	Faculty positive toward general education program	
	Major: education	
	(Involvement measures)[a]	
	Student-faculty interaction	Personal counseling
	Student-student interaction	Watching television
	Writing courses	Part-time job off campus
	Career counseling	
Willingness to re-enroll in freshman college	Leaving home to attend college	Lack of Student Community
	Distance from home to college	Peers: percentage who are Jews
	Institutional Diversity Emphasis	
	Use of teaching assistants	
	(Involvement measures)[a]	
	Student-faculty interaction	Part-time job off campus
	Student-student interaction	Watching television
		Full-time job
Faculty	Distance from home to college	Living in private room or apartment
	Living in residence hall	Self-reliance for financial support
	Grant from college	Research Orientation
	State scholarship	Institutional size
	Faculty: Student Orientation	Use of teaching assistants
	Percentage of all expenditures on student services	Major: engineering
		Peers: Intellectual Self-Esteem

Table 9.2. Summary of Environmental Effects on Satisfaction, cont'd.

Satisfaction with	Positively Affected by	Negatively Affected by
	Peers: percentage in business Social Activism and Community Orientation (Involvement measures)[a] Student-faculty interaction Student-student interaction Writing courses Career counseling	
Curriculum and Instruction	Leaving home to attend college Financial aid Faculty: Student Orientation Faculty positive about general education program Humanities Orientation Social Activism and Community Orientation Peers: percentage in biological sciences Peer SES (Involvement measures)[a] Student-faculty interaction Writing courses Career counseling "Diversity" activitites[b] Studying or homework	Intstitutional size Major: engineering Peers: percentage in engineering
Student Life	Leaving home to attend college Distance from home to college Peers: Liberalism Institutional Diversity Emphasis	Lack of Student Community Percentage of science faculty Thesis requirement Percentage who are Catholics

Table 9.2. Summary of Environmental Effects on Satisfaction, cont'd.

Satisfaction with	Positively Affected by	Negatively Affected by
	Peers: percentage in English Women's studies requirement Faculty: percentage teaching general education courses Peer SES Major: education Institutional size	Percentage who are Jews Major: engineering Major: nursing
	(Involvement measures)[a] Student-student interaction "Diversity" activities[b] Talking with faculty	Watching television
Individual Support Services	Faculty: Student Orientation Distance from home to college Percentage of expenditures for student services	Major: science Major: engineering Reliance on family for financial support Faculty: percentage who team teach Peers: Outside Work Peers: percentage in social science
	(Involvement measures)[a] Career counseling Receiving tutoring Talking with faculty Attending religious services GPA	Watching television
Facilities	Research Orientation Use of teaching assistants Peers: percentage in physical science Peers: percentage in agriculture Peers: Intellectual Self-Esteem	Peers: Materialism and Status Peers: Outside Work Peers: Social Activism Thesis requirement Major-dominated general education program Women's studies requirement

Table 9.2. Summary of Environmental Effects on Satisfaction, cont'd.

Satisfaction with	Positively Affected by	Negatively Affected by
	Peers: percentage in history or political science	Faculty: Student Orientation
	Peers: percentage in biological science	Lack of Student Community
	Peers: percentage in social science	
	Peers: percentage in education	
	Institutional Diversity Emphasis	
	Major: education	
	Major: biological science	
	Minority or Third World course requirement	
	Individualized general education program	
	Written evaulations	
	Over 80 percent men	
	Women's college	
	(Involvement measures)[a]	
	Socializing with students of different ethnicity	Campus activism
General education requirements	Faculty: Student Orientation	Women's studies requirement
	Faculty positive about general education program	Faculty: involving students in research
	Peer SES	Peers: percentage in technical fields
	Peers: Scientific Orientation	
	Major: science or pre-med	
	Grant from college	
	Leaving home to attend college	
	Women's college	
	True-core general education curriculum	
	(Involvement measures)[a]	
	Socializing with students of different ethnicity	Working full-time

Table 9.2. Summary of Environmental Effects on Satisfaction, cont'd.

Satisfaction with	Positively Affected by	Negatively Affected by
	Career counseling Writing courses Partying Attending religious services	

Opportunities to take
  interdisciplinary
  courses
	Faculty: percentage
	  teaching inter-
	  disciplinary courses
	Peer SES
	Faculty: Diversity
	  Emphasis
	Social Activism and
	  Community
	Faculty Morale
	True-core general
	  education curriculum
	Leaving home to attend
	  college
	Need-based aid
	Peers: percentage
	  taking inter-
	  disciplinary courses
		Major: engineering
		Major: nursing
		Student-faculty ratio

	(Involvement measures)[a] Having papers critiqued by instructors Guest in professor's home Writing courses	

Student-Oriented Faculty	Humanities Orientation
	Faculty: percentage
	  teaching inter-
	  disciplinary
	  courses
	Faculty: percentage
	  who are women
	Percent of all
	  expenditures on
	  student services
	Peer SES
	Peers: percentage living
	  on campus
	Major: psychology
	Major: social science
		Institutional size
		Use of teaching assistants
		Research Orientation
		Public university
		Peers: Permissiveness
		Peers: Science Prep-
		  aration
		Faculty: percentage in
		  science
		Peers: percentage who
		  are Asians
		Peers: percentage who
		  are African-Americans
		Public four-year college
		Major: engineering

Table 9.2. Summary of Environmental Effects on Satisfaction, cont'd.

Satisfaction with	Positively Affected by	Negatively Affected by
	True-core general education curriculum Living on campus Distance from home to college Receiving financial aid Peers: percentage receiving financial aid	Peers: percentage in engineering Peers: percentage in health professions Peers: percentage in other technical fields Minority or Third World course requirement Living at home or in private room Use of personal savings to attend college
	(Involvement measures)[a] Student-faculty interaction GPA Career counseling Student-student interaction Number of years completed	Commuting Fraternity or sorority membership
Social Change Orientation	Peers: Social Activism and Community Orientation Peer SES Peers: percentage living on campus Peers: percentage of women Peers: percentage in arts/humanitites Peers: percentage in biological science Peers: percentage in business Black college Women's college Faculty: use of active learning Percentage of all expenditures on student services Receiving financial aid	Peers: Permissiveness Research Orientation Major: science Major: engineering Institutional size

Table 9.2. Summary of Environmental Effects on Satisfaction, cont'd.

Satisfaction with	Positively Affected by	Negatively Affected by
	Leaving home to attend college	
	Distance from home to college	
	(Involvement measures)[a]	
	"Diversity" activities[b]	
	Student-faculty interaction	
	Career counseling	
	Group class projects	
	History courses	
	Student-student interaction	
Trust in the Administration	Faculty: percentage who are women	Use of teaching assistants
	Leaving home to attend college	Peers: Materialism and Status
	Grant from college	Peers: Permissiveness
	Faculty: percentage teaching interdisciplinary courses	Peers: percentage who are Catholics
	Written evaluations	Peers: percentage who are African-Americans
	Peers: percentage who are living on campus	Peers: Liberalism
	Peers: percentage with need-based aid	Major: science
	Minority or Third World course requirement	Major: engineering
	Peers: percentage in business	Research Orientation
	Percentage of all expenditures on student services	Major-dominated general education program
	Women's college	"Progressive" general education curriculum
	Peers: over 80 percent men	
	(Involvement measures)[a]	
	Student-student interaction	Campus activism
	Career counseling	Part-time job off campus
	Math courses	Women's studies course

Table 9.2. Summary of Environmental Effects on Satisfaction, cont'd.

Satisfaction with	Positively Affected by	Negatively Affected by
Diversity Orientation	Peers: Liberalism Peers: Social Activism Faculty: percentage who are women Women's college "Progressive" general education curriculum Peers: percentage with need-based aid Peers: percentage living on campus Faculty: percentage teaching general education True-core general education curriculum Leaving home to attend college Need-based aid (Involvement measures)[a] "Diversity" activities[b] Exercise Career counseling Attending religious services Talking with faculty Writing courses Group class projects	Peers: Materialism and Status Faculty Morale Peers: percentage in health professions Merit-based aid Required internship Major: business Major: engineering
Resources and Reputation Emphasis	Research Orientation Peers: percentage with merit-based aid Peers: Materialism and Status Peer SES Peers: Science Preparation Peers: Intellectual Self-Esteem Thesis required (Involvement measures)[a] Student-faculty interaction	Peers: percentage who are Catholics Peers: over 80 percent men Faculty: Involvement in Administration Faculty Stress Peers: Outside Work True-core general education curriculum

Table 9.2. Summary of Environmental Effects on Satisfaction, cont'd.

Satisfaction with	Positively Affected by	Negatively Affected by
	"Progressive" general education curriculum Use of teaching assistants Taught courses Class presentations Discussing racial issues	

[a]Since the temporal ordering of outcome and involvement measures cannot be precisely determined, causal interpretations should be made with caution.

[b]Includes activities such as discussing racial or ethnic issues, socializing with students from different racial or ethnic groups, participating in campus demonstrations, attending racial or ethnic workshops, and taking women's studies or ethnic studies courses.

of the college experience. Although most satisfaction outcomes are affected by one or more faculty characteristics, we find, once again, the pervasive influence of the peer group. At the same time, many satisfaction and perceptual outcomes are positively influenced both by student-faculty and student-student interaction.

Summary

Undergraduate students express their highest levels of satisfaction (75 percent or higher) with courses in the major, opportunities to participate in extracurricular activities, opportunities to talk to professors, and the overall college experience. The lowest levels of satisfaction (fewer than half of all students) are with regulations governing campus life and with virtually all Individual Support Services: academic advising, career counseling, financial aid services, and job placement services.

In contrast to other types of student outcomes, student satisfaction and the student's perception of the college environment depend much more on actual environmental experiences than on entering student (input) characteristics. Nevertheless, entering freshmen who are well prepared academically come from higher socioeconomic levels, are psychologically healthy, and are most likely to express satisfaction with their college experiences four years later.

Satisfaction with most aspects of the undergraduate experience is facilitated by living on campus rather than at home and by attending college some distance from home. Satisfaction also tends to be high when students attend institutions where the faculty is strongly Student-Oriented. A heavily research-oriented faculty has a negative effect on student satisfaction with faculty and a positive effect on satisfaction with Facilities.

Satisfaction is enhanced by frequent interaction both with faculty and with fellow students. There are also consistent positive associations between student satisfaction, undergraduate GPA, and retention.

Specific areas of satisfaction can be directly influenced by relevant environmental variables. Satisfaction with Individual Support Services, for example, is positively affected by the proportion of educational expenditures devoted to student services. Similarly, student satisfaction with the general education program is enhanced when faculty express positive attitudes toward their own involvement in general education. Satisfaction with student life is negatively affected by a Lack of Student Community on the campus.

The more television students watch, the lower are their levels of expressed satisfaction with student life, individual support services, and the overall college experience. The most pervasive pattern of dissatisfaction, however, is associated with majoring in engineering. Engineering majors report lower levels of satisfaction than students in other majors with Curriculum and Instruction, Relationships with Faculty, Student Life, Individual Support Services, and opportunities to take interdisciplinary courses. Engineering majors also perceive their faculties as not being Student-Oriented and their institutional climates as having low Trust in the Administration and a weak Emphasis on Diversity.

Chapter 10

———•◦•◦•———

Summary of
Environmental Effects

The preceding seven chapters have examined the findings of this study from the perspective of each outcome measure: What environmental variables affect a particular student outcome? In this chapter we look at the results from the perspective of the *environment:* What outcomes are associated with a particular environmental variable or set of environmental variables? What outcomes, for example, will be enhanced or diminished by attending a large rather than a small college? What difference does it make if the student lives on campus, in a private room, or at home? How are students affected when they attend an institution that places a high value on student development? What difference does it make to students when they enroll in an institution with a very strong emphasis on research?

While this chapter will necessarily reiterate (in somewhat different form) many of the findings concerning environmental effects reported in Chapters Three through Nine, the reader will note that certain findings not mentioned in the earlier chapters are reported here. The reason for this discrepancy is what statisticians call "multicollinearity," meaning that many of the environmental variables are correlated with each other. Some of these correlations were highlighted in the discussion of "clusters" of environmental variables in Chapter Two: variables in the same clusters tend to be correlated with each other.

The only environmental effects reported so far (in Chapters Three through Nine) are those that are "direct"; that is, they are unique to the environment in question and cannot be attributed to other environmental variables. What do we mean when we say that a particular environmental characteristic has a "direct" or "indirect" effect? A variable can be considered as having a direct effect when it enters the regression equation and maintains a significant Beta coefficient even after all other variables have entered the equation. (Nonstatistically inclined readers should regard "Beta" coefficients simply as the equivalent of correlation coefficients.) When this happens, the environmental variable is continuing to make a *unique* contribution to the outcome that cannot be accounted for or explained entirely by the effects of other environmental variables. An indirect effect is said to occur when (1) an environmental variable has a significant Beta coefficient after inputs have been controlled, but (2) the coefficient shrinks to nonsignificance when other environmental variables are added to the equation. In other words, when the effect of a particular environmental variable can be completely explained in terms of other "mediating" variables, then its effect on the outcome is said to be entirely indirect.

The Beta coefficients are provided to give the reader some notion of the magnitude of the environmental effect being discussed. However, to avoid cluttering the text with too many numbers, Betas are usually not reported unless they are at least ± .15. In addition, to avoid burdening the reader with too many statistically significant findings that may be of dubious practical significance, environmental effects on outcomes will usually not be mentioned unless the Beta associated with an effect is at least [.05].

The Betas reported here are those produced by the SPSS-X stepwise regression routine, immediately following the step in which the last entering freshman (input) variable comes into the regression equation. At this point in the analysis, all input effects have been controlled, but no environmental variable has yet entered the regression equation. After each step, the computer examines every variable not yet entered into the regression and calculates something called "Beta in." Here, the computer is looking one step ahead to calculate what each environmental variable's Beta coefficient in the regression equation would be if that variable were the one added to the equation at the next step. These Betas are especially important at the step immediately following the entry of the last input variable because they allow us to examine the possible effect of each environmental variable, independently of inputs but before any other environmental variables have entered the regression.

The problem of multicollinearity can be illustrated with a concrete example involving two highly correlated variables: institutional size and public university. These two variables, which are substantially correlated with each other ($r = .65$), form part of the "research and graduate education" cluster discussed in Chapter Two. In the previous chapter we reported that institutional size has a negative effect on student satisfaction with the faculty; attending a public university was not mentioned as having an effect on satisfaction with faculty. Nevertheless, when we look at the "Beta in" immediately after the entry of the last student input variable, we find that each of these environmental measures has a substantial negative effect on satisfaction with faculty. The reason public university was not mentioned in the discussion of environmental effects on satisfaction with faculty is that its "Beta in" becomes nonsignificant when size enters the regression equation. In other words, public university no longer shows any significant effect on satisfaction with faculty once we control for the effects of size. What happened is that public university showed a substantial negative effect (Beta = $-.26$) on satisfaction with faculty immediately after input characteristics were controlled, but the negative effect of institutional size proved to be larger (Beta = $-.33$). Because its Beta was larger at this point, size was the variable that was actually entered at the next step. However, when size was added to the regression equation, the coefficient for public university shrank to nonsignificance. In practical terms, this means that the negative effect of attending a public university can be accounted for by the tendency of such institutions to be larger than others. In terms of causal analysis, we would say that the negative effect of attending a public university on satisfaction with faculty is indirect, being mediated by institutional size.

At this point the reader might ask, if the effect associated with attending a public university can be explained in terms of the public university's larger size, why bother reporting in this chapter that the public university has such an effect? Is not such information superfluous? From the point of view of the prospective college student or parent, the answer to this question would almost certainly be no. Students who are attempting to pick an appropriate college can benefit from knowing they are more likely to be dissatisfied with their faculty if they attend a public university rather than some other type of institution. To them, the explanation of this effect in terms of the public university's larger size is, to a certain extent, irrelevant.

Having information about both variables can also be of use to educators and policy makers. For example, administrators in public universities who might be concerned about the low level of student satisfaction with faculty should know that a certain degree of dissatisfaction may be inevitable, given the institution's large size. Under these conditions, any attempt to raise student satisfaction should probably involve an effort to *simulate* smallness in some manner. On the other hand, if the effect of public universities were to be explained in terms of another highly correlated variable from the "research and graduate education" cluster, such as use of teaching assistants (see Chapter Two), a somewhat different strategy for raising student satisfaction with faculty might be implied. The point here is that, from the perspective of educational policy and educational reform, it is useful for professors and administrators to have information about all the possible environmental variables that might be considered in any effort to enhance student outcomes.

At this point readers might also ask, if the effect of public universities can be explained in terms of other characteristics, such as institutional size, why include a variable like public university at all? Does not this merely cloud our interpretation of the critical causal agent? If we found that every effect asso-

ciated with attending a public university could be explained in
terms of other environmental variables, such as size or reliance
on teaching assistants, this argument might have some merit.
In actuality, however, size does not always have the stronger
relationship to particular outcomes; sometimes both size *and* public university enter the same regression equation. This is the
case, for example, with the perceptual outcome Student-Oriented Faculty (see the preceding chapter). In the analysis of this
outcome measure, public university and institutional size both
have significant Beta coefficients in the final regression equation. Although the high correlation between these two environmental measures causes the Betas for each one to shrink somewhat when the other one enters the equation, both maintain
significant Betas throughout the regression analysis. Therefore,
the negative effect of attending a public university on the student's perception of Student-Oriented Faculty can be explained
in part, but not entirely, by the tendency of public universities
to be larger than other types of institutions. In other words, there
is something about public universities, beyond their large size,
that causes students to report that their faculties are not Student-
Oriented.

The presentation of results given below follows the sequence of environmental variables as described in Chapter Two:
characteristics of the institution, curriculum, faculty environment, and peer environment.

Institutional Characteristics

Results involving the sixteen measures of institutional characteristics will be considered separately under the following headings: type and control, size, graduate emphasis, gender, race,
and resource measures.

Considering first the unique effects of universities, we find
that public and private universities share a number of common
environmental attributes that help to explain most of their effects
on students. Readers should keep in mind that the *maximum possible* correlation of categorical traits like public university or private university with continuous measures like institutional size

is constrained by the percentage of students accounted for by any type. Basically, the more the percentage deviates from 50, the smaller the maximum possible size of the r. Public universities, for example, account for 8 percent of the students in the sample, whereas private universities account for only 5 percent. Thus, if these two types produce correlations of equal size with some institutional characteristics, the correlation involving private university can be considered to be "stronger" than the correlation involving public university.

Several of the environmental attributes shared by both public and private universities are listed here, with the simple correlations in parentheses (public university, private university) after each attribute. Both types are strongly Research Oriented ($r = .50$ for public universities, .48 for private universities), make frequent use of teaching assistants (.58, .47), pay high faculty salaries (.34, .33), put substantial emphasis on resource acquisition and reputational enhancement (.32, .38), and frequently involve undergraduates in faculty research (.31, .28). Their faculties spend relatively little time teaching and advising undergraduates (−.51, −.49), are not student-oriented (−.57, −.32), are relatively uninvolved in teaching general education courses (−.27, −.37), and eschew the use of active learning techniques (−.26, −.36). Both environments put little emphasis on student development and social activism (−.34, −.32).

Public universities are also characterized by certain traits that are less characteristic of private universities. These include large size ($r = .65$ for public universities versus only .12 for private universities), low levels of student-faculty interaction (−.57 versus −.13), substantial racial conflict (.37 versus .17), "progressive" course offerings (.32 versus .09), high student-faculty ratios (.26 versus .09), poor student relations with the administration (−.33 versus −.12), few students receiving need-based financial aid (−.36 versus −.09), and negative faculty attitudes toward the general education program (−.33 versus −.06).

Public universities show a consistent pattern of effects on a variety of student outcomes, although in most instances these effects are indirect; that is, they can be explained by other, highly correlated institutional characteristics, such as large size, strong

Research Orientation, a strong emphasis on Resources and Reputation, heavy use of graduate teaching assistants, Racial Conflict, low faculty time commitment to teaching and student advising, poor student relations with the administration, the lack of a Student-Oriented Faculty, and the absence of an orientation toward Social Activism and Community. As might be expected, attending a public university has its strongest negative effects on satisfaction with faculty (Beta = .26) and on three perceptual outcomes: Student-Oriented Faculty (Beta = -.37), Trust in the Administration, and Social Change Orientation. Attending a public university also has negative effects on satisfaction with curriculum and instruction, the general education program, and student support services. With the exception of Student-Oriented Faculty, all these effects are indirect. Attending a public university has an indirect positive effect on satisfaction with Facilities, no doubt reflecting the large libraries and well-equipped laboratories that one finds in most public universities.

Attending a public university has negative effects on a variety of academic outcomes: MCAT score, Scholarship, GPA, writing ability, analytical and problem-solving ability, critical thinking skills, public speaking ability, Leadership, completion of the bachelor's degree, preparation for graduate school, and actual enrollment in graduate school. Three of these negative effects — on Scholarship, college GPA, and enrollment in graduate school — are direct effects. It is indeed ironic that the very institutions that do most of the graduate and professional education in this country tend to have a negative effect on the student's academic performance and preparation for and actual enrollment in graduate or professional school.

Public universities also have weak, indirect negative effects on being elected to a student office and attending recitals and concerts, and a direct negative effect on majoring in science or engineering. Attending a public university has indirect positive effects on choosing careers in either engineering or medicine and on the belief that the primary benefit of college is to increase one's earning power.

Private universities show a few similarities to public universities in their effects on students, but the two types of institutions also differ considerably in how they affect certain aspects of student development. The similarities appear to result from the tendency of both types of institutions to be large and to have a strong Research Orientation. The two institutional types differ, however, in that the private universities are not as large as the public ones and have lower student-faculty ratios and more student-faculty interaction. These differences may well explain why private universities, unlike the public universities, influence *positively* student retention and interest in graduate school. Attending a private university also strengthens Libertarianism and increases the student's chances of joining a social fraternity or sorority. Private universities also have weak negative effects on Leadership, participation in protests, and tutoring other students.

As far as student perceptions of the environment are concerned, attending a private university has its strongest positive effect on Resources and Reputation Emphasis (Beta = .18). It has negative (but weaker) effects on Diversity Emphasis and perception of the Student Orientation of the Faculty (these negative effects are much weaker than is the case with the public universities).

With the exception of the positive effects on retention and on fraternity and sorority membership, all effects of private universities can be attributed to their strong Research Orientation, large size, and strong Emphasis on Resources and Reputation.

Public four-year colleges include most of the former teachers colleges that expanded their undergraduate and graduate programs and became more general-purpose liberal arts institutions during the 1950s and 1960s. Many also qualify as "comprehensive colleges and universities" under the Carnegie Classification of Higher Education Institutions (Carnegie Foundation, 1987). While most of these institutions have master's programs and many also have doctoral programs and professional schools, undergraduate education remains their primary mission. Although much larger than most private colleges, the public colleges (many of which are called universities) are generally smaller than the "flagship" public universities. They also put much less emphasis on research. The effects of public colleges on students are somewhat less distinctive than the effects of the public universities, perhaps because public colleges are extremely diverse: some are primarily commuter institutions, whereas others are primarily residential; some put a substantial emphasis on research, while others are almost exclusively teaching institutions; a few are very large, while others are quite small in size; many retain a strong emphasis on teacher education, whereas others put very little emphasis on preparing teachers.

The correlations of the type measure "public four-year college" with measures of other institutional characteristics are generally much smaller than the correlations of the two university-type measures, especially considering that the public four-year colleges account for a much larger proportion of the students in our sample (25 percent). This means that these institutions are less easily distinguished from other types of institutions. Why should this be? The most likely explanation is that the four-year colleges, as already noted, comprise a highly diverse set of institutions.

Specifically, the public four-year colleges are characterized by a Lack of Student Community (.30), frequent use of multiple-choice exams (.26), high student-faculty ratios (.24), a well-paid faculty (.28), and a high percentage of resources devoted to instruction (.31). They also score relatively low in Selectivity (−.23), academic competitiveness (−.25), Peer SES (−.30), percentages of students receiving merit-based aid (−.31) *and* need-based aid (−.29), Resources and Reputation Emphasis (−.28), Humanities Orientation (−.23), and Student Orientation of the Faculty (−.25). Finally, Trust in the Administration is low (−.25), and the faculty have a poor opinion of their students' academic ability and preparation (−.36).

Attending four-year public institutions tends to have weak negative effects on satisfaction with faculty, general education requirements, opportunity to take interdisciplinary courses, quality of instruction, and on three perceptual outcomes: Student Orientation of the Faculty, Diversity Orientation, and Social Change Orientation. Satisfaction with Facilities, on the other hand, is positively affected by attending a public college. Unlike the universities, however, the four-year public colleges have a negative effect on perceived Resources and Reputation Emphasis (Beta = −.11).

Attending a public four-year college has a weak negative impact on degree attainment and a weak positive effect on the student's inclination to pursue a career in teaching.

Except for the positive effect on teaching careers and the negative effects on college GPA and Student Orientation of the Faculty, all the previously mentioned effects of attending a public four-year college are indirect and can be attributed to other characteristics of these institutions, such as large size, Lack of Student Community, low Peer SES, weak Humanities Orientation, and lack of a Student Orientation.

Private colleges in our sample comprise three different groups of institutions — independent, Protestant, and Roman Catholic — but all three produce similar patterns of effects on student development. Most of these effects, however, are indirect and can be attributed to small size ($r = -.59$) and strong Student Orientation of the Faculty ($r = .75$). Other characteristics of private colleges include a high percentage of expenditures devoted to student services (.37), low faculty salaries (-.54), low student-faculty ratios (-.36), positive relationships with the administration (.47), and a positive faculty attitude toward students' abilities and preparation (.51). Next, we summarize the effects that are common to all three types of private colleges and then mention a few outcomes that are associated with only one or two of these types.

The effects common to all tend also to be their strongest effects: satisfaction with faculty, general education requirements, quality of instruction, and the perception that the institution is very Student-Oriented. These institutions also have positive effects on the student's perception of a Social Change Orientation and Trust in the Administration and negative effects on Resources and Reputation Emphasis. All three types of institutions also have positive effects on completion of the bachelor's degree and being elected to a student office.

Nonsectarian colleges, in addition to the effects noted earlier, have indirect positive effects on student satisfaction with Individual Support Services and opportunities to take interdisciplinary courses, as well as on MCAT scores and self-reported growth in Cultural Awareness and writing skills. Nonsectarian colleges also have positive effects on participation in protests, attending recitals or concerts, majoring in physical science or social science, and perception of Diversity Orientation, and a negative effect on the view that the principal purpose of college is to increase one's earning power. With the exception of participation in protests, all these effects are indirect. Other characteristics of nonsectarian colleges that serve to mediate these effects include a peer environment that is politically liberal (.36), Permissive (.42), artistically inclined (.38), high in SES (.28), and has a high percentage of Jews (.25) and a low percentage of born-again Christians (−.21). Nonsectarian colleges also have a liberal faculty (.24), a strong Diversity Emphasis (.23), a strong Humanities Orientation (.25), a high level of academic competitiveness (.29), and progressive course offerings (.22); they avoid the Use of Multiple-Choice Exams (−.33).

Roman Catholic colleges also have a weak positive effect on college GPA and weak negative effects on Libertarianism and joining social fraternities or sororities. All these effects are indirect and are mediated by variables such as the high percentage of Catholics in the student body (.63), a low level of Permissiveness (−.28), a high percentage of women on the faculty (.43), a strong Student Orientation (.39), frequent Use of Multiple-Choice Exams (.32), a low level of Racial Conflict (−.30), a weak Emphasis on Resources and Reputation (−.23), a lack of progressive course offerings (−.35), and a strong commitment to Social Activism (.33).

Protestant colleges have positive effects on joining a social fraternity or sorority and attending recitals or concerts and negative effects on MCAT scores and satisfaction with Facilities. The positive effect on joining sororities or fraternities is direct; all others are indirect and attributable to such qualities as a peer group that includes many born-again Christians (.49) and few Catholics (−.40) and that is not politically liberal (−.29), not Permissive (−.34), and that frequently majors in the humanities (.26). Other distinguishing characteristics of Protestant colleges include a high percentage of students receiving merit-based aid (.33) and a faculty that is not Liberal (−.23), is positive about the general education program (.30), is not Research-Oriented (−.41), and has low morale (−.28).

The environmental effects that are shared by these three different types of private colleges are attributable primarily to their small size, strong Commitment to Student Development, residential nature, and weak emphasis on research, resource acquisition, and reputation enhancement. The unique effects of each specific type are due mainly to differences in the characteristics of the student peer groups already noted.

In summary, these findings suggest that institutional type, as such, has little direct effect on student development. Rather, the differential outcomes associated with attending universities rather than colleges, or private versus public versus sectarian institutions, are primarily attributable to differences in these various types of institutions in size, Research Emphasis, Commitment to Student Development, faculty characteristics, and student peer groups. The effects of these other institutional characteristics will be considered in greater depth in subsequent sections of this chapter.

Historically Black Colleges (HBCs)

Relatively few outcome measures are shown to be significantly affected by attending a historically black college (HBC), once the effects of entering student characteristics are controlled. The strongest effects are associated with two perceptual outcomes: Social Change Orientation and Diversity Orientation. Attending an HBC has a positive effect on college GPA, graduating with honors, Intellectual Self-Esteem, participation in protests, tutoring other students, Scholarship, the perception of a Student-Oriented Faculty, and satisfaction with the overall college experience. This last finding is consistent with earlier research on the effects of HBCs (Allen, 1986, 1987; Fleming, 1984). Attending an HBC is also positively associated with choosing majors and careers in science and engineering. The only negative effects of attending an HBC are on satisfaction with institutional Facilities and feeling "overwhelmed by all I have to do." Since African-American students account for more than 90 percent of the enrollment at HBCs, this last finding raises the interesting possibility that attending a *non*black institution may *increase* the African-American student's sense of feeling overwhelmed. Except for the positive effects of HBCs on graduating with honors, attending recitals or concerts, and choosing a career in science, all the other effects are indirect and appear to be attributable to other characteristics of the HBCs, such as low selectivity (−.50), a peer group that is low in SES (−.29) and academic competitiveness (−.27) and high in Social Activism (.49) and Materialism and Status (.39), and a faculty that emphasizes diversity (.22), is heavily involved in administration (.24), and relies heavily on the Use of Multiple-Choice Exams (.40).

Colleges for Women

Attending a college for women is positively associated with baccalaureate completion and with a number of satisfaction outcomes: faculty, overall quality of instruction, general education requirements, Facilities, Individual Support Services, and overall satisfaction. But the strongest effects are on several perceptual outcomes: Diversity Orientation (Beta = .22), Student-Oriented Faculty (Beta = .16), Social Change Orientation (Beta = .14), and Trust in the Administration. Attending a women's college also has positive effects on practically all "leadership" outcomes: the Leadership personality measure, self-reported growth in leadership abilities and public speaking skills, and being elected to a student office. Women's colleges also have positive effects on self-reported growth in Overall Academic Development, Cultural Awareness, writing skills, analytical and problem-solving skills, critical thinking ability, and foreign-language skills. Still other positive effects include participating in protests, and commitment to promoting racial understanding. Negative effects of women's colleges include joining social sororities and two attitudinal outcomes: that racial discrimination is no longer a problem in America, and that the principal value of college is increased earning power.

   In many respects, these patterns of effects replicate many of the findings obtained in longitudinal studies of women's colleges performed some twenty years earlier and summarized in *Four Critical Years*. In particular, these earlier studies show that women were more likely to be satisfied with college, to complete their undergraduate degrees, and especially to participate in leadership activities if they attended women's rather than coeducational colleges. In *Four Critical Years* I speculated about the possibility that women might be more reticent to seek leadership positions if they find themselves competing for these positions with men. Whatever the explanation, it seems clear that the women's movement has not served to eliminate these differential effects between women's and coeducational institutions. It is important to point out that most of the findings reported here are *directly* attributable to attending a women's college; that is, they cannot be entirely explained or accounted for on the basis of other characteristics, such as small size, residential emphasis, and private control.

Predominantly Men's Colleges

Because of the dearth of men's colleges in our sample and in the population at large, we decided instead to include an institutional measure indicating whether the student body comprised at least 80 percent men. In addition to one or two colleges that are still exclusively for men, such a category would include colleges with highly technical curricula (technological universities, service academies, and so on). Attending a predominantly men's college has positive effects on the student's satisfaction with Facilities, Individual Support Services, faculty, general education requirements, overall quality of instruction, and overall college experience. Predominantly men's colleges also have positive effects on two perceptual outcomes — Trust in the Administration, and Social Change Orientation — and a negative effect on the perception of Resources and Reputation Emphasis.

In the behavioral realm, predominantly men's colleges have positive effects on voting in the 1988 election, getting married, and tutoring other students, and negative effects on being elected to a student office and joining a social fraternity or sorority.

Predominantly men's colleges also have weak but significant positive effects in several academic areas: Overall Academic

Development, Leadership, public speaking, job skills, general knowledge, and critical thinking. They also have weak positive effects on self-rated physical health and on the Leadership personality measure.

Attending a predominantly men's college has negative effects on choosing careers in science or engineering. The finding could well be an artifact caused by the inclusion of the service academies in this category. Although high proportions of undergraduates in the service academies major in fields of science and engineering, most of them pursue careers in other fields, such as the military and business; therefore, it may be that the relatively small proportion of their graduates who actually pursue *careers* in science or engineering falls below what would be expected from their entering freshman characteristics.

Institutional Size

As noted in Chapter Two, two different measures of institutional size were used: the total institutional full-time equivalency (FTE) enrollment, and the total undergraduate FTE enrollment. These two measures produce almost identical patterns of effects on student development, although in most instances total enrollment produces slightly larger coefficients than does undergraduate enrollment. Not surprisingly, when one of these two measures enters the regression equation, the other does not. Because the results are generally the same for either measure, the ensuing discussion will refer simply to *size* as the environmental variable.

Size has its strongest and most consistent effects in the affective-psychological realm of student development. Specifically, size has large, indirect negative effects on satisfaction with faculty (Beta = -33) and on the perception of a Student-Oriented Faculty (Beta = $-.46$). It also has negative effects on satisfaction with the quality of instruction, general education requirements, Individual Support Services, opportunities to take interdisciplinary courses, and the overall college experience (the only direct effect). Perceptions of Social Change Orientation, Trust in the Administration, and Diversity Orientation are also negatively but indirectly affected by size. Two satisfaction mea-sures—Facilities and Student Life—are positively and indirectly affected by size, as is the perception of Emphasis on Resource acquisition and Reputational enhancement. Similar effects of size have been reported by Pascarella, Ethington, and Smart (1988) and Smart (1985).

Other affective outcomes that are positively affected by institutional size include the views that the chief benefit of a col-lege education is to increase one's earning power and that the individual can do little to change society. Other outcomes of size that are negatively affected include commitment to develop-ing a meaningful philosophy of life and commitment to promot-ing racial understanding (all indirect). In the behavioral-affective realm, size has direct positive effects on joining a social frater-nity or sorority and being elected to a student office; it has nega-tive and indirect effects on tutoring other students, participat-ing in protests, and attending recitals or concerts. Size also has negative effects on two personality measures: Scholarship (In-tellectual Self-Esteem) and Leadership.

In the cognitive realm, size has positive effects on NTE scores and negative effects on self-reported increases in Overall Academic Development, Cultural Awareness, writing skills, ana-lytical and problem-solving skills, critical thinking skills, general knowledge, leadership skills, public speaking ability, and inter-personal skills. It also has negative effects on GPA, graduating with honors, degree aspirations, self-reported increase in prepa-ration for graduate school, and enrollment in graduate school (direct effect).

Finally, size has direct negative effects on student interest in pursuing careers in both college teaching and scientific re-search and on majoring in the physical sciences.

Emphasis on Graduate Study

The percentage of graduate students making up the entire in-stitutional enrollment produces a pattern of effects very similar to the pattern just described for total enrollment. As a matter of fact, with very few exceptions, every outcome variable showing a significant effect from the percentage of graduate students shows the same effect from total enrollment except that the coefficient associated with enrollment is almost always larger. There are only two exceptions to this generalization. First, both variables have positive effects on Resources and Reputation Emphasis, but the Beta coefficient for percentage of graduate students (.20) is larger than the Beta for total enrollment (.15). The second exception concerns a weak but significant positive effect on percentage of graduate students choosing a career in science or engineering; total enrollment shows no effect one way or another on this outcome.

Student-Faculty Ratio

The student-faculty ratio is one of the most discussed policy issues in higher education. Indeed, faculty arguments for greater administrative funding of faculty positions are often predicated on the assumption that having fewer students per faculty member improves the educational climate. Many institutions emphasize a low student-faculty ratio in their promotional materials, presumably to persuade students that they will get more attention from faculty if the ratio is low.

Although student-faculty ratio proves to have a number of significant effects on student outcomes after student input measures are controlled, all but one of these effects can be accounted for on the basis of other characteristics that are related to the student-faculty ratio (Student Orientation of the Faculty, Intellectual Self-Esteem of the peer group, and so on). The strongest effects of the student-faculty ratio are on the perception of a Student-Oriented Faculty (Beta = −.33) and satisfaction with faculty (Beta = −.23). Keep in mind that these negative coefficients mean that a low student-faculty ratio is associated with a *high* degree of satisfaction. These correlations reinforce the idea that a low student-faculty ratio does indeed have positive implications for student-faculty relationships. The student-faculty ratio also has significant negative effects on practically every other satisfaction measure: Individual Support Services, overall quality of instruction, general education requirements, opportunities to take interdisciplinary courses, and the overall college experience. (The only satisfaction outcomes not significantly associated with student-faculty ratio are Student Life and Facilities.)

The student-faculty ratio also has weaker negative effects on bachelor's degree attainment, plans to attend graduate school, and self-reported growth in all cognitive areas except job skills and knowledge of a field or discipline. Student-faculty ratio is positively associated with voting in the 1988 student election but negatively associated with being elected to a student office, joining a social fraternity or sorority, participating in protests, attending recitals or concerts, and alcohol consumption. Student-faculty ratio also has a positive effect on three beliefs — that the principal purpose of a college education is to increase earning power, that the individual cannot change society, and that racial discrimination is no longer a problem in America — and negative effects on Liberalism, commitment to promoting racial understanding, Scholarship, Leadership, and self-rated emotional and physical health. Further, a high student-faculty ratio is associated with a perception of a strong Resources and Reputation Emphasis and negatively associated with the perceptions of Diversity Orientation and Social Change Orientation.

With the exception of the negative effect of student-faculty ratio on satisfaction with opportunities to take interdisciplinary courses, all these effects are indirect. For the most part, these effects are mediated through the effects of large size, public control (college or university), Research Orientation, and (lack of a) Student-Oriented Faculty.

Expenditures for Student Services

The measure for expenditures on student services consists of the percentage of total "educational and general" expenditures allocated to student services. It is intended to reflect the extent of the institution's commitment to student support services. This measure has its strongest direct positive effects on satisfaction with faculty (Beta = .26) and on the perception of a Student-Oriented Faculty (Beta = .32). It also has direct positive effects on perceptions of Social Change Orientation (Beta = .18) and

Trust in the Administration and on satisfaction with Individual Support Services, the overall quality of instruction, general education requirements, and the overall college experience. The direct positive effect on satisfaction with Individual Support Services (Beta = .18) suggests that investing in student services actually pays off in terms of increased student satisfaction.

The percentage of all expenditures spent on student services has an indirect negative effect on the perception of a Resources and Reputation Emphasis (Beta = −.19) and a direct negative effect on satisfaction with Facilities. The last effect might be a reflection of the zero-sum nature of institutional expenditures: monies spent on student support services may reduce the funds available for facilities.

In the cognitive realm, the percentage of expenditures invested in student services has indirect positive effects on degree completion and on all self-rated growth in leadership abilities, public speaking skills, critical thinking skills, and preparation for graduate school. It also has a weak but direct effect on self-reported growth in writing skills. Investment in student services has weak but significant indirect effects on Scholarship (Intellectual Self-Esteem), tutoring other students, and participating in protests. (Except for the effect on writing skills, all the effects are indirect.) In the vocational area, the percentage of student services expenditures has a direct positive effect on choosing majors in physical science fields and an indirect negative effect on choosing a career in engineering.

Instructional Expenditures

Instructional expenditures, the companion measure to the preceding one, reflects the percentage of total educational and general expenditures invested in instruction. This measure produces a pattern of effects very similar to that for student services expenditures, except that in most instances the Beta coefficients are smaller, and in every instance the effects are indirect.

The reader may wonder why these two expenditure measures do not produce opposing rather than similar patterns of effects, since they represent competing demands on the same resource base. The key to understanding these results lies in the broad category "educational and general expenditures." In addition to student support services and instruction, this resource pool is also invested in research, facilities, and other areas of institutional functioning not directly concerned with student learning and student development (these other areas account for about 13 percent of all expenditures). Apparently, institutions that invest a high percentage of their total resources in student services also tend to invest a relatively high percentage in instruction. Conversely, the institutions that invest heavily in research and facilities tend to invest less in *both* student services and instruction. The results reported here, however, indicate that the investment in student services is a more critical environmental factor than the investment in instruction. One possible explanation of this difference in the relative importance of these two measures is in how institutions define "instructional" costs. The largest single source of such costs is faculty salaries. Apparently, some institutions include all faculty salaries under instructional costs, even though their faculty are expected to do research as a part of their job. Other institutions, by contrast, allocate a certain proportion of faculty salaries to "research" rather than "instruction."

Curriculum

One of the major surprises of this study is the relatively weak influence on student development exerted by the formal general education curriculum. There are some significant effects associated with particular curricular variables, but the magnitude of these effects is almost always much weaker than is the case with measures of either the peer environment or the faculty environment.

True-Core Curriculum

Attending an institution with a true-core curriculum (that is, one that requires all students to take exactly the same courses in order to satisfy general education requirements) has positive effects on several satisfaction measures: opportunities to take interdisciplinary courses, general education requirements, faculty, and overall quality of instruction. A true-core curriculum also has positive effects on perceptions of a Student-Oriented Faculty, Diversity Orientation, Trust in the Administration, and Social Change Orientation, and a negative effect on Resources and Reputation Emphasis. Other positive effects are on joining a social fraternity or sorority and being elected to a student office. Most of these effects appear to be uniquely attributable to having a true-core curriculum, since they cannot be entirely explained by other environmental characteristics.

Major-Dominated General Education Curriculum

Having general education requirements defined by the individual departments has only a few significant effects: major-dominated programs have a positive effect on participation in protests, and negative effects on graduating with honors and perceived Trust in the Administration. All of these effects are direct.

Progressive Offerings

This curricular measure, progressive offerings, reflects the extent to which general education offerings include courses on contemporary issues, such as ethnic studies or gender studies; it is generally associated with large, complex institutions. That the smaller institutions generally score low on this measure may simply reflect their smaller faculties and more limited range of curricular options. The progressive offerings measure produces a pattern of effects very much like that already described for institutional size and public university, although there are fewer significant relationships and the Betas tend to be much smaller. More important, with the exceptions noted next, none of these effects appears to be directly attributable to this curricular variable.

The three notable exceptions to this generalization are the positive effects of progressive course offerings on perceptions of a strong Diversity Orientation (Beta = .17) and Resources and

Reputation Emphasis (Beta = .16) and its negative effect on perceived Trust in the Administration. These direct effects offer interesting material for speculation. The fact that an institution offers many progressive courses may influence a student's perception of the school's Diversity Orientation, but why should these same progressive offerings be negatively associated with Trust in the Administration? Could the existence of such courses breed mistrust in the administration? Or could it be that the faculty and administrators in these institutions have attempted to mollify student dissent by authorizing the inclusion of many such courses?

Personalized and Individualized General Education Program

The existence of a personalized curriculum produces a number of significant correlations with student outcomes after control for student input characteristics, but in most cases the effects are indirect and disappear after other environmental variables are controlled. The personalized and individualized curriculum is positively associated with most areas of satisfaction, participating in protests, Liberalism, and perceptions of Diversity Orientation and Social Change Orientation. The only significant effects that appear to be directly attributable to this curricular measure are a positive effect on satisfaction with facilities and a negative effect on Trust in the Administration.

Integrated or Interdisciplinary General Education Program

An integrated curriculum has even fewer significant effects than the personalized and individualized curricular measure, and virtually all of them are indirect. The largest positive effects have to do with satisfaction with faculty and perception of a Student-Oriented Faculty. The largest negative effects relate to satisfaction with Facilities, but all of these prove to be indirect. The only direct effect is a negative effect on Trust in the Administration.

Structured General Education Program

The degree of structure (versus freedom of choice) in the distributional system of the institution's general educational program produces no effects worthy of note.

The findings related to curricular measures suggest that, with the exception of the true-core curriculúm, the particular form of an institution's general education program has little significance for student development. This does not mean that other curricular characteristics, such as the number of courses students take in particular subject matter fields (see the next chapter), cannot have important effects on student development. Rather, it suggests that the varieties of general educational programs currently used in American higher education do not seem to make much difference in any aspect of the student's cognitive or affective development. This issue will be discussed in more detail in Chapter Twelve.

Other types of curricular variables, such as course requirements and methods of examining, have greater impact on student satisfaction. These are discussed in the following sections.

Written Evaluations

Only a few institutions in American higher education offer written evaluations of student performance as an alternative to traditional grading (only 4 percent of our sample is enrolled in such institutions). Our study, however, reveals several interesting effects that appear to be directly attributable to this particular environmental practice. Perhaps most intriguing is that the use of written evaluations has a positive impact on the student's interest in pursuing a career in college teaching. Since a professor cannot write a competent evaluation of a student without getting to know that person quite well, it is possible that such professors are viewed by some of these students as attractive role models.

The use of written evaluations is also positively associated with four perceptual outcomes: Student Orientation of the Faculty, Diversity Orientation, Social Change Orientation, and

Trust in the Administration. It also has a positive effect on satisfaction with Facilities and on the student's commitment to making a theoretical contribution to science. This pattern of results suggests strongly that written evaluations, despite their labor intensity, offer a promising possibility for enhancing the quality of student-faculty relationships and for developing in students a greater sense of identification with their faculty mentors.

Thesis or Senior Project Requirement

Requiring a thesis or senior project has a direct positive effect on the likelihood that the student will graduate with honors. Apparently, such projects frequently serve as the basis for the awarding of honors. The thesis or project requirement also has positive effects on the student's perception of a Student-Oriented Faculty and satisfaction with faculty, but has negative effects on satisfaction with Student Life and with Facilities. (These two negative effects are direct ones.) Having a terminal project also has an indirect positive effect on the perception of a Resources and Reputation Emphasis and an indirect negative effect on the perception of a Diversity Orientation.

Other Curricular Requirements

Three other curricular requirement measures—comprehensive exam, research requirement, and internship experience—all produce only a few weak effects, virtually all of which disappear when other environmental variables are controlled. The sole exception is a weak positive effect of a required internship on the student's commitment to making a theoretical contribution to science.

Availability of Minority or Third World Courses

The offering of minority courses and women's studies (discussed next) represents a partial dissection of the "progressive offerings" measure examined earlier. Specifically, this variable indicates whether the institution offers any courses focusing on minority or Third World perspectives. The inclusion of such courses has a positive effect on the perception of Diversity Orientation and on the perception of a Social Change Orientation. It also has positive effects on satisfaction both with Facilities and with the overall college experience, and negative effects on being elected to a student office. All these effects appear to be directly attributable to this curricular variable.

Having minority or Third World course offerings also has a number of indirect effects: satisfaction with Student Life and with opportunities to take interdisciplinary courses are positively affected, and degree attainment, satisfaction with faculty, and perception of a Student-Oriented Faculty are negatively affected.

Women's Studies Offerings

A parallel measure to the preceding one, women's studies in the curriculum, produces a very similar pattern of effects. Offering women's studies courses has direct positive effects on the perception of Diversity Orientation, on satisfaction with Student Life and with Facilities, and on self-reported improvements in general knowledge. Offering women's studies also produces a number of other effects similar to those described for minority or Third World offerings, but in all instances these are indirect.

Minority or Third World Course Requirement

In the next two measures, the courses are not just offered but required. Here, as a part of their general education program, students must take a course emphasizing minority or Third World studies (17 percent of the students attended such institutions). All the effects associated with this curricular variable are weak, although a few effects appear to be directly attributable, at least in part, to this curricular measure: positive effects on satisfaction with overall quality of instruction and with the overall college experience, Trust in the Administration, and Diversity Orientation.

Women's or Gender Studies Course Requirement

The next curricular variable is relatively rare; only 6 percent of our sample enrolled in institutions requiring women's or gender studies courses. The variable produces a number of direct effects that are difficult to interpret: negative effects on satisfaction with Student Life, Facilities, and the overall quality of instruction, and positive effects on joining social fraternities or sororities. There are no obvious explanations for these somewhat puzzling findings.

Before leaving the subject of the curricular environment, the reader should keep in mind that two other major sets of curricular variables will be examined later: the percentage of students majoring in various academic fields (see the section on the peer group), and the number of courses taken by the student in various subject matter fields (see Chapter Eleven). In the next section we will also examine in detail some of the instructional practices followed by faculty.

The Faculty Environment

Given the very high correlations among some of the faculty environment measures (Chapter Two), the summaries of results presented in this section will not follow the same sequence of faculty variables as described in Chapter Two. Rather, the discussion will be organized around faculty environmental measures that are highly correlated with each other. We start with faculty variables that are associated with the positive pole of the "research versus student orientation" cluster (see Chapter Two).

Research Orientation

The Research Orientation of the faculty has a number of significant effects on student development, including some of the strongest effects of all of the environmental measures utilized in the study. This environmental variable has its strongest positive effect on the student's perception of the institution's Resources and Reputation Emphasis (Beta = .32) and its strongest negative effects on the Student Orientation of the Faculty (−.41) and satisfaction with faculty (−.34). All three of these effects are directly attributable to Research Orientation. Research Orientation also has direct positive effects on SAT and LSAT scores and substantial and direct negative effects on the perception of Social Change Orientation (Beta = −.20) and Trust in the Administration (Beta = −.17). Other findings (all indirect) include negative effects on satisfaction with overall quality of instruction and with Individual Support Services and a positive effect on satisfaction with Facilities (Beta = .17).

Research Orientation also has substantial negative effects on Leadership, self-reported growth in public speaking skills, being elected to a student office, and tutoring other students. With the exception of election to a student office, these are all direct effects.

Other significant indirect effects of Research Orientation include a positive effect on Libertarianism and negative effects on completing the bachelor's degree, growth in interpersonal skills, satisfaction with the overall quality of instruction and with the overall college experience, graduating with honors, college GPA, and attending recitals or concerts.

Research Orientation also has an indirect positive effect on majoring in engineering and negative indirect effects on majoring in either physical science or business.

These results show clearly that, with the exception of performance on standardized tests, there is a significant institutional price to be paid, in terms of student development, for a very strong faculty emphasis on research.

Average Faculty Salary

Information on average faculty salary was obtained from the 1988 survey of faculty salaries conducted jointly by the National Center for Education Statistics and the College and University Personnel Association. With the very high correlation between this measure and the Research Orientation of the faculty ($r = .86$), it should not be surprising that the pattern of results is almost identical. Average faculty salary, however, has somewhat smaller Beta coefficients and many fewer direct effects. Accordingly, only those outcomes that are directly affected by faculty salaries, or which produce results that are different from those of Research Orientation, are reported here.

The strongest direct effects of average faculty salary are a positive effect on student satisfaction with Facilities (Beta = .23) and a negative effect on perception of the institution's Social Change Orientation (Beta = −.18). The measure of average faculty salaries also has an indirect negative effect on the student's chances of joining a social fraternity or sorority.

Use of Teaching Assistants

Here again, we have a faculty environmental measure, use of teaching assistants, that is highly correlated with Research Orientation and that produces a very similar pattern of effects. As with faculty salaries, we report here only those outcomes that are directly affected by the use of teaching assistants, or that produce findings different from those reported for Research Orientation. The institution's degree of reliance on teaching assistants has a direct positive effect on the student's perception of the institution's Resources and Reputation Emphasis and direct negative effects on self-reported change in leadership skills and interpersonal skills, being elected to a student office, and attending recitals or concerts. Earlier (Chapter Six) we speculated about the possible reasons for this negative effect on leadership. What is it about the heavy use of assistants in teaching undergraduates that seems to inhibit the development of the student's leadership skills? Since teaching assistants are also students, is it possible that they are perceived as "peer leaders" by the undergraduates they teach, such that these undergraduates become overly dependent on the assistants for advice and counsel and thereby less likely to take initiative? While this is admittedly a highly speculative interpretation, the potential importance of this finding suggests that further research on the dynamics of this effect is warranted.

Working with Students on Research

The percentage of faculty who involve undergraduates in their research activities has a pattern of effects that is very similar to that of Research Orientation, except that the coefficients are much smaller and the number of direct effects very limited. There are only two direct effects: a positive effect on the perception of the institution's Resources and Reputation Emphasis (Beta = .25), and a weak negative effect on satisfaction with general education requirements.

Emphasis on Resources and Reputation

As with all the faculty environmental variables discussed so far, Resources and Reputation Emphasis produces a pattern of effects very similar to the pattern reported above for Research Orientation. This environmental measure has direct effects on only four outcome measures. Two of these involve negative effects on satisfaction measures: the quality of instruction, and the overall college experience. The other two direct positive effects are on two outcomes not affected by Research Orientation: joining a social fraternity or sorority, and majoring in engineering.

Percentage of Faculty in Science Fields

The proportion of faculty in science has only two direct effects (both negative) on student outcomes: satisfaction with Student Life, and interest in pursuing a career in school teaching. Otherwise, the pattern of effects (all indirect) closely resembles the pattern for Research Orientation.

Percentage of Faculty Holding Doctorates

The pattern of significant effects for the percentage of faculty with doctorates is similar to that for Research Orientation except that the coefficients are much smaller and none of them is direct. This measure does show weak but significant positive effects on two outcomes not affected by Research Orientation:

satisfaction with the opportunity to take interdisciplinary courses, and participation in campus protests. Both of these effects, however, are indirect.

Racial Conflict

One final environmental measure that produces a pattern of effects similar to that for Research Orientation of the Faculty is Racial Conflict. This measure also produces four direct effects that are different from the effects of Research Orientation. All are positive: participation in protests, Liberalism, joining social fraternities or sororities, and perception of an Institutional Diversity Orientation. While it is understandable that Racial Conflict on the campus might foster student participation in protests and the development of Liberalism, why should it also encourage students to join fraternities or sororities, and why should it be a factor in the perception of a Diversity Orientation on campus? In the case of fraternities or sororities, perhaps the balkanization that often occurs on campuses with a good deal of racial strife may lead to the formation of social organizations that cater to particular racial or ethnic groups or to conservative students who want to isolate themselves from racial interaction. As far as Diversity Orientation is concerned, at least two different interpretations are possible. On the one hand, the existence of Racial Conflict may lead institutions to initiate greater affirmative action efforts and to expand course offerings in the areas of ethnic and women's studies. On the other hand, Racial Conflict may be the *result* of having a strong Diversity Orientation. Given that both Racial Conflict and Diversity Orientation are based on people's *perceptions,* the direction of causation here is unclear.

Student Orientation of the Faculty

We now consider environmental variables that have strong *negative* correlations with Research Orientation. Most of these variables come from the negative pole of the "research versus student orientation" cluster of environmental measures (see Chapter

Two). The Student Orientation of the Faculty produces more substantial direct effects on student outcomes than almost any other environmental variable. Its strongest positive effects are on a variety of satisfaction outcomes: faculty (Beta = .32), quality of instruction (Beta = .22), Individual Support Services (Beta = .18), general education requirements, opportunities to take interdisciplinary courses, and the overall college experience. With the exception of the last two satisfaction measures, all these effects are direct and cannot be attributed to other environmental variables.

The Student Orientation of the Faculty also has a number of direct positive effects on academic outcomes: bachelor's degree attainment (Beta = .16), Scholarship (Intellectual Self-Esteem), and self-reported growth in writing skills, critical thinking abilities, analytical and problem-solving skills, preparation for graduate school, and Overall Academic Development. This environmental variable also has a direct positive effect on the student's decision to major in some field of physical science, as well as indirect positive effects on commitment to developing a meaningful philosophy of life and on self-reported growth in foreign-language skills, leadership abilities, general knowledge, and public speaking skills.

The Student Orientation of the Faculty has indirect positive effects on Leadership, degree aspirations, decision to re-enroll at the same college, being elected to a student office, tutoring other students, participating in protests, attending recitals or concerts, college GPA, and graduating with honors. Finally, Student Orientation of the Faculty has direct negative effects on two satisfaction outcomes, Student Life and Facilities, and an indirect negative effect on the view that the principal purpose of college is to increase one's earning power. In short, this pattern of effects suggests that having a strongly Student-Oriented Faculty pays rich dividends in the affective and cognitive development of the undergraduate.

Social Activism and Community Orientation

The Social Activism and Community Orientation variable produces a pattern of effects very similar to that for Student Orientation of the Faculty. The only unique effects are on Social Activism and Liberalism (both positive) and on the belief that the individual can do little to change society (negative). Social Activism and Community Orientation also has direct positive effects on commitment to developing a meaningful philosophy of life and satisfaction with faculty (Beta = .32), overall quality of instruction (Beta = .21), opportunities to take interdisciplinary courses, and general knowledge.

Hours Spent Teaching and Advising Students

As might be expected, the measure for hours spent teaching and advising produces a pattern of effects very much like that for Student Orientation of the Faculty. The variable has only one unique effect: a positive one on joining a social fraternity or sorority. The only other direct effect is a positive influence on the student's choice of a natural science major.

The absence of effects uniquely attributable to hours per week spent teaching and advising students suggests that the *quality* of faculty-student contacts may be of critical importance. In other words, the sheer number of hours devoted to teaching and advising is of relatively little consequence, once the effects of the Student Orientation of the Faculty are taken into account.

Faculty Commitment to Students' Personal Development; Altruism

As mentioned in Chapter Two, this factor was broken down into two separate measures, one representing commitment to students' personal development and the other related to altruism. As it happens, both variables produce patterns of effects closely paralleling the pattern associated with Student Orientation of the Faculty, and neither variable has any direct effects, with the following exceptions: faculty Altruism has a weak negative effect on commitment to being very well off financially, and faculty commitment to students' personal development has unique (but indirect) negative effects on Hedonism and Liberalism.

Use of Active Learning

As with the four preceding environmental measures, Use of Active Learning produces a pattern of effects that closely resembles the one for Student Orientation of the Faculty, although the coefficients tend to be somewhat smaller. Almost without exception, there are no unique effects of this faculty measure and no direct effects on student outcomes. Apparently, reliance on Active Learning strategies is simply a proxy for Student Orientation of the Faculty.

Positive Perception of the Administration

This faculty environmental measure, Positive Perception of the Administration, also produces a pattern of effects almost identical to the one for Student Orientation of the Faculty. However, there are no unique effects of this faculty measure and no direct effects on student outcomes.

Perceived Academic Competence of Students

Perceived Academic Competence of Students also parallels the Student Orientation of the Faculty measure in its pattern of effects on student outcomes. It produces no direct effects of note, and only one unique indirect effect: a negative impact on student satisfaction with Individual Support Services.

Apparently, perceiving students as academically capable is simply one more manifestation of a Student-Oriented Faculty and not of any great importance in its own right, as far as student development is concerned.

Percentage of Faculty Teaching Interdisciplinary Courses

The percentage of faculty teaching interdisciplinary courses also produces a pattern of effects similar to the pattern associated with Student Orientation of the Faculty, but it yields some interesting unique effects. The largest direct effect is on student satisfaction with opportunities to take interdisciplinary courses

(Beta = .16). This finding is perhaps not remarkable, given that one would expect more such courses to be available if a high proportion of faculty is engaged in teaching them. The percentage of faculty involved in teaching interdisciplinary courses also has direct effects on two perceptual variables: Social Change Orientation, and Trust in the Administration. This environmental measure produces several effects not observed for Student Orientation of the Faculty: positive effects on Liberalism, Political Orientation (liberal versus conservative), and choice of a major in social science; negative effects on majoring in business and on self-reported growth in job skills. All these unique effects, however, are indirect, which means that they disappear after other environmental variables are controlled.

Percentage of Faculty Teaching General Education Courses

This measure, percentage of faculty teaching general education courses, also resembles Student Orientation of the Faculty in its effects on student outcomes, although there are some direct and unique effects. The percentage of faculty teaching general education courses has direct positive effects on satisfaction with Student Life, attending recitals or concerts, perception of an institutional Emphasis on Diversity, and voting in the 1988 presidential election. Otherwise, the pattern of effects (all indirect) is identical to the pattern for Student Orientation of the Faculty. The reader should note that while these effects are highly significant statistically ($p < .0005$), they are quite small in magnitude.

Percentage of Faculty Engaged in Team Teaching

The percentage of faculty engaged in team teaching produces only very weak and indirect effects, closely following the pattern of effects for Student Orientation of the Faculty. It appears that team teaching is simply one more manifestation of having a Student-Oriented Faculty and has no direct significance for student outcomes once other environmental variables are taken into account. Another possibility, of course, is that the overall benefits of genuine team teaching are masked in these data because many faculty use the term to refer simply to "side-by-side" or "taking turns" teaching. Next, we consider the faculty variables that define the "liberalism" cluster of environmental measures as reported in Chapter Two.

Political Orientation of Faculty

As discussed in Chapter Two, this measure is simply the mean score of the institution's faculty on the political orientation item (far left . . . far right). Positive effects are associated with the liberal or left side of the spectrum, whereas negative effects are associated with the conservative or right side of the spectrum. This variable has its strongest direct effects on perception of the institution's Diversity Orientation (Beta = .24) and on the student's own political orientation. The faculty's Political Orientation also has direct negative effects on getting married, graduating with honors, and perceived Trust in the Administration. This suggests that institutions whose faculties are relatively conservative encourage early marriage among their students, graduate a high proportion of students with honors, and produce a relatively high degree of Trust in the Administration.

This environmental measure has a number of other indirect effects that are worthy of mention. Faculty who lean toward the left side of the political spectrum tend to have positive effects on student Liberalism, Libertarianism, participation in protests, Hedonism, commitment to promoting racial understanding, and alcohol consumption; on several satisfaction measures (Facilities, opportunities to take interdisciplinary courses, and Student Life), on self-growth reported in Cultural Awareness; and on commitment to promoting racial understanding. (Readers should keep in mind that the opposite pattern of effects would be associated with a faculty that leans toward the right.) This measure also has indirect positive effects on majoring in natural science or social science and a negative effect on majoring in business. Other negative effects (all indirect) include self-reported growth in public speaking skills and job skills, satisfaction with faculty, joining social fraternities or sororities, and two value items: the belief that racial discrimination is no longer a problem, and the belief that the principal purpose of a college education is to increase one's earning power.

Faculty Liberalism

Whereas the preceding faculty measure is concerned with the political labels embraced by the faculty, this particular measure reflects the faculty's acceptance of liberal views on social *issues.* As would be expected, these two environmental measures are very highly correlated ($r = .95$) and produce quite similar patterns of effects on student outcomes. There are, however, some interesting differences. Faculty Liberalism, for example, has a direct positive effect on student Liberalism. Recall that student Liberalism (see Chapter Five) also reflects the extent to which the student accepts liberal positions on social issues. We thus find that students' views on social issues are directly affected by the faculty's views on the same or similar issues, whereas the student's preference for particular political labels is influenced by the faculty's preference for these same labels. In other words, to make a distinction between views on social issues and preference for political *labels* may seem like splitting hairs, but the distinction appears to be meaningful in the way students' political values are affected by their faculty's political values. There is, in other words, a real difference between political *labeling* and actual views on political *issues.*

Institutional Diversity Emphasis

Emphasis on Institutional Diversity, and the following environmental measure, both have to do with diversity, although there are important differences. This particular measure reflects institutional goals or commitment to policies such as increasing the representation of minorities in the student body, increasing the representation of women and minorities on the faculty, and emphasizing multiculturalism. It has direct positive effects on self-reported growth in Cultural Awareness and on commitment to the goal of promoting racial understanding. It also has direct positive effects on satisfaction in three areas: Student Life, opportunities to take interdisciplinary courses, and the overall college experience. Finally, it has a direct negative effect on the view that racial discrimination is no longer a problem in America.

Institutional Diversity Emphasis also has a number of indirect positive effects on Political Orientation (liberalism versus conservatism), participation in protests, Liberalism, Libertarianism, and satisfaction with Facilities and the quality of instruction. It has indirect negative effects on joining social fraternities or sororities, getting married, and the view that the principal benefit of a college education is to increase one's earning power.

Faculty Diversity Orientation

The faculty's orientation toward diversity reflects the extent to which faculty members incorporate issues of ethnicity or gender in their courses and in their research. Its pattern of effects is similar to the one just described for Institutional Diversity Emphasis, but there are some interesting differences. Like Institutional Diversity Emphasis, Faculty Diversity Orientation has a direct positive effect on self-reported growth in Cultural Awareness. It also has direct positive effects on participating in protests, willingness to re-enroll in the same college, and voting in the 1988 presidential election. Faculty Diversity Orientation has indirect positive effects on satisfaction with faculty and the overall quality of instruction (Institutional Diversity Emphasis showed no significant effect on either of these outcomes). Otherwise, the patterns of effects for these two "diversity" measures are quite similar.

Percentage of Women on the Faculty

This simple measure of faculty characteristics — percentage of women on the faculty — produces one of the most interesting patterns of effects. The percentage of women has direct positive effects on students' satisfaction with faculty (Beta = .17), the perception of a Student-Oriented Faculty (Beta = .21), the perception of a Diversity Orientation (Beta = .20), and Trust in the

Administration. It also has weaker but significant direct positive effects on Scholarship (Intellectual Self-Esteem), degree aspirations, and self-reported growth in knowledge of a field or discipline. Percentage of women on the faculty has indirect positive effects on satisfaction with the overall quality of instruction, self-reported growth in writing skills, being elected to a student office, and college GPA. Negative indirect effects include satisfaction with Facilities and the perception of Resources and Reputation Emphasis.

If nothing else, this pattern of effects offers strong empirical support for efforts to recruit more women on college faculties.

Faculty Morale

It is perhaps surprising that Faculty Morale produces a pattern of results that mirrors the pattern for Research Orientation of the Faculty, but the study results show that faculty who work in institutions with a very strong Research Orientation tend to have higher morale than faculty in non–research-oriented schools. This measure has no direct effects, but an interesting and perhaps ironic finding is that it still produces indirect negative effects on student satisfaction with faculty (Beta = $-.15$) and the perception of a Student-Oriented Faculty (Beta = $-.19$).

Age of the Faculty

While Age of the faculty yields no direct effects, it produces indirect effects on satisfaction with faculty and the perception of a Student-Oriented Faculty. Other weaker but significant indirect effects of possible interest include positive associations with Trust in the Administration and negative effects on satisfaction with Facilities and on the perception of a Resources and Reputation Emphasis.

Humanities Orientation

Another measure that produces an interesting and unique pattern of effects on student outcomes is the Humanities Orientation of the institution. This measure has direct positive effects on self-reported increases in both writing and critical thinking skills. It also has direct positive effects on the student's degree aspirations, attainment of the bachelor's degree (Beta = .15), and perceptions of a Student-Oriented Faculty (Beta = .30) and of a Social Change Orientation (Beta = .20). There is a negative effect on the view that the principal benefit of a college education is to increase one's earning power (Beta = −.11).

Other substantial but indirect effects include satisfaction with faculty (Beta = .20), the overall quality of instruction (Beta = .18), opportunities to take interdisciplinary courses (Beta = .15), and individual support services. The Humanities Orientation also produces positive indirect effects on self-reported change in general knowledge, Overall Academic Development, and Cultural Awareness, and a negative indirect effect on self-reported improvement in job skills. Other indirect effects include Political Orientation (liberalism versus conservatism), Scholarship, self-reported growth in preparation for graduate school, desire to re-enroll in the same college, self-reported growth in listening ability, participation in protests, attending recitals or concerts, Liberalism, Trust in the Administration, and perception of a Diversity Orientation. Negative indirect effects include the view that racial discrimination is no longer a problem in America, joining fraternities or sororities, and Resources and Reputation Emphasis.

Humanities Orientation also has a direct positive effect on majoring in psychology, indirect positive effects on majoring either in natural science or social science, and a negative effect on majoring in engineering.

In many respects, this pattern of effects is highly consistent with the rationale typically advanced to support not only humanities requirements but also the overall concept of a liberal education. Apparently, institutions that carry on the tradition of the humanities affect student development in many ways that are consistent with the underlying philosophy.

Use of Multiple-Choice Tests

This measure of a particular faculty testing practice — specifically, the Use of Multiple-Choice Tests — produces generally weak and scattered effects, but there are two direct positive effects: self-reported improvement in public speaking ability, and choice of a career in school teaching. The last effect may reflect the emphasis on the development and use of multiple-choice tests that one frequently encounters in teacher-training programs.

A few other indirect effects of Using Multiple-Choice Tests are worth noting: positive effects on the views that racial discrimination is no longer a problem and that the chief benefit of college is monetary, and on self-reported growth in listening ability, Cultural Awareness, and critical thinking abilities. Negative effects are found for commitment to promoting racial understanding, participation in protests, Liberalism, Libertarianism, and the perception both of Diversity Orientation and of Resources and Reputation Emphasis.

Time Stress

The final faculty measure, Time Stress, produces direct positive effects on the student's alcohol consumption and choice of a major in psychology. Otherwise, there are no noteworthy effects, either direct or indirect, of this measure.

The Peer Group

Now we come to those aspects of the college environment — peer group characteristics — that produce some of the strongest and certainly the most widespread effects on student development. We begin with a measure that is actually taken from the faculty survey, Lack of Student Community, and then move to a consideration of peer group measures derived from the 1985 freshman survey.

Lack of Student Community

Although this environmental measure, Lack of Student Community, is derived from the faculty survey, it reflects the faculty's opinion about a potentially important aspect of the undergraduate peer group: lack of socialization among students, little contact among students, and student apathy (see Chapter Two).

Lack of Student Community has stronger direct effects on student satisfaction with the overall college experience than any other environmental measure. Negative direct effects include satisfaction with the overall college experience (Beta = $-.15$), willingness to re-enroll in the same college, and satisfaction with Student Life. Other direct relationships include a positive effect on the view that the principal benefit of college is to increase one's earning power and negative effects on emotional health, Libertarianism, and Trust in the Administration.

Lack of Student Community also produces negative indirect effects on satisfaction with faculty (Beta = $-.23$), general education requirements, and overall quality of instruction (Beta = $-.18$). Other substantial negative but indirect effects include bachelor's degree attainment (Beta = $-.18$), perception of a Student-Oriented Faculty (Beta = $-.33$), and self-reported growth in Overall Academic Development, Cultural Awareness, writing skills, general knowledge, critical thinking skills, foreign-language skills, and preparation for graduate school.

Among other things, this pattern of effects clearly supports Carnegie Foundation president Ernest Boyer's call for greater efforts to create a stronger sense of community in our undergraduate institutions (Boyer, 1987). Next, we summarize the outcomes associated with peer group measures from the "SES, social science, and selectivity" cluster of environmental measures (see Chapter Two).

Socioeconomic Status (SES)

Peer group SES produced twenty-one significant direct effects on student outcomes, more than any other peer group or faculty measure. Apparently, the individual student is substantially affected by the overall level of affluence and education of his or her fellow students' families. The types of outcomes affected by Peer SES are wide-ranging and include both cognitive and affective and behavioral and psychological measures. Peer SES has positive direct effects on virtually every aspect of student satisfaction: quality of instruction, general education requirements, opportunities to take interdisciplinary courses, student life, and faculty. The coefficients for faculty and student life actually become larger (increases from .05 to .12 and from .08 to .19, respectively) when other environmental variables (especially Research Orientation) are controlled. In addition, Peer SES also has significant indirect effects on satisfaction with the overall college experience and on willingness to re-enroll in the same college. In short, Peer SES has significant effects (mostly direct) on every area of student satisfaction except Individual Support Services.

Peer SES also has significant direct effects on perceptions of a Student-Oriented Faculty, Social Change Orientation, Trust in the Administration, and Resources and Reputation Emphasis, and a significant indirect effect on the perception of Diversity Orientation.

In the cognitive realm, Peer SES has a number of direct positive effects: GRE Verbal, MCAT, and LSAT, and self-reported growth in Overall Academic Development, general knowledge, analytical and problem-solving skills, listening ability, critical thinking skills, foreign-language skills, and preparation for graduate and professional school. It also has a significant indirect effect on self-reported changes in Cultural Awareness. By contrast, Peer SES has significant (but indirect) negative effects on self-reported growth in public speaking ability and interpersonal skills.

In the psychological-affective realm, Peer SES has direct positive effects on Social Activism, Hedonism, and commitment to promoting racial understanding, and a direct negative effect on the view that racial discrimination in the United States is no longer a problem. Other indirect effects include positive impacts on degree aspirations, Liberalism, and Libertarianism, and an indirect negative effect on the view that the principal benefit of college is to increase one's earning power. In the behavioral-affective realm, Peer SES has a direct positive effect on alcohol consumption and an indirect positive effect on participating in protests. Indirect negative effects include getting married and tutoring other students.

Finally, Peer SES has a direct positive effect on interest in pursuing a career in law and indirect positive effects on majoring in psychology or other social sciences. It has a negative indirect effect on interest in majoring in business.

Why should the socioeconomic status of the peer group have such widespread (and generally favorable) effects on student development? While there are many possible explanations for this broad pattern of effects, it may be that institutions that regularly admit students from highly educated and affluent families have been pressured over the years by these students and their parents to develop programs and practices that are geared specifically to the needs of the undergraduate student. Another explanation is in the characteristics of the peers themselves: since high-SES students may already possess many of the personal characteristics that liberal education programs are designed to foster, such students may constitute ideal role models for one another. These possibilities will be discussed in more detail in the final chapter.

Selectivity

Selectivity is one of the most popular measures of institutional characteristics used in higher education research. It indicates the level of academic preparation of the entering students as reflected in their mean performance on standardized college admissions tests. Considering the substantial correlation between Selectivity and Peer SES ($r = .73$), it is not surprising that Selectivity produces a pattern of effects very much like that just described for Peer SES. The Beta coefficients for Selectivity, however, are much smaller than those associated with Peer SES, and none of the effects was significant. Consequently, it appears that any impact of Selectivity on student development can be accounted for on the basis of Peer SES and other correlated environmental variables.

Intellectual Self-Esteem

Because Intellectual Self-Esteem has a substantial correlation with Peer SES ($r = .58$), it is to be expected that some of its effects would be similar. For example, like Peer SES, Intellectual Self-Esteem has a direct positive effect on perception of Resources and Reputation Emphasis (Beta = .29), and negative effects on college GPA, graduating with honors (Beta = $-.10$), and majoring in business. The last three effects, however, are direct effects of Intellectual Self-Esteem (Peer SES has only indirect effects on these outcomes). The entry of Intellectual Self-Esteem into the regression equation is the main reason that Peer SES does not have direct effects on these three outcomes.

Intellectual Self-Esteem also has direct effects on several other outcomes not affected by Peer SES: voting in the 1988 election (positive), and being elected to a student office (negative). Furthermore, there are some direct negative effects of Intellectual Self-Esteem that actually *reverse* the effects noted above for Peer SES: Social Activism, satisfaction with faculty, and satisfaction with Student Life.

Permissiveness

Permissiveness of the peer group has its strongest positive effect (a direct effect) on Libertarianism. Since these two measures are based in part on the same attitudinal items (legalized abortion and legalization of marijuana), these results offer further support for the notion that during the undergraduate years students tend to change their attitudes in the direction of the dominant attitudes of their peer group. Permissiveness also has direct negative effects on three perceptual outcomes: Student-Oriented Faculty, Social Change Orientation, and Trust in the Administration. (This last Beta coefficient actually increases from $-.09$ to $-.25$ when other environmental variables are controlled.)

Permissiveness also has indirect positive effects on a number of other outcomes: Political Orientation (liberalism versus conservatism), Hedonism, participation in protests, alcohol consumption, Liberalism, self-reported growth in Cultural Awareness and writing ability, and perception of Diversity Orientation and Resources and Reputational Emphasis. Permissiveness has indirect negative effects on getting married and on self-reported growth in public speaking skills, job skills, and preparation for graduate school. It also has indirect positive effects on majoring in social science and indirect negative effects on majoring in business.

Altruism and Social Activism

The Altruism and Social Activism of the peer group has direct positive effects on Perceptions of Diversity Orientation (Beta = .26) and Social Change Orientation (Beta = .29), and indirect positive effects appear on perceptions of a Student-Oriented Faculty (Beta = .25) and Trust in the Administration. It has direct negative effects on joining social fraternities or sororities and satisfaction with Facilities and indirect positive effects on satisfaction with faculty (Beta = .16), overall quality of instruction, opportunities for interdisciplinary courses (Beta = .11), Individual Support Services, and the overall college experience. Altruism and Social Activism also has indirect positive effects on several academic outcomes: attainment of the bachelor's degree, and self-reported growth in writing skills, general knowledge, critical thinking abilities, foreign-language skills, Cultural Awareness, and Overall Academic Development. Other indirect positive effects include Liberalism, commitment to promoting racial understanding, Scholarship, Social Activism, majoring in social science, and the decision to re-enroll at the same college. Indirect negative effects include the views that racial discrimination is no longer a problem and that the principal benefit of a college education is to increase one's earning power.

Materialism and Status

With Materialism and Status, once again we find evidence of the peer group's tendency to change a student's attitudes and values in the direction of the dominant values of the peer group. Thus, Materialism and Status of the peer group has direct positive effects on Status Striving, commitment to the goal of being very well off financially, and the perception of a Resources and Reputation Emphasis. It has direct negative effects on self-reported growth in Cultural Awareness and critical thinking abilities, attending recitals and concerts, Liberalism, and the perceptions of both Diversity Orientation and Social Change Orientation. Weaker direct effects include enrollment in graduate school (positive) and satisfaction with Facilities (negative).

Other indirect positive effects of Materialism and Status include joining social fraternities or sororities and the views that racial discrimination is no longer a problem and that the principal benefit of college is to increase one's earning power. Indirect negative effects include commitment to promoting racial understanding, participating in protests, and satisfaction with faculty, general educational requirements, overall quality of instruction, Individual Support Services, Student Life, and the total college experience.

Feminism

It is somewhat surprising to find that Feminism does not affect the individual student's endorsement of Feminism one way or the other. In fact, peer Feminism shows no direct effect on any student outcome measure. It does show a substantial positive but indirect effect on the perception of Diversity Orientation (Beta = .25) and weaker but positive indirect effects on majoring in social science, participation in protests, Liberalism, Libertarianism, Hedonism, Political Orientation (liberalism versus conservatism), self-reported growth in Cultural Awareness and writing skills, and satisfaction with Facilities, opportunities for taking interdisciplinary courses, and the overall quality of instruction. Weak negative effects (all indirect) are associated with getting married, joining fraternities or sororities, and majoring in business.

Artistic Inclination

Artistic Inclination shows direct negative effects on joining social fraternities or sororities and alcohol consumption. It has positive but weak indirect effects on satisfaction with opportunities for interdisciplinary courses and Facilities, self-reported growth in Cultural Awareness, critical thinking abilities, and listening abilities, Political Orientation (liberalism versus conservatism), participation in protests, Liberalism, Libertarianism, and the perception of Diversity Orientation.

Outside Work

Outside Work has its largest direct but negative effect on attainment of the bachelor's degree (Beta = −.13). Realize that this is a *peer* measure, and that degree attainment is also negatively affected by the *individual's* working at an outside job. In other words, this peer effect operates independently of the effects of the individual's work status. In all likelihood, having a large number of students working at outside jobs (and dropping out as a result) may create an atmosphere in which peer sanctions against leaving college are much weaker than they would otherwise be in an institution where students do not work at outside jobs and where the overall dropout rate is low. What is not clear from this finding is whether the Outside Work measure is serving merely as a proxy for the institution's overall dropout rate, or whether a large number of students actually working at outside jobs creates an environment where peer sanctions against dropping out are weak.

Other direct effects of Outside Work are also mostly negative: Leadership, joining social fraternities or sororities, perception of Resources and Reputation Emphasis, and satisfaction with Individual Support Services and with Facilities. The only direct positive effect is on satisfaction with Student Life, a somewhat surprising result. Perhaps the standards for evaluating Student Life are much lower in institutions where many students work at outside jobs.

Scientific Orientation

Only two direct effects are associated with this peer measure: the Scientific Orientation of the peer group has a positive effect on satisfaction with facilities and a negative effect on the attainment of the bachelor's degree. It has indirect positive effects on majoring in engineering and on the perception of Resources and Reputation Emphasis; its indirect negative effects are on satisfaction with faculty (Beta = −.27) and quality of instruction and on perceptions of a Student-Oriented Faculty (Beta = −.21), Social Change Orientation, and Trust in the Administration.

Political Orientation

The Political Orientation of the peer group is defined simply as the mean score of the entering freshmen on the five-point scale measuring liberalism versus conservatism. The strongest direct effects of this peer group measure are on the political orientation of the individual student, Liberalism, participation in protests, and perception of the Campus Diversity Orientation (Beta = .28). Political Orientation also has direct positive effects on satisfaction with student life and on choosing a career in scientific research.

The mean political orientation of the peer group has indirect positive effects on self-reported growth in Cultural Awareness, Libertarianism, commitment to the goal of promoting racial understanding, and satisfaction with opportunities to take interdisciplinary courses; it has indirect negative effects on joining social fraternities or sororities, getting married, and acceptance of the view that racial discrimination is no longer a problem in the United States.

Financial Aid

Two measures of the financial aid of the peer group were included in the environmental effects analyses: the percentage whose aid is based on merit, and the percentage whose aid is based on need. The percentage of students with merit-based aid has direct positive effects on joining social fraternities or sororities and on perception of a Social Change Orientation, and direct negative effects on perceptions of Diversity Orientation and Scholarship. Since Scholarship is basically a measure of the student's intellectual self-confidence, the last finding suggests that having many peers with academic scholarships can have a depressing effect on the individual student's academic self-concept.

The percentage of students with need-based aid has direct positive effects on completion of the bachelor's degree and on three perceptual outcomes: Student-Oriented Faculty (Beta = .24), Diversity Orientation, and Trust in the Administration.

Curricular Interests of the Peer Group

The peer group's curricular orientation is assessed by means of fourteen different measures, each reflecting the percentage of undergraduate degrees awarded in a particular broadly defined field of study. The most interesting and certainly the most consistent findings have to do with peer group effects on the individual student's choice of a major field or career. Once again, we find evidence that students tend to change in the direction of the dominant interests or values of the peer group. Thus, in almost every instance of a direct parallel between a peer group measure and a student outcome measure, we find a direct positive effect (Betas shown in parentheses): biological science, business, engineering, physical science (Beta = .09), and social science (Beta = .15). The percentage of students majoring in history or political science also has a significant indirect effect on choosing a major in the social sciences.

Peer group effects on career choices are less consistent, although this result is partly attributable to the lack of direct parallels between the peer group measures and the career outcome measures. The percentage of engineering majors does have a direct positive effect on choosing a career in engineering, whereas the percentage of students majoring in education has only a weak and indirect effect on choosing a career in school teaching. Similarly, the percentage of students majoring in the health professions has a weak, indirect positive effect on choosing a career in nursing. Finally, the percentage majoring in history or political science has a weak and indirect positive effect on choosing a career in law.

Concerning the effect of peer interests on other outcomes, the percentage of students majoring in engineering produces the largest number of direct effects. This peer interest measure has direct negative effects on the perceived Student Orientation of the Faculty (Beta = −.27) and on satisfaction with the quality of instruction, Facilities, and the overall college experience. The percentage of engineering majors also has direct negative effects on the student's willingness to re-enroll in the same college and enrollment in graduate school; there is an indirect negative effect on attainment of the bachelor's degree. The proportion of students in engineering also has a direct positive effect on feeling overwhelmed and a weak but indirect positive effect on feeling depressed. There are indirect negative effects on three other perceptual outcomes: Diversity Orientation (−.17), Social Change Orientation (−.19), and Trust in the Administration (−.10). Clearly, these findings indicate that the climate characterizing the typical institution with a strong emphasis on engineering is not ideal for student learning and personal development.

The percentage of students majoring in "other technical" fields also produces a generally negative picture: direct negative effects on perception of a Student-Oriented Faculty and on satisfaction with Facilities, opportunities to take interdisciplinary courses, and general education requirements. These findings suggest that colleges emphasizing purely technical subjects shortchange their general education programs.

A contrasting picture is offered by the percentages of students majoring in English or in other fields of the humanities. Both of these measures have indirect positive effects on bachelor's degree attainment, self-reported growth in many academic areas, student willingness to re-enroll in the same college, and on most areas of satisfaction. The percentage of students majoring in English has a direct positive effect on satisfaction with Student Life, while the percentage of students majoring in other humanities fields has direct positive effects on participation in campus demonstrations and on perceptions of Diversity Orientation (Beta = .19) and Social Change Orientation (Beta = .20).

The percentage of students majoring in agriculture produces several direct negative effects of some interest: bachelor's degree attainment, degree aspirations, and preparation for graduate school. All of these effects are consistent with what one might expect in a student body comprising a large number of future farmers, since farming is one field in which degree attainment and graduate education may be of limited benefit to one's career.

Other direct effects of these peer group measures are of potential interest, including the following: negative effects of the percentage of social science majors on self-reported growth in job skills and public speaking skills; a positive effect of the percentage of students majoring in education on getting married; a positive effect of the percentage of business majors on satisfaction with faculty and on Trust in the Administration; and several effects of the percentage of students majoring in biological sciences (positive effects on earning the bachelor's degree and on perception of Social Change Orientation, and a negative effect on self-reported growth in job skills).

Ethnicity: The Racial Composition of the Peer Group

Three percentage measures are included in the regressions to assess possible effects of the racial composition of the peer group: African-Americans, Asians, and Latinos. With few exceptions, outcomes are generally not affected by these peer measures, and in all but one case the effects are very weak and indirect. Perhaps the most interesting finding is the negative effect of the percentage of Latino students on attainment of the bachelor's degree. This finding is reminiscent of earlier research (Astin, 1982) indicating that Chicanos, in particular, are relatively likely to drop out of high school and college, even after controlling for their academic preparation and other background factors. One possibility is that this measure, the percentage of Latino students in the student body, may well be a crude proxy—like Outside Work—for the overall dropout rate of the institution.

The only other direct effect is the negative effect of the percentage of Asian students on the perception of a Student-Oriented Faculty (Beta = −.21). Otherwise, none of these three measures produces any direct effects, and practically all of the indirect effects are very weak.

Religious Orientation

Three measures of the religious orientation of the student body include the percentages of students who are Jewish, Roman Catholic, or born-again Christians. Most of the significant direct effects are associated with the percentage of born-again Christians, whch has a negative effect on Hedonism, alcohol consumption, and bachelor's degree attainment. The percentage of Jewish students has a negative impact on Trust in the Administration, and the percentage of Roman Catholic students has a negative effect on satisfaction with Student Life. Otherwise, the effects of these three measures are weak and indirect.

Summary

Highlights from this summary of environmental effects on student outcomes can be briefly summarized as follows:

- Perhaps the most compelling generalization from the myriad findings summarized in this chapter is the pervasive effect of the peer group on the individual student's development. Every aspect of the student's development—cognitive and affective, psychological and behavioral—is affected in some way by peer group characteristics, and usually by several peer characteristics. Generally, students tend to change their values, behavior, and academic plans in the direction of the dominant orientation of their peer group.
- The values, attitudes, self-concept, and socioeconomic status of the peer group are much more important determinants of how the individual student will develop than are the peer group's abilities, religious orientation, or racial composition.
- The characteristics and behaviors of the faculty also have important implications for student development. Two faculty characteristics, in particular, have substantial and wide-ranging effects: the extent to which the faculty is Research-Oriented, and the extent to which it is Student-Oriented. As might be expected, these two attributes are negatively related to each other, but they also act independently. Attending a college whose faculty is heavily Research-Oriented increases student dissatisfaction and impacts negatively on most measures of cognitive and affective development. (About the only outcomes not following this pattern are the student's scores on standardized tests, which are positively affected by the Research Orientation of the faculty.) Attending a college that is strongly oriented toward student development shows the opposite pattern of effects.

- While institutional type and control are associated with a number of student outcomes, such institutional characteristics have little direct effect on these outcomes once peer group and faculty characteristics are taken into account.
- Somewhat surprisingly, the form of the institution's general education curriculum has little direct impact on student development. This finding may well reflect the lack of diversity in approaches to general education: better than 90 percent of American colleges and universities use some kind of "distributional" system for implementing the general education curriculum. Only a true-core curriculum (one that requires all students to take exactly the same courses) seems to have distinctive effects on student development: high satisfaction, and positive effects on leadership in particular.

Chapter 11

———•◆•———

Effects of
Involvement

Readers who have not yet read Chapter Ten are advised to read the first five pages of that chapter, since the material provides a good conceptual introduction to the content covered here.

This study has employed two conceptually distinct types of student involvement measures. The first has to do with forms of involvement that can be ascertained at the point when the student initially enters college: freshman place of residence, financial aid, and choice of a probable major field of study. These measures were characterized in Chapter Two as "bridge" measures between input and environmental characteristics, in the sense that they can be considered both as characteristics of the entering student (input) and as attributes of the student's environmental experience. It is in the latter sense that their effects on student development will be summarized in this chapter.

The second, and much more extensive, class of involvement measures includes the so-called intermediate outcomes that can be known only after the student has been in college for some period of time. In Chapter Two we described these measures as falling into five broad categories: academic involvement, involvement with faculty, involvement with student peers, involvement in work, and other forms of involvement.

We shall first summarize the patterns of effects associated with place of residence, financial aid, and freshman choice of a major, and then summarize the effects associated with the five categories of intermediate outcomes.

Place of Residence

Four measures of place of residence have been used: at home, in a college residence hall, in a private room or apartment, and distance of home from college. Most of the direct effects are associated either with living at home or with distance from home to college. That is, once one of these measures enters the equation, the effects of the other three disappear. Thus, most of the effects of living in a college residence hall or in a private room can be attributed to the student's either (a) *not* living at home and/or (b) attending college some distance from home. Both living at home and distance from home affect some outcomes, although the direction of the effects is always reversed (which means simply that living at home often produces an effect that is the same as attending college *close* to home). Living in a campus residence has direct effects on only three outcomes, discussed later, and living in a private room or apartment has no direct effects. In short, these results imply that the principal impact of the student's freshman place of residence occurs because the student is going away from home to attend college.

To summarize, leaving home to attend college has direct effects on satisfaction with Student Life and with the overall college experience, as well as on the student's willingness to attend the same college if the choice had to be made again. It also has direct positive effects on self-reported growth in a number of areas: Cultural Awareness, leadership skills, interpersonal skills, and job skills. Leaving home to attend college has positive effects on the personality traits of Leadership and Hedonism, and a direct negative effect on belief in the idea that the principal value of a college education is to increase one's earning power. In the behavioral realm, leaving home to attend college has direct positive effects on joining social fraternities or sororities, being elected to a student office, attending recitals or concerts, alcohol consumption, and tutoring other students. However, leaving home to attend college also has a negative effect on voting in the 1988 presidential election. Students apparently do not register in their college towns and do not bother to vote by absentee ballot.

The three effects that are directly attributable to living in a campus residence hall are positive effects on attainment of the bachelor's degree, satisfaction with faculty, and willingness to re-enroll in the same college.

These results confirm many of the findings reported in *Four Critical Years:* positive effects of campus residence on retention, joining social fraternities or sororities, Hedonism, and participation in student government. Most of these effects appear to be direct, in the sense that they cannot be attributed to other environmental variables. In other words, while most of the effects of institutional type as reported in *Four Critical Years* now appear to be attributable to other environmental variables, the effects of residential variables as reported in that earlier study do indeed appear to be direct effects. Unlike *Four Critical Years,* however, the current study fails to replicate the impact of campus residence on student liberalism. In all likelihood, this discrepancy in findings is attributable to the changes that have taken place in undergraduate peer groups during the past twenty years: unlike that earlier era, when "liberal" student bodies predominated, today's higher educational system has about equal numbers of liberal and conservative student bodies (see Chapter Three for a more detailed discussion of these changes).

Financial Aid

Although a national study conducted nearly twenty years ago suggested that various forms of student financial aid have significant effects on student retention (Astin, 1975), Pascarella and Terenzini's more recent review (1991) indicates that the evidence concerning the effects of student financial aid is mixed, at best, and contradictory, at worst. One problem with comparing studies of financial aid done at different time periods is that the system of financial aid for undergraduate students in the United States has changed continuously and dramatically during the past several decades. The varieties and amount of the available state and federal aid have increased substantially, along with the complexity of aid packages. Financial "need analysis" and the "packaging" of aid have become an almost arcane activity, and some students are now receiving financial aid from as many as ten different sources.

The increasing complexity and sophistication of the financial aid process help to explain why, in the current sample of students, various forms of financial aid have very few significant effects on student development. In particular, the earlier findings that student retention is enhanced by scholarships and work-study programs and negatively affected by student loans (Astin, 1975) are no longer supported by current data. State assistance and practically every form of federal aid (Pell grants, Perkins loans, college work-study, SEOGs, and Stafford Guaranteed Student Loans) have no discernible effect on student development.

About the only form of financial aid that seems to have measurable direct effects on student development is a grant from the college. Institutionally based scholarships have direct positive effects on college GPA and graduating with honors. College grants also have weak but significant direct effects on the student's decision to major in physical science and to pursue a career as a research scientist. An almost identical pattern of direct effects is associated with the student's freshman report that he or she is receiving aid based on "academic merit." This pattern of effects implies that the *knowledge* that one is receiving merit-based aid from one's institution may serve as a motivating force for higher academic achievement. It also suggests that institutions might be able to increase the number of undergraduates pursuing careers in science if they could award more merit-based aid from institutional resources to deserving students. Having merit-based aid also has a weaker but significant direct effect on Scholarship (Intellectual Self-Esteem).

Receiving aid based on "other special talent" also has a positive effect on the student's Artistic Inclination. As noted in Chapter Four, this finding implies that students can be encouraged to pursue careers in music or the arts if their institutions recognize their special talents through the award of grants or scholarships.

Why would merit-based aid provided by students' institutions in recognition of academic or other special talent have positive effects on students' academic progress, career choice, and self-concept, while state and federal grants—which are far more numerous—fail to show any discernible impact? Perhaps the key lies in the student's *perception* of the aid. In the case of federal and state grants, the student may view such aid pretty much as an entitlement that is awarded on a more or less mechanistic basis. The same may be true even of so-called merit aid that many states now award, simply because the granting of such aid is done largely according to predetermined formulas. Grants from the college, on the other hand, may be perceived as a form of special recognition for the student's *individual* talent and potential. As a consequence, students receiving such aid may feel a greater sense of responsibility to live up to the expectation and promise implied in the award.

Having need-based aid, by contrast, has negative effects on college GPA and graduating with honors. However, both need-based and merit-based aid have direct positive effects on Liberalism. The only other direct effects of financial aid variables on student outcomes are the negative impact of participating in college work-study programs on MCAT performance and the negative impact of parental support on getting married.

Major Field of Study

Of the fourteen categories of freshman choice of a major field that have been examined as possible environmental variables, two (agriculture, and mathematics and statistics) produce no significant effects on student outcomes. (This finding may be the result of the very small numbers of students majoring in either of these fields.) Results for the twelve other categories are summarized below. Only direct effects (those that cannot be attributed to any other environmental variable) are reported here.

Biological Science

Choosing a biological science major as an entering freshman strengthens the student's commitment to making a theoretical contribution to science and increases the likelihood that he or she will pursue a career in scientific research four years later. It has weak but significant negative effects, however, on pursuit of an engineering career, GRE Quantitative score, and the NTE General Knowledge Test.

Other outcomes positively affected by choice of a biological science major include satisfaction with facilities, degree aspirations, enrollment in graduate school, and the perception of a Student-Oriented Faculty. Majoring in biological science has a negative effect on self-reported growth in job-related skills.

Business

Choosing a business major as an entering freshman substantially increases the student's chances of pursuing a business career four years later. It has a negative effect, however, on enrollment in graduate school and on interest in making a theoretical contribution to science. Majoring in business also has weak but significant negative effects on Altruism and Social Activism, commitment to promoting racial understanding, self-reported growth in Cultural Awareness, and the perception of the institution's Diversity Orientation. In many respects, these last effects confirm the stereotype of business schools and departments as bastions of conservatism that give low priority to issues of diversity and multiculturalism.

Education

Majoring in education substantially increases the student's chances of pursuing a teaching career four years later and has a weak negative effect on pursuit of a business career. A number of academically related outcomes seem to be affected by majoring in education: college GPA, graduating with honors, degree aspirations, and self-reported growth in knowledge of a field, job-related skills, and preparation for graduate school. Majoring in education has negative effects, however, on the NTE General Knowledge test and on self-reported growth in foreign-language skills, analytical and problem-solving skills, critical thinking abilities, public speaking skills, and general knowledge. Here is a clear instance in which a particular environmental variable has the same effect on self-reported growth in a cognitive skill (general knowledge) as it does on an actual test of that skill (the NTE General Knowledge Test). These effects also confirm the argument that majoring in education may shortchange the general education component of the student's undergraduate education.

Picking an education major as an entering freshman has positive effects, however, on a variety of satisfaction outcomes: quality of instruction, Student Life, Facilities, overall college experience, and willingness to re-enroll in the same college. Majoring in education also has positive effects on several behavioral outcomes: tutoring other students, raising a family, and getting married.

Engineering

Engineering produces more significant effects on student outcomes than any other major field. Majoring in engineering substantially increases the student's chance of pursuing an engineering career four years later. However, it has negative effects on a variety of satisfaction outcomes: faculty, quality of instruction, Student Life, opportunities to take interdisciplinary courses, and the overall college experience. Majoring in engineering also has widespread negative effects on a variety of academic outcomes: undergraduate GPA, completion of the bachelor's degree, graduating with honors, aspirations for graduate study, enrollment in graduate school, self-reported growth in foreign-language skills, writing skills, listening skills, Cultural Awareness, and scores on the NTE General Knowledge test. (Readers will note that the results for the NTE are sometimes inconsistent with results for other outcomes. Such inconsistencies should probably not be given much weight, considering the highly biased nature of the NTE sample: it included only institutions with large education programs in states that require the NTE, and only students who entered college intending to become school teachers.) On the other hand, majoring in engineering has positive effects on the GRE Quantitative test and on self-reported growth in analytical and problem-solving skills and in job-related skills.

In the affective realm, majoring in engineering has a positive effect on the belief that the principal purpose of college is to increase one's earning power and on the perception of the institution's Resources and Reputation Emphasis, and negative effects on Altruism and Social Activism, Political Orientation (liberalism versus conservatism), Liberalism, participation in campus demonstrations, commitment to promoting racial understanding, and three perceptual outcomes: Social Change Orientation, Student Orientation, and Trust in the Administration.

In short, majoring in engineering enhances the student's quantitative and analytical skills, but it also promotes materialism and conservatism and impedes the development of communication skills, Cultural Awareness, and concern for social issues. In certain respects, this pattern of effects resembles the pattern associated with majoring in business.

Health Professions

Majoring in the health professions has positive effects on self-reported growth in job-related skills and knowledge of a field and negative effects on foreign-language skills and writing ability. Choosing a health profession major as an entering freshman also has a positive effect on commitment to making a theoretical contribution to science, but it has negative effects on retention, entry to graduate school, commitment to promoting racial understanding, and satisfaction with opportunities to take interdisciplinary courses.

Humanities

Majoring in some field of the humanities has positive effects on the student's college GPA and on self-reported growth in foreign-language skills and writing skills. It also has positive effects on interest in pursuing a career in college teaching, Political Orientation (liberalism versus conservatism), and attendance at recitals or concerts. Finally, majoring in the humanities has negative effects on GRE Quantitative scores, on the NTE General Knowledge and Professional Knowledge tests, on the belief that the principal value of college is to increase one's earning power, and on commitment to making a theoretical contribution to science.

Fine Arts

Majoring in fine arts increases the student's chances of pursuing a career in the arts. It also has positive effects on Political Orientation (liberalism versus conservatism), attendance at recitals and concerts, and college GPA. Majoring in the fine arts has negative effects on the GRE Quantitative test and on self-reported growth in analytical and problem-solving skills. (Here is another case in which a self-reported growth measure and a tested growth measure produce similar results.) Majoring in the arts also has negative effects on the NTE General Knowledge and Professional Knowledge tests, on self-reported growth in foreign-language abilities, and on commitment to raising a family and to making a theoretical contribution to science.

Physical Science

Choosing a physical science major at the time of college entry substantially increases the student's chances of pursuing a career in scientific research four years later and strengthens the student's commitment to making a theoretical contribution to science. Majoring in physical science also has a number of positive effects on academic outcomes: GRE Quantitative and Analytical scores, completion of the bachelor's degree, entry to graduate school, and self-reported growth in analytical and problem-solving skills. Here is still another example in which self-reported change and measured change in a cognitive area (in this case, analytical skills) produce similar findings.

Majoring in physical science also has a positive effect on the student's perception of a Student-Oriented Faculty, on tutoring other students, and on commitment to participating in programs to clean up the environment. It has a negative effect on self-reported growth in Cultural Awareness and listening skills.

Psychology

Choosing a psychology major as an entering freshman has positive effects on several academic outcomes: completion of the bachelor's degree, graduating with honors, degree aspirations, and self-reported growth in writing skills and listening skills. It also has a positive effect on the perception of a Student-Oriented Faculty.

Social Science

Majoring in some other field of social science substantially increases the student's chances of pursuing a career in law four years later. It also has positive effects on the perception of a Student-Oriented Faculty, degree aspirations, self-reported growth in writing skills and foreign-language skills, and scores on both the GRE Verbal test and the LSAT. Again, measures of self-reported growth and tested growth (in this case, in verbal skills) produce similar results. Majoring in social science also has a positive effect on the NTE General Knowledge test, but negative effects on tutoring other students and on self-reported growth in job-related skills.

Other Technical Majors

Majoring in "other technical" fields as an entering freshman has two weak effects: a positive effect on pursuing an engineering career four years later, and a negative effect on Libertarianism.

Academic Involvement

Before considering specific results associated with various forms of involvement that qualify as intermediate outcomes, the reader should keep in mind the interpretive ambiguities (discussed at length in Chapters One and Two) that necessarily arise when one attempts to determine whether and how any intermediate outcome affects some student outcome measures. Since there always is the possibility that the outcome measure *changed* between the time it was originally assessed (freshman entry in 1985) and the time of the occurrence of the intermediate outcome, the possibility remains that the direction of causation may, in fact, be reversed. That is, the ensuing change in the outcome might cause the intermediate outcome, rather than the other way around. The likelihood of such reversals in the direction of causation varies, of course, with the particular involvement measure and outcome measure under consideration. I will attempt to point out those situations where causation seems to be in a particular direction, but the readers must ultimately judge for themselves just which effects of involvement variables can be trusted and which ones are suspect. To emphasize the ambiguities involved, I will use primarily phrases like "correlated with" and "associated with," but to relieve the monotony I will occasionally use more causal terminology, such as "affect" or "effect."

With these cautions in mind, we now summarize those outcomes which — following the control of input and environmental variables and number of years completed — show significant partial correlations with involvement measures. We begin the summary with three categories of academic involvement: time allocation, courses taken, and specific learning experiences.

Time Allocation

Three measures of how students spend their time in academic pursuits are expressed by the student's estimate of how many hours per week he or she spent during the previous years in each of the following: attending classes or labs, studying or doing homework, and using a personal computer. Hours per week spent *studying or doing homework* produces the largest and most numerous partial correlations with student outcomes (after the effects of entering student characteristics, environmental variables, and years of undergraduate education completed have been controlled). This involvement measure has significant correlations with more than two-thirds of the outcome measures. Basically, hours spent studying is positively related to nearly *all* academic outcomes: retention, graduating with honors, enrollment in graduate school, all three scores on the NTE, and all self-reported increases in cognitive and affective skills. The strongest effects are on Overall Academic Development and preparation for graduate school (Betas = .15). This measure also has significant associations with *all* measures of satisfaction and with the personality characteristics of Scholarship and Social Activism. It has positive correlations with commitment to the goals of promoting racial understanding, cleaning up the environment, and making a theoretical contribution to science; it is positively associated with all careers in science, engineering, and college teaching. The only outcomes that are negatively correlated with hours per week spent studying are Hedonism, alcohol consumption, smoking cigarettes, the view that the chief benefit of a college education is to increase one's earning power, and the goal of being very well off financially.

This pattern of effects constitutes powerful evidence in support of the theory of involvement (Astin, 1984). Given that this study focuses on human performance in an academic setting, it is fitting that the most basic form of academic involvement — studying and doing homework — has stronger and more widespread positive effects than almost any other involvement measure or environmental measure.

Hours per week spent *using a personal computer* is also associated with a number of student outcomes, but the coefficients are much smaller than is the case with studying and doing homework. The pattern of relationships is much the same, however, with positive effects on most academic outcomes and on most areas of student satisfaction. That using a personal computer has its strongest correlations with self-rated writing ability and self-reported growth in writing skills supports the idea that the student's skill in written composition can be facilitated through the use of word processors.

Hours per week spent *attending classes or labs* has many fewer associations with student outcomes, although the patterns of correlations are similar to those for the previous two time diary items. The strongest correlations are with self-reported growth in knowledge of a field and preparation for graduate school. The only exception to this pattern is the weak but significant negative correlation of this measure with GRE Verbal Scores.

Courses Taken

The number of courses taken in five different broad subject matter fields constitutes the five measures of student involvement under this category. At the outset, it should be noted that the largest correlations of number of courses taken are usually with the relevant major field and career choice. These results are not discussed here simply because they are, in all likelihood, artifacts. For example, among students who enter college planning careers as engineers, those who maintain their engineering choice through the senior year will almost certainly end up taking more mathematics and science courses than will those who switch to some other career choice, such as business. But is it reasonable to argue that the larger number of science and math courses "caused" the final choice of engineering, or that the smaller number of science and math courses "caused" the switch out of engineering? In other words, the number of courses taken in different fields is much more likely to be a *consequence* of the student's follow-up career choice than a cause of it.

Almost without exception, each measure of number of courses taken has some of its strongest correlations with the most appropriate outcome measures. The number of courses taken that emphasize *writing skills,* for example, has its strongest effects on self-reported growth in writing skills (Beta = .31) and in self-rated writing ability (Beta = .20). The next strongest effects are on self-reported growth in general knowledge, critical thinking skills, public speaking skills, and Overall Academic Development. Actually, the number of writing-skills courses taken has significant positive effects on all areas of self-reported growth except job skills, and on all areas of student satisfaction except Facilities. The only exception to this pattern of uniformly positive effects is the weak but significant *negative* correlation of writing-skills courses taken with GRE Quantitative test scores.

Number of courses taken that emphasize *mathematics or understanding numerical data* has its strongest positive effect on self-reported growth in analytical and problem-solving skills (Beta = .18). This measure also has a direct positive effect on the GRE Quantitative test. Since the students took the GRE after they

had taken all or most of the courses in question, we can conclude with some confidence that this is indeed a causal relationship. The reader is also reminded that this is one more example
of a situation in which self-reported growth (that is, in analytical and problem-solving skills) conforms to growth measured
by a standardized test. Number of math or numerical courses
taken also has moderate relationships with tutoring other students and with self-reported growth in job skills and Overall
Academic Development. While this measure has a positive effect
on Scholarship and Status Striving, it has negative effects on
Political Orientation (liberalism versus conservatism), Social
Activism, Artistic Inclination, and Liberalism. It is important
to emphasize that all these "effects" of courses are over and above
the effects of majors such as science and engineering.

Number of courses taken that emphasize *science or scientific inquiry* has its strongest partial correlation with commitment
to the goal of making a theoretical contribution to science (Beta =
.33). Here, the direction of causation is highly ambiguous, since
increasing one's interest in contributing to scientific theory could
just as well be a cause of, rather than a result of, taking a lot
of courses in science. This involvement measure also has positive effects on GRE Verbal scores and on self-reported growth
in Overall Academic Development, analytical and problem-
solving skills, knowledge of a field or discipline, and preparation
for graduate school. Like number of math or numerical courses,
number of science courses taken has a positive correlation with
tutoring other students.

Number of courses taken that emphasize *history or historical
analysis* has its strongest effect on self-reported growth in writing
skills, but it also has positive effects on most other academic outcomes except analytical and problem-solving skills. This involvement measure also has positive effects on Social Activism, Artistic Inclination, and Leadership, as well as on commitment to the
goals of promoting racial understanding and cleaning up the environment. It has negative effects on the goals of making a theoretical contribution to science and being very well off financially.

As would be expected, the last measure of courses taken,
the number emphasizing *foreign-language skills,* has its strongest

effect on self-reported growth in foreign-language skills (Beta = .65). This is the strongest single "effect" in the entire study. Number of foreign-language courses taken also has modest positive effects on the GRE Verbal test, on self-reported growth in Cultural Awareness, and on commitment to promoting racial understanding. It has negative effects on the beliefs that racial discrimination is no longer a problem in the United States, that the chief benefit of a college education is to increase one's earning power, and that the individual can do little to change society.

Specific Learning Experiences

This category includes items concerning specific programs taken (ethnic studies, women's studies, and so on) and participation in special programs (such as study abroad, internship, remedial). Both ethnic studies and women's studies courses produce very similar patterns of effects on student outcomes. The strongest effects have to do either with liberal political attitudes and beliefs or with participation in "diversity" issues: self-reported growth in Cultural Awareness, Social Activism, Political Orientation (liberalism versus conservatism), commitment to promoting racial understanding, participation in campus protests, and Liberalism.

Enrollment in *honors or advanced placement courses* has its strongest positive correlations with the personality measure Scholarship (Beta = .32). While the effects of honors courses on college GPA (Beta = .16) and graduating with honors (Beta = .18) may well be artifacts, it is interesting to note that enrollment in honors programs also has positive correlations with tutoring other students, bachelor's degree attainment, self-reported growth in preparation for graduate school, degree aspirations, and enrollment in graduate or professional school. Enrollment in honors or advanced placement courses also has small positive effects on virtually all areas of satisfaction and all other areas of self-reported growth.

As would be expected, enrollment in *interdisciplinary courses* has its largest positive correlation with satisfaction with opportunities to take interdisciplinary courses (Beta = .26). This measure also has positive effects on the LSAT and all three NTE tests, on most satisfaction measures, on all self-reported growth measures except job skills and foreign-language skills, and on virtually all "diversity" outcomes. Participation in a *study-abroad program* has its strongest effect on self-reported growth in foreign-language skills (Beta = .23). It also has weak but significant positive effects on most satisfaction outcomes and on self-reported growth in Cultural Awareness.

Participation in a *college internship program* has its strongest positive effect on self-reported growth in job skills. It also produces modest positive correlations with college GPA, graduating with honors, completion of the bachelor's degree, and most satisfaction outcomes. Neither taking *reading and study skills classes* nor taking *remedial or developmental courses* is associated with any outcomes of note, with one exception: taking remedial or developmental courses is negatively associated with performance on all three NTE tests.

The last special learning experience in this group, attending a *racial or cultural awareness workshop,* produces a number of correlations with outcomes having to do with student activism and "diversity." The strongest effects are on commitment to promoting racial understanding (Beta = .20), participation in campus demonstrations (Beta = .21), and self-reported growth in Cultural Awareness (Beta = .18). Participation in such workshops is also positively related to almost every other self-reported growth measure, to most satisfaction outcomes, and to the following personality and attitudinal outcomes: Social Activism (Beta = .15), Political Orientation (liberalism versus conservatism), Leadership, commitment to participating in programs to clean up the environment, attending a recital or concert, Liberalism, and being elected to a student office. Attending racial or cultural awareness workshops has negative effects on commitment to being very well off financially and on the following attitudes: racial discrimination is no longer a problem, the chief benefit of a college education is to increase one's earning power, and the individual can do little to change society.

Specific Pedagogical Experiences

This last category of academic involvement measures includes working on independent research projects, receiving tutoring, giving class presentations, taking multiple-choice exams, and taking essay exams.

Working on an *independent research project* has its strongest positive correlations with attainment of the bachelor's degree, commitment to the goal of making a theoretical contribution to science, and self-reported growth in preparation for graduate or professional school. It also has positive correlations with virtually every self-reported growth measure and with satisfaction in all areas except Individual Support Services, Student Life, and Facilities. The only exception to this pattern is a weak negative correlation with the NTE General Knowledge test.

Receiving tutoring in courses is positively associated with satisfaction with Individual Support Services, but it is negatively associated with college GPA, degree completion, graduating with honors, and performance on the GRE Verbal, LSAT, and NTE Communication Skills tests. These latter "effects" may be artifacts, since students who are most likely to receive tutoring are the ones who are having academic difficulties. Perhaps the most interesting relationship involving being tutored, however, is its positive correlation with *providing* tutoring. This unexpected finding might be explained in terms of institutions that have large programs of peer tutoring. Students in such institutions who receive tutoring in the early college years may become tutors when they are upper-division students.

Giving class presentations has its strongest positive effect on self-reported growth in public speaking skills. It also has substantial positive effects on bachelor's degree attainment (Beta = .15), tutoring other students, college GPA, and graduating with honors; its effects are positive on all self-reported growth measures except foreign-language abilities, and on all student satisfaction measures except Facilities.

As would be expected, *taking essay exams* and *taking multiple-choice* exams have very different patterns of correlations. That taking essay exams helps to strengthen a student's writing skills is suggested by its significant positive correlations with self-reported growth in writing skills and self-rated writing ability. Taking essay exams is also positively related to practically all other self-reported growth measures and to satisfaction in all areas except Individual Support Services and Facilities. There are positive associations with attainment of the bachelor's degree, as well as with degree aspirations and several behavioral outcomes: attending recitals or concerts, alcohol consumption, participating in campus demonstrations, and voting in the 1988 presidential election.

By contrast, *taking multiple-choice exams* has negative effects on self-reported growth in writing skills and critical thinking skills. Taking multiple-choice exams has positive effects on Status Striving, commitment to the goal of being very well off financially, and agreement with the proposition that the chief benefit of a college education is to increase one's earning power.

Summary

This pattern of effects provides strong support for the argument that the student's academic and personal development can be enhanced by heavy involvement. Student development seems to be facilitated if the student spends a considerable amount of time studying, attending classes, and using a personal computer, as well as engaging in academically related activities that would be inclined to elicit a high degree of student involvement: honors courses, interdisciplinary courses, study-abroad programs, college internship programs, racial or cultural awareness workshops, independent research projects, class presentations, and taking essay exams. Academic development does *not* seem to be facilitated by frequent use of multiple-choice exams.

Involvement with Faculty

Since each individual measure of involvement with faculty produces a very similar pattern of correlations with student outcomes, this summary will focus primarily on the composite measure of student-faculty interaction, which includes measures such as being a guest in a professor's home, working on a professor's research project, assisting faculty in teaching a class, and hours per week spent talking with faculty outside of class. As would be expected, overall student-faculty interaction has its strongest positive correlations (after controlling for entering student characteristics, environmental variables, and number of years completed) with satisfaction with faculty (Beta = .24) and perception of a Student-Oriented Faculty (Beta = .21). Student-faculty interaction also has substantial positive correlations with all other areas of student satisfaction but especially with the quality of instruction, Individual Support Services, and the overall college experience (Beta = .16). Student-faculty interaction has significant positive correlations with *every* academic attainment outcome: college GPA, degree attainment (Beta = .16), graduating with honors (Beta = .12), and enrollment in graduate or professional school (Beta = .11).

Student-faculty interaction also has positive correlations with every self-reported area of intellectual and personal growth, as well as with a variety of personality and attitudinal outcomes: Scholarship (Intellectual Self-Esteem) (Beta = .16), Social Activism, Leadership (Beta = .15), Artistic Inclination, and commitment to each of three life goals: promoting racial understanding, participating in programs to clean up the environment, and making a theoretical contribution to science. Student-faculty interaction also has positive effects on all self-rated abilities except physical health. By contrast, this involvement measure has negative effects on the following attitudinal outcomes: that the principal value of a college education is to increase one's earning power, and that the individual can do little to change society.

Student-faculty interaction also has a number of positive correlations with behavioral outcomes. Especially notable is the substantial positive effect on tutoring other students (Beta = .25). The most obvious explanation for this effect, of course, is that students who are involved in tutoring other students must necessarily have some additional contact with faculty. Additional behavioral outcomes that are positively affected by student-faculty interaction include being elected to a student office, attending recitals or concerts, and participating in campus demonstrations. Student-faculty interaction also has significant positive effects on two perceptual outcomes: Diversity Orientation and Social Change Orientation.

Finally, student-faculty interaction has a number of fascinating effects on career outcomes. Most notable, perhaps, is the positive effect on choosing a career in college teaching. Clearly, this result suggests that interacting frequently with faculty produces in students a greater sense of identification with their faculty mentors. Student-faculty interaction has positive effects on both career choices and major field choices in all fields of science (but not in engineering, it should be stressed), and negative effects on choice of a career or major in business.

A few other particular effects of individual measures of student-faculty interaction should be noted. Having a class paper critiqued by an instructor, for example, has a substantial positive effect on self-reported change in writing skills (Beta = .18), as well as on self-rated writing ability. Also, assisting faculty in teaching a course has a substantial positive effect on tutoring other students (Beta = .22).

In short, these findings highlight the critical importance to student development of frequent interaction between faculty and students (Astin, 1977; Feldman and Newcomb, 1969; Pascarella and Terenzini, 1991). Given that these apparent benefits of student-faculty contact are observed after we have controlled for the effects of between-institution environmental variables such as Student Orientation of the Faculty (see the previous chapter), it seems safe to conclude that variations in student-faculty contact *within* any given institutional environment can also have important positive implications for student development.

Involvement with Student Peers

As with measures of student-faculty interaction, individual measures of student-student interaction produce a positive pattern of partial correlations with student outcomes. We focus this summary on findings involving the overall measure of student-

student interaction and mention only briefly some of the unique effects attributable to specific student-student interaction items. Keep in mind that the composite measure of student-student interaction includes items such as discussing course content with other students, working on group projects for classes, tutoring other students, participating in intramural sports, being a member of a social fraternity or sorority, discussing racial or ethnic issues, socializing with someone from a different racial or ethnic group, participating in a campus protest, being elected to a student office, and hours per week spent in socializing or in student clubs or organizations.

Student-student interaction has its strongest positive correlations with the Leadership personality measure (Beta = .31) and with self-reported growth in leadership abilities (Beta = .29). It also has substantial positive correlations with self-reported growth in public speaking skills (Beta = .22), interpersonal skills (Beta = .19), Overall Academic Development (Beta = .15), knowledge of a field, analytical and problem-solving skills, critical thinking skills, Cultural Awareness, preparation for graduate and professional school, and general knowledge. The only self-reported change not correlated with student-student interaction is foreign-language skills.

Student-student interaction also has positive correlations with satisfaction with Student Life (Beta = .20), faculty (Beta = .15), and all other satisfaction outcomes except Facilities. It is positively associated with a number of academic outcomes: degree aspirations, college GPA, and graduating with honors. In the affective realm, student-student interaction has positive effects on Scholarship (Intellectual Self-Esteem), Social Activism, Hedonism, and Status Striving. It also has positive effects on all self-ratings, as well as on two behavioral outcomes: attending recitals or concerts (Beta = .16), and alcohol consumption. Student-student interaction has negative effects on feeling depressed, and on the beliefs that the principal value of college is to increase one's earning power and that the individual cannot change society.

Once again, we find a pervasive pattern of positive benefits associated with frequent student-student interaction. Among other things, these findings support the continuing efforts of student affairs professionals to find ways to engage students in extracurricular activities and other programs that encourage student-student interaction.

Two specific forms of student-student interaction, *discussed racial or ethnic issues* and *socialized with someone from another racial or ethnic group,* produce very similar patterns of correlations with student outcomes (following control of inputs and environments): substantial positive correlations with self-reported gains in Cultural Awareness, and smaller positive correlations with most other areas of cognitive and affective development and with most areas of satisfaction. These student activities also have positive residual correlations with commitment to promoting racial understanding, commitment to participating in programs to clean up the environment, and attendance at recitals and concerts. They both also have negative residual correlations with materialistic values and with the belief that the individual can do little to bring about change in society.

As one might expect, participating in *campus demonstrations* has its strongest effects on political or "diversity" outcomes: Political Orientation (liberalism versus conservatism) (Beta = .16), commitment to promoting racial understanding (Beta = .15), commitment to cleaning up the environment, and Liberalism (Beta = .16). Its strongest negative effect is on the view that racial discrimination is no longer a problem in America.

Membership in a *social fraternity or sorority* produces a somewhat different pattern of effects from the overall student-student interaction measure. For example, except for Student Life, being a member of a social fraternity or sorority does not have any significant effects on student satisfaction outcomes. In addition, it has positive effects on self-reported growth in leadership abilities, the Leadership personality measure, Status Striving, Hedonism, and alcohol consumption, and a negative effect on Liberalism.

Participating in *intramural sports* has substantial positive effects on physical health, alcohol consumption, and attainment of the bachelor's degree. It also has significant positive effects on satisfaction with Student Life and on the overall college experience. Both leadership outcome measures are positively affected by participation in intramural sports.

Participating in *intercollegiate sports* also shows positive partial correlations with self-rated physical health, Leadership, and satisfaction with student life, but it also produces negative effects on performance on three standardized tests: GRE Verbal, LSAT, and NTE General Knowledge. In all likelihood, these negative effects have to do with the substantial amount of time and energy that most varsity athletes must devote to nonacademic activities, such as practice and travel.

Working on *group projects for a class* has positive partial correlations with all areas of satisfaction except Facilities and opportunities to take interdisciplinary courses, on all self-ratings, and on all areas of self-reported growth except for foreign-language skills. It has a weak but significant negative effect, however, on GRE Verbal scores. Participating in group projects also has positive correlations with tutoring other students and with choices of careers and majors in business and engineering. These latter results suggest that courses in business and engineering are more likely than undergraduate courses in other fields to involve students in group projects.

Tutoring other students has its strongest correlation with the Scholarship personality measure (Beta = .15). It also has positive correlations with all academic outcomes, as well as with the choice of majors in all fields of science (not in engineering, however) and careers in college teaching, scientific research, precollegiate teaching, and medicine. Finally, tutoring has direct positive effects on both the GRE Quantitative and Analytical test scores. Among other things, these uniformly positive associations of tutoring with most academic and cognitive outcomes underscore the potential value of cooperative learning techniques (see Chapter Twelve).

Involvement in Work

Working at a *full-time job* is associated with a pattern of outcomes that is uniformly negative. The biggest negative effect is on completion of the bachelor's degree (Beta = −.16). Other academic outcomes that are negatively associated with working full-time include college GPA, graduating with honors, enrollment in graduate or professional school, and self-reported growth in Cultural Awareness, interpersonal skills, knowledge of a field or discipline, and preparation for graduate school. Working full-time also has uniformly negative effects on every areas of satisfaction except Facilities, and on willingness to re-enroll at the same college.

In the affective realm, working full-time while attending college has positive effects on Status Striving and on the goal of being very well off financially. In the behavioral realm, it has positive associations with getting married (the direction of causation may well be reversed in this case), smoking cigarettes, and feeling overwhelmed. Working full-time has weak but significant positive effects on pursuing a career in business and weak negative effects on choice of a major in science.

Holding a *part-time job off campus* has a pattern of effects that is almost identical to the pattern associated with working full-time. Having a *part-time job on campus,* however, has a completely different pattern of effects. As a matter of fact, holding a part-time job on campus is positively associated with attainment of a bachelor's degree and with virtually all areas of self-reported cognitive and affective growth. Working at a part-time job on campus also increases the student's chances of being elected to a student office, tutoring other students, and attending recitals or concerts. It has positive effects on Liberalism, Leadership, and a commitment to the goals of promoting racial understanding and participating in programs to clean up the environment. This measure has positive effects on all areas of student satisfaction except Facilities and general education requirements.

Why should part-time employment on campus have such a different pattern of effects from the same kind of employment off campus? In all likelihood, the key to understanding this difference lies in the concept of involvement: compared to students who spend an equivalent amount of time working off campus, students who are employed on campus are, almost by definition, in more frequent contact with other students and possibly with faculty (depending on the type of work). Apparently, this greater degree of immersion in the collegiate environment and culture more than compensates, in terms of student outcomes, for the time that students must devote to a part-time job on campus. Similar trade-offs are simply not available to the student whose part-time job is located off campus.

Other Forms of Involvement

The final category of involvement measures comprises a heterogeneous set of involvement items that could not be classified in the preceding categories: hours per week spent in various activities (watching television, exercising, commuting, and so on), getting married, receiving personal or vocational counseling, and use of alcohol. Again, space will permit only a rough summary of the highlights from each measure.

Watching Television

Hours per week that students spend watching television while enrolled in college is associated with more than two-thirds of the student outcome measures, and the pattern of effects is uniformly negative. We should remember that these effects, like those for other involvement measures, are partial correlations observed after control for student input characteristics (including television-watching habits prior to college entry), college environmental variables, and number of years of college completed. Readers should also keep in mind that the magnitude of these effects is generally quite small, although highly significant statistically. The weakness of the effects may be a function of the limited variability in television-watching habits observed in the college population: many college students watch little or no television, and those who do watch generally do so for only limited periods of time.

Hours per week spent watching television is negatively associated with almost all academic outcomes: college GPA, graduation with honors, and self-reported growth in all areas of academic and personal development except knowledge of a field or discipline. Watching television is also negatively associated with all areas of satisfaction except general education requirements.

Additionally, watching television seems to encourage the development of materialistic values. It has positive correlations with Status Striving, commitment to the goal of being very well off financially, and the view that the principal value of a college education is to increase one's earning power. It also has positive correlations with Hedonism, cigarette smoking, and alcohol consumption.

While hours per week watching television has weak positive correlations with commitment to the goal of raising a family and the belief that the individual can do little to change society, it has negative correlations with the goals of promoting racial understanding, participating in programs to clean up the environment, and developing a meaningful philosophy of life. It also has negative correlations with all self-ratings, and with being elected to a student office, attending recitals or concerts, and tutoring other students. Finally, hours per week spent watching television has a weak positive effect on interest in pursuing a career in business.

This pattern of results closely parallels the findings from studies done at the precollegiate level on the effects of television-viewing habits (Huston and others, 1992). Why should television viewing have such effects? There are several possible explanations. The most obvious explanation, of course, is in terms of the involvement concept: watching television is a passive activity that can isolate students from each other and take time away from activities that might be more conducive to learning and personal development. At the same time, the content of television programming tends to be heavily materialistic, which may help to account for the tendency of television viewing to encourage the development of materialistic values among college undergraduates.

Commuting

Hours per week spent commuting to campus produces a pattern of effects very similar to the pattern described above for off-campus work and full-time work. The more commuting the student does, the less the satisfaction he or she reports in all areas except Facilities. Commuting is also negatively related to attainment of the bachelor's degree, enrollment in graduate or professional school, and self-reported growth in leadership abilities and in interpersonal skills. Commuting also has negative correlations with two personality measures — Hedonism and Leadership — as well as with a number of behaviors: participating in protests, joining fraternities or sororities, attending recitals or concerts, tutoring other students, and consuming alcohol. Some of these activities, of course, are facilitated by being on campus. Finally, commuting also has negative effects on self-ratings of emotional health and positive effects on feeling depressed and feeling overwhelmed. Apparently, substantial commuting seems to raise the level of stress experienced by undergraduate students.

Attending Religious Services

Hours per week spent attending religious services has an interesting pattern of effects on affective and cognitive outcomes. The strongest effects are negative: Hedonism (Beta = −.16), Political Orientation (liberalism versus conservatism), alcohol consumption, and Libertarianism (Beta = −.19). Attending religious services, however, has *positive* effects on Feminism, getting married, being elected to a student office, voting in the 1988 election, and tutoring other students. It has negative effects on MCAT scores, smoking cigarettes, and feeling overwhelmed; there is a positive effect on self-ratings of emotional health. Hours per week spent attending religious services is positively related to satisfaction in every area and has weak but significant positive effects on self-reported growth in Cultural Awareness, leadership skills, public speaking skills, and job skills. Attending religious services also has positive effects on Social Activism and willingness to re-enroll at the same college.

Volunteer Work

Given the current interest in American higher education in encouraging more students to participate in volunteer work, it is useful to explore the pattern of outcomes associated with hours per week that students report spending in volunteer activities.

This measure has its strongest positive correlations with the personality measures of Social Activism and Leadership and with participation in campus demonstrations, tutoring other students, and self-rated growth in leadership abilities. Some of these relationships are perhaps to be expected, given that tutoring other students and participating in leadership activities may well constitute part of what students interpret as "volunteer work." Participation in volunteer work also has positive correlations with a variety of attitudinal outcomes: commitment to developing a meaningful philosophy of life, promoting racial understanding, and participating in programs to clean up the environment. In the academic realm, participating in volunteer work has weak but significant positive correlations with degree aspirations, attainment of the bachelor's degree, and self-reported growth in Cultural Awareness, in public speaking skills, and in interpersonal skills. Participating in volunteer work has negative correlations with commitment to the goal of being very well off financially; there is also a negative effect on the views that the chief benefit of a college education is to increase one's earning power and that the individual has little power to change society. Volunteering has a weak negative correlation with performance on the GRE Verbal test. Finally, participating in volunteer work has positive correlations with choices of careers in medicine and clinical psychology.

Marriage

Getting married while attending college has its strongest positive effect on the goal of raising a family and its strongest negative effects on Hedonism and alcohol consumption. Getting married also has a weak positive effect on the NTE General Knowledge test and weak but significant negative effects on self-reported growth in Cultural Awareness, leadership skills, and interpersonal skills.

Counseling

Two counseling items were used as involvement measures — vocational or career counseling, and personal or psychological counseling. The two measures produce a few common correlations with student outcomes, but the general patterns of effects are very different.

For example, having vocational counseling is substantially correlated with every area of satisfaction except Facilities, and with every area of self-reported growth except foreign-language skills. It has a particularly strong effect on satisfaction with Individual Support Services (Beta = .21). (Personal or psychological counseling, it should be added, has a significant but weaker effect on this outcome: Beta = .07.) Having vocational or career counseling is also positively associated with several personality measures — Leadership, Scholarship, Social Activism, Hedonism, Status Striving — and with perceptions of a Student-Oriented Faculty, Diversity Orientation, Social Change Orientation, and Trust in the Administration. Receiving vocational or career counseling is also positively associated with several behavioral outcomes: being elected to a student office, voting in the 1988 presidential election, tutoring other students, attending recitals or concerts, and alcohol consumption. It also has positive effects on choosing a career in the field of business and on choosing a major in the social sciences.

Receiving personal or psychological counseling, on the other hand, is not associated with satisfaction (except in the area of Individual Support Services, noted above) and had no effect on self-reported growth in any area. By far its strongest positive effect is on feeling depressed (Beta = .17). It also has a significant effect on feeling overwhelmed and a substantial negative effect on self-rated emotional health. Receiving personal or psychological counseling also has weak positive effects on Artistic Inclination, Liberalism, Libertarianism, participation in protests, smoking cigarettes, and majoring in psychology. It is negatively associated with GRE Analytical and MCAT scores. The correlations with emotional health and with feeling depressed and overwhelmed, of course, may be antecedent *causes* of seeking personal or psychological counseling, rather than effects of such counseling.

Alcohol Consumption

Alcohol consumption produces a rather unusual pattern of relationships. In the academic realm, drinking is negatively related to college GPA and graduating with honors, but positively related to the attainment of the bachelor's degree. Drinking has been negatively associated in past studies with academic performance (Astin, 1971), but here we also find that it is positively associated with retention. In view of some of the other outcomes that are associated with alcohol consumption (below), perhaps this positive retention effect operates, once again, through the involvement principle: despite the negative effect of drinking on academic performance, it may facilitate involvement with peers.

For example, alcohol consumption has positive relationships with joining social fraternities or sororities, attending recitals or concerts, participating in campus demonstrations, and self-reported growth in interpersonal skills, leadership abilities, and Overall Academic Development. It has positive correlations also with Leadership. (Recall from Chapter Six that alcohol consumption is strongly associated with hours per week spent "partying".)

Alcohol consumption has one of its strongest correlations with smoking cigarettes (Beta = .16). It also has positive correlations with Libertarianism, commitment to the goal of being very well off financially, and feeling depressed; its negative correlations are with getting married and Feminism.

Summary

This review once again underscores the tremendous potential that student involvement has for enhancing most aspects of the undergraduate student's cognitive and affective development. Learning, academic performance, and retention are positively associated with academic involvement, involvement with faculty, and involvement with student peer groups. When it comes to cognitive development, we find widespread support for the self-evident but frequently overlooked principle that "students learn what they study." That is, overall academic development is proportional to the amount of time that students devote to studying, while growth in a particular area of knowledge or skill is proportional to the number of courses taken that focus on these same areas of knowledge or skill.

A wide spectrum of cognitive and affective outcomes is negatively affected by forms of involvement that either isolate the student from peers or remove the student physically from the campus: living at home, commuting, being employed off campus, being employed full-time, and watching television.

In the next chapter, we shall consider some of the implications of these and other findings for educational policy and practice.

Chapter 12

━•◆•━

Implications for
Educational Theory
and Practice

The principal aim of this book is to provide a better empirical and theoretical basis for faculty, administrators, and policy makers to improve the effectiveness of higher education policy and practice. We also hope that the results will help students to make better choices among educational institutions and programs. This final chapter presents some of the practical and theoretical implications of the findings under the following headings: The Peer Group; The Faculty; Institutional Type; Curriculum, Pedagogy, and Testing; The Diversity Issue; and Resource Allocation. To provide a context for discussing each of these topics, the chapter begins with a brief summary of how contemporary college students change during the undergraduate years.

Student Change During College

The national longitudinal data on which this study is based show clearly that students change in many ways after they enter college. In the affective realm, they develop a more positive self-image, as reflected in a greater sense of interpersonal and intellectual competency, and they show substantial increases in

396

Social Activism, Feminism, alcohol consumption, and support for legal abortions. Students also show substantial increases in their commitment to participate in programs to clean up the environment, to promote racial understanding, and to develop a meaningful philosophy of life.

Perhaps the most notable decline observed during the college years is in the student's sense of psychological well-being. Students also show substantial declines in business interests and materialistic values: the notion that the chief benefit of a college education is monetary, and commitment to the goal of being very well off financially.

Many, but not all, of these affective changes appear to be attributable primarily to the college experience, rather than to maturation or social change. This is especially true in the case of increases in intellectual and interpersonal self-confidence, Social Activism, alcohol consumption, and Feminism and of the declines in materialism. The role of the college experience in the student's declining sense of psychological well-being is unclear.

When it comes to cognitive development, students experience a substantial decline in their grade point averages between high school and college. Nevertheless, they report substantial growth in most areas of knowledge and skills, especially in knowledge of a field or discipline. The one exception here is mathematical or quantitative ability, which may even decline slightly during the undergraduate years.

Unlike earlier generations of college students, students today show little evidence of the "liberalizing" effect of the undergraduate experience, at least as defined by labels such as "liberal" or "conservative." In other words, the liberal-conservative balance shows little change during the four years after students enter college. Moreover, the decline in business interests and status needs is smaller than it was two decades ago. This failure to replicate earlier studies appears to be attributable to dramatic changes in entering freshman classes during the past two decades: whereas entering college students of earlier generations showed a distinct preference for the "liberal" over the "conservative" label, today's college students are about equally divided in their preferences for these two labels. During this same period there has also been a dramatic increase in student interest in careers and majors in business. As a result of these changes, the student entering college today has about an equal chance of encountering a "liberal" versus a "conservative" peer group.

The Peer Group

Viewed as a whole, the many empirical findings from this study seem to warrant the following general conclusion: *the student's peer group is the single most potent source of influence on growth and development during the undergraduate years.* While the importance of the peer group has been pointed out earlier by most reviewers of the voluminous research on student development (Astin, 1977; Bowen, 1977; Chickering, 1969; Feldman and Newcomb, 1969; Pascarella and Terenzini, 1991), this is the first time that research has been able to compare and contrast peer group effects with effects of faculty, curriculum, and institutional type, and to pinpoint how particular outcomes are affected by specific *characteristics* of the peer group.

When it comes to the student's affective development, one generalization seems clear: *students' values, beliefs, and aspirations tend to change in the direction of the dominant values, beliefs, and aspirations of the peer group.* This represents a clear confirmation of two closely related theories of peer group effects: Feldman and Newcomb's "accentuation of initial differences" (1969, pp. 333–356), and Astin and Panos's "theory of progressive conformity" (1969, pp. 125–129). Indeed, there are many instances in which individual student development is directly affected by a parallel measure of the peer group:

Individual Student Outcome	*Parallel Peer Group Measure*
Political Orientation (liberalism versus conservatism)	Political Orientation (liberalism versus conservatism)
Libertarianism	Permissiveness
Social Activism	Altruism and Social Activism
Status Striving	Materialism and Status

Major Choice in Biological Science	Percentage Majoring in Biological Science
Major Choice in Business	Percentage Majoring in Business
Major Choice in Engineering	Percentage Majoring in Engineering
Major Choice in Physical Science	Percentage Majoring in Physical Science
Major Choice in Social Science	Percentage Majoring in Social Science

Besides these direct parallels between peer group measures and the outcome measures that they affect, there are many peer group effects that dramatize the wide-ranging ways in which the individual student can be affected by the peer group:

Individual Student Outcome Measure	Direction of Effect	Peer Group Measure
Perception of Resources and Reputation Emphasis	+	Materialism and Status
Cultural Awareness	–	Materialism and Status
Liberalism	–	Materialism and Status
Liberalism	+	Political Orientation (liberalism versus conservatism)
Perception of Diversity Orientation	+	Political Orientation (liberalism versus conservatism)
Perception of Diversity Orientation	+	Altruism and Social Activism
Perception of Social Change Orientation	+	Altruism and Social Activism
Performance on Standardized Tests	+	Intellectual Self-Esteem
Satisfaction with College	+	Peer SES
Hedonism	–	Percentage of Born-Again Christians
Retention	–	Outside Work

A Theory of Peer Group Effects

Just how do peer group effects serve to facilitate learning and personal development? While this is no doubt a subtle and complex process that merits a good deal more study and research than has been possible in this book, it is interesting to speculate on what some of the mechanisms might be. First, let us consider the question of what a "peer group" really is. There are probably at least two perspectives from which to address this question: the individual or *psychological* point of view, and the group or *sociological* point of view.

From the perspective of the individual, a peer group is a collection of individuals with whom the individual *identifies* and *affiliates* and from whom the individual seeks *acceptance* or *approval*. "Identification" can be an especially fuzzy concept. What, precisely, do we mean when we speak of identification? The sense in which the word is used here refers to the person's *beliefs:* that I am like these other people in certain key respects and that they are like me. These similarities can cover an almost limitless range of personal qualities: age, interests, race, gender, social class, employment, beliefs, values, or life circumstances (student, commuter, single parent, sophomore, chemistry major, athlete, honor student, part-time student, and so on). Identification and affiliation, of course, go hand in hand with the need for acceptance and approval: one generally seeks acceptance and approval from those associates who are regarded as being like oneself.

Identification and affiliation would seem to be especially important conditions if any group of people is to qualify as a "peer group" from the individual's perspective. An undergraduate majoring in theater, for example, may identify with motion picture stars in the entertainment industry, but these stars hardly qualify as a peer group unless and until that student actually becomes a working actor or entertainer. But what if the student subsequently gets occasional work as an extra in motion pictures? Is this kind of "affiliation" sufficient to qualify the student as a "peer" of leading men and women? This question suggests still another requirement for peer group membership: there must be some element of comparable or equal *status* for any group to qualify as a peer group. Indeed, even the word *peer* suggests comparability in status. Thus, our former theater student might be considered as belonging to the peer group of extras or even of actors, but not of movie stars. Even though our young actor may identify with stars, seek their acceptance and approval, and even work with them from time to time, she would probably not regard herself as their peer or regard stars as a peer group. Stars, of course, along with our young actor, would see themselves as members of that larger peer group known as actors. Only in this more generic sense can our former drama student be considered a peer of star actors.

Viewed from a collective or sociological perspective, a peer group would be defined as any group of individuals in which the members identify, affiliate with, and seek acceptance and approval from *each other*. The word *acceptance* has two different meanings here. At its most basic level, acceptance refers to the group's acknowledgment that any individual does, in fact, possess the minimal characteristics needed to qualify for membership. In this sense, then, acceptance by peers is a necessary condition for individual membership in a peer group. The second meaning of acceptance has to do more with approval: the extent to which the individual's beliefs, conduct, and accomplishments conform to the norms and expectations of others in the group. A student, for example, may undergo the requisite pledging and initiation rituals to qualify as a "brother" in a particular social fraternity, but exhibit attitudes and behavior that generate disapproval (nonacceptance) from the other brothers.

The concepts of acceptance and approval have somewhat different implications from the individual's perspective. A student who does not seek acceptance and approval from a particular peer group cannot really be considered a member of that group, even if she affiliates or interacts with that group and is "accepted" (in both senses) by members of the group. In other words, identification with, and especially the desire to seek acceptance and approval from, any group are both necessary conditions for that group to qualify as a peer group for that student.

How, then, does the peer group exert influence on its individual members? The key to understanding this process may well lie in the norms and expectations of the group members. A politically liberal student who joins a social fraternity populated primarily by members with conservative beliefs will be tempted to change his beliefs as a means of gaining approval and acceptance. An engineering student who affiliates primarily with other engineering students, in contrast to one whose peers are primarily from the liberal arts, will find it more difficult to switch to some other major, since such a change runs a greater risk of peer disapproval. The norms of the engineering students, in other words, are strongly in the direction of pursuing engineering as a career, whereas the norms of liberal arts students in general offer little support for the pursuit of such a career.

This discussion suggests several elaborations of the theories of accentuation of initial differences and progressive conformity that could be tested in future research. Beyond the basic prediction that "students tend to become more like their peers," here are several other testable hypotheses:

- The peer groups having the greatest impact will be those with whom the individual most strongly identifies (this is an especially important issue, given the very large number of *possible* peer groups that one finds in a single institution).
- The impact of the peer group will be proportional to the extent to which the individual seeks acceptance and approval from that group.
- The magnitude of any peer group effect will be proportional to the individual's frequency and intensity of affiliation or interaction with that group.

Some other possible corollaries that could be tested would include the following:

- Individual members of a peer group who exhibit beliefs and behaviors that are at variance with peer group norms will be more likely to *leave* that peer group than will students whose beliefs and behavior are consistent with peer group norms.
- Individual peer group members with deviant beliefs or behavior will be less likely to leave the peer group if they *change* their beliefs and/or behavior in the direction of group norms.

This discussion also helps to explain why student-student interaction in general tends to facilitate the student's intellectual and personal development. It should be realized, first of all, that interaction signifies "affiliation," one of the conditions that has been proposed here as being necessary for peer group membership. Students who do not interact frequently with fellow students are most likely interacting frequently with other, nonstudent groups, such as co-workers, family members, or friends outside the academic institution. How would the norms and expectations of these nonstudent groups be likely to differ from the norms and expectations of the students? In the first place, students would tend to place a higher priority than nonstudents on values and behaviors that are appropriate to the student role: studying, learning, intellectual development, and the pursuit of careers that require undergraduate and postgraduate degrees. (Such values, incidentally, would tend to be especially strong in high-SES peer groups, and especially weak in peer groups that are heavily involved in Outside Work.) In other words, frequent student-student interaction should tend to reinforce those values and behaviors that distinguish students from nonstudents, whereas interacting more frequently with nonstudents would tend to reinforce a different set of values.

The role of the peer group can also be seen by considering why certain peer group factors did not affect their counterpart individual outcome measures. Why does Feminism of the peer group, for example, fail to show an effect on the individual student's feminism? In all likelihood, the answer to this question lies in the *lack of variability* in the peer group measure: even in the *least* "feminist" student bodies, the majority of students endorse feminist viewpoints with respect to equal pay and the role of women. In other words, regardless of which institution any student enters, the norm for the peer group will be a feminist perspective. Since the effect of any environmental *measure* depends, in part, on how *variable* that measure is (an "effect," as defined by the regression analysis, is always a *differential* effect of different levels of the environmental variable), it is difficult for the peer group measure of Feminism to show any effect because it lacks variability from institution to institution. This does not mean, however, that some individual students' feminist attitudes are not affected by the peer group. Indeed, the overall feminism of students does increase substantially during college (Chapter Five), a change most likely attributable to the peer group: since virtually all peer groups are strongly feminist, many students who enter college espousing nonfeminist beliefs will be inclined to change these beliefs in order to conform more to peer group norms.

"Input" Effects

After reflecting for some time on the myriad findings summarized in Chapters Three through Nine, it occurred to me that many of the "effects" of input variables may also be attributed to *peer group* effects. I refer here specifically to the effects of demographic variables such as gender, race, and SES. What are these effects, and how might they reflect the differential impact of peer groups?

To begin with gender, there are significant gender effects on nearly two-thirds of the eighty-two outcome measures used in this study. Some of the most interesting gender differences are in the area of political views: women become more politically liberal during the undergraduate years, whereas men become more conservative. This finding actually *reverses* the gender effect noted in *Four Critical Years,* when men were found to become relatively more liberal than the women during the undergraduate years. In all likelihood, this reversal has something to do with the women's movement: women's rights and equality for women in the United States have come to be identified with the left side of the political spectrum. (The Equal Rights Amendment, for example, was strongly supported by most liberals and Democrats and strongly opposed by many conservatives and Republicans.) Such an interpretation is supported by the observation that women also show greater increases than men in Feminism during the undergraduate years. Interestingly enough, women are also more likely than men to marry soon after entering college and to increase their commitment to the value of raising a family.

Some of the largest gender differences occur in the area of psychological well-being: the declines in psychological well-being (feeling depressed, feeling overwhelmed, low self-rating on emotional health) are all stronger among women than among men during the undergraduate years. In other areas of personality development, men show larger increases than women do in Hedonism, Status Striving, and Leadership. They also become more committed than women to several life goals (developing a meaningful philosophy of life, becoming involved in programs to clean up the environment, making a theoretical contribution to science) and more committed to the views that racial discrimination is no longer a problem and that the individual can do little to change society. In the behavioral area, men also show greater increases in alcohol consumption and are more likely to become involved in tutoring other students.

There are also many gender differences in cognitive development. Men become relatively more proficient on both the Verbal and Quantitative scales of the GRE. Women, on the other hand, get better grades in college (even after control for their better high school grades) and are more likely to complete the bachelor's degree and to graduate with honors. Since men have higher SAT scores and women higher secondary school grades at the point of entry to college, these differential changes during college serve to widen gender gaps that exist at the point of college entry.

The college experience also seems to exaggerate many other freshman gender differences: during college, women are more likely than men to remain in the fields of school teaching, nursing, and psychology and more likely to drop out of the fields of medicine, law, and engineering. During the undergraduate years, women also report relatively stronger increases in interpersonal skills, job-related skills, Cultural Awareness, knowledge of a particular field, and foreign-language ability, whereas men report relatively stronger gains in public speaking ability.

In summary, it seems clear that colleges do not serve to eliminate or even reduce many of the stereotypic differences between the sexes. That is, women enter college already differing considerably from men in self-rated emotional and psychological health, standardized test scores, GPAs, political attitudes, personality characteristics, and career plans, and most of these differences widen during the undergraduate years. Thus, even though men and women are presumably exposed to a common liberal arts curriculum and to other common environmental experiences during the undergraduate years, it would seem that their educational programs preserve and strengthen, rather than reduce or weaken, stereotypic differences between men and women in behavior, personality, aspirations, and achievement. A similar conclusion was reached nearly twenty years ago in *Four Critical Years*.

How, then, can these gender effects be attributable to peer group effects? Very simply, women are most likely to affiliate with women during college, and men are most likely to affiliate with men. These differential affiliation patterns are created in part by structural factors — single-sex colleges, student housing, and so on — but there are also powerful self-selection factors at work: each sex tends to form same-sex friendships and same-sex peer groups during the undergraduate years. As a consequence, women are more likely to be influenced by the values and behavior of other women, and men are more likely to be influenced by the values and behavior of other men. Such an interpretation is supported by the observation that *virtually every gender difference observed at input widens with time*.

This "peer group effect" interpretation also helps to explain why the changes in political views by gender are different today than was the case with the findings reported in *Four Critical Years*. Whereas men as a group were more liberal at college entry than were women during the late 1960s, today the women freshmen are more liberal. Thus, the college women of today are exposed to more liberal same-sex peers than are college men.

A similar peer group interpretation accounts for the differential effects of race. White and African-American students show contrasting patterns of change on a number of affective variables. In particular, white students tend to become more politically conservative during the undergraduate years, whereas black students tend to become more politically liberal. The two groups also grow much farther apart in their agreement with the proposition that racial discrimination is no longer a problem and in their commitment to the goal of promoting racial understanding. Consistent with these trends is the finding that African-American students become more likely to engage in campus protests during college, whereas white students become less likely to be campus activists. As is the case with gender, this pattern of differential change indicates that the college experience, rather than narrowing political differences between the two major racial groups in this country, actually serves to exacerbate already existing differences observed at the point of college entry. That these differential changes by race are attributable to peer group effects is suggested by the tendency for the races to segregate themselves during the undergraduate years (either institutionally or via student clubs and organizations; see, for example, Duster, 1991). Part of this segregation is voluntary (students choose their own associates and their own organizations), but it is also caused in part by the structure of the American higher education system: not only do we have many colleges that enroll almost exclusively white students and many others that enroll primarily African-American students (the historically black colleges, for example), but there are also demographic and geographical factors that tend to concentrate African-American and other minority students in certain institutions.

Finally, we come to the effects of the student's socioeconomic status. SES has its strongest effect on completion of the bachelor's degree. It is important to emphasize that this and all other effects of SES are *over and above* the effects of all ability measures and other input characteristics. The student's SES is also related to satisfaction with all aspects of the undergraduate experience except Individual Support Services and Facilities. It has positive effects on GPA, entry to graduate school, and willingness to re-enroll in the same college. (The last two measures are affected more by parental education than by parental income.) SES also has significant effects on self-reported growth in critical thinking ability, knowledge of a field or discipline, analytical and problem-solving skills, interpersonal skills, and Overall Academic Development. In short, these findings show that students from high-SES families can look forward to more positive outcomes in college, regardless of their abilities, academic preparation, or other characteristics.

That these effects may be largely attributable to the peer group is suggested by the fact that American college students are substantially segregated by SES during the undergraduate years. Unlike the situation with race and gender, where self-selection of peers within the institution plays an important part, this segregation is largely structural in origin: the great institutional variation in Selectivity (which is strongly correlated with SES) means that many high-SES students attend colleges populated mainly by other high-SES students, and that many lower-SES students attend colleges where there is a much greater mix of students in terms of SES (Astin, 1985). To gain further insight into the phenomenon, let us turn now to consider the effect of *Peer* SES.

Peer SES

That the effects of the individual student's SES are really mediated by Peer SES is suggested by the very similar pattern of effects of Peer SES: positive effects on satisfaction, on most areas of cognitive growth and development, and on alcohol consumption, Liberalism, and Libertarianism (see Chapter Ten). We can gain even further insight into these effects by looking at the other institutional correlates of Peer SES.

While Peer SES is strongly related to Selectivity ($r = .73$) and Intellectual Self-Esteem ($r = .58$), these last two measures (which correlate .68 with each other) are of minimal consequence once we have taken into account the effects of Peer SES. Why should the socioeconomic status of the peer group have such consistently positive effects on student satisfaction, Liberalism, Social Activism, Feminism, Hedonism, and most measures of cognitive growth and development? For one thing, peer groups that are high in SES score high in Feminism ($r = .46$), Hedonism (.49), and Permissiveness (.43), are well prepared in science (.48), and live on campus (.48). They are also likely to major in social science (.58), English (.50), or physical science (.23). Moreover, they frequently take interdisciplinary courses (.64) and women's studies courses (.41), as well as foreign-language (.67), history (.58), and writing courses (.49), and frequently engage in independent research (.41). Peer groups that are low in SES frequently work at outside jobs ($r = -.45$), have need-based aid ($-.46$), major in education ($-.46$), and take remedial or developmental courses ($-.56$) and reading/study-skills courses ($-.44$).

Peer SES is also strongly correlated with the percentage of Ph.D.s on the faculty (.62), the faculty's political orientation (liberalism versus conservatism; $r = .52$), the Research Orientation of the Faculty (.52), average faculty salaries (.48), and the Institutional Emphasis on Resources and Reputation (.43). It is of particular interest that these last three faculty characteristics produce patterns of effects on student outcomes that are very different from the pattern associated with Peer SES, discussed later. Indeed, the strength of the effect of peer SES usually increases when any of these three faculty measures enters the regression equation.

Why do we find this particular pattern of peer group, environmental, and faculty measures correlating with peer SES? First, it should be realized that there is a lot of consistency in the kinds of student bodies enrolling at particular institutions, even over long periods of time (Astin, 1985). In other words, we can assume that most institutions that currently enroll high-SES students have been enrolling such students for years. What are the likely consequences, then, of enrolling a high-SES student body year after year over a considerable period of time? For one thing, by having high-SES parents and alumni, the institution is in an excellent position to raise money. Parents and alumni would be able not only to afford making substantial contributions but also to appreciate the importance of helping to support educational institutions. Here is at least a partial explanation of the high faculty salaries, the high proportion of Ph.D.s on the faculty, and the emphasis on resource acquisition. For another, high-SES students and their parents are likely to expect and demand that the institution be student-oriented.

The finding that Peer SES is positively related to the faculty's Research Orientation, even though the two measures have different effects on student development, can probably be explained by the emergence within public higher education of a number of prestigious "flagship" universities, such as the Universities of California, Washington, Michigan, Wisconsin, Texas, and North Carolina. Because they are highly selective in their admissions policies and nationally prestigious, these universities attract and admit students from high-SES backgrounds. Why have these high-SES peer groups and their parents not pressured universities to strengthen their undergraduate programs? The answer to this dilemma may lie in the great prestige of these universities and their low cost. In contrast to private institutions, where high-SES students and their parents pay a large part of the educational costs, the major public research universities represent a substantial educational bargain. Could it be that high-SES students and their parents feel much freer to make demands on those institutions where they are paying a large part of the costs? Could it be that students and parents are more willing to tolerate the low priority given to undergraduate education in exchange for the prestige that goes with a degree from one of these public universities?

The Faculty

Next to the peer group, the faculty represents the most significant aspect of the student's undergraduate development. In this study we have identified two characteristics of faculty that produce contrasting patterns of effects: Research Orientation and Student Orientation. Since both of these measures have strong correlations with a number of other faculty measures, the effects of many of these measures disappear once we account for Research Orientation and Student Orientation. For example, Research Orientation has strong correlations with average faculty salaries ($r = .86$), reliance on graduate teaching assistants (.83), involvement of undergraduates in faculty research (.74), percentage of faculty holding Ph.D.s (.72), Resources and Reputation Emphasis (.67), "progressive" curricular offerings (.56), Racial Conflict (.55), size (.60), selectivity (.56), percentage of graduate students in the student body (.51), public university (.50), and private university (.48). It has strong negative correlations with hours per week spent teaching and advising ($-.83$), commitment to student development (−.72), Student Orientation of the Faculty (−.69), Use of Active Learning techniques in the classroom (−.52), percentage of resources invested in student services (−.52), and percentage of faculty engaged in teaching general education courses (−.52).

The correlates of Student Orientation of the Faculty are in many respects the reverse of what we find with Research Orientation. Thus, the Student Orientation has its strongest positive correlations with Social Activism and Community Orientation (.78), private four-year college (.75), hours per week spent teaching and advising students (.71), Positive Perception with the Administration (.69), positive faculty attitudes toward the general education program (.64), Commitment to Student Development and Social Activism (.60), and percentage of resources invested in student services (.55). Negative correlates of Student Orientation of the Faculty include use of graduate teaching assistants (−.74), size (−.71), average faculty salary (−.64), Racial Conflict (−.61), public university (−.57), and student-faculty ratio (−.56).

These contrasting patterns of correlations show that the tension between research and teaching in U.S. higher education is very real. The Faculty's Research Orientation and Student Orientation reflect not only how they spend their time but also their personal goals and values and their interest in and accessibility to students. Clearly, the issue of research versus teaching is not likely to be resolved by establishing a Teacher of the Year award or by admonishing faculty to take their teaching and mentoring responsibilities more seriously. More fundamental change is needed.

Even though Research Orientation and Student Orientation are substantially correlated in a negative direction ($r = -.69$) and have similar (but opposite) patterns of effects on student development (see Chapter Ten), it is important to realize that they are to a certain extent independent and that each contributes independently to predicting student outcomes. This means that it is possible for some institutions to score high on both factors and for others to score low on both factors. A weak emphasis on research is not an inevitable consequence of having a Student-Oriented Faculty, for example, nor is a weak Commitment to Student Development an inevitable consequence of having a strongly Research-Oriented Faculty.

It should also be emphasized that this strong negative association between Research Orientation and Student Orientation reflects *institutional* characteristics. When we look at individual faculty *within* a single institution, we find little correlation, or even a very weak positive correlation, between research productivity and teaching effectiveness (Centra, 1981; Feldman, 1987; Pascarella and Terenzini, 1991). These single-institution studies suggest that there is no inherent contradiction in a faculty member's being both research-oriented and effective in teaching. The problem would seem to reside in *institutional* policies: most institutions that hire large numbers of Research-Oriented Faculty apparently give little priority to effective undergraduate teaching.

The institutions that personify the combination of strong Research Orientation and weak emphasis on student development are, of course, the major public universities. Institutions that personify the reverse pattern include primarily small private colleges with limited resources. My late colleague Calvin Lee and I wrote a book about such colleges more than two decades ago, under the title *The Invisible Colleges* (Astin and Lee, 1971). Those rare institutions that combine a strong orientation toward research with a strong student orientation include a number of affluent and selective private colleges and a few of the smaller private research universities.

Are there any institutions that combine a low emphasis on research with a weak orientation toward students? Perhaps the closest approximation to this particular configuration would be some of the four-year public colleges (see Chapter Ten), although it should be kept in mind that this is a highly heterogeneous category of institutions that is difficult to stereotype.

In short, this discussion suggests that while a low priority on undergraduate teaching and student development tends to be one of the consequences of a strong research orientation, it is not a necessary consequence of assigning a high priority to research.

Institutional Type

While *Four Critical Years* emphasized the differential effects of institutional type (public versus private, four-year college versus university, and so on), this newer study has shown that most effects of institutional type are indirect; that is, that they are mediated by faculty, peer group, and involvement variables. Most of the pedagogical problems currently facing our public institutions — universities as well as colleges — are, it seems to me, the result of the dilemmas that confront any institution that tries simultaneously to serve multiple functions. Most of these priority dilemmas are best understood when viewed in historical context.

In many ways, the British "college" supplied the prototypical model for undergraduate education in the United States. The colonial colleges and the many hundreds of private colleges that were founded in the next 250 years were in several respects predicated on that model: a primary commitment to educating the undergraduate, a residential setting that not only removes the student from the home but that also permits and encourages close student-student and student-faculty contact, smallness, and a sense of history and tradition that generates a strong sense of community. This sense of community is manifested in many ways, including alumni loyalty, the strong student interest and involvement in team sports, and the friendly rivalries that evolve between neighboring colleges.

This study has shown, once again, that this traditional model of undergraduate education leads to favorable educational results across a broad spectrum of cognitive and affective outcomes and in most areas of student satisfaction. Perhaps most important, however, is the finding that institutional *structure,* as such, is not the key ingredient; rather, it is the kinds of peer groups and faculty environments that tend to emerge under these different structures.

Recently I discussed these findings with one of our leading higher education scholars. In effect, this investigator dismissed the findings as "irrelevant" to the higher education scene in contemporary America, saying that "the modern American university is not a residential liberal arts college." I must admit that this kind of response, which is very similar to what many community college officials said after *Four Critical Years* was released, strikes me as a kind of non sequitur. For one thing, it ignores the reality that *all* types of institutions *claim* to be engaged in the same enterprise: the liberal education of the undergraduate student. While it is true that certain kinds of institutions also do other things—research, vocational education, and graduate education, to name just a few—does having multiple functions "give permission" to an institution to offer baccalaureate education programs that are second-rate? Does engaging in research and graduate education justify shortchanging undergraduate education? Does engaging in vocational education justify offering mediocre transfer education?

Certainly, the public that pays for much of what goes on in public higher education would not be inclined to buy such arguments. Most states are quite generous in their funding of undergraduate education programs, and there are funding formulas that try to take into account the differential cost of undergraduate and graduate education and the time that university professors are expected to devote to research. Nevertheless, there is a widespread (but seldom publicly stated) belief among university administrators that some of the funds allocated for undergraduate education must be siphoned off to support graduate education and research. Many administrators seem to believe that the public would not support graduate education and research if the public knew its real costs.

It has never been self-evident to me that the public would be unwilling to support the true costs of graduate education and research, whatever they might be. University-based research and graduate education in the United States are unparalleled anywhere in the world. American scientists and scholars are among the world's leaders in practically every academic field, and virtually every country in the world sends large numbers of its brightest men and women to the United States for graduate training. In some fields, the *majority* of persons earning doctoral degrees are citizens of other countries. That our federal and state governments would stop supporting such a great national resource if they knew its "true costs" is by no means a foregone conclusion. The real problem, it seems to me, is that many academic administrators feel that the only way to protect and preserve graduate education and research is at the expense of undergraduate education.

To dismiss the educational virtues of the residential liberal arts college model as "irrelevant" to the problems of undergraduate education in the university or in the community college is to miss one of the key findings of this study: institutional type and structure (size, private versus public, university versus college) are *not* direct causal factors in most student outcomes. Rather, these structural characteristics *tend* to create particular environmental circumstances — Research Orientation, Student Orientation, Humanities Orientation, certain peer group factors — that in turn affect student outcomes. Some research universities are much more "student-oriented" than others, and some private residential colleges are much more "research-oriented" than others. At the same time, some institutional leaders are much more conscious than others of the critical role that the peer group can play in undergraduate education. A fuller appreciation of the potential of the peer group as a facilitator of the learning process could, I believe, serve to improve undergraduate education in *all* types of institutions.

How does the "peer group effect" operate in the traditional residential college? For one thing, students have an easier time seeing each other as peers because they are of similar age (eighteen to twenty-two) and find themselves in similar circumstances: uprooted from the home (many for the first time), living in an unfamiliar environment, being confronted with a common set of intellectual challenges (the curriculum), and experiencing (many for the first time) a great deal of personal freedom in the conduct of their lives. The sense of community and peer identification that results from these shared qualities is further facilitated by the residential experience, since it brings students into close physical proximity to each other. The "relevance" of all this for research universities and community colleges is not in the specifics just enumerated (some of which would be very difficult to replicate), but rather in the underlying principle: *students in similar circumstances and with common needs and interests have been afforded an opportunity to interact and learn together.*

While this kind of peer community has developed more or less naturally in many small, private, residential colleges that serve primarily eighteen- to twenty-two-year-olds, what has happened to create such different peer group relations in other types of institutions? Take the state colleges and universities as a case in point. Since many of these institutions began as relatively small, (often) residential institutions serving primarily eighteen- to twenty-two-year-olds who shared an interest in teaching careers, they naturally enjoyed many of the advantages of the private residential college. Over the years, however, these institutions have changed in many ways that tend to undermine strong peer relationships: they have become much larger and much more diverse in curricular emphasis and have enrolled large numbers of adults, commuters, transfers, part-time students, and students who are employed full-time. Many have also begun to emphasize research and graduate education.

A similar story can be told about community colleges. Originally founded as relatively small institutions with the primary mission of providing young people of traditional college age with the first two years of a liberal arts education, these institutions now serve primarily a different clientele: older, part-time, adult, and vocational or terminal occupational students.

While defenders of these institutions like to talk romantically about the educational virtues of having such a diversity of students in the classroom, in reality it is very difficult to create anything resembling a "peer group" out of such a hodge-podge of students. Each difference — in interests, in circumstances (full-time versus part-time, marital status, and so on), and especially in age — makes it more difficult for students to identify with each other and to form common bonds. The age difference is a particular problem, I think, because it interferes with the development of friendships and social relationships outside the classroom. For better or for worse, friendships and social life in our society are heavily age-based. All of these limitations imposed by student diversity are, of course, exacerbated by the absence of a residential experience.

While part-time attendance, night and weekend courses, and the absence of any pressure to participate in the campus social life might all be regarded as important conveniences by the adult student who needs a few more credits for a degree or who is pursuing a vocational credential, the recent high school graduate who is pursuing the baccalaureate degree on a full-time basis pays a heavy price. The most obvious manifestation of this problem is that eighteen- to twenty-two-year-olds attending community colleges and other types of commuter institutions drop out of college at much higher rates than would be expected from their abilities, aspirations, and family backgrounds (see Chapter Seven and Adelman, 1992; Astin, 1975, 1977, 1982; Dey and Astin, 1989).

The constraints imposed by student diversity and the lack of residential facilities should not blind us to the ways to form strong peer groups within community colleges and other types of commuter institutions. Some community colleges, for example, operate vocational or occupational programs that have very high retention rates, most likely because they generate powerful peer bonds among the student participants. Even though the students may be diverse with respect to age, academic preparation, and social background, they are apparently able to form a strong sense of community and peer identification because the programs are small, the students share common career interests and are exposed to a common set of curricular experiences, and full-time attendance is required. That many of the students can also have families and even work at outside jobs is made possible because these programs often offer night and weekend classes. The role of the faculty, student support services, and classroom size and organization in such programs is not entirely clear because there is little published research on such programs. Nevertheless, it is probably reasonable to conclude that the classes are relatively small and that regular faculty, rather than teaching assistants, take primary responsibility for classroom teaching and academic advising.

In summary, this discussion suggests at least a partial explanation for the increasing difficulties that many contemporary community colleges and public four-year colleges encounter in trying to provide effective programs for transfer or baccalaureate students of traditional college age: as these institutions have attempted to serve a clientele that is increasingly diverse with respect to age, social background, academic preparation, interests, career aspirations, and conditions of attendance, it has become increasingly difficult for the students to form the kinds of peer group bonds that facilitate involvement.

The major public research universities present a history that differs from the recent history of public four-year colleges and community colleges. For the most part, these institutions have managed to maintain a fairly homogeneous undergraduate student clientele: traditional college age, well prepared academically, high SES, and full-time. Most public universities also continue to offer residential facilities, especially for freshmen. The main reason these institutions have not had to adapt to the changing character of the undergraduate student population is that the public colleges and community colleges have assumed most of the responsibility for serving these more diverse students. If anything, the "flagship" universities in most states became even more selective and elite as access to higher education was expanded during the 1950s, 1960s, and 1970s.

The public university's increasing difficulties in offering a high-quality undergraduate education can be traced primarily to the massive expansion of university-based research that occurred during the decades following the end of the Second World War and to the concomitant ascendance of the academic disciplines and of academic specialization. Fueled by massive investments of federal research dollars and by growing institutional ambitions to become academically "excellent," an intense competition involving the major public and private universities emerged during the 1950s and has continued up until the present time. The principal manifestation of this competition is the quest for academic "stars." Researchers and scholars who are regarded as the highest achievers by their disciplinary peers have become a highly sought-after commodity in academe, beneficiaries of a bidding war that offers not only high salaries but also a variety of "perks" that include such things as low teaching loads and generous support for laboratories and graduate research assistants. Stars are highly valued, of course, because they can bring large amounts of money into the university and because their presence enhances the university's national image and prestige. Top scholars and researchers, in other words, help the university to become "rich and famous." In earlier writings (Astin, 1985), I have characterized these as the "resources" and "reputation" approaches to achieving excellence.

This drive by the public universities to enhance their resources and reputations has had important implications for undergraduate education. Since the stars who have been the targets of the bidding war are heavily committed to their research and scholarship, they are attracted to offers that minimize the amount of undergraduate teaching and advising that they are required to do (graduate teaching and advising is less of an issue, since graduate students are often viewed as potential helpers and colleagues in research). As a consequence, faculty in research universities do considerably less teaching of undergraduates than do faculty in other types of institutions, and many of them do *no* advising of lower-division undergraduates. This task has been assigned to professional academic advisers in many research universities, and even upper-division undergraduates are advised by nonfaculty in many academic departments. Moreover, the lower-division instruction that is done by faculty in most research universities is frequently carried out in large lecture sessions where personal contact between faculty and student is unlikely to occur; individual consultation with students, including grading of papers and examinations, is usually done instead by graduate assistants.

The net result of these trends has been not only to create a large physical and psychological distance between the research university faculty and their undergraduate students but also to confer a kind of second-class status on the undergraduate. The undergraduate, so it seems, is not regarded as important enough to merit the personal attention of the university community's most esteemed members: the faculty. No wonder, then, that student satisfaction with faculty is lower in the public university than in any other kind of institution (see Chapter Nine).

These problems with student-faculty relations in the public research university are exacerbated by other structural factors, including the sheer size, complexity, and impersonality of the institution. Although new freshmen at most research universities have the advantage of living on campus in residence halls (some universities actually require it), those facilities are usually very large and not well designed to facilitate the development of meaningful peer group relationships. At the same time, the huge student body and the enormous variety of majors that are offered make it unlikely that substantial numbers of resident students will be able to form peer group relationships based on common interests or on common curricular experiences. With random assignment of students to such residence halls, the probability that freshman roommates will be taking even one class in common is very low.

Possible Solutions

There are many possible approaches to ameliorating some of the problems confronting undergraduate education in the research university and in other kinds of institutions that overemphasize research or that have a weak peer group structure. A necessary first condition, of course, is to have institutional *leadership* that understands these problems and is willing to make significant efforts to deal constructively with them. The problem of leadership has clear implications for trustees and other officials who select institutional leaders: unless presidential search committees give a high priority to such personal qualities, it will be very difficult to improve and reform higher education in the United States, especially in the public sector. Besides the findings reported in this book, there are a number of other models for "effective colleges" that can help to guide both search committees and the new leaders they select (for example, Baird, 1976; Chickering, 1969; Chickering and Gamson, 1987; Kuh and others, 1991; Study Group, 1984; Pace, 1984, 1987).

There are many possible strategies that institutional leaders can follow in dealing constructively with the faculty and peer group issues discussed here. In the research universities, for example, there are ways in which undergraduates can actually benefit from the faculty's research efforts if the researchers involve them directly as junior participants in the conduct of research and scholarship. Highly promising programs of this kind have already been implemented, with considerable success, at places like the Massachusetts Institute of Technology (MIT) and the University of California, Los Angeles (UCLA). Another approach is to diversify faculty job descriptions. As long as faculty in the research universities are expected simultaneously to perform research, teaching, advising, university service, and outside professional activities, teaching and advising will continue to receive low priority. Given the great diversity of faculty interests and abilities, there is no reason that universities cannot negotiate individual contracts with faculty members that would permit them to do more teaching, mentoring, and advising, less research, more university service, and so on. Contracts can also include provisions for sustained periods of time — several years, if necessary — during which a faculty member would be expected to perform *only* teaching or advising or *only* research, and be evaluated accordingly. The possibilities are limitless. As long as the sum total of faculty effort accomplishes the necessary teaching and mentoring, such diversification of faculty contracts and job descriptions would almost certainly strengthen the university's pedagogical activities and reinvigorate the faculty.

A critical but poorly understood issue in the "teaching versus research" controversy is the method of *assessment* used to evaluate faculty for hiring, promotion, and tenure. Assessment of research and scholarship almost always relies primarily on an examination of the creative *products* of the faculty member, whereas assessment of teaching focuses instead on superficial *process* variables (syllabi, student evaluations of classroom performance, and — less frequently — direct observations of classroom behavior). Teaching is hardly ever assessed in terms of its products (student learning and development). In a sense, this would be like attempting to assess a professors's research by looking in her office, watching her in the library or laboratory, or observing how she sits in front of the word processor.

Lee Shulman (1992) has pointed out an important truth about how we assess research in relation to teaching: whereas research is considered a *public* activity that results in creative products or performances that can be directly observed and assessed by others, teaching remains a highly *private* activity where direct observation and involvement by others is not only infrequent but actively discouraged and resisted by faculty and departments. Shulman believes that the key to making teaching more public and therefore giving it much greater weight in the faculty review process is through the use of more sophisticated assessment procedures, especially portfolios. The use of teaching portfolios transforms the process of assessing teaching into a kind of scholarly research enterprise, in which the faculty member engages in a continuous process of assessing and documenting what is going on in the classroom and accumulating this documentation into a portfolio. Among other things, teaching portfolios can include the following kinds of information:

- Plans and intentions: examples of course outlines and syllabi, assignment sheets, and so on, together with personal commentary from the professor concerning course goals and objectives
- Samples of student portfolios or other products that document concretely what students have been accomplishing and learning through their classroom activities
- Videotapes, possibly with additional written or recorded commentary by the professor
- Ratings, comments, and other feedback from students
- Observations and commentary from colleagues about materials in the portfolio

A comprehensive compilation of ideas for teaching portfolios has been recently published by the American Association for Higher Education (Edgerton, Hutchings, and Quinlan, 1991).

There are also many ways in which institutions can be much more creative in facilitating the formation of peer groups. Rather than generating a long list of possible ideas for the formation of peer groups, it may be more useful here simply to reiterate some of the principles that need to be kept in mind in creating more potent peer group relationships in an institution. For example, if the preliminary theory of peer group effects presented earlier in this chapter is valid, then the prime considerations for the formation of peer groups would seem to be twofold: (1) to find a common ground on which *identification* can occur (the possible common grounds are numerous: career interests, curricular interests, avocational interests, political interests, and so on); (2) to provide *opportunities to interact on a sustained basis.* This second principle means that institutions need to create structures or policies that will require or encourage student peers to interact with each other.

The critical importance of peer group relationships to both cognitive and affective learning suggests that student affairs personnel can play a much more active role in strengthening the undergraduate educational experience, especially at large commuter institutions or at research universities. Given their substantial experience in working with students and student peer groups in a variety of settings, student affairs professionals represent an extremely valuable resource for generating creative plans to strengthen peer group relationships on the campus.

Curriculum, Pedagogy, and Testing

In this section we shall consider three major topics: effective pedagogy, general education programs, and standardized tests.

Effective Pedagogy

Beyond the self-evident finding that "students learn what they study," what other generalizations concerning curriculum and pedagogy are warranted by the findings of this study? If we look specifically at cognitive development, there are three types of courses that seem to produce generally favorable outcomes: courses emphasizing science or scientific inquiry, courses emphasizing the development of writing skills, and interdisciplinary courses. Institutions have much to gain by increasing the number of such courses in the curriculum.

A number of pedagogical practices likewise seem to be associated with favorable cognitive outcomes: time devoted to studying and homework, tutoring, cooperative learning, honors or advanced placement courses, racial or cultural awareness workshops, independent research projects, giving class presentations, taking essay exams, having class papers critiqued by professors, use of personal computers, frequent student-faculty interaction, and frequent student-student interaction. Again, finding ways to encourage such activities will substantially enhance student learning.

In the area of affective development, the following practices seem to produce positive results: time devoted to studying and homework, majoring in the humanities, courses emphasizing history and historical analysis, foreign-language courses, women's studies courses, ethnic studies courses, interdisciplinary courses, attending racial or cultural awareness workshops, study-abroad programs, volunteer work, part-time employment on campus, campus activism, student-faculty interaction, and student-student interaction.

There are also certain identifiable practices that seem to have *negative* impacts on students' cognitive and affective development practices: watching television, taking multiple-choice exams, working full-time, working off campus, and commuting. Discouraging or minimizing such activities will not only enhance learning but also reduce the dropout rate. Once again, all of these findings reinforce the critical role of student "involvement" in the college experience.

General Education Programs

Do the findings of this study suggest any ways in which general education programs can be strengthened? To explore this question, our HERI staff reviewed the literature on the goals of general education and identified a subgroup of twenty-two of the eighty-two outcome measures from this study that seem to have the most direct relevance to the stated goals of general education. The list included both cognitive and affective outcomes, as well as cognitive-psychological outcomes (for example, standardized test scores) and behavioral outcomes (for example, completion of the bachelor's degree, enrollment in graduate school).

What we found, first of all, was that the particular manner in which the general education curriculum is structured makes very little difference for most of these twenty-two outcomes. Since over 90 percent of all general education programs use a "distributional" system, basically these findings mean that the major varieties of implementation strategies for distributional systems do not appear to make much difference. In other words, what specific options are offered, how much freedom of choice is allowed, and whether particular types of courses are required do not appear to have any substantial effect on how students develop during their undergraduate years. To a certain extent, this suggests that we may be spinning our wheels when we devote so much faculty time and energy to discussions and debates about the content and form of general education. As mentioned in Chapter Ten, the major exception to this generalization is the true-core interdisciplinary approach to general education, in which all students are required to take precisely the same set of courses. This unique approach to general education, which accounts for less than 5 percent of all undergraduate general education programs, does appear to have generally favorable effects on many of the twenty-two general education outcomes. The beneficial outcomes of a true-core curriculum may be mediated by the peer group: having students take exactly the same general education courses provides a common experience that can stimulate student discussion outside class and facilitate the formation of strong bonds among student peers.

In short, it appears that how the students *approach* general education (and how the faculty actually *deliver* the curriculum) is far more important than the formal curricular content and structure. More specifically, the findings strongly support a growing body of research suggesting that one of the crucial factors in the educational development of the undergraduate is the degree to which the student is actively engaged or *involved* in the undergraduate experience. As noted above, two critical factors are (1) the extent to which the student interacts with student peers, and (2) the extent to which students interact with faculty. General education outcomes are thus enhanced when students devote a lot of time to study, when they socialize with diverse student peers, when they serve as tutors for each other, and when they engage each other in discussions of contemporary issues. All of these positive factors signify active involvement and engagement in the educational process. On the negative side, we find that the student's general educational development is retarded or impeded when the student lives at home, commutes to campus, spends a lot of time watching television, or works at an off-campus job. All these factors, in turn, signify low involvement.

The data also clearly underscore the importance of the *peer group*. Beyond the benefits of frequent interaction with fellow students, we find that the student's educational development is enhanced when the peer group has relatively high socioeconomic status and when it places a high value on Altruism and Social Activism. On the other hand, we find less favorable outcomes when the student peer group lacks a sense of community and when it places a high value on Materialism and Status.

The results also highlight the critical role played by faculty. The most important factor appears to be the amount of personal contact between faculty and students, but the *quality* of that contact also appears to be of substantial importance. More specifically, a faculty that places a high value on Student Development, that values Altruism and Social Activism, and that has a positive attitude toward the general education program is facilitative to student learning and development. Heavy reliance on teaching assistants or excessive involvement in research, on the other hand, do not appear to be conducive to favorable general education outcomes.

Since the manner in which the general education curriculum is implemented seems to be much more important than its actual form or content, it would appear that we need to rethink radically our traditional institutional approach to general education. Curricular discussions, it seems, are focused far too much on issues of form and content. We academicians love to discuss and debate content. Since most of us are strongly identified with our disciplines and fancy ourselves as experts in specific content areas, we are inclined to lobby hard to have our favorite content represented in the general education curriculum. These competitive instincts very often consume a disproportionate share of the institutional energy that goes into planning and designing our general education programs, and what results is more likely to be a sort of political compromise than an integrated and coherent educational experience.

These research findings suggest that curricular planning efforts will reap much greater payoffs in terms of student outcomes if we focus less on formal structure and content and put much more emphasis on pedagogy and other features of the *delivery system,* as well as on the broader interpersonal and institutional context in which learning takes place.

Especially intriguing are the possibilities suggested by the findings concerning peer group effects. If the peer group can be one of the most powerful sources of influence on the student, why not take advantage of this fact in designing not only our curricular delivery systems but also our co-curricular programs?

Take instructional method as an example. The traditional lower-division class involves a good deal of lecturing, possibly some class discussion, some individual out-of-class work, course exams, and letter grades. Under such a system, individual students work pretty much on their own, and peers are basically viewed as competitors. However, under what we have come to call cooperative learning methods, where students work together in small groups, students basically teach each other, and our pedagogical resources are multiplied. Classroom research has consistently shown that cooperative learning approaches produce outcomes that are superior to those obtained through traditional competitive approaches, and it may well be that our findings concerning the power of the peer group offer a possible explanation: cooperative learning may be more potent than traditional competitive methods of pedagogy because it motivates students to become more active and more involved participants in the learning process. This greater involvement could come in at least two different ways. First, students may be motivated to expend more effort if they know that their work is going to be scrutinized by peers; and, second, students may learn course material in greater depth if they are involved in helping teach it to fellow students.

The potency of the peer group has still other implications for general education. For example, when an institution embarks on a review of its general education program, it may want to include students and student affairs personnel as active participants in the process. Student affairs professionals are clearly in a position to affect peer group relations in such diverse areas as housing, counseling, student government, student activities, and student organizations. Student leaders, for their part, can provide valuable insights into how peer relations among students can be enhanced as a means of strengthening the students' general educational development.

It is easy to understand why we academics put so much emphasis on curricular content and why we worry so much about the form of our general education programs. Most of us discovered very early in school that we were skilled at mastering the curricular content that we were exposed to by our teachers and in our textbooks, and we were well rewarded for demonstrating this skill in class and on exams and standardized tests. What professional success we might be able to achieve in our disciplines is often dependent on our ability to master highly specialized content in our fields or subfields. So when we get appointed to the general education committee, our natural instinct is to battle, on behalf of our particular fields or disciplines or specialized knowledge, for a piece of the action. The knowledge explosion and the proliferation of specialized fields and subfields in recent years have served only to exacerbate these competitive exchanges that inevitably occur when we set out to review our general education programs.

The real question, I suppose, is whether we and our faculty colleagues are willing to consider the possibility that the student's "general education" consists of something more than the content of what is taught and the particular form in which this content is packaged.

Standardized Tests

One of the most intriguing and potentially important findings of this study is that the environmental factors and involvement experiences that affect performance on standardized tests such as the GRE and the MCAT are almost entirely different from those that affect most other cognitive and affective outcomes—such as college grades, retention, self-perceived intellectual growth, enrollment in graduate or professional school, values and attitudes, and satisfaction with college. Given our heavy reliance on standardized tests at all levels of education in the United States, it is important to realize that educational reform efforts designed primarily to improve students' ability to perform well on standardized tests may not contribute to any of the other outcomes and may, in some cases, detract from them. Take just one striking example: courses that emphasize the development of writing skills. Since taking many such courses appears to have a negative effect on GRE Quantitative performance and does not enhance performance on any other standardized test (including verbal tests like the LSAT and GRE Verbal), and since taking a great many math courses benefits performance on the GRE Quantitative test, a policy geared exclusively toward improving standardized test scores might well substitute math courses for writing courses. While such a policy would probably produce a net improvement in student performance on math tests, it might produce negative effects on writing ability, retention, satisfaction, aspirations for advanced study, and other outcomes.

The point here is not necessarily to denigrate the use of standardized multiple-choice tests in assessing educational outcomes—such tests are clearly of value in assessing certain kinds of student performance—but rather to point out that they measure rather narrowly defined skills and do *not* appear to be good indicators of student development in many important areas. In the jargon of information theory, standardized multiple-choice tests have very high "fidelity" (of all the outcome measures, they produced by far the strongest pretest-posttest correlations over the four-year period) but very low "band width" (that is, they overlapped very little with most of the other outcome measures).

The Diversity Issue

One of the most controversial issues in American higher education these days is "diversity." Many if not most colleges and universities have for several decades now been making efforts to diversify by increasing the representation of women and members of historically underrepresented racial groups in their faculties, staffs, and student bodies and by expanding curricular content to include more material from women, ethnic minorities, and non-Western cultures. At the same time, many institutions have attempted to create a "multicultural" perspective on campus by sponsoring new student organizations, workshops, seminars, speakers, festivals, and other cultural and intellectual activities that focus on issues of gender, race, ethnicity, and culture.

During the past few years, conservative critics from both inside and outside the academy have raised serious objections to these efforts on a variety of grounds: that the curriculum is being politicized, that emphasizing diversity promotes divisiveness on the campus, that admission of students and hiring of faculty and staff are no longer done on the basis of merit, that free speech and academic freedom are in peril, and that the entire undergraduate experience is being compromised. These critics, with help from the news media, have also popularized the phrase *political correctness* (PC), which they use to encompass all the focus on diversity to which they object.

While this is not the place to debate the PC issue, it is important to realize that people on all sides of the issue have been arguing with each other pretty much in the abstract. However, from an *educational* perspective, one would ideally like to know whether emphasizing or not emphasizing diversity issues has any real consequences for students. How are students actually affected by the practices that the PC critics find so objectionable?

The summaries provided in Chapters Ten and Eleven suggest that many cognitive and affective outcomes are in fact affected by diversity policies and activities. Do these effects form any consistent pattern? Let us briefly summarize the main trends.

As far as institutional policies and practices are concerned, this study has included two major indicators: Institutional Diversity Emphasis (having to do primarily with affirmative action and promotion of multiculturalism on the campus), and Faculty Diversity Orientation (having to do mainly with the content both of the research that faculty members do and of the courses that they teach). The study also included several indicators of the individual student's direct experience with diversity activities: taking women's or ethnic or Third World courses, participating in racial or cultural awareness workshops, discussing racial or ethnic issues, and socializing with someone from another racial or ethnic group. Generally speaking, all these institutional and individual environmental experiences were associated with greater self-reported gains in cognitive and affective development (especially increased cultural awareness), with increased satisfaction in most areas of the college experience, and with increased commitment to promoting racial understanding. The same variables are also negatively associated with the development of materialistic values and with the belief that the individual can do little to change society. Perhaps the only outcome that might be considered "negative" is the positive effect of the diversity variables on participation in student protests. However, participation in protests is itself associated with generally favorable outcomes (see Chapter Eleven and Hurtado, 1990).

One other student outcome that is positively associated with individual diversity activities (but not with Faculty or Institutional Emphasis on Diversity) is political liberalism. The conservative PC critics might view this effect as negative, but the advocates of diversity might see it as a positive effect!

In short, the weight of the empirical evidence shows that the actual effects on student development of emphasizing diversity and of student participation in diversity activities are overwhelmingly positive. Clearly, the dire claims about the detrimental effects of emphasizing diversity are not supported by the data. On the contrary, the findings of this study suggest that there are many developmental benefits that accrue to students when institutions encourage and support an emphasis on multiculturalism and diversity.

Resource Allocation

Students of management and higher education administration have developed a fairly elaborate belief system about higher education "resources," which is only partially supported by these empirical findings. Indeed, some of these beliefs seem to be contradicted by the findings. For example, it is generally agreed among persons who study resource allocation issues in higher education that the following resource measures are indicative of a high-quality educational program: percentage of faculty holding doctorates, average faculty salaries, and the student-faculty ratio. When it comes to percentage of faculty holding doctorates and faculty salaries, the findings of this study raise serious questions about the efficacy of such measures of "quality." As mentioned in the preceding discussion of faculty characteristics, both of these measures are associated with generally negative cognitive and affective outcomes, primarily because they are both proxies for the Research Orientation of the faculty. In other words, how much you pay your faculty and what proportion of them hold doctoral degrees are much more indicative of how strongly oriented the faculty are toward research than reflective of pedagogical effectiveness. If anything, such measures are *negatively* associated with educational effectiveness.

A very different pattern of outcomes is associated with student-faculty ratio. Educational policy maintains that a *low* student-faculty ratio is a favorable index of educational quality. Our findings generally support such an assumption, although the mechanism whereby a low student-faculty ratio results in favorable educational outcomes is somewhat complex. Specifically, it appears that the effects of a low student-faculty ratio are mediated primarily by Student Orientation of the Faculty and, to a lesser extent, by the Humanities Orientation and by infrequent use of teaching assistants. The direction of causation here is not entirely clear, however. Do a strong Orientation toward Students and a strong Humanities Orientation *necessitate* a low student-faculty ratio, or does a low student-faculty ratio *make possible* a strong Student Orientation and strong Humanities Orientation? The mediating effect of the use of teaching assistants is perhaps a bit more clear: one of the reasons major research universities (especially public universities) have relatively high student-faculty ratios is that they make frequent use of teaching assistants, especially in lower-division courses. When these teaching assistants are excluded from the calculations, the student-faculty ratio appears to be high in comparison with the ratios generated by small liberal arts colleges.

A potentially important resource issue that receives very little attention in discussions of resource allocation is the proportion of the institution's expenditures that are invested in student services. As indicated in the summary for this variable presented in Chapter Ten, investing a relatively high proportion of institutional expenditures in student services pays off in terms of the number of favorable cognitive and affective outcomes that result. Clearly, here is an area in which institutions have an opportunity to strengthen their educational effectiveness by a reallocation of resources. Given that student services account for a relatively small proportion of educational and general expenditures (usually between 3 percent and 8 percent), it would appear that modest increases (in absolute terms) in such resources could reap significant benefits.

Another potentially important issue concerns student financial aid. This study produced a considerable amount of evidence indicating that the awarding of institutional grants or scholarships in recognition of academic or "other special" talent (such as musical, artistic) reaps significant benefits in terms of increased self-esteem, retention, and perseverance in fields of science and the arts. The massive federal and state grant programs do not seem to produce any measurable effects; it would appear that institutional funds awarded in recognition of a particular student's individual merit produce much better results than entitlement programs that parcel out aid according to predetermined, impersonal formulas.

The implications for federal aid are clear: if the federal government wishes to increase, say, the number of promising students who pursue careers in science, it might be much more successful if it awarded block grants to institutions and let these institutions award the funds to specific students on the basis of individual merit.

Another resource issue concerns the impact of the residential experience. Like the original *Four Critical Years,* this study once again underscores the value and potency of the residential experience. In all likelihood, the effectiveness of residential living is mediated through the peer group, given that living in a campus residence hall almost certainly brings the student into closer and more intimate contact with fellow students. It is unfortunate that many states, in their desire to accommodate as many undergraduate students as possible in the interest of "expanding access," have not also understood the critical importance of the residential experience for the eighteen-year-old student who is pursuing higher education for the first time. When I first encountered empirical evidence supporting the beneficial effects of the residential experience on student retention (Astin, 1975), I suggested the possibility that public systems of higher education might want to conduct cost-benefit analyses to assess the pros and cons of additional residential hall construction on commuter campuses. While only one state, to my knowledge, has actually done this, it is still an analysis that seems well worth the effort, given the widespread benefits associated with the residential experience that were revealed in this latest study. At the same time, it is unfortunate that many institutions with residential facilities have never fully exploited this resource. Because students spend so much of their time in residence halls, these facilities should be used to increase their academic involvement. Faculty members might be encouraged to spend more time in residence halls, perhaps even to teach classes and hold office hours there. The possibilities are numerous (Baird, 1976) and limited only by the creativity and imagination of the residence hall planners.

Some Final Thoughts

When I was concluding work on *Four Critical Years,* some sixteen years ago, it occurred to me that many of the policies that seemed to govern the expansion of public higher education during the years following the Second World War were really at variance with what was suggested by the research. Instead of building more small institutions we opted instead for fewer very large ones. Instead of expanding residential undergraduate education we opted for commuter education. Instead of continuing to emphasize full-time undergraduate education we encouraged more part-time attendance. My conclusion at that time was that these contradictions existed because policy makers had been guided more by *economic* than by *educational* considerations:

large institutions are presumably more economical because they permit us to capitalize on economies of scale; commuter education is preferred over residential education because dormitory facilities are too expensive to construct and maintain; and part-time attendance is preferable to full-time attendance because it permits students to work full-time while attending college. As I have reflected on these dilemmas since that book was originally published, it has become increasingly clear that the problems of strengthening and reforming American higher education are fundamentally problems of *values*. Policy makers can justify these more economical approaches to undergraduate education as long as they value the "bottom line" more than they do the quality of education offered. Research universities can continue shortchanging undergraduate education as long as they value the acquisition of resources and the enhancement of reputation more than they do the educational and personal development of the undergraduate (what I have come to call the "talent development" conception of institutional excellence).

Values are fundamental to just about everything we do in undergraduate education: whom we admit, and on what basis; *what* we teach them, and *how* we teach it; what *rules* and *requirements* will govern our students' conduct; how to *test* and *certify* our students; *whom* to hire, and the *criteria* for hiring, tenuring, and promoting them; the manner in which we treat each other as professional colleagues; the *topics* we choose for our research and scholarship; and how we faculty use our discretionary time. What is especially important about American higher education is that most of our institutions, despite complaints about external threats to institutional autonomy, retain an enormous amount of autonomy over all these decisions. We are, in other words, relatively free to modify or reform any or all of these activities according to whatever set of values we choose to pursue.

Institutions espouse high-sounding values, of course, in their mission statements, college catalogues, and public pronouncements by institutional leaders. The problem is that these explicitly stated values — which always include a strong commitment to undergraduate education — are often at variance with the actual values that drive our decisions and policies. The real issue in reforming undergraduate education, it seems to me, is to effect a better rapprochement between our explicitly stated values and the values that really drive our institutional policies and decisions.

Many value debates in higher education focus far too much on *means* and far too little on *ends*. Nowhere is this misplaced emphasis better illustrated than in the case of the curriculum. Practically all the current debate over "political correctness" in the curriculum is a debate about content. If we really mean it when we say that we are educational institutions, these debates would be much more productive if they were reformulated more in terms of *outcomes*. Thus, the current study clearly suggests that, when viewed in terms of educational outcomes, an institutional emphasis on "diversity" issues has widespread beneficial effects.

I am also intrigued by the findings concerning factors that affect student commitment to the goal of "developing a meaningful philosophy of life" (Chapter Five). Could declining student interest in this value during the past two decades be explained in terms of those involvement variables with which it correlates? That is, have many students lost interest in developing a meaningful philosophy of life because they read and write less, study less, participate less in religious activities, and watch more television than did their counterparts of twenty years ago? To me, this value has always symbolized the existential dilemmas that college students have traditionally confronted in their studies, readings, and peer group bull sessions: What is the meaning of life? What am I doing here? What is *my* purpose in life? How can I lead a meaningful and satisfying existence during my time on earth? The fact that this "philosophy of life" value is related to involvement in political activism and concern with racial issues, and that commitment to this value is strengthened by exposure to a college environment that stresses social activism and community, is especially intriguing. Is it possible that social activism and concern for the plight of others and for community heighten young people's awareness of these existential dilemmas?

In pursuing an economic or materialistic view of education, we tend to forget the basic values that lead us to recommend a "liberal education" for all undergraduates. The real meaning of a liberal education goes far beyond just teaching the student how to be a doctor, a lawyer, a diplomat, or a business executive. A liberal education is really about encouraging the student to grapple with some of life's most fundamental questions. Some of these questions are mentioned in the preceding paragraph, but there are many others: What do I think and feel about life, death, God, religion, love, art, music, history, and science? What kinds of friends and associates do I want in my life? What kinds of peer groups do I want to affiliate with?

In many ways the philosophy underlying a liberal education is a testimony to the value of the peer group. In other words, a liberal education assumes that a little bit of serendipity is a good thing. Allow young people to go away from home and to live together in an academic environment for a while, and some good things will happen. Give these young people a good deal of freedom, coupled with some new challenges and new responsibilities, and some good things will happen. Often we really have no idea what these good things will be, but the students will seldom disappoint us.

Resource A

———•·•·•———

Multiple Correlations
at Selected Steps

Table A.1. Multiple Correlations at Selected Steps.

		Stage of Multiple R		
Outcome	Step 1	All Inputs	Environments	Final Step
Chapter 3				
Political Orientation	.42	.53	.54	.59
Chapter 4				
Typology: Scholar	.63	.68	.69	.80
Typology: Social Activist	.43	.50	.51	.59
Typology: Hedonist	.52	.56	.57	.74
Typology: Status Striver	.48	.54	.54	.58
Typology: Artist	.61	.66	.68	.69
Typology: Leader	.53	.56	.57	.69
Self-Rating: Drive to achieve	.41	.46	.53	.54
Self-Rating: Writing ability	.52	.56	.56	.61
Self-Rating: Emotional health	.39	.44	.44	.49
Self-Rating: Physical health	.48	.50	.51	.57
Self-Rating: Listening ability	.19	.29	.32	.33
Felt depressed	.29	.36	.36	.42
Felt overwhelmed	.24	.32	.33	.40

Table A.1. Multiple Correlations at Selected Steps, cont'd.

	Stage of Multiple R			
Outcome	Step 1	All Inputs	Environments	Final Step
Chapter 5				
Goal: Develop meaningful philosophy	.37	.44	.44	.49
View: Racial discrimination not a problem	*.19*	.33	.34	.38
View: College increases earning power	.32	.42	.44	.48
View: Individual can't change society	.24	.29	.30	.32
Goal: Be well off financially	.47	.53	.54	.57
Goal: Raise a family	.44	.47	.47	.50
Goal: Promote racial understanding	.42	.51	.51	.62
Goal: Clean up environment	.33	.37	.38	.43
Goal: Make contribution to science	.40	.46	.46	.47
Affective factor: Liberalism	*.33*	.52	.55	.59
Affective factor: Libertarianism	*.23*	.38	.40	.44
Affective factor: Feminism	*.13*	.16	.16	.18
Chapter 6				
Participated in campus demonstrations	.28	.39	.43	.78
Member of fraternity or sorority	.26	.32	.45	.59
Got married	.17	.26	.29	.35
Elected to student office	.18	.23	.29	.50
Voted in 1988 election	*.15*	.26	.28	.31
Tutored another student	.23	.30	.33	.57
Smoked cigarettes	.54	.55	.55	.59
Attended musical concert	.27	.36	.38	.47
Drank beer, wine, or liquor	.48	.54	.56	.71
Chapter 7				
Graduated with honors	*.32*	.38	.41	.60
Average undergraduate GPA	.48	.56	.58	.65
Earn bachelor's degree	*.29*	.41	.48	.69
Admission to graduate school	*.17*	.34	.35	.41
GRE Verbal	.86[a]	.87	.87	.88
GRE Quantitative	.87[a]	.89	.90	.90
GRE Analytical	.73[a]	.77	.77	.78
GRE Composite	.88[a]	.91	.91	.92
MCAT	.76[a]	.85	.87	.89
LSAT	.72[a]	.74	.76	.77
NTE Communication Skills	.71[a]	.74	.74	.78
NTE General Knowledge	.77[a]	.79	.80	.83
NTE Professional Knowledge	.60[a]	.66	.67	.73

Table A.1. Multiple Correlations at Selected Steps, cont'd.

Outcome	Step 1	All Inputs	Environments	Final Step
			Stage of Multiple R	
Self-Change: Academic Development	.19	.26	.27	.43
Self-Change: Cultural Awareness	.15	.26	.30	.42
Self-Change: Leadership Abilities	.18	.24	.28	.42
Self-Change: Public speaking abilities	.15	.22	.25	.40
Self-Change: Interpersonal skills	.11	.19	.21	.31
Self-Change: Job-related skills	.09	.23	.26	.36
Self-Change: Writing skills	.13	.26	.28	.45
Self-Change: General knowledge	.12	.19	.20	.29
Self-Change: Problem-solving skills	.16	.23	.24	.36
Self-Change: Knowledge of field	.15	.22	.22	.38
Self-Change: Critical thinking ability	.14	.23	.25	.35
Self-Change: Foreign-language ability	.12	.26	.28	.66
Self-Change: Preparation for graduate school	.21	.30	.31	.45
Chapter 8				
Degree Aspirations	.35	.46	.47	.55
Career: Physician	.49	.51	.51	.54
Career: Lawyer	.35	.41	.41	.43
Career: Teacher	.45	.48	.49	.50
Career: Nurse	.62	.62	.62	.63
Career: College teacher	.13	.24	.25	.29
Career: Business	.41	.48	.48	.55
Career: Engineer	.49	.51	.53	.56
Career: Research scientist	.28	.35	.35	.42
Chapter 9				
Satisfaction Factor: Faculty	.10	.25	.46	.56
Satisfaction: General education requirement	.11	.21	.29	.32
Satisfaction: Overall quality of instruction	.15	.27	.37	.42
Satisfaction: Overall College Experience	.13	.26	.31	.49
Perception: Student-Oriented Faculty	.11	.28	.59	.66
Satisfaction: Individual Support Services	.10	.21	.30	.40
Satisfaction: Student Life	.13	.24	.36	.44
Satisfaction: Facilities	.13	.19	.40	.42

Table A.1. Multiple Correlations at Selected Steps, cont'd.

Outcome	Stage of Multiple R			
	Step 1	All Inputs	Environments	Final Step
Satisfaction: Opportunity for interdisciplinary courses	.15	.26	.34	.44
Would re-enroll in freshman college	.14	.25	.30	.46
Faculty perceptions: Diversity Orientation	.12	.23	.46	.51
Faculty perceptions: Resource/ Reputation Emphasis	.18	.29	.48	.50
Faculty perceptions: Social Change Orientation	.19	.33	.49	.53
Faculty perceptions: Trust of Administration	.10	.23	.29	.42

[a]Multiple correlations involving SAT Verbal and SAT Mathematical.
Note: Step 1 coefficients that are not direct pretests are noted in italics.

Resource B

━━━●◆●◆●━━━

Longitudinal Changes in the Weighted and Unweighted Samples

Table B.1. Longitudinal Item Changes in the
Weighted and Unweighted Samples: Personality and Self-Concept.

Item	Unweighted Sample (N = 24,847)			Weighted Sample Change
	1985 Percent	*1989 Percent*	*Change*	
(Scholar)				
Academic ability[a]	81.0	83.0	+3.0	+7.4
Intellectual self-confidence[a]	66.0	71.8	+5.8	+5.0
Mathematical ability[a]	54.9	49.5	−5.4	−1.4
Planning a graduate degree	72.5	77.3	+4.9	+4.7
(Social Activist)				
Helping others in difficulty[b]	65.1	69.5	+4.4	+5.4
Influencing social values[b]	33.4	48.9	+15.5	+14.6
Participating in community action programs[b]	24.9	33.7	+8.8	+7.5
Influencing the political structure[b]	17.2	22.5	+5.3	+4.8
(Artist)				
Creating artistic works (such as painting)[b]	11.0	14.6	+3.6	+3.5
Becoming accomplished in a performing art[b]	12.8	10.5	−2.3	−2.0
Writing original works[b]	14.5	17.6	+3.1	+3.4
Artistic ability[a]	27.0	31.9	+4.9	+5.7

Table B.1. Longitudinal Item Changes in the Weighted
and Unweighted Samples: Personality and Self-Concept, cont'd.

Item	Unweighted Sample (N = 24,847)			Weighted Sample Change
	1985 Percent	1989 Percent	Change	
(Hedonist)				
Marijuana should be legalized[c]	19.9	23.5	+3.6	−1.0
Drank beer	64.8	74.8	+10.0	+9.0
Smoked cigarettes frequently	4.6	7.3	+2.7	+1.1
Stayed up all night	72.7	62.6	−10.1	−8.2
(Leader)				
Leadership ability[a]	59.6	65.0	+5.4	+5.4
Popularity[a]	44.1	46.6	+2.5	+2.2
(Status Striver)				
Being very well off financially[b]	63.8	53.9	−9.9	−7.1
Obtaining recognition from colleagues[b]	56.0	52.0	−4.0	−1.6
Becoming an authority in my field[b]	72.6	66.2	−6.4	−2.8
Being successful in my own business[b]	43.8	36.1	−7.7	−7.8
Having administrative responsibility for the work of others[b]	38.9	43.1	+4.2	+8.0

[a]Self-rating "above average" or "top ten percent."
[b]Rated "essential" or "very important."
[c]Agree "strongly" or "somewhat."

Table B.2. Longitudinal Item Changes in the
Weighted and Unweighted Samples: Self-Ratings.

Item	Unweighted Sample (N = 24,847)			Weighted Sample Change
	1985 Percent	1989 Percent	Change	
Writing ability	53.6	63.0	+9.4	+8.9
Drive to achieve	74.7	73.7	−1.0	+2.7
Physical health	61.7	56.9	−4.8	−5.0
Emotional health	63.4	59.8	−3.6	−6.1

Source: Data from Wingard, Treviño, Dey, and Korn (1991).

Table B.3. Longitudinal Item Changes in the
Weighted and Unweighted Samples: Psychological Well-Being.

Item	Unweighted Sample (N = 24,847)			Weighted Sample Change
	1985 Percent	1989 Percent	Change	
Felt depressed	8.6	13.1	+4.5	+6.8
Felt overwhelmed by all I had to do	20.2	33.4	+13.2	+13.5

Table B.4. Longitudinal Item Changes
in the Weighted and Unweighted Samples: Attitudes.

Item	Unweighted Sample (N = 24,847)			Weighted Sample Change
	1985 Percent	1989 Percent	Change	
(Liberalism)				
A national health care plan is needed to cover everybody's medical costs.	55.2	66.1	+10.9	+8.8
The federal government is not doing enough to control environmental pollution.	82.3	91.2	+8.9	+8.4
Wealthy people should pay a larger share of taxes than they do now.	73.4	74.1	+0.7	−0.7
The death penalty should be abolished.	28.9	29.4	+0.5	−2.7
Busing is OK if it helps to achieve racial balance in the schools.	49.8	50.2	+0.4	−4.2
The federal government should raise taxes to reduce the deficit.	25.7	31.7	+6.0	+5.1
Abortion should be legalized.	58.5	73.9	+15.4	+17.6
(Feminism)				
Women should receive the same salaries and opportunities for advancement as men in comparable positions.	94.9	97.1	+2.2	+3.7
The activities of married women are best confined to the home and family.	84.8[a]	92.6[a]	+7.8[a]	+8.4[a]
(Other)				
The chief benefit of a college education is that it increases one's earning power.	59.9	38.9	−21.1	−17.0
Realistically, an individual person can do little to bring about changes in our society.	31.6	30.6	−1.0	−1.7

[a]Percentage *dis*agreeing

Source: Weighted data abstracted from Wingard, Treviño, Dey, and Korn (1991).

Table B.5. Longitudinal Item Changes
in the Weighted and Unweighted Samples: Values.

Item	Unweighted Sample (N = 24,847)			Weighted Sample Change
	1985 Percent	1989 Percent	Change	
Becoming involved in programs to clean up the environment	19.4	35.8	+16.4	+14.3
Developing a meaningful philosophy of life	49.1	58.0	+8.9	+7.9
Helping to promote racial understanding	36.6	41.1	+4.5	+4.1
Raising a family	70.8	71.0	+0.2	+1.9
Making a theoretical contribution to science	15.8	12.4	−3.4	−0.2
Being very well off financially	63.8	53.9	−9.9	−7.1

Table B.6. Longitudinal Item Changes
in the Weighted and Unweighted Samples: Behaviors.

Item	Unweighted Sample (N = 24,847)			Weighted Sample Change
	1985 Percent	1989 Percent	Change	
Drank beer	64.8	74.8	+10.0	+9.0
Tutored another student	58.1	53.4	−4.7	+3.9
Smoked cigarettes[a]	4.6	7.3	+2.7	+1.1
Attended a recital or concert	83.4	76.4	−7.0	−8.3

[a]"Frequently" only.
Source: Weighted data from Wingard, Treviño, Dey, and Korn (1991).

References

Adelman, C. *The Standardized Test Scores of College Graduates, 1964-1982.* Washington, D.C.: National Institute of Education, 1984.

Adelman, C. *The Way We Are: The Community College as American Thermometer.* Washington, D.C.: U.S. Department of Education, 1992.

Allen, W. *Gender and Campus Race Differences in Black Student Academic Performance, Racial Attitudes and College Satisfaction.* Atlanta: Southern Education Foundation, 1986.

Allen, W. "Black Colleges vs. White Colleges: The Fork in the Road for Black Students." *Change,* 1987, *19,* 28-34.

Allport, G. W., Vernon, P. E., and Lindzey, G. *Study of Values: Manual.* (3rd ed.) Boston: Houghton Mifflin, 1960.

Anaya, G. "Cognitive Development Among College Undergraduates." Unpublished doctoral dissertation, Department of Education, University of California, Los Angeles, 1992.

Anderson, K. "The Impact of Colleges and the Involvement of Male and Female Students." *Sociology of Education,* 1988, *61,* 210-221.

Angoff, W. H., and Johnson, E. G. "The Differential Impact

of Curriculum on Aptitude Test Scores." *Journal of Educational Measurement,* 1990, *27*(4), 291–305.

Astin, A. W. "An Empirical Characterization of Higher Education Institutions." *Journal of Educational Psychology,* 1962, *53*(5), 224–235.

Astin, A. W. "Further Validation of the Environmental Assessment Technique." *Journal of Educational Psychology,* 1964, *55*(4), 267–275.

Astin, A. W. *The College Environment.* Washington, D.C.: American Council on Education, 1968.

Astin, A. W. "The Methodology of Research on College Impact, Part I." *Sociology of Education,* 1970a, *43,* 223–254.

Astin, A. W. "The Methodology of Research on College Impact, Part II." *Sociology of Education,* 1970b, *43,* 437–450.

Astin, A. W. *Predicting Academic Performance in College.* New York: Free Press, 1971a.

Astin, A. W. "Two Approaches to Measuring Students' Perceptions of Their College Environment." *Journal of College Student Personnel,* 1971b, *12*(2), 169–172.

Astin, A. W. *Minorities in American Higher Education: Recent Trends, Current Prospects, and Recommendations.* San Francisco: Jossey-Bass, 1982.

Astin, A. W. "The Impact of Dormitory Living on Students." *Educational Record,* 1973, *54*(3), 204–210.

Astin, A. W. "Measuring the Outcomes of Higher Education." In H. Bowen (ed.), *Evaluating Institutions for Accountability.* New Directions for Institutional Research, no. 1. San Francisco: Jossey-Bass, 1974.

Astin, A. W. *Preventing Students from Dropping Out.* San Francisco: Jossey-Bass, 1975.

Astin, A. W. *Four Critical Years.* San Francisco: Jossey-Bass, 1977.

Astin, A. W. *Minorities in American Higher Education.* San Francisco: Jossey-Bass, 1982.

Astin, A. W. "Student Involvement: A Developmental Theory for Higher Education." *Journal of College Student Personnel,* 1984, *25,* 297–308.

Astin, A. W. *Achieving Educational Excellence.* San Francisco: Jossey-Bass, 1985.

Astin, A. W. *The Black Undergraduate: Current Status and Trends in the Characteristics of Freshmen.* Los Angeles: Higher Education Research Institute, University of California, 1990.

Astin, A. W. *Assessment for Excellence: The Philosophy and Practice of Assessment and Evaluation in Higher Education.* New York: Macmillan, 1991.

Astin, A. W. "An Empirical Typology of College Students." *Journal of College Student Development,* forthcoming.

Astin, A. W., Astin, H. S., Bayer, A. E., and Bisconti, A. S. *The Power of Protest.* San Francisco: Jossey-Bass, 1975.

Astin, A. W., and Dey, E. L. *Causal Modeling with Blocked Regression Analysis (CAMBRA).* Los Angeles: Higher Education Research Institute, University of California, 1992.

Astin, A. W., Dey, E. L., and Korn, W. S. *The American College Teacher.* Los Angeles: Higher Education Research Institute, University of California, 1991.

Astin, A. W., Dey, E. L., Korn, W. S., and Riggs, E. R. *The American Freshman: National Norms for Fall 1991.* Los Angeles: Higher Education Research Institute, University of California, 1992.

Astin, A. W., Green, K. C., Korn, W. S., and Schalit, M. *The American Freshman: National Norms for Fall 1985.* Los Angeles: Higher Education Research Institute, University of California, 1986.

Astin, A. W., and Holland, J. L. "The Environmental Assessment Technique: A Way to Measure College Environments." *Journal of Educational Psychology,* 1961, *52,* 308–316.

Astin, A. W., Korn, W. S., and Berz, E. R. *The American Freshman: National Norms for Fall 1990.* Los Angeles: Higher Education Research Institute, University of California, 1991.

Astin, A. W., and Lee, C. *The Invisible Colleges.* New York: McGraw-Hill, 1971.

Astin, A. W., and Molm, L. D. "Correcting for Response Bias in Follow-Up Surveys." Unpublished manuscript, Graduate School of Education, University of California, Los Angeles, 1972.

Astin, A. W., and Panos, R. J. *The Educational and Vocational Development of College Students.* Washington, D.C.: American Council on Education, 1969.

Astin, A. W., Panos, R. J., and Creager, J. A. *National Norms for Entering College Freshmen — Fall 1966.* Washington, D.C.: American Council on Education, 1967.

Astin, A. W., Treviño, J. G., and Wingard, T. L. *The UCLA Campus Climate for Diversity.* Los Angeles: Higher Education Research Institute, University of California, 1991.

Baird, L. "Structuring the Environment to Improve Outcomes." In O. Lenning (ed.), *Improving Educational Outcomes.* New Directions for Higher Education, no. 16. San Francisco: Jossey-Bass, 1976.

Bowen, H. *Investment in Learning: The Individual and Social Value of American Higher Education.* San Francisco: Jossey-Bass, 1977.

Boyer, E. *College: The Undergraduate Experience in America.* New York: HarperCollins, 1987.

Brown, R. "Manipulation of the Environmental Press in a College Residence Hall." *Personnel and Guidance Journal,* 1968, *45,* 555–560.

Budd, J. M. "Higher Education Literature: Characteristics of Citation Patterns." *Journal of Higher Education,* 1990, *61*(1), 2.

Carnegie Foundation for the Advancement of Learning. *Classification of Institutions of Higher Education.* Princeton, N.J.: Carnegie Foundation for the Advancement of Learning, 1987.

Cartter, A. M., and Brown, M. D. *Manpower Survey of 1967–1969 College Entrants.* Los Angeles: Graduate School of Education, University of California, 1976.

Centra, J. *Research Productivity and Teaching Effectiveness.* Princeton, N.J.: Educational Testing Service, 1981.

Chickering, A. W. *Education and Identity.* San Francisco: Jossey-Bass, 1969.

Chickering, A. W. *Commuting Versus Resident Students: Overcoming the Educational Inequities of Living Off Campus.* San Francisco: Jossey-Bass, 1974.

Chickering, A. W., and Gamson, Z. F. "Seven Principles for Good Practice in Undergraduate Education." *The Wingspread Journal,* 1987, *9* (June Special Section), 2.

Christian, C. E. "Patterns of College Experience: An Empirical Typology of Students and College Interaction." Unpublished doctoral dissertation, University of California, Los Angeles, 1977.

Clark, B., and Trow, M. "The Organizational Context." In T. Newcomb and E. Wilson (eds.), *College Peer Groups: Problems and Prospects for Research*. Chicago: Aldine, 1966.

Cooley, W. W., and Flanagan, J. C. (eds.). *Project TALENT: One-Year Follow-Up Studies*. U.S. Department of Health, Education and Welfare Cooperative Project no. 2333. Pittsburgh: School of Education, University of Pittsburgh, 1966.

Davis, J. A. *Undergraduate Career Decisions: Correlates of Occupational Choice*. Chicago: Aldine, 1965.

Dey, E. L. "An Empirically Based Student Typology." Unpublished manuscript, Higher Education Research Institute, University of California, Los Angeles, 1989.

Dey, E. L. "Perceptions of the College Environment: An Analysis of Organizational, Interpersonal, and Behavioral Influences." Unpublished doctoral dissertation, University of California, Los Angeles, 1991.

Dey, E. L., and Astin, A. W. *Predicting College Student Retention: Comparative National Data from the 1982 Freshman Class*. Los Angeles: Higher Education Research Institute, University of California, 1989.

Dey, E. L., Astin, A. W., and Korn, W. S. *The American Freshman: Twenty-Five Year Trends*. Los Angeles: Higher Education Research Institute, University of California, 1991.

Drew, D. E. "A Profile of Jewish Freshmen." *ACE Research Reports*, 5(4). Washington, D.C.: American Council on Education, 1970.

Drew, D., and Astin, A. W. "Undergraduate Aspirations: A Test of Several Theories." *American Journal of Sociology*, 1972, 77, 1151–1164.

Drew, D. E., King, M. R., and Richardson, G. T. *A Profile of the Jewish Freshman: 1980*. Los Angeles: Higher Education Research Institute, University of California, 1980.

Duster, T. *The Diversity Project: Final Report*. Berkeley: Institute for the Study of Social Change, University of California, 1991.

Edgerton, R., Hutchings, P., and Quinlan, K. *The Teaching Portfolio: Capturing the Scholarship in Teaching*. Washington, D.C.: American Association for Higher Education, 1991.

Educational Testing Service. *Guide to the Use of the Graduate Record*

Examinations Program, 1987–88. Princeton, N.J.: Educational
Testing Service, 1987a.

Educational Testing Service. *Summary of Admissions Testing Program Scores, 1965–66 Through 1986–87.* Princeton, N.J.: Educational Testing Service, 1987b.

Feldman, K. "Research Productivity and Scholarly Accomplish-
ment of College Teachers as Related to Their Instructional
Effectiveness: A Review and Exploration." *Research in Higher
Education,* 1987, *26*(3), 227–298.

Feldman, K., and Newcomb, T. *The Impact of College on Students.* San Francisco: Jossey-Bass, 1969.

Fleming, J. *Blacks in College: A Comparative Study of Students' Success in Black and White Institutions.* San Francisco: Jossey-Bass,
1984.

Gurin, G. "The Impact of the College Experience." In S. Withey
(ed.), *A Degree and What Else? Correlates and Consequences of a
College Education.* New York: McGraw-Hill, 1971.

Holland, J. *The Psychology of Vocational Choice: A Theory of Personality Types and Model Environments.* Waltham, Mass.: Blaisdell,
1966.

Holland, J. *Making Vocational Choices: A Theory of Careers.* Engle-
wood Cliffs, N.J.: Prentice-Hall, 1973.

Hurtado, S. "Campus Racial Climates and Educational Outcomes." Unpublished doctoral dissertation, University of
California, Los Angeles, 1990.

Hurtado, S., Astin, A. W., and Dey, E. L. "Varieties of General
Education Programs: An Empirically Based Taxonomy." *Journal of General Education,* 1991, *40*(1), 133–162.

Huston, A. C., and others. *Big World, Small Screen: The Role of
Television in American Society.* Lincoln: University of Nebraska
Press, 1992.

Hyman, H., Wright, C., and Reed, J. *The Enduring Effects of
Education.* Chicago: University of Chicago Press, 1975.

Johnson, D. W., Johnson, R. T., and Smith, K. A. *Cooperative
Learning: Increasing College Faculty Instructional Productivity.* ASHE-
ERIC Higher Education Report no. 91-1. Washington, D.C.:
Association for the Study of Higher Education, 1991.

Katchadourian, H., and Boli, J. *Careerism and Intellectualism Among*

College Students: Patterns of Academic and Career Choice in the Under-graduate Years. San Francisco: Jossey-Bass, 1985.

Keniston, K. "The Sources of Student Dissent." *Journal of Social Issues,* 1967, *23,* 108–137.

Kohlberg, L. *The Meaning and Measurement of Moral Development.* Worcester, Mass.: Clark University Press, 1981.

Kuh, G., and others. *Involving Colleges: Encouraging Student Learning and Personal Development Through Out-of-Class Experience.* San Francisco: Jossey-Bass, 1991.

Locke, S., and Colligan, D. *The Healer Within.* New York: Dutton, 1986.

National Center for Education Statistics. *Faculty in Higher Education Institutions, 1988.* Contractor Report. Data Series DR-NS OPF-87/88-I.27. Washington, D.C.: National Center for Education Statistics, March 1990.

Newcomb, T. M., and others. *Persistence and Change: Bennington College and Its Students After 25 Years.* New York: Wiley, 1967.

Opp, R. "The Impact of College on NTE Performance." Unpublished doctoral dissertation, University of California, Los Angeles, 1991.

Pace, C. R. *Measuring the Quality of College Student Experiences.* Los Angeles: Higher Education Research Institute, University of California, 1984.

Pace, C. R. *Good Things Go Together.* Los Angeles: Center for the Study of Evaluation, University of California, 1987.

Pace, C. R., and Stern, G. G. "An Approach to the Measurement of Psychological Characteristics of College Environments." *Journal of Educational Psychology,* 1958, *49,* 269–277.

Pascarella, E. T. "College Environmental Influences on Students' Educational Aspirations." *Journal of Higher Education,* 1984, *55*(6), 751–771.

Pascarella, E. T. "College Environmental Influences on Learning and Cognitive Development: A Critical Review and Synthesis." In J. Smart (ed.), *Higher Education: Handbook of Theory and Research,* Vol. 1. New York: Agathon, 1985a.

Pascarella, E. T. "The Influence of On-Campus Living Versus Commuting to College on Intellectual and Interpersonal Self-

Concept." *Journal of College Student Personnel,* 1985b, *25*(4), 292–299.

Pascarella, E. T. "Racial Differences in Factors Associated with Bachelor's Degree Completion: A Nine-Year Follow-Up." *Research in Higher Education,* 1985c, *23*(4), 351–373.

Pascarella, E., Ethington, C., and Smart, J. "The Influence of College on Humanitarian/Civic Involvement Values." *Journal of Higher Education,* 1988, *59,* 412–437.

Pascarella, E. T., Smart, J., and Ethington, C. "Long-Term Persistence of Two-Year College Students." *Research in Higher Education,* 1986, *24*(1), 47–71.

Pascarella, E. T., and Terenzini, P. T. *How College Affects Students.* San Francisco: Jossey-Bass, 1991.

Pascarella, E. T., and Wolfle, L. "Persistence in Higher Education: A Nine-Year Test of a Theoretical Model." Paper presented at the annual meeting of the American Educational Research Association, Chicago, 1985.

Perry, W. *Forms of Intellectual and Ethical Development in the College Years: A Scheme.* New York: Holt, Rinehart & Winston, 1970.

Rees, M. "The Ivory Tower and the Market Place." In S. M. McMurrin (ed.), *On the Meaning of the University.* Salt Lake City: University of Utah Press, 1976.

Schumer, H., and Stanfield, R. "Assessment of Student Role Orientations in a College." Paper read at the 74th annual meeting of the American Psychological Association, 1966.

Sewell, W. H., and Shah, V. P. "Parents' Education and Children's Educational Aspirations and Achievements." *American Sociological Review,* 1968, *33,* 191–209.

Shulman, L. *Toward a Pedagogy of Cases: Case Methods in Teacher Education.* New York: Teachers College Press, 1992.

Smart, J. "Holland Environments as Reinforcement Systems." *Research in Higher Education,* 1985, *23,* 279–292.

Smart, J. "College Effects on Occupational Status Attainment." *Research in Higher Education,* 1986, *24*(1), 73–95.

Smart, J. "College Influences on Graduates' Income Levels." *Research in Higher Education,* 1988, *29*(1), 41–59.

Steele, J. "Evaluating College Programs Using Measures of Student Achievement and Growth." *Educational Evaluation and Policy Analysis,* 1989, *11*(4), 357–375.

Study Group on the Conditions of Excellence in American Higher Education. *Involvement in Learning: Final Report of the Study Group on the Conditions of Excellence in American Higher Education.* Washington, D.C.: National Institute of Education, 1984.

Thornton, A., Alwin, D., and Camburn, D. "Causes and Consequences of Sex-Role Attitudes and Attitude Change." *American Sociological Review,* 1983, *2*(48), 211–227.

Thornton, A., and Freedman, D. "Changes in Sex Role Attitudes of Women, 1962–1977: Evidence From a Panel Study." *American Sociological Review,* 1979, *44*(5), 831–842.

Trent, J. W., and Medsker, L. L. *Beyond High School: A Study of 10,000 High School Graduates.* Berkeley: Center for Research and Development in Higher Education, University of California, 1967. (Published subsequently by Jossey-Bass, San Francisco, 1968.)

Warren, J. R. *Patterns of College Experiences.* U.S. Department of Health, Education and Welfare Cooperative Research Project S-327. Claremont, Calif.: College Graduate School and University Center, 1966.

Wingard, T. L., Treviño, J. G., Dey, E. L., and Korn, W. S. *The American College Student, 1989: National Norms for 1985 and 1987 College Freshmen.* Los Angeles: Higher Education Research Institute, University of California, 1991.

Index